LAW AND THE 100-YEAR LIFE

Law and the 100-Year Life addresses the growing trend of Americans living longer and healthier lives, with many reaching the age of 100. An aging nation presents new challenges for society, which must be reimagined to accommodate longer and more varied careers, multiple marriages, and defining moments of education. This volume explores the possibility of a "third demographic dividend," a new period of productivity following middle age, and the potential for law and policy to support or divide aging citizens. Leading scholars across various fields come together to explore topics related to aging, such as health law and trusts and estates, as well as less obvious but equally important areas like housing, criminal justice, and education. This title is also available as open access on Cambridge Core.

Anne L. Alstott is Jacquin D. Bierman Professor at Yale Law School. She is the author of a number of books, including *The Public Option* (with Ganesh Sitaraman, 2019) and *A New Deal for Old Age* (2016).

Abbe R. Gluck is Alfred M. Rankin Professor of Law and founding Faculty Director of the Solomon Center for Health Law and Policy at Yale Law School. She is also Professor of Internal Medicine at Yale School of Medicine and founding director of the Drell/Nitikman Elder Law Project at Yale. Her work on health care, Congress, complex civil litigation, and federalism is among the most cited in the nation.

Eugene Rusyn is a senior fellow at the Solomon Center for Health Law and Policy at Yale Law School. His research interests include health law, environmental law, legal history, and the study of government bureaucracy.

Law and the 100-Year Life

TRANSFORMING OUR INSTITUTIONS FOR A LONGER LIFESPAN

Edited by

ANNE L. ALSTOTT
Yale University

ABBE R. GLUCK
Yale University

EUGENE RUSYN
Yale University

CAMBRIDGE
UNIVERSITY PRESS

CAMBRIDGE
UNIVERSITY PRESS

Shaftesbury Road, Cambridge CB2 8EA, United Kingdom

One Liberty Plaza, 20th Floor, New York, NY 10006, USA

477 Williamstown Road, Port Melbourne, VIC 3207, Australia

314–321, 3rd Floor, Plot 3, Splendor Forum, Jasola District Centre, New Delhi – 110025, India

103 Penang Road, #05-06/07, Visioncrest Commercial, Singapore 238467

Cambridge University Press is part of Cambridge University Press & Assessment, a department of the University of Cambridge.

We share the University's mission to contribute to society through the pursuit of education, learning and research at the highest international levels of excellence.

www.cambridge.org
Information on this title: www.cambridge.org/9781009466028

DOI: 10.1017/9781009466004

When citing this work, please include a reference to the DOI 10.1017/9781009466004

First published 2025

A catalogue record for this publication is available from the British Library

Library of Congress Cataloging-in-Publication Data
NAMES: Alstott, Anne, 1963- editor. | Gluck, Abbe R., editor. | Rusyn, Eugene, editor.
TITLE: Law and the 100-year life : transforming our institutions for a longer lifespan / edited by Anne L. Alstott, Yale University, Connecticut; Abbe R. Gluck, Yale University, Connecticut; Eugene Rusyn, Yale University, Connecticut.
OTHER TITLES: Law and the hundred-year life
DESCRIPTION: Cambridge, United Kingdom ; New York, NY: Cambridge University Press, 2024.
IDENTIFIERS: LCCN 2024030854 (print) | LCCN 2024030855 (ebook) | ISBN 9781009466028 (hardback) | ISBN 9781009465991 (paperback) | ISBN 9781009466004 (epub)
SUBJECTS: LCSH: Older people–Legal status, laws, etc.–United States. | Older people–Services for–Government policy–United States. | Older people–Care–Government policy–United States. | Older people–United States–Economic cnditions. | Aging–Government policy–United States. | Longevity–Government policy–United States.
CLASSIFICATION: LCC KF390.A4 L327 2024 (print) | LCC KF390.A4 (ebook) | DDC 342.7308/774–dc23/eng/20240712
LC record available at https://lccn.loc.gov/2024030854
LC ebook record available at https://lccn.loc.gov/2024030855

ISBN 978-1-009-46602-8 Hardback
ISBN 978-1-009-46599-1 Paperback

Contents

List of Contributors *page* ix

Introduction 1
Eugene Rusyn, Abbe R. Gluck, and Anne L. Alstott

PART I IMPLICATIONS ACROSS THE LEGAL SYSTEM

1 **How the 100-Year Life Challenges the Legal Model of the Human Life Cycle** 15
Anne L. Alstott

2 **The 100-Year Life and the New Family Law** 26
Naomi Cahn, Clare Huntington, and Elizabeth Scott

3 **Education and the 100-Year Life: The Linchpin for Thriving and Enjoyment** 39
Kimberly Jenkins Robinson

4 **Aging Out of Criminal Justice** 52
Shon Hopwood

5 **The 100-Year Life Meets the Future of Work** 60
Cynthia Estlund

PART II PROTECTING RIGHTS AND PREPARING FOR THE FUTURE

6 **The New Old Civil Rights** 77
Kenji Yoshino

7 **Age, Inequality, and Political Representation** 96
Ganesh Sitaraman

8 **Age-Based Classifications in an Age of Centenarians** 111
Nina A. Kohn

9 **Working to Death: Labor Law and Collective Voice in the 100-Year Life** 121
Kate Andrias

10 **The Savings Mirage** 134
Sara Sternberg Greene

11 **Trusts and the 100-Year Life** 146
John Morley

12 **The Right to Grow Old** 153
Jamal Greene

PART III HEALTH, WORKFORCE, AND INNOVATION: THE INVESTMENTS REQUIRED FOR A HEALTHY LIFESPAN

13 **The 100-Year-Old American and Our Health System** 173
Yaron Covo, Abbe R. Gluck, and Linda P. Fried

14 **Making the Best of Long-Term Care for Seniors** 190
Katherine Pratt

15 **Immigration and the 100-Year Life** 203
Eleanor Brown

16 **Science Fiction, Legal Fiction, Political Fiction, and the 100-Year Life** 216
Daniel J. Hemel

17 **Bioethics, Reproduction, and Extending Life** 229
I. Glenn Cohen

PART IV THE 100-YEAR LIFE AND OUR BROADER ENVIRONMENT

18 **Weathering the 100-Year Life** 245
Eugene Rusyn and Douglas A. Kysar

19 **Local Government Law for the 100-Year Life** 258
Noah M. Kazis

20 **Transportation Policy for the 100-Year Life** 271
Gregory H. Shill

21 **Property and the 100-Year Life** 283
Taisu Zhang

22 **Scaling Down Senior Living: The Postpandemic Future of Housing for Elderly People** 296
Joanna L. Martin and Lior Jacob Strahilevitz

Contributors

Anne L. Alstott is Jacquin D. Bierman Professor at Yale Law School. Alstott is the author of a number of books, including *The Public Option* (with Ganesh Sitaraman, 2019) and *A New Deal for Old Age* (2016). Alstott received a JD from Yale Law School in 1987 and an AB in Economics, summa cum laude, Phi Beta Kappa (junior year), and with departmental honors, from Georgetown University in 1984. She began her teaching career at Columbia University School of Law, where she taught from 1992 to 1996. She joined the Yale Law School faculty with tenure in 1997 and remained there until 2008, when she left to join the Harvard Law School faculty, again with tenure. In 2011, she returned to Yale. Alstott has won five teaching awards, one at Columbia and four at Yale.

Kate Andrias is Patricia D. and R. Paul Yetter Professor of Law at Columbia Law School. She teaches and writes about labor and constitutional law, with a focus on problems of economic and political inequality.

Eleanor Brown is a professor at Fordham University and an affiliated faculty member at the Rock Ethics Institute of Penn State. Her research interests are at the intersection of race, property, and immigration. She was previously a chair of the Jamaica Trade Board. Brown was appointed by Andrew Holness, the Jamaican prime minister, to the CARICOM Commission. She has served on the boards of several publicly traded Caribbean companies. Brown holds a bachelor's degree in molecular biology from Brown University and was a Rhodes scholar at Oxford. She earned her JD from Yale and was a Reginald Lewis fellow at Harvard.

Naomi Cahn is Codirector of the Family Law Center at the University of Virginia School of Law, where she is Justice Anthony M. Kennedy Distinguished Professor of Law. She is the author or coauthor of numerous books and articles, including *Fair Shake: Women and the Fight to Build a Just Economy* (2024, coauthored with June Carbone and Nancy Levit).

I. Glenn Cohen is one of the world's leading experts on the intersection of bioethics (sometimes also called "medical ethics") and the law, as well as health law. His current projects relate to AI, big data, health information technologies, mobile health, reproduction/reproductive technology, research ethics, organ transplantation, rationing in law and medicine, health policy, FDA law, translational medicine, and medical tourism. He is the author of more than 200 articles and chapters and the author, coauthor, editor, or coeditor of more than twenty books.

Yaron Covo is a senior research fellow at the Solomon Center for Health Law and Policy, Yale Law School. He holds JSD and LLM degrees from Columbia Law School, where he was a Fulbright fellow, and an LLB from Tel Aviv University.

Cynthia Estlund is Crystal Eastman Professor at the New York University School of Law. Her most recent book is *Automation Anxiety: Why and How to Save Work* (2021). She has published widely on the law and regulation of work, including three earlier books (*A New Deal for China's Workers?* [2017], *Regoverning the Workplace: From Self-Regulation to Co-regulation* [2010], and *Working Together: How Workplace Bonds Strengthen a Diverse Democracy* [2003]), two coedited volumes, and more than eighty articles, book chapters, reviews, and essays.

Linda P. Fried is Dean of Columbia University's Mailman School of Public Health, serving since 2008. Since 2021 she has also served as Director of the university-wide Butler Columbia Aging Center. A geriatrician and epidemiologist, Fried has dedicated her career to the science and accomplishment of healthy longevity. Prior to 2008, Dr. Fried served as Director of Geriatric Medicine and Gerontology and of the Center on Aging and Health at Johns Hopkins Medical Institutions. She is an elected member of the US National Academy of Medicine and was past president of the Association of American Physicians. Recent honors include being named, in 2023, a chevalier of the Legion of Honor of France.

Abbe R. Gluck is Alfred M. Rankin Professor of Law and Faculty Director of the Solomon Center for Health Law and Policy at Yale Law School, and Professor of Medicine at Yale School of Medicine. She is one of America's leading experts in health law, Congress, litigation, and federalism, and has served in numerous senior government positions, including recently as Special Counsel to the President and lead lawyer for the White House COVID-19 Response Team. She is founding Faculty Director of the Yale Medical Legal Partnership, including the Yale Geriatric MLP, and The Adrienne Drell '92 M.S.L. and Franklin Nitikman '66 LL.B. Elder Law Project at Yale Law School.

Jamal Greene is Dwight Professor of Law at Columbia Law School, where he teaches courses in constitutional law, comparative constitutional law, and the law of the political process. He is the author of *How Rights Went Wrong: Why Our Obsession with Rights Is Tearing America Apart* (2022), as well as numerous articles and book chapters on constitutional law and theory. He served as a law clerk to Hon. Guido Calabresi on the US Court of Appeals for the Second Circuit and to Hon. John Paul Stevens on the US Supreme Court. He earned his JD from Yale Law School in 2005 and his AB from Harvard College in 1999.

Sara Sternberg Greene is Katharine T. Bartlett Distinguished Professor of Law at Duke University School of Law. She is a sociologist and legal scholar who uses primarily qualitative empirical methods to study the relationship between law, poverty, and inequality. Her work focuses on how low-income families understand, experience, and interact with the law, how legal institutions may inadvertently perpetuate poverty and inequality, and how structural conditions create barriers to accessing law and justice for low-income families. Greene received her BA from Yale University, her JD from Yale Law School, and her PhD in sociology and social policy from Harvard University.

Daniel J. Hemel is a professor of law at New York University School of Law. His research explores topics in taxation, intellectual property, administrative and constitutional law, and nonprofit organizations. His recent articles include "Valuing Medical Innovation," published in the *Stanford Law Review* in 2023 (with Lisa Ouellette), and "Regulation and Redistribution with Lives in the Balance," published in the *University of Chicago Law Review* in 2022. He has held visiting professorships at Harvard, Stanford, and Yale Law Schools and previously served on the faculty of the University of Chicago School of Law.

Shon Hopwood is an associate professor of law at Georgetown University Law Center. Shon's unusual legal journey began not at law school but at federal prison, where he learned to write briefs for other prisoners, including two petitions for certiorari that were later granted review by the US Supreme Court. Shon is an advocate for criminal justice reform and writes about federal courts and criminal procedure. Shon received a JD from the University of Washington School of Law as a Gates public service law scholar. He clerked for Judge Janice Rogers Brown at the US Court of Appeals for the District of Columbia Circuit. He cowrote a memoir entitled *Law Man: Memoir of a Jailhouse Lawyer* (2017).

Clare Huntington is Barbara Aronstein Black Professor of Law at Columbia Law School. Huntington is a nationally recognized expert in family law and poverty law. Her wide-ranging scholarship explores the institutions and empirical foundations of the legal system's approach to relationships. Her research focuses on early childhood development, aging, and the challenges facing nonmarital families because of the law's myopic focus on marriage.

Noah M. Kazis is an assistant professor of law at the University of Michigan Law School. His research focuses on land use, housing, and local government law. He studies legal and policy mechanisms to make cities and suburbs more affordable, equitable, and integrated, as well as the internal institutional structures of local governments.

Nina A. Kohn is David M. Levy Professor of Law and a distinguished scholar in elder law at Syracuse University. An expert in elder law, she is the author *of Elder Law: Practice, Policy, and Problems* (2020).

Douglas A. Kysar is Joseph M. Field '55 Professor of Law at Yale Law School. His teaching and research areas include torts, environmental law, climate change, products liability, and risk regulation. He received his BA summa cum laude from Indiana University in 1995 and his JD magna cum laude from Harvard Law School in 1998.

Joanna L. Martin is a palliative care physician at Jesse Brown VA Medical Center in Chicago and a clinical assistant professor at Northwestern University Feinberg School of Medicine. Dr. Martin is board-certified in internal medicine, geriatric medicine, and hospice and palliative medicine. She is a clinician educator with expertise in quality improvement.

John Morley is Augustus E. Lines Professor of Law at Yale Law School. He teaches and writes about the structure of organizations, including donative and business trusts. He was the reporter for the Uniform Directed Trust Act and an author of many articles on trusts and estate planning.

Katherine Pratt writes on tax and public policy topics and teaches tax and business law courses. She has received Loyola's Excellence in Teaching Award twice. She is an American College of Tax Counsel fellow, an American Tax Policy Institute trustee, a former member of the Board of Directors and Strategic Planning Committee of the National Tax Association, and a former chair of the Teaching Taxation Committee of the ABA Tax Section. She earned her BA from the University of Florida, her JD from UCLA, and her tax LLM and corporate LLM from New York University.

Kimberly Jenkins Robinson is Martha Lubin Karsh and Bruce A. Karsh Bicentennial Professor of Law at the University of Virginia School of Law, where she is the inaugural Director of the Education Rights Institute. She is the editor of *A Federal Right to Education: Fundamental Questions for Our Democracy* (2019) and coeditor, with Charles Ogletree, Jr., of *The Enduring Legacy of Rodriguez: Creating New Pathways to Equal Educational Opportunities* (2015). She was a former attorney for the General Counsel's Office of the US Department of Education and represented school districts with Hogan Lovells (then Hogan & Hartson).

Eugene Rusyn is a senior fellow at the Solomon Center for Health Law and Policy at Yale Law School. He holds a BA from New York University and a JD from Yale Law School.

Elizabeth Scott is Harold R. Medina Professor of Law Emerita at Columbia University School of Law. Her areas of scholarly interest are family and juvenile law. Much of her research is interdisciplinary, applying social science and neuroscience research and developmental theory to legal policy issues involving children and families. She is the coauthor (with Laurence Steinberg) of *Rethinking Juvenile Justice* (2008), which received the 2010 award for the best social policy book from the Society for Research in Adolescence. Scott is the Chief Reporter of a new "Restatement of Children and the Law" and the coauthor of a widely used casebook, *Children in the Legal System* (6th ed. 2020).

Gregory H. Shill is a professor of law and Michael and Brenda Sandler Faculty Fellow in Corporate Law at the University of Iowa College of Law. He is an expert in transportation law and policy as well as business law, and he cohosts an urban economics podcast, *Densely Speaking: Conversations about Cities, Economics & Law*.

Ganesh Sitaraman holds the New York Alumni Chancellor's Chair at Vanderbilt Law School and is Director of the Vanderbilt Policy Accelerator for Political Economy and Regulation. He is the author of numerous books, including *The Crisis of the Middle-Class Constitution* (2017).

Lior Jacob Strahilevitz is Sidley Austin Professor of Law at the University of Chicago. He writes about property and land use law, privacy law, and law and technology. He is a coauthor of the most widely adopted property law textbook in the US, as well as several other books and dozens of law review articles. His most recent long-form article examining aging and the law of property is "Property Law for the Ages," 63 *William & Mary Law Review* 561 (2021, with Michael Pollack).

Kenji Yoshino is Chief Justice Earl Warren Professor of Constitutional Law and Faculty Director of the Meltzer Center for Diversity, Inclusion, and Belonging at New York University School of Law. He is the author of four books, most recently *Say the Right Thing: How to Talk about Identity, Diversity, and Justice* (coauthored with David Glasgow, 2023).

Taisu Zhang is a professor of law at Yale Law School and works on comparative legal and economic history, private law theory, and contemporary Chinese law and politics. He is the author of two books, *The Ideological Foundations of Qing Taxation: Belief Systems, Politics, and Institutions* (2023) and *The Laws and Economics of Confucianism: Kinship and Property in Pre-industrial China and England* (2017).

Introduction

Eugene Rusyn, Abbe R. Gluck, and Anne L. Alstott

Recent studies suggest that many Americans will be able to live longer than ever – reaching 100 in record numbers and experiencing a greater quality of life throughout.[1] Such a demographic shift would transform society and the law across domains from medical care to employment to education and beyond.

Given the far-reaching implications of the 100-year life, this book provides the first comprehensive look at how the law will affect, and be affected by, the new longevity. We cast a very broad net, including topics both closely related to aging (such as health law, elder law, and trusts and estates) and less obvious but still critical areas for study (such as family law, housing, and infrastructure provision).

We recognize that *law* may not be some readers' first association with the 100-year life. Many contemplating their own extended longevity might naturally think about individual adaptations like savings, health plans, and family support. Taking a broader view, one might consider changes by employers, retirement systems, the healthcare system, and even networks of public transit and housing that must anticipate an older clientele. Indeed, it is precisely this range of topics that Lynda Gratton and Andrew Scott considered in their important book, *The 100-Year Life*,[2] which was part of the inspiration for this project. But law is integral to all of those topics, and a wide-ranging exploration of how legal developments intersect with such an inquiry – that is, how the law impacts, and will be impacted by, these trends and transformations – has not yet been undertaken.

Law is not simply the rules written in the books, although those will likely have to adapt to the new longevity, too. Law also constitutes a form of social infrastructure that will shape both individual and social adaptations to greater lifespan. It is law that creates the structures in which people make individual decisions, and it is law that shapes the options for work, entrepreneurship, family, housing, and many other collective endeavors. For example, the retirement age, which is set by law, will affect

[1] *See* Lynda Gratton & Andrew Scott, The 100-Year Life: Living and Working in an Age of Longevity (2016).

[2] *Id.*

economic options for workers, their families, and employers. The law also regulates access to a wide range of social and economic goods, including higher education, housing, and employment. Even family life, which we think of as quintessentially private, is shaped by law: It helps structure the obligations children have to their aging parents and that spouses have to each other.

As we consider the implications of the 100-year life, law faces two challenges. First, the fact of increasing longevity will strain some existing legal structures, like the Social Security retirement age, now set at sixty-seven. Accordingly, one task of this volume is to identify these strains and consider options for addressing them. Second, there is an affirmative question: Beyond patching up existing rules, how might legal policymakers change the law to ensure that the 100-year life offers even more well-being and opportunities than lifespan does today? Can we produce a "third demographic dividend," as some of our authors put it: a third period of productivity following the so-called prime of life in middle age?[3] Depending on how the law structures health care, employment, and disability – to take just a few examples – the 100-year life might bestow healthy, productive years on most Americans. It could produce second or third careers, new family structures, new ways of thinking about education, and so on. Or it might divide citizens into haves and have-nots, with much of the population suffering insecurity in their health and finances.

As the world continues adapting to the after-effects of the COVID-19 pandemic and the ongoing opioid crisis, the 100-year life may seem implausible. Average life expectancy in the US has fallen in the past decade even as it trails behind that of comparable countries.[4] The first years of the pandemic are illustrative. Between 2019 and 2022, US life expectancy fell by 1.3 years – from 78.8 to 77.5.[5] During the same period, comparable countries in the Organisation for Economic Co-operation and Development (OECD) experienced an average decline of nearly 0.5 years, from 82.6 to 82.2.[6] Indeed, among the same group, the US has the lowest life expectancy at birth for both men (74.8 compared to the average of 80.0) and women (80.2 compared to the average of 84.4) based on the most recently available data.[7] Meanwhile, racial disparities are stark – with declines in US life expectancy between

3 Yaron Covo, Abbe R. Gluck & Linda P. Fried, *The 100-Year-Old American and Our Health System, in* LAW AND THE 100-YEAR LIFE, 186–188 (Anne L. Alstott, Abbe R. Gluck & Eugene Rusyn eds., 2025).

4 *Life Expectancy in the U.S. Dropped for the Second Year in a Row in 2021*, CTRS. FOR DISEASE CONTROL & PREVENTION (Aug. 31, 2022), https://www.cdc.gov/nchs/pressroom/nchs_press_releases/2022/20220831.htm.

5 Chelsea Cirruzzo, *US Life Expectancy Rises after 2-Year Dip*, POLITICO (Mar. 31, 2024), https://www.politico.com/news/2024/03/21/cdc-us-life-expectancy-rises-after-two-year-dip-00148193.

6 *How Does U.S. Life Expectancy Compare to Other Countries?* KFF (Jan. 30, 2024), https://www.kff.org/slideshow/life-expectancy-in-the-u-s-and-how-it-compares-to-other-countries-slideshow.

7 Shameek Rakshit et al., *How Does U.S. Life Expectancy Compare to Other Countries?* PETERSON-KFF HEALTH SYS. TRACKER (Jan. 30, 2024), https://www.healthsystemtracker.org/chart-collection/u-s-life-expectancy-compare-countries.

2019 and 2022 ranging from 1.1 years for Asian people (from 85.6 to 84.5 years) to 3.9 years for American Indian and Alaska Native people (from 71.8 to 67.9 years).[8]

But the 100-year lifespan projection remains directionally valid, despite COVID and the opioid crises, because it rests on a century-long uptrend in longevity. It remains to be seen whether COVID will permanently lower the life expectancy of the elderly or will, instead, morph into a lesser threat. The same is true of the fentanyl epidemic, which as of this writing remains a significant danger to younger Americans. Data, nevertheless, show that the overall trend toward longer average lives remains strong when we look at, say, a century or half-century rather than a decade.[9] At the same time, the ranks of the longest-lived Americans increased appreciably over the same period. Between 1960 and 2021, the number of Americans at or over eighty-five grew at a faster rate than the general population – by more than six times.[10]

Still, an important theme of this book is that policymakers should recognize that a longer lifespan may not always be a blessing for individuals and for the earth. The experience of the 100-year life is likely to be heterogeneous. It is critical for the law to anticipate and cushion the impact of longevity for those with limited financial resources, those who have disabilities, those who experience poor health, as well as for categories that have not yet received due attention from the law, such as those living alone, caregivers, or people within or emerging from carceral settings.

In the chapters that follow, prominent legal scholars in a variety of fields take a fresh look at how their disciplines might change with increased population longevity. Each chapter addresses our two core questions. How will the 100-year life create or relieve stresses on existing law? And how might the law best be changed to anticipate the new pressures and generate the new opportunities that the 100-year life will bring?

I.1 KEY THEMES

Several key themes recur throughout this book, cutting across subjects.

I.1.1 *Longer Lives in a Time of Rapid Social Change*

The contours of family life in the US and across the developed world have changed radically in the last generation. For example, only about half of American adults are married – a marked change from the 80 percent or more who were married in, say,

8 Latoya Hill, Nambi Ndugga & Samantha Artiga, *Key Data on Health and Health Care by Race and Ethnicity*, KFF (June 11, 2024), https://www.kff.org/racial-equity-and-health-policy/report/key-data-on-health-and-health-care-by-race-and-ethnicity.

9 Elizabeth Arias et al., *Provisional Life Expectancy Estimates for 2021*, Vital Stat. Rapid Release, No. 23 (2022), https://www.cdc.gov/nchs/data/vsrr/vsrr023.pdf.

10 Reed Abelson & Jordan Rau, *Facing Financial Ruin as Costs Soar for Elder Care*, KFF (Nov. 14, 2023), https://kffhealthnews.org/news/article/dying-broke-facing-financial-ruin-as-costs-soar-for-elder-care.

1960. Meanwhile, the percentage of childless Americans is rising.[11] All of these changes will affect, and may be affected by, increasing longevity. The assumptions built into Social Security, for example, are badly outdated. The system's benefit structure rests on the assumption that most workers and parents are married. The result is that too many single workers and single parents face disadvantage.[12] Similarly, the Medicare system still incorporates the outdated presumption that older people have a live-in spouse or adult children who can provide care when they are discharged from the hospital. These outdated assumptions also need to be updated to take into account and improve on where older people live as they age and who cares for them.

Working life has also undergone major transformations. The demise of lifelong employment and the rise of gig work have major implications for workers' financial security. The guaranteed pensions that accompanied long-term employment have largely disappeared, leaving most workers in Generation Z and thereafter to rely on whatever they have saved in a 401(k) or on their own. The rise in college attendance in the last generation has boosted earnings for some but has saddled many more with high levels of student debt that, in turn, make savings more difficult. Workforce changes, occasioned by technological developments like artificial intelligence (AI), may require retraining multiple generations of workers. On the positive side, options for flexible work have benefited older workers, who increasingly pursue a "Third Age" of entrepreneurship, volunteer work, and career retraining.

I.1.2 *Underinvestment*

Whether in the geriatric healthcare workforce, innovations, retirement savings, longevity-friendly housing, public health efforts to prevent chronic disease, or infrastructure like public transportation, we have an epidemic of underinvestment in the areas essential to a healthy lifespan. Chronic underfunding could leave older Americans more vulnerable to major changes ahead. As automation and AI upend the workforce, funding programs that help adults learn new skills and change occupations will be essential. Meanwhile, investing in climate-resilient communities and helping relocate those in vulnerable regions *before* disaster strikes will save lives and cost less than waiting for the next storm.

I.1.3 *Longevity amid Rising Inequality*

Inequality already impacts several critical dimensions of American life. Compared to the mid twentieth century, a greater share of the country's economic product now

[11] Exactly 19.6 percent of Americans between fifty-five and sixty-four reported being childless in 2018, a larger percentage than for older demographics (15.9 percent of those aged sixty-five to seventy-four and 10.9 percent for those over seventy-five). Tayelor Valerio et al., U.S. Census Bureau, Childless Older Americans: 2018 (2021).

[12] Anne L. Alstott, A New Deal for Old Age: Toward a Progressive Retirement (2016).

goes to families in the top percentiles. Longevity itself is unequally distributed: Higher-income people can expect to live a decade or more than their lower-income counterparts.[13] Health and disability also skew to the better-off, with less-educated workers living at or near the poverty line reporting higher rates of functional decline with age.[14] Underlying these inequalities are differences in earnings, working conditions, housing, and access to health care.

Indeed, poverty is a pressing concern for some among the elderly. Poverty rates for elderly women exceed those for elderly men. The reality of being old and poor is common – with one study finding that approximately one-third of elderly Americans live at or below 200 percent of the Federal Poverty Line.[15] Racial disparities accentuate the problem – with data indicating that half of Black and Latinx elderly Americans live at or below 200 percent of the Federal Poverty Line.[16]

I.1.4 *Being Young in an Aging Society*

Today, the large Baby Boom generation is near or past retirement age. Greater longevity is already challenging the law in myriad ways that affect not just new retirees but also their children. On the family front, the "sandwich generation" of middle-aged people must fund and provide care for children and older family members simultaneously. When compared with peers who only care for an older parent, sandwich-generation caregivers are twice as likely to report financial difficulty and more likely to report substantial emotional difficulty.[17]

In the workplace, the delayed retirement of some Boomers seems to be limiting the upward mobility of the young. And yet in some fields like government work, the retirement of senior people can leave younger groups without much-needed guidance and institutional memory. Meanwhile, some older Americans may seek to stay in the workforce longer because they cannot afford several decades of retirement – with longer *working* lives potentially exacerbating job scarcity for younger workers.

I.1.5 *The Politics of Gerontocracy*

A growing population of older Americans is likely to impact the political system. If – as is now true – older people vote more, serve more in government, and are

[13] Raj Chetty et al., *The Association between Income and Life Expectancy in the United States, 2001–2014*, 315 JAMA 1750 (2016).

[14] NAT'L RSCH. COUNCIL, AGING AND THE MACROECONOMY: LONG-TERM IMPLICATIONS OF AN OLDER POPULATION, 68–69 figs. 4-1 and 4-3 (2012).

[15] *Id.*

[16] National Council on Aging, *Get the Facts on Economic Security for Seniors* (Feb. 22, 2024), https://www.ncoa.org/article/get-the-facts-on-economic-security-for-seniors.

[17] Donovan Maust, *"Sandwich Generation" Study Shows Challenges of Caring for Both Kids and Aging Parents*, UNIV. OF MICH. INST. FOR HEALTHCARE POL'Y & INNOVATION (Dec. 7, 2022), https://ihpi.umich.edu/news/sandwich-generation-study-shows-challenges-caring-both-kids-and-aging-parents.

wealthier, the effect could be gerontocracy – defined as rule by the elderly. Inequalities already present in *who* lives longer will be exacerbated by the possibility that those Americans will amass and wield power to the detriment of younger and less-wealthy citizens. Indeed, as of this writing the median age in the Senate is sixty-three, and nearly one in five congresspeople is seventy or older.[18] Local elections also favor older long-time residents.

Gerontocracy may result in policies adversely affecting and out of step with young voters. Climate change offers a case in point, as older Americans are less likely than younger ones to identify the issue as a priority and to support policies aimed at addressing it.[19] The misalignment between who wields present power and who will bear future harms points to a potential crisis of political legitimacy to come.

I.1.6 *What to Pass On and What to Protect*

Increased life expectancy will likely deepen the importance of inheritance – furthering intergenerational economic dependency and boosting the socioeconomic status of the elderly. The rise of practices like "giving while living" – wherein parts of an estate are distributed to heirs while one is still alive through mechanisms such as property purchases and tax-free cash transfers of estate money – suggest that resulting wealth distributions could further entrench inequities along the way.

And then there is the different political problem altogether of ageism. To counter this and related harms, a positive "right to grow old" could ensure a certain minimum quality of life to people as they age, while programs supporting the elderly could be tailored to their vulnerabilities, recognizing that needs vary *within* age cohorts. Closely related will be new ethical questions, such as the right to parent and the right to die as we get older.

I.2 CONTRIBUTORS

The 100-year life will profoundly impact law and policy. The diverse contributors to this book illuminate the enormous range of questions it raises and how they might be answered.

Part I *Implications across the Legal System*

Part I offers a broad introduction to how the 100-year life disrupts assumptions across core areas of law that structure our lives, like family law, education, work, and

[18] Charlie Hunt, *Analysis: Why Are There So Many Older Lawmakers than Young Ones in Congress?* PBS NEWS (July 11, 2024), https://www.pbs.org/newshour/politics/analysis-why-are-there-so-many-more-older-lawmakers-than-young-ones-in-congress.

[19] Cary Funk, *Key Findings: How Americans' Attitudes about Climate Change Differ by Generation, Party and Other Factors*, PEW RSCH. CTR. (May 26, 2021), https://www.pewresearch.org/short-reads/2021/05/26/key-findings-how-americans-attitudes-about-climate-change-differ-by-generation-party-and-other-factors.

criminal justice. In doing so, it asks us to reimagine the way law frames age itself: both how life is structured over time – including what major milestones happen when – as well as when different needs emerge, even for people of the same age.

The stage is set by **Anne L. Alstott**, whose chapter argues that the conventional three-stage model of human life – from childhood to adulthood to old age – is being challenged by social and economic changes that the 100-year life will likely amplify. Laws tailored around typical life patterns protect those who conform – by finishing their education early in life, marrying in young adulthood and joining a stable workplace, and retiring by sixty-seven – while disadvantaging those who do not. If law does not adapt to new life patterns, it will worsen existing inequalities. Alstott draws on the examples of higher education, family and inheritance, and retirement to illustrate how lives are already diverging from assumptions embedded in law, as well as to suggest needed reforms.

Naomi Cahn, **Clare Huntington**, and **Elizabeth Scott** spotlight ongoing changes in the American family – with individuals marrying later and perhaps more often, creating blended families comprised of various generations with varied parentage, and taking on unique caregiving configurations. The authors argue that even in the face of societal changes, families will remain the primary setting for caregiving and caretaking – whatever form those families take. As a result, the authors suggest that legal reform should recognize the range of family relationships older Americans are likely to choose among.

As families adapt to longer life expectancy, ensuring equitable access to education becomes increasingly vital. **Kimberly Jenkins Robinson** reveals why by, first, explaining the integral role played by education in ensuring that individuals can live a long life. Robinson notes that educational opportunity gaps will hinder both the lifespans and options – among careers, earnings, and health – of many poor and minority individuals. She then presents a series of proposals for how education law and policy can be reformed to close these gaps.

Shon Hopwood investigates the criminal justice system and lays out how everything from sentencing to the conditions of prisons should be reconsidered given longer lifespans. He notes that the annual cost of incarcerating people over fifty-five is roughly three to five times that of younger people – all while older individuals released from prison have the lowest rates of rearrest. Despite this, between 1999 and 2016, the number of prisoners aged fifty-five and older grew by 280 percent. Hopwood argues that the 100-year life necessitates reforms including rehabilitation and vocational programs that would help the incarcerated succeed once released and a reconsideration of what constitutes adequate punishment for a crime in the first place – both the length of sentences and what crimes should lead to imprisonment.

Cynthia Estlund closes Part I by considering the future of work. She identifies a fundamental challenge: To afford more years of retirement, most people will have to work longer. Intergenerational competition could increase while integration at work may become more challenging given the steady introduction of new technologies requiring specialized skills. At the same time, the presence of a growing older workforce could increase the tendency of employers to dismiss or refuse to hire aging workers.

Part II *Protecting Rights and Preparing for the Future*

Part II explores rights and readiness for the future. Bookended by discussions of how antidiscrimination law and constitutional law can better protect the 100-year life, questions of inequality, ageism, organizing the older workforce, and reckoning with savings are considered – both to prepare for a longer life and with an eye toward what younger generations might inherit.

Kenji Yoshino opens the section by arguing that, to realize the full potential of this transformative moment, our age discrimination paradigm should transcend the traditional civil rights model around race and sex. This new approach should respond to the distinctive fears about mortality that older individuals conjure. Indeed, it is these fears that partly justify why courts should care more about ageism.

Ganesh Sitaraman explores the intersection – and potential consequences – of increased life expectancy and growing wealth inequality. He suggests that rising life expectancy will be unequally shared due to differences in wealth, education, and geography. These inequities, as we have noted, will impact representative government, with potentially destabilizing consequences.

Nina A. Kohn argues that the 100-year life should encourage a shift away from age-based policies that will disproportionately disadvantage already disadvantaged groups who may have worse health and more restricted capabilities than their richer peers. Kohn calls for an approach whereby social welfare interventions target the vulnerability of a population to the issue(s) the intervention is meant to address.

Given the precarity facing older workers, labor law may offer tools for protecting an older workforce. **Kate Andrias** notes that seniors are more likely to work as independent contractors than younger workers, often taking these jobs to supplement inadequate retirement savings. Yet the law lacks a clear framework for independent contractors – as well as retirees and unemployed workers. Reforms empowering older workers and retirees to negotiate collectively could help support the 100-year life.

Sara Sternberg Greene considers older Americans facing retirement with limited resources, noting that those who enter old age with little or no savings often face medical problems without adequate coverage and are forced to continue working to afford housing and food. To help ameliorate these harms, Greene argues that we must confront "the savings mirage." The government does not provide citizens making near-poverty-level wages with a solid financial foundation prior to retirement. At the same time, it effectively prevents those making low wages from building a nest-egg for retirement via antisavings policies, such as asset limitations for basic safety net programs. Absent substantial policy reform, Greene suggests that we face an elderly poverty epidemic.

John Morley argues that those expecting to live to 100 will likely have less to transfer at death – partly because living longer will require expending more resources, leaving less to pass on – and may prefer to distribute holdings to descendants and beneficiaries before death. Attempts to meet the challenge of lifetime transfers will be complicated by the existing legal and policy regime, particularly involving taxation. Morley concludes by arguing that, while the law of trusts and estates will remain an essential feature of the legal system, it will increasingly take on the function of a backstop rather than a preferred means for dividing estates.

Closing Part II, **Jamal Greene** considers a "right to grow old" under the US Constitution. Greene acknowledges that this would require recognizing governmental duties that are atypical in American constitutional law. Nevertheless, he suggests that objections could be countered through strategies successfully applied in courts around the world, including proportionality review and polycentric constitutionalism.

Part III *Health, Workforce, and Innovation: the Investments Required for a Healthy Lifespan*

Part III surveys healthcare infrastructure, innovation, and bioethics, targeting areas where our society has underinvested given the demographic changes under way. Contributors discuss services central to an older population like long-term care – from how it is funded to ways to grow relevant workforces – as well as how major scientific breakthroughs needed to extend life could be secured through and beyond intellectual property law, before exploring challenging bioethical questions raised by longer life.

A citizenry of centenarians will need effective and affordable access to health care. **Yaron Covo**, **Abbe R. Gluck**, and **Linda P. Fried** open Part III by discussing necessary investments to make longer lives healthier. Investing in much more public health to prevent disease, managing chronic conditions, and expanding the geriatric workforce are critical reforms, as is reconsideration of the long-term care and housing needs of the aging population. Pressing all of these levers, they argue, is needed to reap the "third demographic dividend" whereby society realizes the benefits – both economic and noneconomic – of having a healthy and engaged older population.

Expanding on long-term care, **Katherine Pratt** identifies a glaring shortfall in the US social insurance system: The federal government does not provide universal social insurance for long-term care in old age. Noting that an estimated two-thirds of individuals aged sixty-five or older will require long-term services and supports (LTSS) at some point in their lives, Pratt assesses alternative means of accessing and funding LTSS, before concluding by suggesting ways how policymakers can help improve the "healthspan" of future seniors.

To meet the needs of a growing elderly demographic, **Eleanor Brown** argues that immigration law must be reformed. Noting that the growth in paid home care has been largely staffed by migrant labor – with some care workers operating outside the legal scope of their visas – Brown suggests the creation of a new immigration system for care workers.

Daniel J. Hemel considers how intellectual property (IP) law affects the goal of a longer lifespan that is also healthier. Hemel points out that while IP and patents, in particular, are seen as key mechanisms for encouraging scientific research, they are an imperfect fit for interventions that slow the aging process. Hemel spotlights the need for major public sector investment in aging research – a moonshot program for longevity – to make up for these structural limitations.

Finally, **I. Glenn Cohen** takes up two pressing bioethical questions raised by the 100-year life, beginning with whether life extension itself is worth pursuing. Breakthroughs might not be equally distributed, while developing breakthroughs would consume resources that might be better spent elsewhere – such as improving the lives of the currently disadvantaged. Cohen then pivots to a different question facing those living longer: whether to have children late in life. After briefly considering how this could happen, Cohen raises two debates in reproductive bioethics. He focuses on the rights claim to reproduce, particularly as to state support for reproduction, before closing with whether reproduction late in life is harmful to children born out of it.

Part IV *The 100-Year Life and Our Broader Environment*

Part IV maps the interplay of local government, housing, transportation, and property law in shaping the 100-year life – from localities responding to climate change to zoning reforms designed to encourage aging in place.

Demographic trends will play out in a rapidly changing world. **Eugene Rusyn** and **Douglas A. Kysar** open Part IV by considering how climate change will impact elderly Americans – from housing and long-term care to the financing of retirement – and suggest needed policy reform, such as a streamlined long-term support program for displaced older people. They also argue that older Americans might contribute to environmental justice through litigation, bringing novel cases that seek to compel government action on climate change rooted in the unique harms they face.

Noah M. Kazis argues that the interests of older citizens are disproportionately represented at the local level. This – coupled with a divide between age groups on core local functions, particularly education and infrastructure – creates the potential for conflicts that local government is ill-suited to resolve. Kazis considers a variety of potential reforms – ranging from equalizing voters' patterns of participation to reassigning some local responsibilities to state and national governments – that could help local government represent and serve all its citizens.

Gregory H. Shill lays out how transportation and land use policy have created a built environment where the centrality of driving can undermine the 100-year life. Roadside deaths claim American lives at disproportionately young ages, cutting life expectancy. Meanwhile, those who reach old age face an average of seven to ten years when driving becomes too dangerous – limiting their access to everything from groceries to health care, thereby degrading independence and worsening quality of life. Shill suggests interventions that tackle both problems, opening the 100-year life to more people while making it better throughout.

Looking to the future with a comparative lens, **Taisu Zhang** tracks the likely impact of aging populations moving toward cities on property law and land use regulations. Zhang contrasts the US property system, defined by private self-governance, with that of nations in East and Southeast Asia – home to a disproportionately high number of the world's largest and richest megacities, as well as some of the most aggressive and powerful property governance regimes. He concludes that despite the need for a greater state role in responding to elder-driven urbanization, the US will likely double down on its current exclusion-driven regime – much like governance-oriented nations like China and Japan will demand ever greater government intrusion.

Joanna L. Martin and **Lior Jacob Strahilevitz** conclude Part IV by considering the impact of the COVID-19 pandemic on providing safe housing for an elderly population. The authors spotlight housing models that allowed residents to weather COVID relatively well and which, as a result, they suspect the elderly will prefer over traditional nursing homes. They focus on "Green House" nursing homes, noting that this and other popular options will be impeded by existing zoning laws. They close with suggestions for reform.

*

Law, thus broadly conceived, has an essential role to play in who will age, how they age, where they age, and more. The chapters in this book are meant to provoke creative and ambitious thinking about the law's potential as a tool, rather than an obstacle, to a better 100-year-life.

Nothing less than transformative – and trans-substantive – thinking is needed to match the revolutionary social, political, and economic changes that await. Whether we meet the challenge will determine if the 100-year life is defined by inequity or greater opportunity – securing longer health as well as lifespans, and a thriving polity within and across generations for years to come.

PART I

Implications across the Legal System

1

How the 100-Year Life Challenges the Legal Model of the Human Life Cycle

Anne L. Alstott

Many areas of the law rely, explicitly or implicitly, on a three-stage model of the human life cycle. According to this familiar construct, the first stage is childhood, the second is adulthood, and the third is old age. Childhood ends with high school graduation, and old age begins with retirement. In their book, Lynda Gratton and Andrew Scott point out that increasing longevity will challenge the three-stage life cycle, as human beings who expect to live for a century begin to reshape their lives accordingly.[1] In this chapter, I consider the related topic of how the prospect of the 100-year life might – and should – change assumptions about the life cycle that are now built into the law.

The three-stage model of the life cycle plays an organizing role in the law; it is a simplifying construction, a set of unwritten assumptions about the life course, that helps impose order and make rules possible.[2] Like any model, it relies on averages and generalities. And so, according to the law, childhood ends at age eighteen (voting) or twenty-one (drinking), for instance, even though adolescents vary in their maturity levels. The world of work begins at about age sixteen (when child labor laws no longer apply), even though some people (think child actors or college graduates) begin work earlier or later. Old age begins at age sixty-seven, with the full retirement age for Social Security, even though many older adults enjoy fine health and work into their seventies and eighties.

The three-stage model of the life cycle plays both a descriptive and a prescriptive role in the law. Those whose lives fit neatly into the three stages find themselves protected by law; those whose lives diverge may be excluded from legal protections

1 Lynda Gratton & Andrew Scott, The 100-Year Life: Living and Working in an Age of Longevity (2016).

2 To take another example, consider the rules of family law, which define a parent as an immediate biological forbear or a formal adopter. These rules describe many people who provide the close and continuous care that human children require, but they exclude others: The rules of parenthood are, first and foremost, *legal* tools that demarcate the powers of adults with respect to children. *See* Anne Alstott, Anne Dailey & Douglas NeJaime, *Psychological Parenthood*, 106 Minn. L. Rev. 2363 (2022).

and benefits.[3] Teen parents, for example, pose a paradox for the law, because they are simultaneously entitled (under federal constitutional law) to govern their own children while being subject to the control of their own parents (or the state).[4] Adult children pose another legal puzzle: Federal tax benefits for children generally end when children turn seventeen or eighteen, even though one-third of young adults between eighteen and thirty-four now live with their parents.[5] Early retirees face a financial disadvantage, even when poor health or economic catastrophe forecloses their work options. And retirement law sometimes treats work and retirement as mutually exclusive, denying older people the ability to work while also taking retirement benefits.[6]

In this chapter, I show that social and economic changes have already undermined the three-stage model of the life cycle, and that those changes will likely accelerate as society comes to terms with the prospect of the 100-year life. The result is that the law's rules are increasingly inaccurate, as a descriptive matter, and unjust, as a normative matter.

Today, adolescence extends into the twenties for many young people, who spend years in and out of higher education and living with their parents. Marriage and work, the major institutions that once defined adulthood, have morphed as well. More and more people never marry; those who do often have several marriages. Blended families and single parenthood have become common, and many people have children in their thirties and forties and beyond. The stable workplace has given way to gig jobs, midlife unemployment, and precarious service jobs.

Even in old age, life has changed. Today, affluent workers enjoy good health and wide opportunities into their seventies and beyond, while ordinary workers face poor

3 Another legal punishment takes the form of exclusion from the three-stage model. Sometimes, exclusion and punishment are deliberate and explicit. For instance, the Fair Labor Standards Act (limiting child labor) and the Social Security Act (creating a federal retirement system) exempted farm workers and domestic workers, groups that were disproportionately Black. *See* Phyllis Palmer, *Outside the Law: Agricultural and Domestic Workers under the Fair Labor Standards Act*, 7 J. Policy Hist. 416 (1995); Social Security Act of 1935 § 210. These legal omissions denied these workers the protected spheres of childhood and retirement and left them with a version of the cradle-to-grave employment that dated from slavery.

4 Maya Manian, *Minors, Parents, and Minor Parents*, 81 Mo. L. Rev. 127 (2016); Kendra J. H. Fershee, *A Parent Is a Parent, No Matter How Small*, 18 Wm. & Mary J. Women & L. 425 (2012).

5 Jonathan Vespa, *Jobs, Marriage and Kids Come Later in Life*, US Bureau of the Census, https://www.census.gov/library/stories/2017/08/young-adults.html.

6 Private pensions may not permit current workers, even if past age sixty-five, to claim benefits while also drawing a salary. *FAQs about Retirement Plans and ERISA*, US Dep't of Lab., https://www.dol.gov/sites/dolgov/files/EBSA/about-ebsa/our-activities/resource-center/faqs/retirement-plans-and-erisa-for-workers.pdf. The Social Security rules reduce benefits for some retirees who continue to work. The current version of the earnings test reduces benefits only for early retirees and compensates with a higher benefit after full retirement age. *See Retirement Earnings Test*, Social Security Administration, https://www.ssa.gov/policy/docs/program-explainers/retirement-earnings-test.html.

health and shrinking employment options, often in their fifties. Social Security's rules, designed for an earlier era, increasingly reward the life patterns of the highly paid and penalize the life patterns of low earners.[7]

The 100-year life will further upend the three-stage life cycle and likely demand a new model – a new set of descriptive and prescriptive propositions about the life course. And the model adopted will influence how Americans experience the new, longer life cycle. One set of laws might consign people to live out extra years in pain and penury, while another set might help most people enjoy longer years of health and vitality. And so, even though predictions about the 100-year life involve some speculation, it is the kind of speculation that we should undertake. The power of the law will distribute rewards and punishments according to the model of the life cycle we choose.

In this chapter, I expand on these ideas using examples drawn from three areas of law: higher education, family and inheritance, and retirement. For each, I document why the three-stage model is inaccurate and why that inaccuracy produces objectionable results. And I will speculate about the issues the law should address in anticipation of the 100-year life.

1.1 HIGHER EDUCATION AS A LIFELONG TRANSITION MECHANISM

The three-stage life cycle frames higher education as once-in-a-lifetime career preparation. On this model, late adolescents obtain their degrees and then use them in a career lasting decades. But Lynda Gratton and Andrew Scott point out that the 100-year life is likely to change the higher education system, as long-lived adults make multiple transitions among jobs over their lifetimes.[8]

The once-in-a-lifetime norm is not written in law, and so middle-aged and older people can, in theory, return to school and change careers. But the US system of higher education finance is built on the once-in-a-lifetime norm. Two-thirds of students seeking a bachelor's degree take out loans, even at state universities, and the average borrower graduates with more than $30,000 in debt.[9] Among all student debtors, 20 percent owe more than $60,000.[10] Students who earn graduate degrees take on far more debt: On average, those earning medical degrees now graduate with nearly $250,000 in student debt, and those earning law degrees graduate with $150,000.[11]

7 Anne L. Alstott, A New Deal for Old Age (2016) (chapters 2 and 3).
8 *See* Gratton & Scott, *supra* note 1.
9 *Loans for Undergraduate Students and Debt for Bachelors Degree Recipients*, National Center for Education Statistics (last updated May 2023), https://nces.ed.gov/programs/coe/indicator/cub.
10 Kadija Yilla & David Wessel, *Five Facts about Student Loans*, Brookings Inst. (2019), https://www.brookings.edu/blog/up-front/2019/11/12/five-facts-about-student-loans.
11 *Trends in Graduate Student Loan Debt*, National Center for Education Statistics (Aug. 2, 2018), https://nces.ed.gov/blogs/nces/post/trends-in-graduate-student-loan-debt.

These price tags deter a second round of higher education, and the tuition cost is only part of the expense. Living costs for late adolescents are relatively low, because they tend to be single, live in cheap, shared housing, and (in many cases) have access to parental resources. By contrast, midlife students are more likely to have children of their own, to own homes, and to shoulder other obligations (e.g., caring for aging parents). To secure another round of higher education, these students would have to save or borrow enough to fund tuition plus all these costs.

All this would not be a problem if higher education could continue to be a once-in-a-lifetime task undertaken in early adulthood. But the prospect of the 100-year life should prompt us to ask whether we should, instead, see higher education as one (of many) lifelong transition mechanisms.

The Great Recession and, most recently, the COVID-19 pandemic have illustrated the economic shocks that can decimate whole industries without warning. More gradual, longer-term trends toward the outsourcing and mechanization of jobs also point toward the need for transition mechanisms.

If later-in-life access to higher education is to be made real, then hard questions about education finance must be addressed. At a minimum, tuition costs should be held in check, and financial aid should be readily available to older workers, even though they have shorter working periods in which to repay their debt. More ambitiously, the states (perhaps supported by federal funds) could radically reduce tuition at state colleges and universities.

Stepping back, the larger issue is whether we ought to take seriously the idea of *higher education as a social risk-sharing device* rather than a once-in-a-lifetime private purchase. Seen in that light, midlife college tuition might properly be included in a social insurance scheme of some kind. And this requires a more thorough reimagining of the risks of a (very long) working life.

The twentieth-century Social Security system continues to insure most US workers (and their families) against three big economic risks: disability, retirement, and early death. The unemployment insurance system insures against short-term unemployment. But there is no universal, public program for workers who fall victim to economic shocks and find that their skills are simply worth little in the marketplace.

Reimagining the role of higher education in our social insurance system is a big agenda but an important one, and the prospect of the 100-year life intensifies the need to undertake it.

1.2 SERIAL MONOGAMY AND LASTING PARENTHOOD

Families have changed remarkably since the mid twentieth century. At that time, most people married in young adulthood and remained married to the same partner through old age. Children came along when their parents were young adults and were expected to be self-sufficient and well into their own adulthood once parents reached old age. These patterns were remarkably consistent across social classes from World War II until the 1970s.[12]

These patterns fit the three-stage model of the life cycle. The first stage is one's own childhood; the second is the childrearing years; and the third is retirement and old age, when children are long gone. In this model, marriage marked the longest-lasting and most important relationship in any lifetime; a lasting marriage anchored the nuclear family and defined one's economic and social life.[13]

This model of the family strongly influenced family law and inheritance law, which treated – and continue to treat – the spousal relationship as primary. Divorce in the US was relatively rare until the late twentieth century. Beginning in the 1970s, as divorce rates rose, legal reformers took as their major task to recognize and protect mothers by providing alimony and child support. Intestacy laws also aimed to protect spouses, with typical laws giving priority to spouses over children in inheritance.[14]

Along similar lines, Social Security enacted rules to protect spouses, awarding a spousal benefit equal to half the higher earner's own benefit. Medicaid rules, too, presumed a close and lasting spousal bond: The notorious asset rules treat a couple's assets as entirely shared – and require the couple to spend down its assets before claiming assistance for a spouse who needs, say, nursing home care.

These laws remain on the books even though family patterns have dramatically changed in two general ways.[15] First, there is far more diversity in family patterns and in the content of family life across life stages. Many adults never marry; among those who do, divorce is common. Cohabitation is common and widely accepted in every age group. Children live with married and unmarried parents, with step-parents, and with grandparents.[16]

Second, for many people, the spousal relationship has become secondary to the parent–child relationship. More and more people never marry, and more have children outside marriage. Lifelong marriage is becoming rare, while serial marriage and blended families have become quite common. At the same time, the parent–child bond has been strengthened. Today's parents tend to be emotionally closer to their children, to remain connected into the children's adulthood. And more and

[12] Anne L. Alstott, *Updating the Welfare State: Marriage, the Income Tax, and Social Security in the Age of the New Individualism*, 66 Tax L. Rev. 695 (2013).

[13] *Id.*

[14] *See, e.g.*, Uniform Probate Code (UPC) § 2-102 (providing for 100 percent inheritance by the spouse if all of the decedent's descendants are also the spouse's descendants, and roughly one-half if there are unshared descendants). *See also* UPC § 2-301 (protecting spousal inheritance in case of a premarital will).

[15] In their chapter in this volume, Naomi Cahn, Claire Huntington, and Elizabeth Scott provide a detailed review of changing demographics and implications across a wide range of family laws.

[16] *See* Alstott, *supra* note 12, at 708–720.

more young adult children remain financially dependent on their parents well past age eighteen.[17]

And so, the law is outdated already, even before we confront the 100-year life. The rules of family law, at least arguably, should provide default rules that reflect the social practices and intentions of most people. Meeting that aspiration is more difficult now than in the twentieth century, because family patterns are more variable. Even so, we could redesign key components of the law to better mirror current patterns. Consider three examples that illustrate the adverse consequences of the current mismatch between actual lives and the law's imagined three-stage model.

First, millions of grandparents rear their grandchildren for long periods.[18] These arrangements can encounter legal trouble across several fronts. One issue concerns custody, when absent parents return and want "their children" back. When the law privileges parents' biological tie over grandparents' on-the-ground parenting work, the result is that children can be separated from their loving caregivers, despite the adverse effects of such separation.[19] Another issue concerns parental permissions for medical treatment and education; the law does not readily or automatically substitute grandparents even when they are doing the day-to-day work. Still another issue concerns retirement and survivor benefits: Grandparents may claim a "parent's" benefit to supplement their retirement benefit, but only if the child's parents are dead or officially disabled – a condition often not met even when parents are de facto absent.

Second, intestacy laws are badly out of step with many lives.[20] The law tends to ignore even long-term cohabitants, who cannot (in many states) claim a share of the estate or make healthcare decisions for their partner.[21] At the same time, the law tends to (over)privilege some formal marriages, awarding the surviving spouse a hefty share of the estate, even if (say) a later-in-life marriage and both spouses would prefer to see their own children (from prior relationships) inherit. Medicaid treats all formally married couples as joint owners of all assets, even if one or both spouses have children from a past relationship. Social Security, too, ignores cohabitation and adult children and privileges formal marriage.

Third, child support obligations often end, by statute, when children are eighteen, even though most children attend some kind of postsecondary education and

17 Karen L. Fingerman, *Millennials and Their Parents: Implications of the New Young Adulthood for Midlife Adults*, 1 Innovation in Aging (2017).

18 Eli Rapoport et al., *Family Well-Being in Grandparent- versus Parent-Headed Households*, 146 Pediatrics (2020).

19 The facts of the famous case *Painter v. Bannister* illustrate the problem; the result in that case, which rules for the grandparents, remains legally contestable. 140 N.W.2d 152 (Iowa 1966).

20 *See* Naomi R. Cahn & Amy Ziettlow, *"Making Things Fair": An Empirical Study of How People Approach the Wealth Transmission System*, 22 Elder L.J. (2015).

21 *See Common Law Marriage by State*, National Conference of State Legislatures, https://www.ncsl.org/research/human-services/common-law-marriage.aspx.

many live at home well past eighteen. The law varies across states, but in a number of states, parents are not legally obligated to contribute to a child's college expenses. The result is that a custodial parent often cannot count on a noncustodial parent to contribute.

Savvy families can contract around some of these issues. A guardianship agreement can grant day-to-day authority to grandparents (but only if parents consent). A will can specify the decedents' desired outcome; most states, for instance, permit a (postmarital) will to disinherit a spouse entirely. Divorcing parents typically have the option (though not the obligation) to formalize an agreement about child support after age eighteen.

But default rules are powerful, because very few people realize that they need to opt out and manage to do so. And the most vulnerable people are least likely to know about the importance of contracting around adverse default rules.[22]

It is far from clear how the 100-year life will affect trends in family life, but it seems unlikely that a longer lifespan will somehow return us to mid twentieth-century patterns. A longer life may well magnify trends toward serial relationships: People with (say) ninety years of healthy, active life to anticipate might routinely opt for two, three, or more marriages or marriage-like relationships.[23] A longer lifespan plus evolving reproductive technology could radically alter the life cycle related to childbearing and childrearing as well. Even today, it is common for people in their forties to have babies, and the technology exists to extend into the fifties and beyond.

Freed from the "biological clock," and anticipating a much longer lifespan, women and men might undertake radically new patterns of career and childbearing. Some might wait until their forties or fifties to start a family, establishing secure careers beforehand. Others might spread out childbearing, having (say) one child in one's thirties and another in one's fifties. Still others might do the childrearing part first, having children while young and relying on long years later to establish careers. This is all speculation, yet we ought to take care that the law does not impede the evolution of family life – and productive innovations.

1.3 THE NEW INEQUALITY OF OLD AGE

In the mid twentieth century, the three-stage life cycle was also reasonably descriptive of old age. Until relatively recently, the experience of old age was not so very different for the rich and for the poor. Through the mid twentieth century, the great majority of people of all income classes aged in a similar way. Most men died in

[22] For an analysis of default rules in family law, *see* Margaret Brinig, *Penalty Defaults in Family Law: The Case of Child Custody* (Feb. 2005), University of Iowa Legal Studies Research Paper No. 05-08; Adrienne D. Davis, *Regulating Polygamy: Intimacy, Default Rules, and Bargaining for Equality*, 110 Colum. L. Rev. 1955 (2010).

[23] *See* Gratton & Scott, *supra* note 1.

their sixties of heart attacks and strokes, and most women followed in their seventies.[24]

Since then, longevity has marched upward. In 1940, a sixty-five-year-old could expect to live another thirteen years. By 2008, a sixty-five-year-old could expect to live another nineteen years, a gain of six years.[25] But gains in longevity have not been equally distributed, and the result is that the mid twentieth-century model fits the lived experience of fewer and fewer Americans. The longevity gap between high- and low-earning men at age fifty is now thirteen years – meaning that, of all men who reach age fifty, the richest fifth can expect to live thirty-nine more years, while the poorest fifth can expect to live only twenty-six more years.[26]

Inequality in old age isn't just a matter of lifespan. Lifelong advantage and disadvantage cumulate, and we see disparities across measures of well-being and opportunity. Lower-earning workers face job instability, with frequent periods of un- and underemployment. They are more likely to hold physically demanding jobs, including low-paid and stressful jobs in the service sector.[27] As a group, they are more likely to suffer hypertension, obesity, diabetes, early stroke, and heart disease.[28] And they are more likely to reach their early sixties unable to perform physical jobs and with limited skills for transitioning to new work.[29]

Higher earners, by contrast, tend to enjoy robust health and stable jobs. Their white-collar jobs give them a high degree of autonomy and do not require physical work. Financially secure, these healthy older people have reinvented old age, often rejecting "retirement" in favor of new careers, travel (before COVID-19), and entrepreneurship. Indeed, sociologists coined the term "Third Age" to describe the new vitality of this group in their sixties and seventies and even eighties. With longer lives and better health, many older people no longer retire in the classic sense and, instead, reinvent themselves with new careers, travel, and entrepreneurship.[30]

[24] Centers for Disease Control, National Vital Statistics Reports, Vol. 61, No. 3 (Sep. 24, 2012), at 46, http://www.cdc.gov/nchs/data/nvsr/nvsr61/nvsr61_03.pdf.

[25] *Id.* (By 2008, women had gained eight years of life after age sixty-five, while men had gained just six.)

[26] National Academies of Science, Engineering, and Medicine, The Growing Gap in Life Expectancy by Income 3 (2015).

[27] David M. Cutler, *Declining Disability among the Elderly*, 20 Health Affairs 11–27 (Nov./Dec. 2001).

[28] Mauricio Avendano & M. Maria Glymor, *Stroke Disparities in Older Americans: Is Wealth a More Powerful Indicator Than Income and Education?* 39 Stroke 1533 (2008).

[29] Vicki Freedman et al., *Behavioral Adaptation and Late-Life Disability: A New Spectrum for Assessing Public Health Impacts*, 104 Am. J. Pub. Health e88, e92 tbl.3 (Feb. 2014) (finding that 73 percent of Medicare enrollees in 2011 with incomes of $60,000 or more were either fully able or had successfully accommodated a disability, and finding, by contrast, that only 42 percent of those with incomes less than $15,000 and 48 percent of those with incomes between $15,000 and $30,000 fell into that high-functioning category).

[30] *See* Phyllis Moen & Donna Spencer, *Converging Divergences in Age, Gender, Health, and Well-Being: Strategic Selection in the Third Age, in* Handbook of the Social Sciences 127 (2005). *See also* Phyllis Moen, *Midcourse: Navigating Retirement and a New Stage of Life, in*

Inequality in old age has a financial dimension as well. Retirement savings (setting aside Social Security entitlements for the moment) are strikingly unequal. Low-earning workers (and many middle earners) reach retirement with few pension rights and little personal savings. Only half of retirees now have any pension income at all.[31] Workers with private pensions often have sufficient retirement income (together with Social Security) to retire comfortably, but workers without private pensions often do not.[32]

At the same time, the changes in family life described in Section 1.2 have begun to affect older Americans, with additional inequalities based on family structure. Individuals in (roughly) the bottom half of the income distribution are less likely to marry, more likely to divorce if they do marry, more likely to cohabit, and more likely to be single parents. At the high end of the income spectrum, by contrast, people still marry at high rates, remain married for longer periods, and tend to have children with their spouse (rather than a blended family with children from multiple parental relationships).[33]

These growing inequalities mean that the three-stage model of the life cycle no longer describes life for many, even most Americans. And it means that the old model cannot readily be replaced with a single, newer version. The last third of the life cycle plays out very differently depending on one's socioeconomic background. Roughly speaking, lower earners need a model that cushions the financial impact of job instability and unemployment, anticipates early disability, and permits dignified retirement relatively early in one's sixties. The life cycle for higher earners, in sharp contrast, should recognize their greater opportunities, better health, and relative job stability.

To illustrate how the outdated model of the life cycle challenges legal design for old age, consider two policy problems. First is the design of Social Security. As I have documented in other work, Social Security was designed to be progressive, but its progressive redistribution is premised on outdated assumptions.[34] More specifically, the designers of the program had the luxury of designing a one-size-fits-all system in which workers varied only along one dimension – earnings – and otherwise lived similar lives.

HANDBOOK OF THE LIFE COURSE 269 (Jeylan T. Mortimer & Michael J. Shanahan eds., 2003); *see generally* Shin-Kap Han & Phyllis Moen, *Clocking Out: Temporal Patterning of Retirement*, 105 AM. J. SOC. 191 (1999).

31 Virginia P. Reno & Elisa A. Walker, *Social Security Benefits, Finances, and Policy Options: A Primer*, NATIONAL ACADEMY OF SOCIAL INSURANCE (2013), at 8, http://www.nasi.org/sites/default/files/research/2013_Social_Security_Primer_PDF.pdf.

32 Virginia P. Reno & Joni Lavery, *Social Security and Retirement Income Adequacy*, National Academy of Social Insurance Brief No. 25 (2007), at 8, https://www.nasi.org/wp-content/uploads/2009/11/SS_Brief_025.pdf.

33 Andrew J. Cherlin, *The De-institutionalization of American Marriage*, 66 J. MARRIAGE AND FAM. 848 (2004); Alstott, *supra* note 12.

34 ALSTOTT, *supra* note 7.

The result is that Social Security's rules now redistribute in complex and inconsistent ways.[35] All else equal, the retirement program favors (among others) steady work, low earnings, formal marriage, traditional gender roles in marriage, and long lives.[36] The retirement program disfavors (among others) the unmarried, temporary work, unemployment, two-earner married couples, and short lives.[37]

Is Social Security still progressive overall? The answer is not obvious. Studies that lump in disability benefits with survivors' and retirement benefits find that Social Security is modestly progressive.[38] But disability and survivors' benefits are especially progressive, because lower earners are more likely to die early or experience disability. The retirement system standing alone is far less progressive.[39] What is clearer is that the progressivity of the Social Security retirement program is declining as retirees who lived in the mid twentieth century give way to Baby Boomers and their successors, who live very different lives.[40]

Reforms to bolster progressivity will be complex and demanding. The moving pieces include the retirement age, the disability system, and the spousal benefit. For instance, the system could be designed to allow lower earners to retire at an early age with little or no penalty while expecting better-off workers to work longer. A higher retirement age puts additional pressure on the disability system (which today need not address people over age sixty-seven). And the spousal benefit might be replaced with a variety of family accommodations, including an optional survivor benefit (not limited to spouses) or a caregiver's benefit available to single as well as married people.[41]

The 100-year life is a useful prompt to action. If current trends continue, the last third or so of one's century of life may look very different, depending on one's cumulative advantage or disadvantage. And so there is likely to be no "retirement" in the mid twentieth-century sense of a lockstep stage of life, recognizable to and lived by all.

35 C. Eugene Steuerle, Karen E. Smith & Caleb Quakenbush, *Has Social Security Redistributed to Whites from People of Color?* Urban Institute Brief No. 38 (2013), at 2, http://www.urban.org/UploadedPDF/412943-Has-Social-Security-Redistributed-to-Whites-from-People-of-Color.pdf.

36 C. Eugene Steuerle, Adam Carasso & Lee Carasso, *How Progressive Is Social Security and Why?* Urban Institute (2004), http://www.urban.org/publications/311016.html.

37 *Id.*, at 1–2.

38 Social Security Administration researchers report that old age, survivors, and disability insurance, taken as a whole, is "modestly progressive on a lifetime basis." Andrew G. Biggs, Mark Sarney & Christopher R. Tamborini, *A Progressivity Index for Social Security*, SSA Issue Paper No. 2009-01 (2009), http://www.ssa.gov/policy/docs/issuepapers/ip2009-01.html.

39 Congressional Budget Office, *Is Social Security Progressive?* (Dec. 15, 2006) (finding that retirement benefits are less progressive than OASDI as a whole; the progressivity of the benefits formula is offset, but not entirely, by the shorter lives of low earners, which would reduce the value of the life annuity).

40 *See* Biggs et al., *supra* note 38 (finding that "progressivity has declined in recent decades" and that progressivity will decline for cohorts retiring in the 2010s).

41 *Id.*

1.4 CONCLUSION

The prospect of the 100-year life should prompt us to recognize and reform the three-stage model of the life cycle across areas of law. The 100-year life poses both new pitfalls and new opportunities, and the law will play a critical mediating role. A casual observer might suppose that the forces that create the 100-year life and shape its course are natural, not man-made. But the law can, and does, strongly shape health and the economy, and so we can envision a better – and a worse – version of the 100-year life.

The dangers are clear enough. Current trends, if unchecked, will usher in a 100-year life riven with inequalities. For low-income populations, the extra years will be hard ones: Even today, these workers disproportionately suffer early disability, frequent unemployment, and chronic disease. They reach old age often unable to keep working physically but also unable to retire financially. The prospect of, say, ten or twenty additional years in such conditions is a bleak one.

But the law could also usher in a brighter scenario. With reforms in health care, in social insurance, and in antipoverty efforts (just to take a few examples), the law could attack the causes of these inequalities. Measures to improve access to higher education throughout the life course could increase social mobility and resilience to economic changes. And a redesigned social insurance system could do far better to cushion remaining inequalities by directing greater benefits to low earners and those with disabilities while redistributing them from the advantaged class that enjoys long lives, good health, and ample work options.

2

The 100-Year Life and the New Family Law

Naomi Cahn, Clare Huntington, and Elizabeth Scott

In this chapter, we explore the likely impact of increased life expectancy on family law. We focus primarily on family formation and structure, a core aspect of family law. Based on existing demographic trends, we predict that families will continue to function as the primary setting for intimacy and care for older adults, but increased longevity will likely have a profound impact on the shape of families. Although marriage continues to be the family form privileged by law, marriage rates are already declining, and fewer older adults forming new families will choose marriage. Instead, older adults increasingly are likely to prefer cohabitation or nonconjugal families of choice; many will also live in multigenerational families or live alone. The law currently does not support these nonmarital families. This chapter argues that lawmakers must consider both doctrinal and policy reforms to support individuals in following their preferences for intimacy in old age. To this end, we suggest general goals for law reform as well as specific proposals.

These reforms are critically important because, in our libertarian legal regime, families continue to bear the burden of providing the care most older adults will need. This burden falls disproportionately on low-income families and families of color, who face significant racial and income inequities and who are least likely to marry. As the proportion of older adults grows, the struggles of these families to provide care will increase. Thus, an important goal of family law reforms responding to increased life expectancy will be to support the formation and functioning of *all* families and to assist them in providing care to older family members. In this chapter, we focus on how the law can help older adults create the families they want. These reforms will support intimacy – however an older person defines it – and family caregiving.

At the outset, it is critical to consider just what "family law" might mean. In the early 1960s, Jacobus tenBroek observed that, although family law is neutrally applied regardless of income, there are actually two systems, one set of regulations that applies to the wealthy, who are able to opt out of default rules and have little political oversight, and one set that applies to the use of public funds and affects lower-income families, who are subject to stringent monitoring by the state apparatus.[1] To be sure, most of the reforms we propose do not address the second system. On the other hand, our proposed reforms to family formation might help stem the growing inequity of family structures by facilitating the ability of lower-income adults to form legal families according to their values and preferences and by providing those families with benefits that marital families enjoy. In this way, adapting family law to the 100-year life can begin to break down the dual system of family law. In other work, we explore at length the many ways the government can directly assist family members across the income spectrum to provide care to older family members.[2]

2.1 FAMILY DEMOGRAPHIC TRENDS

Life expectancy is indeed increasing, such that 50 percent of children born today are predicted to live 100 years or more.[3] But disparities exist; life expectancy varies by race, ethnicity, sex, and income, and this likely will continue. Hispanic older people have the longest life expectancy, followed by white and then Black adults.[4] Women live longer than men, and high-income individuals live longer than those with low incomes.[5] Disparities also exist in health outcomes. Black, Hispanic, and lower-income adults have poorer health outcomes than white and higher-income adults.[6]

Against this backdrop, an account of trends in family formation and structure assists us in forecasting the impact of increased longevity on family law. While

1 Jacobus tenBroek, *California's Dual System of Family Law: Its Origin, Development, and Present Status: Part I*, 16 STAN. L. REV. 257, 257–258 (1964).

2 *See* Naomi Cahn, Clare Huntington & Elizabeth Scott, *Family Law for the One-Hundred-Year Life*, 132 YALE L. J. 1691 (2023). As we argue, these reforms also must avoid the dual system of family law.

3 *The New Map of Life: 100 Years to Thrive*, STAN. CTR. ON LONGEVITY 2 (2021), https://longevity.stanford.edu/wp-content/uploads/2021/11/NMOL_report_FINAL-5.pdf.

4 Elizabeth Arias & Jiaquan Xu, *United States Life Tables, 2020*, 71 NAT'L VITAL STATS. REPS., No. 2 (Aug. 8, 2022), at 3 tbl.A (showing that Hispanic individuals who reach age sixty-five are expected to live another 21.4 years, as compared to 19.4 years for white individuals and eighteen years for Black individuals). The Census data on longevity do not report on Asian individuals. For a source that describes life expectancy at birth for Asian people and Pacific Islanders, *see* Off. of Minority Health, *Asian American Health*, US DEP'T OF HEALTH & HUM. SERVS. (Oct. 12, 2021), https://minorityhealth.hhs.gov/omh/browse.aspx?lvl = 3&lvlid = 63.

5 *See* Arias & Xu, *supra* note 4, at 3 tbl.A. For sources discussing the relationship between income and longevity, *see* Raj Chetty et al., *The Association between Income and Life Expectancy in the United States, 2001–2014*, 315 J. AM. MED. ASS'N 1750, 1754 fig. 2 (2016) (finding a 14.6-year gap in life expectancy between men at the bottom of the income distribution and men at the top and a 10.1-year difference for women and showing a steady increase in life expectancy with each incremental gain of income).

6 *See* Michael E. Martinez & Tainya C. Clarke, *Percentage of Adults in Fair or Poor Health, by Age Group and Race and Ethnicity: National Health Interview Survey, United States, 2019*, 70 MORBIDITY & MORTALITY WKLY. REP. 333, 333 (2021).

extrapolation from the present to the future is difficult, a large body of demographic data on families offers the best tools available to predict the challenges the law will face as life expectancy increases. The future of families is likely to build on several trends, described below.

2.2.1 *The Numbers*

Family structure and form are changing in ways that will likely affect the future of families as life expectancy increases. First, families are smaller today. Average household size and fertility rates have decreased, producing fewer children to care for aging parents.[7] But most older adults have adult children; for those creating new families, these children are from earlier relationships.[8]

Second, in general, marriage rates have declined, and cohabitation rates have increased. The percentage of people who are not married has increased for all racial groups, although it has remained relatively stable for Asians.[9] Correspondingly, the rate of cohabitation for all age groups and social classes is increasing, including those over the age of fifty; the cohabitation rate for those over the age of sixty-five tripled from 1996 to 2017, although the rate is far lower than that of younger adults.[10] Unlike younger cohabiters, who typically marry or break up relatively quickly, older cohabiting relationships are relatively stable, lasting an average of ten years and usually ending with the death of one partner rather than a decision to separate.[11] However, despite the general increase in cohabitation rates for all groups, family structures increasingly are stratified by levels of education. College-educated couples are more likely to marry, and couples with less education are more likely to cohabit.[12] This stratification in family form is relatively new.

7 *See* Aaron O'Neill, *Total Fertility Rate in the United States from 1800 to 2020*, STATISTA (June 21, 2021), https://www.statista.com/statistics/1033027/fertility-rate-us-1800-2020.

8 *See First-Ever Census Bureau Report Highlights Growing Childless Older Adult Population*, US CENSUS BUREAU (Aug. 31, 2021), https://www.census.gov/newsroom/press-releases/2021/childless-older-adult-population.html (80 percent of older adults have children).

9 USAFacts, *The State of American Households: Smaller, More Diverse and Unmarried*, US NEWS & WORLD REP. (Feb. 14, 2020), https://www.usnews.com/news/elections/articles/2020-02-14/the-state-of-american-households-smaller-more-diverse-and-unmarried.

10 Benjamin Gurrentz, *Cohabitating Partners Older, More Racially Diverse, More Educated, Higher Earners*, US CENSUS BUREAU (Sep. 23, 2019), https://www.census.gov/library/stories/2019/09/unmarried-partners-more-diverse-than-20-years-ago.html.

11 *See* Susan L. Brown & Matthew R. Wright, *Marriage, Cohabitation, and Divorce in Later Life*, 1 INNOVATION IN AGING 2, at 4 (2017).

12 *See* JUNE CARBONE & NAOMI CAHN, MARRIAGE MARKETS: HOW INEQUALITY IS REMAKING THE AMERICAN FAMILY (2014); Richard V. Reeves & Christopher Pulliam, *Middle Class Marriage Is Declining, and Likely Deepening Inequality*, BROOKINGS INST. (Mar. 11, 2020), https://www.brookings.edu/research/middle-class-marriage-is-declining-and-likely-deepening-inequality.

In 1960, 72 percent of all adults were married, and these rates did not differ much by educational attainment.[13]

Third, divorce and remarriage are common. The divorce rate has flattened or declined for college-educated couples generally but is increasing for those aged fifty and above.[14] Between 1990 and 2017, the divorce rate doubled for those aged fifty-five to sixty-four and tripled for those aged sixty-five and older,[15] although the divorce rate of older adults is still below those of younger cohorts. Remarriage rates overall are decreasing, suggesting that divorced individuals may be more likely to enter informal unions than remarry.[16] This is especially true for older adults, who are more likely to cohabit with a new partner than remarry.[17]

Finally, older adults are more likely to live in nondyadic families than in earlier times. Older adults increasingly live in multigenerational households, which include at least two adult generations, or grandparents and grandchildren who are younger than twenty-five.[18] More than one-fifth of those over the age of sixty-five live in such a household.[19] The trend toward multigenerational households is likely to continue as lives lengthen because aging parents both provide and need care. Living patterns for older adults are shifting in other ways too. Increasingly, older people live in informal groups that currently are not recognized as families. Nonconjugal congregate living has increased with a growing number of options, such as

[13] *See* D'vera Cohn et al., *Barely Half of U.S. Adults Are Married: A Record Low*, Pew Rsch. Ctr. (Dec. 14, 2011), https://www.pewsocialtrends.org/2011/12/14/barely-half-of-u-s-adults-are-married-a-record-low/.

[14] *See* Renee Stepler, *Led by Baby Boomers, Divorce Rates Climb for America's 50+ Population*, Pew Rsch. Ctr. (Mar. 9, 2017), https://www.pewresearch.org/fact-tank/2017/03/09/led-by-baby-boomers-divorce-rates-climb-for-americas-50-population.

[15] *See id.*; Colette Allred, *Age Variation in the Divorce Rate, 1990 & 2017*, Bowling Green State Univ. (2019), https://www.bgsu.edu/ncfmr/resources/data/family-profiles/allred-age-variation-div-rate-fp-19-13.html.

[16] *See* Krista K. Payne, *Change in the U.S. Remarriage Rate, 2008 and 2016*, Bowling Green State Univ. (2018), https://www.bgsu.edu/content/dam/BGSU/college-of-arts-and-sciences/NCFMR/documents/FP/payne-change-remarriage-rate-fp-18-16.pdf.

[17] *See* Susan L. Brown, I-Fen Lin, Anna M. Hammersmith & Matthew R. Wright, *Repartnering Following Gray Divorce: The Roles of Resources and Constraints for Women and Men*, 56 Demography 503, 513 figs. 1 & 2 (2019); Deborah Carr & Rebecca L. Utz, *Families in Later Life: A Decade in Review*, 82 J. Marriage & Fam. 346, 351 (2020); Gurrentz, *supra* note 10; Renee Stepler, *Number of U.S. Adults Cohabiting with a Partner Continues to Rise, Especially among Those 50 and Older*, Pew Rsch. Ctr. (Apr. 6, 2017), https://www.pewresearch.org/fact-tank/2017/04/06/number-of-u-s-adults-cohabiting-with-a-partner-continues-to-rise-especially-among-those-50-and-older.

[18] *See Family Matters: Multigenerational Living Is on the Rise and Here to Stay*, Generations United (2021), 1, 2, 7, https://www.gu.org/app/uploads/2021/04/21-MG-Family-Report-WEB.pdf.

[19] *See id.*, at 8. Families of color and families with foreign-born members are more likely to live in multigenerational households than white families are.

intentional cohousing communities,[20] voluntary kin groups,[21] and naturally occurring retirement communities; some of these family arrangements support aging-in-place, a goal of many seniors,[22] and all promote ongoing social and emotional connections. Of course, many older people also live in nursing homes, assisted living, or continuing-care retirement communities.[23]

Finally, the number of individuals, particularly seniors, living alone has increased. More than a quarter of Americans over the age of sixty live alone,[24] although many live near an adult child or other family member.[25] Women are more likely than men to live alone, while both African American men and women live alone at rates that are higher than those of white older adults.[26] The rates for LGBTQ+ seniors living alone are higher than for cisgender and heterosexual older adults,[27] a trend that is likely changing with greater societal acceptance of same-sex relationships.

2.1.2 *Implications of Increased Longevity for Family Formation and Structure*

These trends form a context for speculating about the impact of substantial increases in longevity on family formation and structure. Family relationships continue to be critically important as a source of intimacy and mutual care for this demographic group, and so, not surprisingly, older adults who have lost earlier family relationships to death, divorce, or dissolution are forming new families. As life expectancy increases, more older adults will be forming families later in life. But the goals of older adults in creating new families differ from those of their younger counterparts.

[20] *See* Melissa Stanton, *6 Creative Housing Options: The Choices for How and Where to Live as an Older Adult Are Growing*, AARP (July 2014), https://www.aarp.org/livable-communities/info-2014/creative-age-friendly-housing-options.html.

[21] Dawn Braithwaite et al., *Constructing Family: A Typology of Voluntary Kin*, 27 J. Soc. & Pers. Relationships 388 (2010).

[22] Joanne Binette & Kerri Vasold, *2018 Home and Community Preferences: A National Survey of Adults Ages 18-Plus*, AARP (July 2019), https://www.aarp.org/research/topics/community/info-2018/2018-home-community-preference.html.

[23] *See Nursing Home Care*, Ctrs. for Disease Control (Dec. 15, 2022), https://www.cdc.gov/nchs/fastats/nursing-home-care.htm.

[24] Jacob Ausubel, *Older People Are More Likely to Live Alone in the U.S. Than Elsewhere in the World*, Pew Rsch. Ctr. (Mar. 10, 2020), https://www.pewresearch.org/fact-tank/2020/03/10/older-people-are-more-likely-to-live-alone-in-the-u-s-than-elsewhere-in-the-world.

[25] *See* Janice Compton & Robert A. Pollak, *Proximity and Coresidence of Adult Children and Their Parents in the United States: Description and Correlates*, 91 Annals of Econ. & Stat. 99 (2015); AARP, *Caregiving in the U.S.* (May 2020), 21, https://www.aarp.org/content/dam/aarp/ppi/2020/05/full-report-caregiving-in-the-united-states.doi.10.26419-2Fppi.00103.001.pdf.

[26] Ausubel, *supra* note 24 (explaining that 20 percent of older women, but only 10 percent of men, live alone); Rodney Brooks, *Old, Black and Alone: A Grim Forecast*, Next Ave. (Nov. 22, 2017), https://www.nextavenue.org/old-black-alone-grim-forecast.

[27] *See* Soon Kyu Choi & Ilan H. Meyer, *LGBT Aging: A Review of Research Findings, Needs, and Policy Implications*, Williams Inst. (2016), https://williamsinstitute.law.ucla.edu/wp-content/uploads/LGBT-Aging-Aug-2016.pdf.

Older adults seldom form families for the purpose of having and rearing children, a primary function of families for younger people.

Perhaps partly for this reason, the demographic trends suggest that while most older adults today were once married, many may choose other family forms later in life. The appeal of marriage as a secure setting to raise children is less relevant as people age, and older adults may not want to assume the financial commitments that typically go with marriage. Even those who prefer marriage for religious or other reasons may vary in the extent of financial sharing and commitment they desire. Also, increasing numbers of older adults are living in multigenerational families. And a small but growing number of seniors are forming families of choice – informal, typically nonconjugal groups that provide intimacy or companionship and mutual care of dependency needs, the two core functions of families. Further, as we live longer lives, an increasing number will live alone; these individuals will need substitutes for family if they are to fulfill their need for care and intimacy.

A key implication of these demographic trends is that older adults are a varied group with diverse preferences for the family form that satisfies their needs later in life. In general, seniors who establish new families, either marital or nonmarital, will likely have varied expectations for the levels of commitment and financial sharing desired. Some may want to undertake a broad commitment, with financial sharing and other expectations typical of first marriages. But many more may want a relationship of intimacy and companionship without financial sharing or with sharing only for the duration of the relationship.

There is another distinctive feature of older adults forming new families. Many older persons who create new families have close bonds with children and other family members from earlier relationships, and they may want to continue to give priority to those bonds. In other families, however, filial bonds may have become attenuated over time, resulting in reduced feelings of obligation for both generations.

2.2 THE INADEQUACY OF CURRENT FAMILY LAW

Current family law doctrine is poorly suited to respond effectively to increased life expectancy against the backdrop of these trends. By privileging marriage and failing to recognize or protect other family forms, the law is likely to defeat the preferences of many individuals forming families later in life. This harm will fall disproportionately on low-income and Black older adults, who are least likely to choose marriage and whose families will struggle most with the burden of care. The privileging of marriage may also undermine the expectations of older adults in relation to adult children.

Marriage continues to be uniquely privileged as a family form, enjoying strong legal protection, financial advantages conferred by government, and enforcement of financial obligations between spouses.[28] In general, legal marriage is tailored to the preferences and needs of younger individuals starting families, and it is designed to provide a stable, secure setting for raising children. It is not well suited to the needs of those entering marriage later in life. Thus, default rules presume long-term commitment and aim to protect dependent spouses and children by providing for the sharing of marital property and spousal support on divorce. Spouses also enjoy inheritance rights that cannot be altered unilaterally. The default rules for medical and other surrogate decision-making also favor a spouse over other family members. These rights and duties can be changed, but parties must affirmatively agree to opt out, and most couples do not. And some override rules, such as the doctrine of necessaries, which benefits third-party creditors, are not subject to spousal agreement but are imposed by the state to ensure a level of basic support.

While some older couples may wish to assume the rights and duties of marriage, many older adults who might choose to marry later in life may not wish to undertake these legal obligations. Seniors often want their children, and not new spouses, to inherit their property, and many would not expect to be saddled with spousal support. Most would not want to divide marital property on divorce. Further, the priority of spouses as surrogate medical decision-makers may conform to the preferences of some older spouses in second marriages, but others may prefer a child, other relative, or friend to assume this role. The presumption of financial interdependence affecting eligibility for long-term care under Medicaid is yet another disincentive to marriage.

Current law is also problematic because it draws a sharp line between marital and nonmarital relationships; that is, parties either opt into marriage and all of its rights and responsibilities, or they choose nonmarital relationships, which carry no financial obligations or assumptions of sharing and no legal recognition of emotional and social connections. The evidence indicates that older adults across the income span increasingly choose nonmarital relationships. And while cohabiting couples can execute contracts to clarify their financial understandings and other documents to protect their emotional connection, very few couples do. Two individuals living together and fulfilling each other's intimacy and dependency needs also do not count as a legally recognized family for the purposes of government privileges or benefits. For example, regardless of their age, cohabitants will not qualify for family leave under federal law to care for an ill partner.[29] Nor, if the ill partner has children, will they typically qualify as the preferred decision-makers in the event of incapacity. While many older individuals will choose informal nonmarital unions, in part because they want more limited expectations of financial sharing and fewer mutual obligations than marriage, they will find that their relationships enjoy virtually no legal support or recognition.

[28] *United States v. Windsor*, 570 U.S. 744 (2013).

[29] 29 U.S.C. § 2612(a)(1) (2018).

Under current family law, individuals in nondyadic and nonconjugal family relationships, both multigenerational and age-based, also receive little or no recognition as families.[30] Individuals in these groups seldom formally execute contracts and are excluded from even the benefits afforded to cohabiting couples. Moreover, in some localities, these families of choice may be excluded from living in single-family residential zones under local ordinances. Multigenerational families cannot be explicitly excluded, but these groups may be subject to other zoning restrictions, and, generally, they receive little legal support or recognition, despite their valuable role in providing care across generations. These "new" family forms are likely to become more common for older individuals, but they currently function largely outside the protection of family law.

The upshot is that family law fails to support the interests of older adults because it is centered on marriage, a union that is of declining interest to older adults. Family relationships are important to the well-being of older adults, but many individuals who want to form new family relationships later in life do not want to assume these commitments and financial obligations. For these older adults, the relationships they choose receive little legal protection or recognition.

2.3 WHY LAW REFORM IS IMPORTANT

Families play a critically important role in satisfying individuals' core needs for care and intimacy. Dependency needs vary across different life stages and are most acute in infancy and childhood and again in old age, when individuals' ability to care for themselves often declines. In many other advanced countries, the government plays a major role in providing substantial support for dependency needs, but a libertarian presumption of self-sufficiency is embedded in American law and policy, resulting in a substantial burden on families to provide care and assistance. Families also fulfill the human need for intimacy and social connection. Much research supports that older persons who lose intimate connections show declines in both physical and psychological health.[31] Family relationships, whether in conventional legal families or in families of choice, become ever more important as seniors are less able to actively cultivate social relationships outside of the family.[32]

Many older individuals will experience illness and disability and need care and support, and all will need psychological support and human connection.

[30] An exception might be grandparents' standing to seek visitation in most states, but this remains contested.

[31] *See* Jialu L. Streeter, Sarah Raposo & Hsiao-Wen Liao, *The Importance of Social Relationships for Longevity*, Stan. Ctr. on Longevity, https://longevity.stanford.edu/sightlines-project-social-engagement-special-report.

[32] *See id.*

If individuals lack emotional or economic support, the state will bear an increased burden to fulfill these needs, which currently it fails to do. (Other chapters also address those failures.) While the 100-year life may prompt a larger governmental role in providing care and support for the aging population, strengthening legal support for families remains critical. Thus, society has an interest in facilitating family formation for older individuals and in supporting groups that fulfill family functions.

Attaining this goal will require a commitment to legal reforms that acknowledge and support the variety of family relationships that seniors are likely to choose. Many have criticized family law's privileging of marriage, an approach grounded in traditional assumptions about marital roles and commitment. It has long been recognized that this approach harms individuals in nonmarital families, particularly lower-income individuals, and also hurts single people. As we have shown, it is a particularly poor fit for the needs and preferences of older persons, both those who choose marriage and those who prefer other conjugal or nonconjugal family forms, as well as those who age alone.

2.4 AN AGENDA FOR REFORM

2.4.1 *Broad Goals of Reform*

A major goal of legal reform in response to the 100-year life will be to adopt a more pluralist and less libertarian family law that serves the interests of people across incomes, across races, and across the lifespan. The new family law would support a range of families, facilitating individuals' ability to create families adapted to their needs and desires efficiently and without undue effort. Flexibility will be needed to accommodate a range of preferences for financial sharing and other aspects of interdependency. Reforms can also offer assurance to older persons forming new families that their intentions toward members of earlier families, particularly children, will be legally protected.

At a broader policy level, individual fulfillment in old age as well as social welfare will depend on a fundamental shift toward a more active state role supporting individuals and families in fulfilling the critical role of providing care and facilitating human connection. A part of this reform is a regime in which nonmarital families receive the government privileges and benefits that marital families enjoy.

Recognition of, and support for, a broad range of families is particularly urgent for lower-income and Black families, who are unlikely to receive the benefits of marriage and who bear the greatest burden of care for older family members. As a result of a lifetime of inequity, older adults in these families are more likely than those in wealthier families to have health challenges requiring substantial care, and that care will usually be provided by family members. Not surprisingly, these family caregivers provide more hours of care than those in higher-income families and are more likely to leave paid employment to provide care.[33] Moreover, low-income families often do not have the resources to supplement family care with paid caregivers, increasing the burden and stress on family caregivers.

In other work, we explore the caregiving needs of older adults in greater depth and argue that there is far more the state can, and should, do to support family caregiving.[34] In the following, we focus on reforms that allow older adults to form families, both marital and nonmarital, that meet their needs across income and class. The ultimate goal of these reforms is to provide the government benefits and support that marital families enjoy also to nonmarital families.[35]

2.4.2 *Specific Family Law Reforms*

A range of family law reforms will usefully support older adults in realizing their goals for intimacy. While the need for reform is highlighted by the 100-year life, many reforms will benefit younger family members as well.

A key type of reform is the development of mechanisms that facilitate the more streamlined execution of parties' intentions regarding family formation, obligations, and expectations. Prenuptial agreements, cohabitation contracts, wills, powers of attorney, and medical directives are all helpful in allowing older individuals to determine the legal rights and duties that define their relationships. But, while creating documents that override default presumptions is usually not difficult, most individuals do not execute contracts or otherwise formalize their intentions, because it takes effort and expense to do so; low-income individuals particularly are unlikely to formalize their expectations for family relationships.

Rather than rely on individual initiatives, governments could take steps to facilitate formal expressions of intentions easily and cheaply. We have proposed elsewhere a two-part registration system that would go far toward achieving this goal. Our proposed system would allow cohabiting couples and other nonmarital groups to register their intentions to form families and to undertake mutual commitments and obligations that suit their needs ("family group registration") and also allow couples entering legal marriage to opt out of particular marital rights and obligations (the "marital menu").[36] Such a regime could be a key part of a pluralist family law that recognizes the wide variety of preferences regarding family form and functioning.

Individuals in nonmarital family groups may not want to assume the obligations of marriage (and nondyadic groups will not be eligible), but they may want to clarify

[33] *See* AARP, *supra* note 25, at 31.

[34] *See* Cahn et al., *supra* note 2.

[35] In short, a goal of reform should be to break down the boundary between tenBroek's two systems of family law and give low-income families access to the benefits of the first system. *Supra* note 1.

[36] Cahn et al., *supra* note 2.

expectations and assume some mutual family obligations and commitments. The proposed family group registration option would allow family groups to select obligations and benefits that could range from various kinds of financial sharing to surrogate decision-making to inheritance rights. A model of sorts exists in a Colorado law authorizing individuals in nonmarital relationships to register for "designated beneficiary" status. That option, limited to couples, allows each individual to decide on specific relationship rights and duties recognizing emotional connection and financial interdependence.[37] It could be adapted to facilitate the formation and recognition of a broader range of family groups.

The second part, a "marital menu," would allow couples obtaining a marriage license to opt out of legal default rules providing for marital property, spousal support, spousal inheritance rights, medical proxies, and other obligations.[38] Effectively, the marital menu is a streamlined substitute for a premarital agreement, allowing couples to opt out of marital obligations efficiently and cheaply. For many older couples, particularly those with adult children, this reform would offer substantial benefits.

This proposal faces two challenges if it is to facilitate progress toward the important goal of serving the needs of older adults across the income span. First, a registration system will not be useful if people are not aware of it, or if it is viewed as too complex. Even more concerning, the system risks replicating inequity if only higher-income groups benefit from its services. Lower-income couples currently are less likely to formalize their relationships, and thus, it is important that registration be made inexpensive and accessible for all couples and groups. Providing information in locations and through channels that are likely to reach lower-income individuals is one means to assure awareness of opportunities for family formation across the income span.[39] This information should also increase awareness of the legal and social benefits of family formation, as well as of the availability of registration. The process must also be clear and straightforward, as any need for legal advice will serve as a deterrent.

This relates to the second challenge, which begins with the creation of the registration system but embodies an ambitious longer-term goal. Given that families provide a critically important function in providing care for a growing population of older adults, the law's goal should be to extend to all registered families the legal benefits and government support that marital families enjoy. Tangible benefits may

[37] Colo. Rev. Stat. § 15-22-105 (2020).

[38] Note that it would not affect state or federal public benefits that are associated with marriage; thus, for example, the couple would still be considered married for tax purposes.

[39] To make older adults aware of the options for family formation, informational material can be made available in physicians' offices, Social Security offices, senior centers, and other locations frequented by older adults. Information could also be distributed with Medicare forms and in periodicals that target older adults, such as AARP publications.

encourage individuals to formalize family relationships, signaling their commitment and creating more stable settings for mutual intimacy and care in aging. Providing these couples with the support that married couples enjoy is good social policy and will benefit a broader range of individuals than current law could. Other families will benefit from marital privileges and benefits as well.

Lawmakers likely will be cautious in extending benefits and privileges to a broader range of families, perhaps fearing strategic behavior or a substantial fiscal burden. But strategic behavior seems less likely in this age cohort, and concern about the budgetary impact of these reforms is short-sighted in light of the financial and social value of care provided by family members. As a start, registration should trigger government recognition needed for the registered group to function as a family and provide support for family care that other families enjoy. For example, zoning regulation should define "family" broadly enough to include all families and allow land use that facilitates the needs of multigenerational families.[40] Regulations protecting family members in rental housing should also be broadly construed. Further, the protection given by the Family and Medical Leave Act could be extended to support a broader range of family and chosen family caregivers. Ultimately, government benefits that reinforce families and provide support for family care should be extended to all families.

Recognizing that registration may deter family formation, lawmakers might shift default rules to benefit established informal families and extend to them a limited set of benefits that go to other families. For older couples in long-term cohabiting relationships, for example, default rules recognizing emotional connections could apply. These default rules might include presumptions about surrogate healthcare decision-making and hospital visits while also ensuring protection of the interests of children from earlier relationships. There might also be some type of homestead exemption (perhaps a life estate) to ensure continuity in living arrangements at the death of a partner who owns the home. In multigenerational families, greater protection of the relationships of grandparents and grandchildren living together may be important.[41]

2.5 CONCLUDING THOUGHTS

The challenges posed by increased life expectancy cannot be resolved simply by recognizing a broad range of families and facilitating the ability of older adults to form families according to their needs and preferences – or even by extending the government benefits enjoyed by marital families to all families. We argue in other

[40] *See* Lisa Prevost, *The A.D.U. Experiment*, N.Y. Times (Dec. 10, 2021), https://www.nytimes.com/2021/12/10/realestate/the-adu-experiment.html.

[41] Elizabeth Scott, *Marriage, Cohabitation and Collective Responsibility for Dependency*, 219 U. Chi. Legal F. 225 (2004).

work that for older adults across the income span to live dignified and rewarding lives without unduly burdening their families, other reforms, including substantial government investments in family care and support, will be necessary. Changes to Social Security, tax law, Medicare, Medicaid, and other programs can provide support to low-income families and begin to address the race and class inequities that otherwise are likely to only be amplified as life expectancy increases.

3

Education and the 100-Year Life

The Linchpin for Thriving and Enjoyment

Kimberly Jenkins Robinson

Each nation's approach to education will determine if the 100-year life is a blessing or a curse. As the 100-year life becomes more commonplace rather than an exception, nations should strive to empower every individual to develop the intellectual capacity and wisdom that will be needed to make decisions that will support thriving over a longer life rather than merely surviving or, worse yet, suffering. This goal should guide nations in two ways. First, nations should reduce opportunity and achievement gaps that have hindered too many students' professional and personal lives for generations. The longer life expectancy of today's students will result in these gaps imposing even greater harms than previously. Second, nations should aim for educational opportunities that enable individuals to choose a life path that leads to human flourishing. Therefore, the 100-year life should lead nations to overhaul how they design and operate their education systems, particularly in light of the sharp declines in academic achievement that followed the COVID-19 pandemic.[1]

In this chapter, I examine how the US should reform its education system to support the 100-year life. As an initial matter, I explore how a high-quality education is essential for enabling individuals to make smart and life-enhancing decisions that a fruitful 100-year life will require. I then analyze how educational opportunity gaps, if not reduced and ultimately closed, will hinder the lifespans and opportunities of many individuals from low-income households and persons of color. I explain the importance of closing these gaps by highlighting the influence of education on career opportunities, earnings, and health, which are three critical components for thriving throughout a 100-year life. Indeed, at the outset, it

[1] *Largest Score Declines in NAEP Mathematics at Grades 4 and 8 Since Initial Assessments in 1990*, The Nation's Report Card (2022), https://www.nationsreportcard.gov/highlights/mathematics/2022; *Scores Decline in NAEP Reading at Grades 4 and 8 Compared to 2019*, The Nation's Report Card (2022), https://www.nationsreportcard.gov/highlights/reading/2022/; Sarah D. Sparks, *Explaining That Steep Drop in Math Score on NAEP: 5 Takeaways*, Educ. Wk. (Oct. 24, 2022), https://www.edweek.org/teaching-learning/explaining-that-steep-drop-in-math-scores-on-naep-5-takeaways/2022/10.

is important to understand that improving school quality will serve as one of the key determinants of whether an individual will be able to live to 100 years because improvements in school quality – specifically, increasing the length of the school year, raising teacher wages, and reducing class sizes – have been shown to reduce the mortality rate.[2]

I then propose education law and policy reforms to reduce these gaps in ways that enable individuals to thrive and enjoy a 100-year life. I contend that a federal right to education is a comprehensive reform for this moment because it is particularly well positioned to accomplish this goal. I explore how the prospect of a 100-year life should inform assessment of competing scholarly proposals for recognition of this right and its content. I conclude with a vision for how embracing the increasing prevalence of the 100-year life can guide us to reimagine education.

3.1 EDUCATION DRIVES THRIVING OVER THE 100-YEAR LIFE

The 100-year life will transform many aspects of life as we know it – including how each individual pursues her life work, how she manages her finances, and how she invests in relationships, to name only a few of the transformations. A strong educational foundation will be critical for managing each of these areas of life in ways that support human flourishing. For instance, consider Jane, the fictional individual that *The 100-Year Life* creates to imagine life for an individual born in 1998. Jane will enter a rapidly changing world of work. Over her lifetime, technological innovation will cast a shadow over the job market through its elimination of some jobs and the creation of others. Jane must be flexible to adapt to the evolving employment landscape by choosing jobs that have either an absolute or a comparative advantage over artificial intelligence (AI).

Investing in education will enable Jane to build the skills and knowledge she will need to navigate this evolving workplace. Jane's long lifespan at a time when technology is rapidly changing will mean that education will play a key role as Jane enters college and graduate school or vocational training to prepare for a fulfilling career that is greatly impacted by technological innovation. Later in Jane's life, she must invest time and energy in developing new knowledge, skills, and specializations that respond to the evolving employment landscape. She will be particularly incentivized to pursue a postgraduate education to gain both the in-depth knowledge and demonstration of commitment that she will need to survive, at least initially, in a competitive job market.

Jane also must work smartly and embrace transformation as a core value for her working life, which will have great implications for her education. Technological advances will force individuals to seek new education and training when their fields

[2] Shahar Sansani, *The Effects of School Quality on Long-Term Health*, 30 ECON. ED. REV. 1320, 1329 (2011).

of employment are rendered obsolete. Such advances also will result in workplace skills losing value more quickly than in previous generations. As a result, Jane will need to become a lifelong learner who regularly reinvents herself as she acquires new knowledge and skills.[3] A report, *The Age of Agility: Education Pathways for the Future of Work* by America Succeeds, describes the required shift as one in which "each one of us will have to take ownership of a lifetime of learning, a constant process of retraining and reeducating ourselves as the world around us lurches into the uncertain future."[4]

In addition, Jane is more likely to need to return to higher education for additional formal education after spending significant time in the workforce than individuals in prior generations. Rapid technological innovation also will require employers to make greater investments in professional development and training so that employees are equipped to respond to the employer's evolving needs. Future scholarship might explore how to structure and implement the types of higher education that returning adults will need to thrive in this rapidly evolving workforce.

Research confirms that to empower herself with the skills she needs for the future workforce, Jane will need to acquire a set of durable skills, which are defined as "a combination of how you use what you know – skills like critical thinking, communication, collaboration, and creativity – as well as character skills like fortitude, growth mindset, and leadership."[5] These durable skills not only are in high demand by employers now but also have the lowest probability of being automated. These skills, which individuals keep with them from job to job, enable individuals to respond to change with resilience rather than resignation. Rapid innovation demands that individuals develop durable skills as well as academic and digital literacy skills.

Jane must face head-on the reality that her longer lifespan demands earning more over her lifetime. She must acknowledge the needs of her future self and create the saving and consumption patterns that will enable her to pay for her long life. Jane's longer life also requires her to invest in the education and training that yield the financial rewards that will enable her to enjoy her retirement. If Jane does not make such investments in her education and training, she will quickly find herself either unemployed or in positions that are insufficiently remunerative to sustain her and her family for the additional years that her longer life entails. She will have no choice but to work for more years than prior generations. Otherwise, she will become either a burden to her family or the responsibility of the government, with little freedom to design the life that she desires.

In addition, Jane will need to build and sustain relationships that support a happy long life. Marriage can provide her with a life partner to share this longer journey

[3] Jinyoung Kim & Cyn-Young Park, *Education, Skill Training, and Lifelong Learning in the Era of Technological Revolution: A Review*, 34 Asian-Pac. Econ. Literature 3, 7–8 (2020).

[4] Jason Gaulden & Alan Gottlieb, Am. Succeeds, The Age of Agility: Education Pathways for the Future of Work 5 (2017).

[5] Lauren Cole et al., Am. Succeeds, The High Demand for Durable Skills 5 (2021).

and provide financial support as she ages. A spouse or partner may be more critical for Jane than for previous generations because a spouse or partner can support the household as Jane steps in and out of professional opportunities to acquire the education and training she needs to remain relevant and successful in the job market. To support a successful marriage, she will need "a great deal more skill and the capacity to make commitments and negotiate resources over a long period of time."[6] She will need to make smart choices with her partner and invest in sustaining her relationship over a long period of time.

In the next section I explore how opportunity and achievement gaps within the United States could create insurmountable roadblocks to a successful 100-year life for many students from low-income households and students of color.

3.2 EDUCATIONAL OPPORTUNITY AND ACHIEVEMENT GAPS WILL UNDERMINE THE POTENTIAL FOR A THRIVING 100-YEAR LIFE FOR GENERATIONS OF YOUNG PEOPLE

Although the 100-year life presents an array of opportunities, from multiple careers to more intergenerational relationships over a longer life, it may also become a crushing burden without the skills and capacity to capitalize on these opportunities. Socioeconomic and racial opportunity gaps throughout the US establish different educational worlds for our students, with some students enjoying the educational opportunities that lead to a prosperous and engaged future while others are placed on the road to nowhere. Too often, the nature and scope of educational opportunity gaps are overlooked due to the greater focus on achievement gaps. Yet, it is these opportunity gaps that drive the achievement gap that separates the outlook for many students from low-income households and students of color from their more affluent and white peers.[7]

Educational opportunity and achievement gaps will inflict even greater harms over a 100-year life because they can rob individuals of the knowledge and skills they need to reimagine and embrace novel career opportunities, to engage in financial planning for longevity, and to invest in their health and well-being, to name a few of the critical investments needed for an enjoyable 100-year life. Education is often heralded as the engine of opportunity. Yet, if existing opportunity and achievement

6 Lynda Gratton & Andrew Scott, The 100-Year Life: Living and Working in an Age of Longevity 297 (2016).

7 Kimberly Jenkins Robinson, *An American Dream Deferred: A Federal Right to Education*, *in* A Federal Right to Education: Fundamental Questions for Our Democracy 327, 329, 332 (Kimberly Jenkins Robinson ed., 2019) [hereinafter A Federal Right to Education]; James E. Ryan, Five Miles Away, a World Apart: One City, Two Schools, and the Story of Educational Opportunity in Modern America 3–4, 145–178, 305 (2010); Prudence L. Carter & Kevin Welner, *Achievement Gaps Arise from Opportunity Gaps*, *in* Closing the Opportunity Gap: What America Must Do to Give Every Child an Even Chance 1, 3 (Prudence L. Carter & Kevin Welner eds., 2013) [hereinafter Closing the Opportunity Gap].

gaps are not closed, education will serve as an engine of opportunities for some but a doorway to despair for others.

Given the potential for educational opportunity gaps to inflict even greater harm upon students as the 100-year life becomes more commonplace, this section describes the current anatomy of these gaps and then explains some of the ways that these gaps could hinder individuals from living a fulfilled 100-year life. Understanding educational opportunity gaps is particularly essential because the perception of these gaps' existence varies by race and class. Although the vast majority of whites – 81 percent – believe that students of color receive the same opportunities in education as they do, just 43 percent of Black people believe this. Similarly, low-income parents are significantly less likely than wealthier ones to believe that schools provide adequate support for students from low-income backgrounds.[8] The research and data are clear that students of color and students from low-income families far too often receive substantially inferior educational opportunities compared to their peers, which will hinder their ability to thrive over a 100-year life.

The technology gaps in educational opportunities and disparate access to courses that enable students to engage effectively with technology will serve as pivotal roadblocks to individuals enjoying the 100-year life. Scholars emphasize that young people need to embrace reskilling to adapt to emerging technologies. Our future workforce will need training that enables them not only to produce new products and applications but also to understand technology's societal impact and to use their training to advance ethical and sustainable technological and scientific advancements. As noted earlier, durable skills will be essential, as well as a wide array of additional skills, such as comprehending science and technology, understanding how to collaborate with AI, and developing skills that AI cannot duplicate.[9]

Yet, contrast the needs of our future workforce with the realities in today's schools. Consider the startling reality that more than 40 percent of teachers in Title I schools, which are those with significant student poverty, do not assign schoolwork that relies

[8] Pathways in Educ. & YouGov, *Parent Views on Education, Equality* (2016), www.educationsurveyresults.org.

[9] Lina Markauskaite et al., *Rethinking the Entwinement between Artificial Intelligence and Human Learning: What Capabilities Do Learners Need for a World with AI?* 3 COMPUTS. AND EDUC.: A.I. 3, 6 (2022); Alexandre Oliveira Junior et al., *Hands-On Learning Modules for Upskilling in Industry 4.0 Technologies*, 2022 IEEE 5TH INT'L CONF. ON INDUS. CYBER-PHYSICAL SYS. 2; COLE ET AL., *supra* note 5, at 7; David Chrisinger, *The Solution Lies in Education: Artificial Intelligence & the Skills Gap*, 27 ON HORIZON 1, 3 (2019); Brian E. Penprase, *The Fourth Industrial Revolution and Higher Education*, *in* HIGHER EDUCATION IN THE ERA OF THE FOURTH INDUSTRIAL REVOLUTION, 207, 217–218, 224 (Nancy W. Gleason ed., 2018); Tom Vander Ark, *Growing Talent for the 4th Industrial Revolution*, EDUC. WK. (Nov. 29, 2017), https://www.edweek.org/education/opinion-growing-talent-for-the-4th-industrial-revolution/2017/11 (explaining the need for "a focus on science, technology and creativity in education").

upon internet access due to concerns that such assignments would worsen inequalities. Close to 60 percent of Title I teachers state that the absence of home access to computers and the internet hinders student learning.[10]

The technological opportunity gaps are compounded by opportunity gaps in funding, teacher quality, and course offerings. Students from low-income households and students of color are being shortchanged in funding, the quality of teachers, access to rigorous courses, and other educational opportunities. For instance, a study by EdBuild found that school districts that serve 75 percent or more students of color receive $23 *billion less* than school districts that serve 75 percent or more white students, despite serving the same number of students.[11] Likewise, a study by school finance expert Bruce Baker and his associates found that 75 percent of African American students and 71 percent of Latino students attend schools in districts that are underfunded, as measured by the funding needed to reach average US test scores, while just over a third (35 percent) of white students and almost half (44 percent) of Asian students attend underfunded districts. The size of the funding gap also varies by race, with African American students experiencing the largest funding gap, receiving 17.2 percent less funding than is considered adequate, and Latino students experiencing an 11 percent funding gap. In contrast, Asian students typically receive 14.8 percent more funding than what is considered adequate and white students receive 21.9 percent more.[12]

Students in the nation's poorest districts similarly receive the short end of the stick when it comes to school funding. The two quintiles of districts with the highest poverty rates receive, respectively, 13.1 percent less and 11.4 percent less than adequate funding, while the two quintiles with the lowest poverty receive, respectively, 32.4 and 9 percent more than adequate funding. Given that one in five students in the US live in low-income and nonwhite districts, these opportunity gaps will shackle a generation of young people as they are preparing to run a much longer race.[13]

Students from low-income households and students of color also have access to far fewer quality and effective teachers, which matters because teacher quality greatly impacts student achievement. Research confirms that less experienced teachers and those who gain certification through alternative teacher certification

[10] Kelsey Clark et al., *Closing the Digital Divide Benefits Everyone, Not Just the Disconnected: An Analysis of How Universal Connectivity Benefits Education, Health Care, Government Services, and Employment*, Bost. Consulting Grp. & Common Sense 8 (2022), www.commonsensemedia.org/sites/default/files/research/report/2022-cs-bcg-closing-digital-divide_final-release-3-for-web.pdf.

[11] EdBuild, $23 *Billion* (2019), https://staging.edbuild.org/content/23-billion/full-report.pdf.

[12] Bruce D. Baker et al., Albert Shanker Inst. & Rutgers Univ. Graduate Sch. Education, The Adequacy and Fairness of State School Finance Systems 35 (5th ed. Dec. 2022).

[13] *Id.* at 27; EdBuild, *supra* note 11.

programs inflict an adverse impact on student achievement.[14] These teachers are employed at higher rates in schools with high concentrations of students from low-income households and students of color. A child in a school with high concentrations of minority students is almost four times as likely to be educated by an inexperienced teacher and twice as likely to have an uncertified teacher. As the concentration of students of color increases, so too does the percentage of teachers who took an alternative route to teacher certification.

Students in high-poverty schools also receive instruction from a higher-than-average percentage of alternative-route teachers. Schools serving higher concentrations of students of color and students who live in low-income households receive instruction from teachers who are less qualified based on nearly every measure of qualification.[15] These disparities in teacher quality adversely affect the achievement outcomes of students from low-income households and students of color. Conversely, consistently receiving instruction from high-quality teachers, as determined by their expertise in a subject matter, experience, effectiveness, and education level, significantly improves outcomes for high school students, such as their likelihood of earning a bachelor's degree.[16]

Other impactful disparities in educational opportunities also hinder the educational experiences of students from low-income households and students of color.[17] The opportunity for coursework that prepares students for a successful entry into college is far less available to students of color and students from low-income households. While calculus is offered in 60 percent of majority-white high schools, it is offered in only 36 percent of majority-Black high schools. Algebra I for seventh- and eighth-graders is provided in 42 percent of majority-Black schools, while

[14] Linda Darling-Hammond & Jeannie Oakes, Preparing Teachers for Deeper Learning, 3 (2019); Linda Darling-Hammond, *Education and the Path to One Nation, Indivisible*, Learning Pol'y Inst. 8 (Feb. 27, 2018), https://learningpolicyinstitute.org/product/education-path-one-nation-indivisible-brief ("Studies at the state, district, school, and individual student level have found that teachers' academic background, preparation for teaching, certification status, and experience, significantly affect their students' learning gains.").

[15] *Understanding Teacher Shortages: 2018 Update*, Learning Pol'y Inst. (Aug. 24, 2018), https://learningpolicyinstitute.org/product/understanding-teacher-shortages-interactive (defining "high-minority schools" as those with the top 25 percent of minority student enrollment for the state and "low-minority schools" as those in the bottom 25 percent of schools for minority enrollment within a state); *Understanding Teacher Shortages: Notes and Sources*, Learning Pol'y Inst., https://learningpolicyinstitute.org/understanding-teacher-shortages-notes-sources#_edn19; Darling-Hammond, *supra* note 14, at 4, 7–8; Joel McFarland et al., U.S. Dep't Education, The Condition of Education 20–21 (2018), https://nces.ed.gov/pubs2018/2018144.pdf.

[16] Se Woong Lee, *Pulling Back the Curtain: Revealing the Cumulative Importance of High-Performing, Highly Qualified Teachers on Students' Educational Outcome*, 40 Educ. Evaluation & Pol'y Analysis 359, 372–374 (2018).

[17] Linda Darling-Hammond, *Inequality and School Resources: What It Will Take to Close the Opportunity Gap*, *in* Closing the Opportunity Gap, *supra* note 7, at 77, 84; Darling-Hammond, *supra* note 14, at 7–8.

66 percent of majority-white schools offer it. Data from the Office for Civil Rights at the Department of Education reveals that schools with high Latino and African American enrollment lag behind other schools in offering courses in science and mathematics.[18] These data also confirm that while 52.4 percent of white students enrolled in an Advanced Placement class in the 2017–2018 academic year, only 9.3 percent of African American students enrolled in such a course. Furthermore, wealthier schools provide greater access to foreign languages, as well as comprehensive music and art programs and science-based hands-on learning, while poorer schools often do not offer foreign languages even in high school and fail to consistently deliver music, art, and science learning opportunities. Wealthier communities also enjoy greater access to resources and technology.[19] As the 100-year life is increasing the importance of a high-quality educational experience, these and other opportunity gaps drive achievement gaps that will leave many students from low-income households and students of color without the educational foundation that they will need to gain entry to and complete college or to compete successfully in the world of work.[20] Beginning a career with a great academic disadvantage would not just hinder Jane's initial employment opportunities and earnings if she only graduates from a high school but also hamper her ability to enter higher education and thereafter explore new employment opportunities.

Opportunity and achievement gaps also will encumber individuals' earnings and health, to name just a couple of the additional impacts linked closely to an

[18] Off. for C.R., US Dep't of Educ., *2017–18 State and National Tables* (2021), https://ocrdata.ed.gov/estimations/2017-2018. The 2017–2018 data are the most recent data that the Office for Civil Rights was reporting on its website at the time of writing.

[19] David Hinojosa, *Essential Building Blocks for State School Finance Systems and Promising State Practices*, Learning Pol'y Inst. 17–18 (Dec. 2018), https://learningpolicyinstitute.org/media/290/download?inline&file = Essential_Building_Blocks_State_School_Finance_Systems_REPORT.pdf; Darling-Hammond, *supra* note 14, at 7; Dick Startz, *Equal Opportunity in American Education*, Brookings Inst., Brown Ctr. Chalkboard (Jan. 15, 2019), https://www.brookings.edu/blog/brown-center-chalkboard/2019/01/15/equal-opportunity-in-american-education/; Joyce Winslow, *America's Digital Divide*, Pew (July 26, 2019), https://www.pewtrusts.org/en/trust/archive/summer-2019/americas-digital-divide.

[20] Carter & Welner, *supra* note 7, at 2–6; *The Great Divergence: Growing Disparities between the Nation's Highest and Lowest Achievers in NAEP Mathematics and Reading between 2009 and 2019*, US Dep't of Educ., NAEPPlus+: The Official Blog of the Nation's Report Card (Oct. 30, 2019), https://nces.ed.gov/nationsreportcard/blog/mathematics_reading_2019.aspx; Jonathan Rabinovitz, *Local Education Inequities Across U.S. Revealed in New Stanford Data Set*, Stan. News (Apr. 29, 2016), https://news.stanford.edu/2016/04/29/local-education-inequities-across-u-s-revealed-new-stanford-data-set/ ("The most and least socioeconomically advantaged districts have average performance levels more than four grade levels apart."); Michael Hansen et al., *Have We Made Progress on Achievement Gaps? Looking at Evidence from the New NAEP Results*, Brookings Inst., Brown Ctr. Chalkboard (Apr. 17, 2018), https://www.brookings.edu/blog/brown-center-chalkboard/2018/04/17/have-we-made-progress-on-achievement-gaps-looking-at-evidence-from-the-new-naep-results ("Reducing the achievement gap by 0.2 standard deviations could be loosely interpreted as reducing the gap by about a half-year of typical academic instruction.").

individual's education. Jane will need more income and savings to sustain her 100-year life. The amount of education, particularly higher education, that she receives will directly determine her income and earnings. The substantial differences in income between a high school dropout and a college graduate accumulate over time to drive large lifetime earning gaps that will impact whether Jane can support her need to take breaks from work so as to retrain in order to reap the advantages of emerging opportunities, as well as to fund a pension and pay off her mortgage before retirement. Jane's lifetime earnings also will need to sustain her quality of life through a longer retirement. Jane would be wise to pursue and secure a college degree at minimum because such a degree provides additional benefits beyond higher earnings, including greater job security, retirement plans, and a 47 percent greater likelihood of obtaining employer-provided health insurance.[21]

To thrive throughout a 100-year life, Jane also will need to invest in her health and well-being in sustained ways. Maximizing her education provides a vehicle for protecting her health because research confirms that education and health are strongly linked, with investments in additional education being correlated with improved health. Education may serve this function because it encourages positive behaviors, such as eating vegetables and fruits, exercising, and wearing a seat belt, and discourages negative behaviors, such as smoking, a sedentary lifestyle, a substandard diet, and alcohol abuse.[22] Jane's investment in higher education also can delay the onset of "accelerated cognitive decline."[23] Higher educational attainment provides access to resources such as knowledge, prestige, power, and social relationships that Jane can employ to prevent adverse health outcomes. Additionally, Jane can use the accumulation of wealth that education provides to strengthen her health through such actions as acquiring or improvising resources to achieve desirable health outcomes.[24]

21 Philip Trostel, It's Not Just the Money: The Benefits of College Education to Individuals and to Society 1, 10, 13, 16–21 (2015); Sandy Baum, Higher Education Earnings Premium: Value, Variation, and Trends 2 (2014).

22 Erich Striessnig, Too Educated to Be Happy? An Investigation into the Relationship between Education and Subjective Well-Being 23 (2015); Trostel, *supra* note 21, at 29–30; David M. Cutler & Adriana Lleras-Muney, *Understanding Differences in Health Behaviors by Education*, 29 J. Health Econ. 1, 24 (2010); Carina A. Furnée et al., *The Health Effects of Education: A Meta-Analysis*, 18 Eur. J. Pub. Health 417, 420 (2008). *Cf.* Titus J. Galama et al., *The Effect of Education on Health and Mortality: A Review of Experimental and Quasi-Experimental Evidence*, Nat'l Bureau of Econ. Rsch. Working Paper No. 24225 (2018), at 26 (finding that education sometimes reduces smoking or obesity).

23 Sean A. P. Clouston et al., *Education and Cognitive Decline: An Integrative Analysis of Global Longitudinal Studies of Cognitive Aging*, 75 Js. Gerontology: Series B e151, e156 (2020).

24 John Mirowsky & Catherine E. Ross, Education, Social Status and Health 197 (2003); Jo C. Phelan et al., *Social Conditions as Fundamental Causes of Health Inequalities: Theory, Evidence, and Policy Implications*, 51 J. Health & Soc. Behav. S28 (2010); Anna Zajacova & Elizabeth M. Lawrence, *The Relationship between Education and Health: Reducing Disparities through a Contextual Approach*, 39 Ann. Rev. Pub. Health 273, 277 (2018); Striessnig, *supra* note 22.

The research and data are clear that Jane's educational opportunities and attainment will provide the linchpin for her thriving professionally, financially, and physically throughout a 100-year life. Therefore, law and policy should aim to close the opportunity and achievement gaps that could hinder Jane from maximizing her educational opportunities and outcomes.

3.3 EDUCATION LAW REFORM IN THE SHADOW OF THE 100-YEAR LIFE

Given the demands of the 100-year life, the US should adopt law and policy reforms that ensure that Jane receives the high-quality education that she will need to sustain her professional, economic, and health needs as a future centenarian. The strong connections between education and an individual's professional, economic, and physical well-being mean that investments in improving educational opportunities and outcomes will yield exponential benefits. Law and policy shape the landscape of educational opportunities and achievement and can be reformed to support individuals' living and thriving over longer lives.

In this section, I recommend law and policy reforms for education that the US could adopt to support a 100-year life. Before doing so, it is essential to note two critical points. First, a full presentation of the education reforms that are needed to support individuals living to 100 years or more would take many volumes. These reforms could include reducing poverty and its adverse impacts on education and providing high-quality childcare, universal high-quality preschooling, and free access to higher education, to name only a few of the possibilities. Second, no single law, policy, or reform can solve the nation's education challenges. These challenges are vast and varied, and defy any single reform.

I highlight four essential education law and policy reforms that the US should consider as it examines how it will create and support a growing population of centenarians: (1) recognizing a federal right to education, (2) adopting equitable and adequate funding to support a high-quality education, (3) transitioning away from tracking and toward an approach to education that expands access to rigorous curricula and robust teaching and learning practices for all students, and (4) restructuring education federalism to support these reforms.

A federal right to education could provide the type of comprehensive framework that is essential for supporting Jane and future generations to live a productive and enjoyable 100-year life. My recently published edited volume, *A Federal Right to Education: Fundamental Questions for Our Democracy*, explores the possibilities and pitfalls of a federal right to education. Although a full exploration of those ideas is beyond the scope of a single book chapter, I highlight here some critical ideas focused on how such a right could transform educational opportunities that support a 100-year life.

A "rights" framework provides an essential lens for addressing the challenges of our education system. Although all fifty states recognize a right to education, those rights fail to guarantee that students receive access to a high-quality education. Instead, the rights range from a mere access right to a more robust right that aims to provide students the opportunities they need to achieve state standards. This reality leaves many students' education to the whims of state political majorities that too often tolerate deeply entrenched educational opportunity gaps.[25] Competing views on what a federal right to education should guarantee, such as essential educational resources, a right to compete, or a right to "an equally adequate, adequately equal education," should be examined through the lens of the 100-year life and what it will take to sustain it.[26]

Fortunately, several pathways exist for the US to recognize and protect a federal right to education, from a Supreme Court decision grounded in originalism to a constitutional amendment. However, the need to equip individuals to adapt to an ever-changing workforce and professional demands, as well as to rapidly evolving technological advances, reveals that a statutory right to education provides the best path forward to support the educational opportunities needed to sustain individuals over the 100-year life. I explore in *A Federal Right to Education* how Congress could adopt a federal right to education and employ its flexibility as a legislature to create a collaborative enforcement model that views litigation as a last resort to reduce the litigation burden of recognizing such a right. More importantly, a statutory right to education would enable Congress to adapt the content of the right to novel workforce and technological demands through review and revision of the statutory guarantee.[27]

25 Kimberly Jenkins Robinson, *The Essential Questions Regarding a Federal Right to Education*, *in* A FEDERAL RIGHT TO EDUCATION, *supra* note 7, at 1–9; Kristine L. Bowman, *The Inadequate Right to Education: A Case Study of Obstacles to State Protection*, *in* A FEDERAL RIGHT TO EDUCATION, *supra* note 7, at 65, 65–77.

26 LINDA DARLING-HAMMOND, *Assuring Essential Educational Resources through a Federal Right to Education*, *in* A FEDERAL RIGHT TO EDUCATION, *supra* note 7, at 235, 241 (recommending that a federal right to education guarantee "a competent, certified well-trained teacher," "a well-trained competent principal," and "the resources necessary to support the effective instructional program within that school so that the educational needs of all children, including at-risk children, can be met"); Carmel Martin et al., *Lessons from State School Finance Inform a New Federal Right to a High-Quality Education*, *in* A FEDERAL RIGHT TO EDUCATION, *supra* note 7, at 283, 291–295 (contending that a federal right to education should ensure a high-quality education that provides additional resources to students with the greatest needs and that employs an outcomes-based model for state accountability for school funding systems); Rachel F. Moran, *The Constitution of Opportunity: Democratic Equality, Economic Inequality, and the Right to Compete*, *in* A FEDERAL RIGHT TO EDUCATION, *supra* note 7, at 261–262 (recommending a federal right to education that protects a meaningful opportunity for students to compete with their peers); Joshua E. Weishart, *Protecting a Federal Right to Educational Equality and Adequacy*, *in* A FEDERAL RIGHT TO EDUCATION, *supra* note 7, at 303, 304 (recommending that a federal right to education should guarantee "an equally adequate, adequately equal education").

27 Robinson, *supra* note 7, at 9–10; Kimberly Jenkins Robinson, *A Congressional Right to Education: Promises, Pitfalls, and Politics*, *in* A FEDERAL RIGHT TO EDUCATION, *supra* note

Second, the US must insist that states adopt school funding systems that would support educational opportunities that prepare students to both attain and enjoy a 100-year life. School funding provides the foundation for the nation's education system, yet our nation's approach to school funding is undeniably broken. School funding is far too often linked to the whims of political majorities and a student's wealth, race, or neighborhood and far too infrequently to the needs of students. The US needs to adopt laws and policies that remedy the key shortcomings of state education systems, which include, among others:

1. lower funding to districts serving students with greater needs;
2. insufficient linkage of funding systems to desired educational outcomes;
3. low funding levels; and
4. inadequate oversight of state funding systems.[28]

The three branches of the federal government have at their disposal an array of tools to take aim at these shortcomings, and all three branches should work together to remedy them. For example, Congress has required states and districts to report per-pupil spending data, including personnel spending data, by source of funds in state report cards in the Elementary and Secondary Education Act. Congress can employ the Elementary and Secondary Education Act as a vehicle for incentivizing states to remedy funding inadequacies, inequities, and inefficiencies. Alternatively, Congress could address these shortcomings through new legislation focused on incentivizing school funding reform. The president can also use political pressure to urge states to remedy these shortcomings. Finally, the Department of Education can provide research and technical assistance to states and districts to explain why and how states should remedy these funding inequities and inadequacies, as well as financial assistance to aid in closing funding gaps.[29]

Third, tracking – a long-standing educational practice that results in many students from low-income households and students of color being placed into dead-end tracks while their peers are placed in tracks that lead to college and career – should be phased out to support more individuals thriving over a 100-year life. Tracking oftentimes begins in the early grades in the US, and lower track placement typically leads students to lower-quality teachers, a less rigorous curriculum, and watered-down educational goals. These lower tracks are antithetical to the

7, at 186; Derek W. Black, *Implying a Federal Constitutional Right to Education, in* A Federal Right to Education, *supra* note 7, at 135; S. Educ. Found., *No Time to Lose: Why the United States Needs an Education Amendment to the US Constitution, in* A Federal Right to Education, *supra* note 7, at 208.

[28] Robinson, *supra* note 7, at 4–5; Kimberly Jenkins Robinson, *No Quick Fix for Equity and Excellence: The Virtues of Incremental Shifts in Education Federalism*, 27 Stan. L. & Pol'y Rev. 201, 206 (2016).

[29] Every Student Succeeds Act, 20 U.S.C. §§ 6311(h)(1)(C)(x), 6311(h)(2)(C); Kimberly Jenkins Robinson, *Restructuring the Elementary and Secondary Education Act's Approach to Equity*, 103 Minn. L. Rev. 915, 984–988 (2018).

high-quality educational opportunities that all students will need to thrive over a 100-year life. Fortunately, some school districts are beginning to successfully detrack, and studies confirm that detracking benefits not only students from low-income households and students of color but also all students. Law and policy reform can incentivize states and districts to end tracking by passing legislation that disincentivizes the practice, or through enforcement of federal and state law and policy that prohibits practices that inflict a disparate impact on the basis of race, color, or national origin.[30]

Finally, successful implementation of the comprehensive array of education law and policy reforms that would make a 100-year life possible will require greater federal leadership and involvement in education and thus a restructuring of education federalism. Education federalism currently favors state and local control of education and a limited federal role in education. This narrow federal role enables states to choose to neglect the needs of students from low-income households and students of color from communities that are oftentimes unable to leverage political influence to secure the high-quality educational opportunities that students need to succeed and thrive. Education federalism also has served as a major roadblock to efforts to advance equal educational opportunity. Restructuring education federalism will provide a necessary and essential launching pad for comprehensive education reforms that deliver a high-quality education to all students to support future generations attaining and enjoying a 100-year life.[31]

3.4 CONCLUSION

The prospect of most people enjoying a 100-year life, as well as sharp declines in academic outcomes following the pandemic, provides new urgency to closing US opportunity and achievement gaps in order to empower the professional and personal experiences of thriving over this longer life. Our economy, democracy, and society will depend even more on the types of comprehensive reforms outlined in this chapter to support human flourishing and enjoyment of a 100-year life.

[30] Title VI of the Civil Rights Act of 1964, 42 U.S.C. § 2000d; Carol C. Burris & Kevin G. Welner, *Closing the Achievement Gap by Detracking*, 68 Phi Delta Kappan 594 (2005); Kamilah Legette, A *Social-Cognitive Perspective of the Consequences of Curricular Tracking on Youth Outcomes* (2020), https://www.ncbi.nlm.nih.gov/pmc/articles/PMC7810159/.

[31] Kimberly Jenkins Robinson, Protecting Education as a Civil Right: Remedying Race Discrimination and Ensuring a High-Quality Education 16–25 (2021); Kimberly Jenkins Robinson, *Disrupting Education Federalism*, 92 Wash. U. L. Rev. 959, 962, 976–978, 985 (2015); Darling-Hammond, *supra* note 14, at 7–9.

4

Aging Out of Criminal Justice

Shon Hopwood

A 100-year life expectancy will radically change our American criminal justice system – much for the worse and, hopefully, some for the better. It will require us to consider who we send to prison, for how long, and how we treat those in prison, knowing that most will be released someday to become our neighbors. It will also require us to consider what is a just punishment, considering that life sentences become harsher the longer the life.

The US already has the world's highest incarceration rate.[1] If every single state were a country, most would incarcerate "more people per capita than virtually any independent democracy on earth."[2] This "mass incarceration" problem began in the 1980s and has only abated slightly over the past decade.[3] Mass incarceration means we house nearly 2 million people in thousands of prisons, jails, and juvenile correctional facilities.[4] This results partially from the US sentencing people to prison for more types of crimes and for longer periods than most other countries. Once incarcerated, people in prison are subjected to an incredibly violent prison system with little rehabilitation programming prior to their release. Consequently, people leave correction systems and reenter society worse off, rather than corrected.

It was once thought that our incarceration rate was inversely proportional to our crime rate. But criminologists and economists now believe that the link between higher incarceration and lower crime rates is not nearly as strong as previously thought.[5] Because there were many variables (such as increased economic opportunities) that led crime to decline in the 1990s, criminologists now believe that

[1] Emily Widra & Tiana Herring, *States of Incarceration: The Global Context 2021*, Prison Pol'y Initiative (Sep. 2021), https://www.prisonpolicy.org/global/2021.html.

[2] *Id.*

[3] *See* E. Ann. Carson, *Prisoners in 2020: Statistical Tables*, Bureau Just. Stat. (Dec. 2021), https://bjs.ojp.gov/content/pub/pdf/p20st.pdf.

[4] Wendy Sawyer & Peter Wagner, *Mass Incarceration: The Whole Pie 2023*, Prison Pol'y Initiative (Mar. 14, 2023), https://www.prisonpolicy.org/reports/pie2023.html.

[5] *See* Don Steman, *The Prison Paradox: More Incarceration Will Not Make Us Safer*, Vera Inst. Just. (July 2017), 1–2, https://www.vera.org/downloads/publications/for-the-record-prison-paradox_02.pdf; David Roodman, *The Impacts of Incarceration on Crime*, Open Philanthropy

increased incarceration had no "statistically significant effect" on reducing violent crime in the 1990s and the 2000s.[6] These views from experts studying our system holistically are borne out by recent data showing that, between 2007 and 2017, thirty-four states reduced both their crime rates and their prison populations.[7] So expanding our criminal justice and prison systems has not made us any safer.

Longer lifespans could greatly expand our mass incarceration problem. Over 7 million Americans have at some point been imprisoned; over 12 million Americans have been convicted of a felony but not been imprisoned; and about 45 million Americans have been convicted of misdemeanors.[8] It is also estimated that over 113 million Americans have had someone in their close or immediate family who has been incarcerated during their lifetime.[9] Our communities, especially communities of color, are also more heavily policed now than in the past.[10] As people live longer, and as our neighborhoods are increasingly policed, people will have more contact with our criminal justice system, and there is a serious concern that we will incarcerate even greater numbers of citizens.

The expansion of our criminal justice and prison systems comes at great cost to impacted families. People with felony or misdemeanor convictions see their annual earnings significantly reduced. People who have served time in prisons have their annual earnings reduced by 52 percent over the course of their lives. Those earning losses entrench poverty and worsen already large economic disparities between different races and socioeconomic classes.

Prison also takes a toll on the physical and mental health of incarcerated people. Around 600,000 people leave American prisons each year. Few people leaving our prison systems escape trauma. Our prisons are often understaffed, which increases the amount of violence within our prison systems.[11] Prisons do not provide adequate

PROJECT (Sep. 2017), 7, https://www.openphilanthropy.org/files/Focus_Areas/Criminal_Justice_Reform/The_impacts_of_incarceration_on_crime_10.pdf.

6 Roodman, *supra* note 5.

7 Cameron Kimble & Ames Grawert, *Between 2007 and 2017, 34 States Reduced Crime and Incarceration in Tandem*, BRENNAN CTR. FOR JUST. (Aug. 6, 2019), https://www.brennancenter.org/our-work/analysis-opinion/between-2007-and-2017-34-states-reduced-crime-and-incarceration-tandem.

8 Terry-Ann Craigie, Ames Grawert & Cameron Kimble, *Conviction, Imprisonment, and Lost Earnings: How Involvement with the Criminal Justice System Deepens Inequality*, BRENNAN CTR. FOR JUST. (Sep. 15, 2020), 2, https://www.brennancenter.org/sites/default/files/2020-09/EconomicImpactReport_pdf.pdf.

9 Christal Hayes, *"This Isn't Just Numbers – But Lives": Half of Americans Have Family Members Who've Been Incarcerated*, USA TODAY (Dec. 6, 2018), https://www.usatoday.com/story/news/politics/2018/12/06/half-americans-have-family-who-have-been-jailed-new-study-shows/2206521002.

10 *See* Alan Feuer, *Black New Yorkers Are Twice as Likely to Be Stopped by the Police, Data Shows*, N.Y. TIMES (Sep. 23, 2020).

11 *See* Shon Hopwood, *How Atrocious Prisons Conditions Make Us All Less Safe*, BRENNAN CTR. FOR JUST. (Aug. 9, 2021), https://www.brennancenter.org/our-work/analysis-opinion/how-atrocious-prisons-conditions-make-us-all-less-safe.

mental health care, and when people with mental illness have an episode, the system often uses solitary confinement to manage the problem, even though it has been shown to exacerbate mental illness.[12] With lifespans increasing, we might unintentionally create or exacerbate mental health problems in those released from our prisons.

And it is not just our prisoners who are impacted. Over half of those in American prisons are parents. Incarceration fractures relationships between parents and children. Parents in state prisons reported "roughly 1.25 million minor children, meaning the number of people in state prison almost exactly mirrors the number of impacted minor children."[13] The results are often disastrous, as children with an incarcerated parent have higher suicide rates, more antisocial behavior, more mental health problems, and a higher chance of someday committing crimes and experiencing incarceration. Put differently, there are a number of social harms that come with being the world's largest cager of human beings.

Our mass incarceration problem is driven by an abundance of life without parole sentences. One in seven people currently in a US prison is serving a life sentence – meaning either life without parole, life with some sort of parole, or virtual life (a sentence of fifty years or more).[14] In 2021, there were over 200,000 people serving life sentences.[15] Already, over 30 percent of lifers are fifty-five years old or more, making our prisons geriatric centers.[16] Worse yet, over 8,000 people are serving virtual life sentences for crimes committed as minors, despite research on adolescent brain development that reveals that minors' younger age leads to a diminished capacity to comprehend the risks and consequences of their actions.[17]

Take one case as an example of this phenomenon: Joe Ligon was fifteen when he met four other teenagers in South Philadelphia. They started drinking, and Ligon drank alcohol for the first time. They looked for money to buy more wine, and their escapade ended with Ligon's codefendants fatally stabbing two men. A judge sentenced him to life in prison without the possibility of parole. After the US Supreme Court ruled that all juvenile life sentences without parole were unconstitutional, a judge ordered Ligon's release after he had served an unfathomable sixty-eight years in prison. Ligon entered prison when Dwight D. Eisenhower was president and left prison, at the age of eighty-two, during the Biden administration. As people live

[12] *See* Tiana Herring, *The Research Is Clear: Solitary Confinement Causes Long-Lasting Harm*, Prison Pol'y Initiative (Dec. 8, 2020), https://www.prisonpolicy.org/blog/2020/12/08/solitary_symposium.

[13] Leah Wang, *Both Sides of the Bars: How Mass Incarceration Punishes Families*, Prison Pol'y Initiative (Aug. 11, 2022), https://www.prisonpolicy.org/blog/2022/08/11/parental_incarceration.

[14] Ashley Nellis, *No End in Sight, America's Enduring Reliance on Life Sentences*, Sent'g Project (Feb. 17, 2021), 4, https://www.sentencingproject.org/app/uploads/2022/08/No-End-in-Sight-Americas-Enduring-Reliance-on-Life-Imprisonment.pdf.

[15] *Id.*

[16] *Id.*

[17] *Id.*

longer, these life (or majority-of-life) sentences will only increase our mass incarceration problem, filling our prisons with people who, if they commit their crimes as juveniles, could serve decades in custody before their release.

The number of older people in our prisons has grown exponentially. Between 1999 and 2016, the number of prisoners fifty-five years and older grew by 280 percent.[18] Incarceration itself accelerates aging due to inadequate medical care before prison and substandard care in prison, in addition to the stress linked to prison violence. And although we are incarcerating more people over the age of fifty-five, those older adults have the lowest rates of rearrest after release from prisons, meaning they pose some of the lowest risks of reoffending.[19] Imposing long sentences on people less likely to reoffend (those over fifty-five years old) thus means an expansion of our criminal justice system without any positive societal gain in public safety.

The consequences of expanding our mass incarceration problem and turning prisons into geriatric centers are profound. The annual cost of incarcerating people over the age of fifty-five is roughly three to five times as much as incarcerating younger people. In 2009, California spent more than $42 million in one year on medical care and the continued incarceration of just thirty-two older prisoners who were chronically ill.[20]

These costs strain our law enforcement budgets. Total US government expenses on prisons and jails are roughly $80 billion. In the federal system alone, mass incarceration has led to the Federal Bureau of Prisons' (BOP) ever-growing budget. BOP's budget has grown so much that it has begun "crowding out" other Department of Justice (DOJ) priorities, such as hiring additional federal law enforcement officers to investigate and prosecute lawbreakers.[21] The more people there are living longer in prison, the more it will cost to maintain prison systems. With longer lifespans, it will be vital for us to reduce the number of aging people in our prisons.

An ever-expanding lifespan will also require us to reevaluate what is an adequate punishment for particular crimes, including the length of sentences and what crimes are worthy of sending someone to prison. Right now, the US sends more people to prison for more offenses and imposes longer sentences than any country

[18] Matt McKillop & Alex Boucher, *Aging Prison Populations Drive Up Costs*, PEW CHARITABLE TRS. (Feb. 20, 2018), https://www.pewtrusts.org/en/research-and-analysis/articles/2018/02/20/aging-prison-populations-drive-up-costs.

[19] *See* Emily Widra, *The Aging Prison Population: Causes, Costs, and Consequences*, PRISON POL'Y INITIATIVE (Aug. 2, 2023), https://www.prisonpolicy.org/blog/2023/08/02/aging.

[20] Ashley Demyan, *Elderly People in Prison Present Little Risk, but Staggering Costs*, VERA INST. JUST. (July 6, 2015), https://www.vera.org/news/elderly-people-in-prison-present-little-risk-but-staggering-costs.

[21] *See* Sally Q. Yates, *McNamara Memorial Lecture at Fordham University* (Nov. 14, 2016), https://www.justice.gov/opa/speech/deputy-attorney-general-sally-q-yates-delivers-mcnamara-memorial-lecture-fordham.

on the planet. Prior to the 1980s, prison sentences were reserved mostly for violent offenses. But starting in the 1980s, the US began prosecuting and seeking decades-long sentences for nonviolent and property offenses, thereby creating a system of mass incarceration.

As people, including those in prison, live longer, we will have to reevaluate the length of prison sentences. One result might be that our policymakers increase sentences as people live longer. If a person lives to 100, then a sentence of ten years does not seem as large a punishment. The hope, however, is that, as people live longer, our policymakers will shorten sentences and focus on more efficient and fair ways to reduce crime. That hope was signaled by an ACLU telephone poll in 2016 that showed 72 percent of Americans would be more likely to vote for politicians who support eliminating harsh mandatory minimum sentencing laws, and 71 percent agree that incarceration is often counterproductive to public safety.[22]

Despite the increased number of people serving life or virtual life, approximately 95 percent of people who are incarcerated will one day be released and return to our communities. With 100-year lifespans, we will have to radically change the conditions in our prisons. Current prison conditions are awful. American prisons are incredibly dangerous, with the ever-present threat of violence, including sexual violence. Many prisons are grossly understaffed and overpopulated. A DOJ report found that, in a single week, the Alabama prison system had four stabbings (resulting in one death), three sexual assaults, several physical assaults, and one person's bed set on fire as he slept.[23] As the *New York Times* noted, "One prisoner had been dead for so long that when he was discovered lying face down, his face was flattened. Another was tied up and tortured for two days while no one noticed. Bloody inmates screamed for help from cells whose doors did not lock."[24]

Right now, the great irony of the criminal justice system is that the longer someone spends in "corrections," the less likely they are to come out a corrected, law-abiding citizen. By that I mean, the longer a person spends in prison, the more traumatized and unstable their return to society will be, due to the harshness of being incarcerated. The last thing society needs is for people in custody to do life imprisonment on the installment plan, whereby people go to prison, return to the community, commit new offenses (while creating new victims), and then return to prison, to be repeated as long as they live.

Many of our criminal justice systems track recidivism rates, which measure how many people released from prisons will be rearrested again within three years.

[22] *91 Percent of Americans Support Criminal Justice Reform, ACLU Polling Finds*, Am. C.L. Union (Nov. 16, 2017), https://www.aclu.org/press-releases/91-percent-americans-support-criminal-justice-reform-aclu-polling-finds.

[23] *See* Katie Benner & Shaila Dewan, *Alabama's Gruesome Prisons: Report Finds Rape and Murder at All Hours*, N.Y. Times (Apr. 3, 2019), https://www.nytimes.com/2019/04/03/us/alabama-prisons-doj-investigation.html.

[24] *Id.*

A study in 2012, tracking thirty-four states, showed that 62 percent of people released from state prisons were rearrested within three years, and 71 percent rearrested within five years.[25] To make matters worse, 81 percent of prisoners twenty-four or younger were rearrested within five years of release.[26] That is an extraordinary amount of failure – failure that directly leads to increased crime and victimization.

With ever-expanding lifespans, we need to double down on rehabilitation programs inside our prison systems. One reason our prisons are so violent is the idleness that occurs in them. As mass incarceration grew, many states rejected the role of rehabilitation and reduced the number of available rehabilitation and educational programs. In Florida, with the nation's third largest prison system, there are virtually no education programs for prisoners, even though research shows that those programs reduce violence in prison and the recidivism rate for those released from prison. Prisons lessen personal autonomy and increase institutional dependence. This leads people to rely upon a virtual welfare state with free room and board that only a prison can offer, thus rendering them less able to cope with economic demands upon release. We need robust educational and vocational training in prisons to train people to live successful and law-abiding lives post-prison. As prisoners age and the prison population thereby grows, prison will become less useful as a "rehabilitation device" for those who might benefit from one, which could, in turn, increase recidivism, but not among the prisoners who are living longer in prison.

In an age of Google searches and an ever-expanding criminal justice system, many people released from prison are punished long after they serve their sentences. As we live longer, we also need a reexamination of the collateral consequences of a felony conviction. Collateral consequences are legal penalties that take away rights, access to services, or impose some other disadvantage. Currently, people with a felony conviction can be legally discriminated against in employment, housing, welfare, and voting and are barred from certain professions. These lifelong punishments are not factored into our sentencing practices. And these collateral consequences often lead to high unemployment and large amounts of homelessness for those returning to the community from a custodial sentence, thereby increasing the chance of recidivism. Formerly incarcerated people, of course, need stable employment and housing to live successful and law-abiding lives. And when those returning to the community feel like they have employment opportunities and upward mobility, they reoffend at much lower rates.

One area where federal courts might increase protections for those serving draconian sentences is the Eighth Amendment arena. Whether a punishment is

[25] Matthew R. Durose & Leonardo Antenangeli, *Recidivism of Prisoners Released in 34 States in 2012: A 5-Year Follow-Up Period (2012–2017)*, Bureau Just. Stat. (July 2021), at 1, https://bjs.ojp.gov/sites/g/files/xyckuh236/files/media/document/rpr34s125yfup1217.pdf.

[26] *Id.*

"cruel and unusual" is generally determined using a proportionality test that weighs the severity of the offense committed against the harshness of the punishment. So far, the Supreme Court has not used the prohibition on cruel and unusual punishment to strike down long sentences for adults. In *Ewing v. California*,[27] the defendant challenged a twenty-five-years-to-life sentence under California's notorious three-strikes law for stealing three golf clubs valued at $399 each. The Court found that this sentence was neither cruel nor unusual and upheld it.

But in recent years, the Court has cut back the potential punishments facing juveniles, including the death penalty and life without parole sentences, even for homicide crimes. In doing so, the Court applied an "evolving standards of decency" test, finding that the death penalty and life without parole for juveniles were against the consensus of state practices and that the death penalty was a disproportionate punishment for juveniles.[28] The Court largely based its ruling on the idea that juveniles are not as culpable as adults who commit similar crimes and receive similar sentences due to their lack of maturity and underdeveloped sense of responsibility in considering the long-term consequences of their actions. The Court later struck down mandatory life without parole sentences for juveniles convicted of murder.[29] A life sentence without parole ignores that someone who commits a violent act at seventeen is unlikely to commit the same act at forty.

Brain science has advanced since these decisions. Scientists have concluded that reckless and impetuous behavior is a characteristic not just of minors but also of young adults. Young adults (those eighteen to twenty-five) are often in a transition phase and lack the maturity and foresight needed to refrain from risky behavior, such as committing crimes. There is hope that, as brain science advances, the Supreme Court will one day forbid long sentences even for those who reach the age of twenty-five due to their lessened culpability and maturity.

As for older adults, there is growing body of literature suggesting that people continue to change throughout adulthood depending, in part, on external stimuli.[30] Even adults can "age out" of crimes and be rehabilitated. If adults have the capacity to change, and if character is not static, maybe one day our policymakers will determine that longer prison sentences are not necessary to keep us safe. State legislatures and Congress should reexamine sentencing schemes with a focus on data-driven sentencing and public safety rather than mere punitiveness.

As people live longer, policymakers must also reconsider scaling back our criminal justice system; otherwise, we could see an even greater expansion of jails and prisons. Policymakers could do so by reclassifying some felonies as misdemeanors, which would reduce the length of sentences. They also could decriminalize some

[27] 538 U.S. 11 (2003).

[28] *Roper v. Simmons*, 543 U.S. 551 (2005).

[29] *Miller v. Alabama*, 567 U.S. 460 (2012).

[30] *See* M. Eve Hanan, *Incapacitating Errors: Sentencing and the Science of Change*, 97 Denver L. Rev. 151, 171–185 (2019).

actions, such as simple drug possession, thereby reducing the risk of violent confrontations between police and citizens. They could invest in alternatives to incarceration, such as probation, home confinement, and community service. On the back end of the system, policymakers could reduce collateral consequences that lead to higher rates of recidivism, such as barriers to employment and stable housing options. Or they could pass clean-slate legislation that removes the stigma of a criminal conviction once someone has returned to society and demonstrated rehabilitation.

The gift of a longer life is ultimately the gift of time. Longer lifespans will likely lead to more overpopulation, more crowded urban centers, and fewer resources and economic opportunities for the majority of people, all of which increase crime. Questions about how best to keep the public safe will abound. The hope is that, the longer we live, the more wisdom we will acquire and the more we will realize that a system of mass incarceration is inconsistent with our values of fairness and public safety.

5

The 100-Year Life Meets the Future of Work

Cynthia Estlund

The 100-year life, if it becomes a reality, will bring daunting challenges as well as highly skewed gains. First, longer lives will be a blessing only if they come with gains in mental and physical health that last well into the last decade of those lives, and the extra years of life and health are likely to be distributed very unequally both across and within societies. Indeed, recent declines in life expectancy in the US point to the disturbing possibility that poorer and less-educated Americans might be looking at both shorter and less healthy lives for the foreseeable future.[1] Growing inequality thus casts a shadow over this chapter's exploration of the implications of longer lifespans for the future of work and work law in the US – the world's richest and, on some accounts, most unequal country.[2]

Among the more profound challenges of the 100-year life will be to our already-frayed patchwork system of retirement security.[3] It is hard to imagine how either most individuals or the society as a whole will be able to fund more than three decades of reasonably comfortable retirement on the basis of four decades or so of workforce participation.[4] Without a very large (and arguably unjustified[5]) shift of societal resources toward supporting nonworking seniors, most of those who can extend their working lives beyond what is now normal retirement age will have to do so. That might upset expectations, depending on how fast it happens, and it will put an especially heavy burden on those whose work is physically demanding. It might

[1] *See* Ctrs. for Disease Control, *Life Expectancy in the U.S. Dropped for the Second Year in a Row in 2021* (Aug. 31, 2022), https://www.cdc.gov/nchs/pressroom/nchs_press_releases/2022/20220831.htm; *see generally* Anne Case & Angus Deaton, Deaths of Despair and the Future of Capitalism (2021).

[2] *See* Jack Ewing, *United States Is the Richest Country in the World, and It Has the Biggest Wealth Gap*, N.Y. Times (Sep. 23, 2020), https://www.nytimes.com/2020/09/23/business/united-states-is-the-richest-country-in-the-world-and-it-has-the-biggest-wealth-gap.html. Inequality concerns are at the forefront of Kate Andrias's chapter in this volume (Chapter 9).

[3] On the dire state of existing retirement systems, *see* Katherine Newman, Downhill from Here: Retirement Insecurity in the Age of Inequality (2019).

[4] That problem is explored at length in Lynda Gratton & Andrew Scott, The 100-Year Life: Living and Working in an Age of Longevity (2016).

[5] *See infra* Part IV.

even generate political turmoil of the sort recently seen in France over proposals to increase the retirement age to sixty-four.[6]

Longer working lives might in turn exacerbate competition for jobs that do not require scarce or advanced skills. For their part, older workers will be hindered in that labor market competition – more than they already are – by doubts about their capabilities. Longer working lives will require us to reassess the law of age discrimination in employment (discussed at greater length in Kenji Yoshino's chapter) and to devise new ways to ensure intergenerational equity in employment. Longer working lives will also recast the debate over job security protections and will highlight the need to make work and work schedules less demanding, especially as workers age. This chapter will explore these challenges and how they will intersect with changing technology and its impact on the nature and number of jobs.

5.1 FROM LONGER LIVES TO LONGER *WORKING* LIVES

All existing public and private pension systems, including personal retirement savings plans, depend ultimately on working adults generating the revenues that support nonworking retirees. Some of those revenues come from workers' employers, but let us treat that as deferred compensation and part of what workers generate through their work. Let us also put aside the *deus ex machina* device of injecting massive additional funds from general tax revenues; that might prove necessary, but seeing why will require first working through the problems faced under existing models. On those models, workers support their own future nonworking selves through private retirement savings, and current workers collectively support the retirement incomes of current retirees through Social Security and other public and private pension plans. All of these elements of retirement security – public and private, voluntary and mandatory – depend on maintaining a sustainable ratio between the number of active workers and of retirees, and between years of active labor market participation and years of retirement.[7] The 100-year life will test the limits of what is sustainable.

To take a crucial example, consider Social Security, whose rather modest benefits – on average, just $1,614 a month, or $19,370 a year in 2022[8] – are the only source

[6] *See* Elaine Ganley, *French Protests Push for Withdrawal of Macron's Pension Plan*, AP News (Mar. 11, 2023), https://apnews.com/article/france-retirement-pension-protests-macron-c3dc4eaoefb6ofcof5fdd4b8f3d72d51; *see also* Catherine Porter & Aurelien Breeden, *Record Protests in France as Anger over Macron's Pension Plan Persists*, N.Y. Times (Mar. 7, 2023), https://www.nytimes.com/2023/03/07/world/europe/macron-france-retirement-protests.html.

[7] *See generally* Nicholas Barr & Peter Diamond, Pension Reform: A Short Guide (2009); Nicholas Barr, *Pensions: Overview of the Issues*, 22 Oxford Rev. Econ. Pol'y 1 (2006).

[8] Ctr. for Budget & Policy Priorities, *Top Ten Facts about Social Security*, https://www.cbpp.org/research/social-security/top-ten-facts-about-social-security (accessed Mar. 13, 2023).

of retirement income for many US workers, including most workers of color.[9] (As of 2020, according to the US Census Bureau, over 40 percent of those aged fifty-six to sixty-four, and larger shares of younger cohorts, had no private retirement savings.[10]) In 1940, shortly after Social Security began to provide basic pensions at age sixty-five, average life expectancy in the US was sixty-two years, and the ratio between covered workers and beneficiaries was 159 to 1.[11] By 2020, average life expectancy had risen to seventy-nine years, and by 2021, the worker-to-beneficiary ratio had fallen to about 2.8 to 1.[12] Thus far, reforms have been modest: a rise in the normal retirement age to sixty-seven (for those born after 1960),[13] and higher payroll taxes to support those longer retirement periods.[14] More of both kinds of reforms will surely be needed.

Employer-sponsored retirement plans, for those lucky enough to have them, face similar demographic pressures. Such plans grew in the mid twentieth century, encouraged by tax subsidies and impelled in some sectors by collective bargaining, but they were never made mandatory[15] and were largely unregulated until the Employee Retirement Income Security Act of 1974 (ERISA).[16] Back in the day, most employer-sponsored and collectively bargained pension plans were, like Social Security, "defined benefit" plans: They promised workers a specific monthly pension depending on age and years of service at the time of retirement; rising life expectancies thus necessitated higher employer contributions. That fact, and perhaps also ERISA's tighter regulation of defined benefit plans, helped to spur employers' sharp shift in recent decades to "defined contribution" plans, in which employers promise no particular benefit levels in the future but contribute some small percentage of each paycheck to individuals' retirement savings.[17] Those plans banish the problem of unfunded employer liabilities, but they put the whole risk of

9 NEWMAN, *supra* note 3, at 6. Indeed, until 1954 most Black workers in the South were excluded from Social Security, too, because of the New Deal exclusions of agricultural and domestic workers. *See* Wilbur J. Cohen et al., *Social Security Act Amendments of 1954: A Summary and Legislative History*, 17 SOC. SEC. BULL. 3 (1954).

10 *See* Maria G. Hoffman et al., *New Data Revel Inequality in Retirement Account Ownership*, US CENSUS BUREAU (Aug. 31, 2022), https://www.census.gov/library/stories/2022/08/who-has-retirement-accounts.html#:~:text=Demographics%20of%20Ownership&text=About%20half%20(49.5%25)%20of,23%20owned%20a%20retirement%20account.

11 On worker-to-beneficiary ratio in 1940, *see Social Security History*, SOCIAL SECURITY ADMIN., https://www.ssa.gov/history/ratios.html. On life expectancies, *see Life Expectancy (From Birth) in the US from 1860 to 2020*, STATISTA (2020), https://www.statista.com/statistics/1040079/life-expectancy-united-states-all-time.

12 *See* Social Security Admin., *Fast Facts and Figures about Social Security* (2022), https://www.ssa.gov/policy/docs/chartbooks/fast_facts/2022/fast_facts22.pdf.

13 Social Security Amendments of 1983, Pub. L. No. 98-21, § 201, 97 Stat. 65.

14 *Id.* § 123(a).

15 *See* NEWMAN, *supra* note 3, at 4–5.

16 Pub. L. No. 406, 88 Stat. 829.

17 *Id.* at 4–5; 67 *Percent of Private Industry Workers Had Access to Retirement Plans in 2020*, US BUREAU OF LAB. STAT. (Mar. 1, 2021), https://www.bls.gov/opub/ted/2021/67-percent-of-private-industry-workers-had-access-to-retirement-plans-in-2020.htm (just 15 percent of private sector workers had defined benefit plans).

financial mismanagement, underfunding, and underperformance on individuals, who are often ill-equipped both to manage assets and to weather economic downturns.[18] In the meantime, many public pension plans – which are unregulated by ERISA and mostly still of the defined benefit type – have begun to teeter or even topple under the weight of nearly $4 trillion in estimated unfunded liabilities.[19]

How will this picture change with the advent of the 100-year life? The basic actuarial challenge of longer lifespans is quite simple: If the normal retirement age held steady, the burden of supporting longer retirement periods would require either higher contributions and savings during working lives (meaning lower disposable incomes for current workers), or lower benefit levels for retirees. A simple example from Gratton and Scott underscores the challenge: Suppose an individual born in 1998 (age twenty-five as of 2023), with a life expectancy of 100, hopes to retire at age sixty-five on an income that is *half* her average income during her working years (plus whatever Social Security provides). To reach that goal, she would have to accumulate savings (and employer contributions if she is lucky) amounting to *25 percent of her income during her entire remaining working life.*[20] Some high earners – those whose income amply exceeds their living costs – will be able to save enough during their working lives to support a long and comfortable retirement. (Ironically, many of those high earners might choose to postpone retirement, given their high economic and psychic returns from work.) But it is hard to see how working people who are just making ends meet will be able to accumulate those private retirement savings.

The alternative to reducing incomes either during individuals' working lives or in retirement is to extend working lives. (Indeed, all of the above might be necessary.) Most people will have to keep working longer, if they can, in order to save enough for their own retirements and, at the societal level, to maintain a sustainable ratio of active workers to retirees and of work years to retirement years. Every additional year of paid work does double duty in terms of retirement security, both increasing pension contributions and savings and shrinking the retirement period that those funds will have to cover.

Again, it would be possible to address this problem by injecting much greater public funds into Social Security (or, more ambitiously, into something like universal basic income (UBI) throughout individuals' lifespans). That would stave off destitution for the least well-off retirees, though it would fall short of maintaining living standards for most people. And it would shift part of the burden of funding pensions off the platform of employment, which might make sense for a variety of

[18] Newman, *supra* note 3, at 5.

[19] On pension cuts after Detroit's 2014 bankruptcy, *see* Newman, *supra* note 3, at 77–103. On total unfunded liabilities, *see* Joshua D. Rauh, Hidden Debt, Hidden Deficits: 2017 Edition (2017), https://perma.cc/N8UP-NN55.

[20] Gratton & Scott, *supra* note 4, at 58–59.

reasons (which I explore elsewhere).[21] But the appeal of such solutions will depend partly on what the alternative of longer working lives would look like. So before considering large-scale redistributive public funding of pensions, let us assume here that, one way or another, workers and their employers will continue to fund pensions through a combination of savings, payroll taxes, and employer contributions. With the advent of the 100-year life, that will translate into longer working lives for many.

Some people will be unable to work longer due to age-related infirmities – including cognitive decline[22] – or simply the wear and tear from decades of physically demanding work. Their economic fates will mostly ride (in the US) on the future shape of Social Security's retirement program. The rest of this chapter will focus instead on the implications of a growing cohort of older workers and would-be workers, especially in light of other likely changes in work and labor markets.

5.2 HOW WORKPLACE TECHNOLOGY WILL INTERACT WITH LONGER WORKING LIVES

As lifespans grow over the next few decades, other trends in the landscape of work will not stand still. In particular, some observers expect overall demand for labor to decline gradually but inexorably as innovations in robotics, artificial intelligence, and machine learning encroach on the comparative advantages of human workers.[23] That is hardly conventional wisdom among economists. By 2019, however, leading labor economists at MIT had concluded that, unlike in past waves of technological innovation, automation was already destroying more mid skill jobs than it was creating and was a major cause of labor market polarization.[24] They still projected growing demand for highly skilled labor, and for workers in health care and elder care across the skill spectrum, given the needs of an aging population.[25] But without huge advances in education and training, high demand for skilled labor might translate into job *vacancies* that are out of reach for the vast majority of workers. And the other side of an aging population explored above – that is, a probably

[21] *See* Cynthia Estlund, Automation Anxiety: Why and How to Save Work 119–24 (2021); Cynthia Estlund, *What Should We Do after Work? Automation and Employment Law*, 128 Yale L.J. 254 (2018).

[22] For a thoughtful overview of the likely implications of cognitive decline in the workplace, given both greater longevity and longer working lives, *see* Sharona Hoffman, *Cognitive Decline and the Workplace*, 57 Wake For. L. Rev. 115 (2022).

[23] For one compelling account, *see* Daniel Susskind, A World without Work 115–119 (2020). I delve into the various forecasts in chap. 2 of Estlund, *supra* note 21.

[24] *See* David Autor, David A. Mindell & Elisabeth B. Reynolds, *The Work of the Future: Shaping Technology and Institutions*, MIT Work of the Future Task Force (2019), at 25–26, https://perma.cc/AN4B-PFE5.

[25] *See id.* at 19, 36.

growing *supply* of labor from older workers and job-seekers – does not factor into the MIT forecast. Those two caveats alone might point toward a sizable job gap in a decade or two.

We have not yet factored in other potential countervailing demographic trends that, according to the 2019 MIT report, "point towards rising labor scarcity in the decades ahead."[26] In particular, *lower birth rates* in developed countries mean fewer new entrants to the labor force (putting aside immigration). But longer life expectancies throw a curveball into predictions of labor scarcity.[27] The MIT researchers note that growth in the older population will increase demand for workers in health care and elder care, but they don't consider the prospect of *longer working lives* – that is, older workers seeking or holding onto jobs past "normal" retirement age. In some aging societies of Europe and Asia, a growing cohort of *healthy* older workers (as well as productivity improvements arising from automation) could help offset the shrinking flow of new entrants into the labor market.[28] The US population is younger and is aging more slowly than that of much of the developed world.[29] Still, longer working lives would make job deficits more likely than MIT experts predicted in 2019.

Two other developments since the MIT report – the splashy debut of "generative AI" such as Chat-GPT, and COVID-19 – might further swell job losses. The impact of generative AI is the quintessential "moving target" whose advances and failures feature daily in newsfeeds. Yet few doubt that it boosts the potential for automating the work of those who analyze data or produce words (or computer code) for a living, among others.[30]

As for COVID-19, leading experts on automation, including the MIT folks, quickly tagged it as an accelerant of job destruction via several pathways.[31] First, economic downturns, whatever their cause, tend to spur adoption of labor-saving

[26] *Id.* at 17.

[27] *See generally* GRATTON & SCOTT, *supra* note 4; Anne Alstott, *Law and the Hundred-Year Life*, 26 ELDER L.J. 131 (2016).

[28] *See* Leng Leng Thang, *Populating Aging, Older Workers, and Productivity Issues: The Case of Singapore*, 27 J. COMP. SOC. WELFARE 17, 26–30 (2011); Shekhar Aiyar et al., *The Impact of Workforce Aging on European Productivity*, IMF Working Paper 16/238 (2016), at 16–18.

[29] "Fig. 2.1, Working Better with Age," ORG. FOR ECON. CO-OPERATION & DEV. (Aug. 30, 2019), https://www.oecd-ilibrary.org/employment/working-better-with-age_c4d4f66a-en.

[30] For an early survey of competing views, *see* Emma Goldberg, *A.I.'s Threat to Jobs Prompts Question of Who Protects Workers*, N.Y. TIMES (May 23, 2023).

[31] *See, e.g.*, Carl Benedikt Frey, *Covid will Only Increase Automation Anxiety*, FIN. TIMES (Apr. 21, 2020), https://www.ft.com/content/817228a2-82e1-11ea-b6e9-a94cffd1d9bf; David Autor & Elisabeth Reynolds, *The Nature of Work after the COVID Crisis: Too Few Low-Wage Jobs*, HAMILTON PROJECT (2020), https://perma.cc/48XB-Q5NJ; Mark Muro et al., *The Robots Are Ready as the COVID-19 Recession Spreads*, BROOKINGS (Mar. 24, 2020), https://perma.cc/F59P-RRAG; Susan Lund et al., *COVID-19 and Jobs: Monitoring the US Impact on People and Places*, MCKINSEY (Apr. 29, 2020), https://perma.cc/N9QJ-NVVL.

technologies.[32] Second, COVID highlighted the risks – and not only the health risks – associated with human labor. After all, "robots don't need face masks, health care, or social distancing, and they don't go on strike for better conditions."[33] Third, COVID triggered a dramatic shift in the large retail sector both toward automation of brick-and-mortar retail and toward e-commerce, both of which reduce demand for human labor.[34] It "compress[ed] into a few short months what would otherwise have unfolded over multiple years."[35] Fourth, the spike in remote work and meetings would usher in lasting "reductions in office occupancy, daily commuting trips, and business excursions" and "steep declines in demand for ... workers who feed, transport, clothe, entertain, and shelter people when they are not in their own homes."[36] By and large, these early predictions have been borne out.[37] Apart from its human death toll, the lasting legacy of COVID-19 might include sizable job losses,[38] notwithstanding the post-COVID rise of labor shortages[39] (which, as noted earlier, carry their own tendency to spur automation).[40]

All in all, a more automated future of less work – especially for those without advanced skills – appears likely enough that we should begin to ponder and plan for that future.[41] In particular, if automation depresses demand for ordinarily skilled human labor over the next few decades, then older workers who cannot afford to retire will be competing with younger workers for a shrinking number of decent

32 *See* Brad Hershbein & Lisa B. Kahn, *Do Recessions Accelerate Routine-Biased Technological Change? Evidence from Vacancy Postings*, 108 Am. Econ. Rev. 1737, 1762–1767 (2019); Nir Jaimovich & Henry E. Siu, *Job Polarization and Jobless Recoveries*, 102 Rev. of Econ. & Stats. 129 (2020).

33 *See* Erika Hayasaki, *Covid-19 Could Accelerate the Robot Takeover of Human Jobs*, MIT Tech. Rev. (June 17, 2020), https://perma.cc/Y3FR-8XYM.

34 *See* Frey, *supra* note 31; Zoe Thomas, *Will Covid-19 Speed Up the Use of Robots to Replace Human Workers?* B.B.C. (Apr. 19, 2020), https://www.bbc.com/news/technology-52340651; Josep M. Argiles-Bosch, Josep Garcia-Blandon & Diego Ravenda, *Cost Behavior in E-Commerce Firms*, Electron. Commer. Res. (2022), https://doi.org/10.1007/s10660-021-09528-2.

35 Autor & Reynolds, *supra* note 31, at 3. COVID also accelerated automation in brick-and-mortar retail. *See* Ben Casselman, *Pandemic Wave of Automation May Be Bad News for Workers*, N.Y. Times (July 3, 2021), https://www.nytimes.com/2021/07/03/business/economy/automation-workers-robots-pandemic.html.

36 Autor & Reynolds, *supra* note 31, at 2–4.

37 Kristen Broady, Darlene Booth Bell, Anthony Barr & Ryan Perry, *The Covid-19 Pandemic Spurred Growth in Automation*, Fed. Reserve Bank of Chicago Working Paper 2023-06 (Feb. 27, 2023), https://www.chicagofed.org/publications/working-papers/2023/2023-06.

38 Lei Ding & Julieth Saenz Molina, *"Forced Automation" by COVID-19? Early Trends from Current Population Survey Data*, Federal Reserve Bank of Philadelphia Discussion Paper (Sep. 2020), https://perma.cc/KQ2N-53UR.

39 *See* Orsetta Causa, Michaell Abendschein, Nhung Luu, Emilia Soldani & Chiara Soriolo, *The Post-COVID-19 Rise in Labour Shortages*, OECD Economics Dep't Working Paper No. 1721 (July 7, 2022), https://www.oecd-ilibrary.org/docserver/e60c2d1c-en.pdf?expires=1688664326&id=id&accname=guest&checksum=2BFFC99B176200E1CFDB19C9751E95C5.

40 *See* Hershbein & Kahn, *supra* note 32.

41 As I do at length in a recent book, Estlund, *supra* note 21.

jobs. That is, the convergence of demographic and technological trends could produce a double whammy: fewer work opportunities for a larger number of job-seekers.

Technology will affect the nature as well as the number of jobs. To begin with, more jobs will require working with technology, and the pace of technological change is more likely to speed up than slow down. That will tend to reduce the relative value of cumulative work experience versus newly minted skills. Back in the heyday of "lifetime employment," labor economists sought to explain long job tenures and rising wages in core sectors of the economy.[42] They argued that the experience and tacit knowledge that workers accumulated on the job increased their productivity for many years (though not quite until retirement); long-term job security (until the then-standard and even mandatory retirement age) served to encourage workers to stay and share their tacit knowledge with younger workers. But those patterns were undercut in part by technological change: The value of accumulated experience declined as the skill demands of jobs began to change in ever-shorter cycles.[43] As that pattern continues, older workers will be burdened by both the reality of aging brains and skill sets and stereotypes about their facility with new technologies.[44]

All of these technologically driven trends underscore the need for much better institutions of basic education and new and better pathways for adults to learn new skills on and off the job and to change occupations over the course of their careers. That is an article of faith among those who study technology's evolving impact on work;[45] and it is one obvious implication of the 100-year life.[46] More and better training will ameliorate but not eliminate the challenges of changing workplace technologies for older workers, as well as the job gap that might open up with growing machine capabilities.[47]

[42] *See* Edward P. Lazear, *Why Is There Mandatory Retirement?* 87 J. of Pol. Econ. 1261 (1979); Edward P. Lazear, *Agency, Earnings Profiles, Productivity and Hours Restrictions*, 71 Am. Econ. Rev. 606 (1981). On some implications for employment law, *see* Stewart J. Schwab, *Life-Cycle Justice: Accommodating Just Cause and Employment at Will*, 92 Mich. L. Rev. 8, 13–15 (1993).

[43] *See* Peter Capelli, The New Deal at Work (1999); Katherine V. W. Stone, From Widgets to Digits: Employment Regulation for the Changing Workplace 67–86 (2004).

[44] *See* Hoffman, *supra* note 22; Jessica K. Sink & Richard Bales, *Born in the Bandwidth: "Digital Native" as Pretext for Age Discrimination in Hiring*, 31 ABA Journal Lab. & Emp. Law 521 (2016).

[45] Autor et al., *supra* note 24, at 36–40; *A Future That Works: Automation, Employment, and Productivity*, McKinsey Global Inst. (Jan. 2017), 113–116, https://perma.cc/X9BX-9RWQ; Mark Muro et al., *Automation & Artificial Intelligence: How Machines are Affecting People and Places*, Brookings (Jan. 2019), https://perma.cc/QC7T-F4BU.

[46] *See generally* Gratton & Scott, *supra* note 4; Alstott, *supra* note 27.

[47] *See* Estlund, *supra* note 21, at 21–39.

Technology will affect the nature as well as the number of jobs and can be deployed in ways that either help or hurt older workers. On the one hand, machines can take over physically demanding tasks in some jobs (as they have been doing for centuries). For example, robots can do the literal heavy-lifting of human bodies in elder care and of mattresses in hotel room cleaning.[48] Reducing cumulative physical wear and tear might enable some workers to extend their working lives. On the other hand, many employers use technology to intensify the pace of work by monitoring every working moment and movement and squeezing out seconds and minutes of downtime.[49] The resulting "burnout" could undercut older workers' ability to keep at it. The use of such technologies at Amazon's Bessemer warehouse was both a major impetus and a major impediment to union organizing, which takes place largely through conversations among coworkers.[50] These dimensions of workplace technology underscore both the importance and the difficulty of ensuring that workers have a meaningful voice at work, as explored by Kate Andrias in this volume and by Brishen Rogers elsewhere.[51]

There are obvious upsides of technological change. Automation is likely to significantly boost productivity and yield enormous economic dividends. Those dividends *could* be redistributed to ordinary workers in the form of higher incomes, more leisure, or both and could further mitigate the daunting challenge of longer working lives. Or they might continue to flow overwhelmingly to the top of the income scale, as they have in recent decades. Let's now shift to the policy plane.

5.3 TWO STRATEGIES FOR EXTENDING WORKING LIVES: SECURING JOBS AND SPREADING WORK

Let us assume that, a few decades hence, most people will be in the active labor market, either working or seeking work, into their seventies or beyond. Some will seek "self-employment" – nominally or actually independent work outside the relatively protective umbrella of employment, including work in the expanding "gig economy." That might be a decent option for some older workers with specialized skills or capital to invest in a business, but it will be at best a fallback

[48] Stuart Dredge, *Robear: The Bear-Shaped Nursing Robot Who'll Look After You When You Get Old*, GUARDIAN (Feb. 27, 2015), https://www.theguardian.com/technology/2015/feb/27/robear-bear-shaped-nursing-care-robot.

[49] *See* BRISHEN ROGERS, DATA AND DEMOCRACY AT WORK (2023); Darrell M. West, *How Employers Use Technology to Surveil Employees*, BROOKINGS INST. (Jan. 5, 2021), https://www.brookings.edu/articles/how-employers-use-technology-to-surveil-employees/.

[50] Steven Greenhouse, *"We Deserve More": An Amazon Warehouse's High-Stakes Union Drive*, GUARDIAN (Feb. 23, 2021), https://www.theguardian.com/technology/2021/feb/23/amazon-bessemer-alabama-union; Michael Sainato, *Amazon Intensifies "Severe" Effort to Discourage First-Ever US Warehouse Union*, GUARDIAN (Feb. 3, 2021), https://www.theguardian.com/technology/2021/feb/03/amazon-intensifies-severe-effort-discourage-first-warehouse-union.

[51] *See* Andrias, Chapter 9, in this volume; ROGERS, *supra* note 49; Brishen Rogers, *The Law and Political Economy of Workplace Technological Change*, 55 HARV. C. R.-C.L. L. REV. 531 (2020).

option for workers without those advantages, whatever their age. I'll focus here on what longer working lives are likely to mean within the sphere of employment.

In order to continue working later in life, workers will have to hold onto jobs longer or find new jobs late in life. Both job-keeping and job-seeking are affected by age discrimination and stereotypes, and sometimes by real deterioration in skills or capabilities. Discrimination against older job *applicants* is especially likely, as stereotypes tend to carry more weight when employers have less information about, and no actual experience with, an individual.[52] And hiring discrimination is especially difficult to uncover, challenge, and deter through antidiscrimination law: Nonhiring decisions are relatively opaque to rejected applicants and are difficult and unlikely to be challenged.[53] Older job applicants already meet hiring resistance, partly due to age discrimination; their even older counterparts in the future are likely to encounter at least as much resistance. But the magnitude of that problem will depend partly on older workers' ability to hold onto their jobs and avoid dismissals or layoffs, and that depends not only on the efficacy of discrimination laws but also on protections against arbitrary or unjustified dismissal.

Nearly all economically developed nations require employers to justify most dismissals based on legitimate reasons such as poor performance, misconduct, or economic necessity.[54] In the US, by contrast, the vast majority of workers can be fired at will – at any time and without justification.[55] Employment at will is the rule, and job security the exception, in both private and public sector employment, and exceptions are largely confined to the shrinking union sector and the civil service. In theory, individuals can bargain for job security, but that rarely happens for reasons explored by legions of US employment law scholars.[56] Employment at will no

[52] David Neumark et al., *Age Discrimination and Hiring of Older Workers*, Federal Reserve Bank of San Francisco (Feb. 27, 2017), https://perma.cc/P529-G55U; Patricia Cohen, *New Evidence of Age Bias in Hiring, and a Push to Fight It*, N.Y. Times (June 7, 2019), https://www.nytimes.com/2019/06/07/business/economy/age-discrimination-jobs-hiring.html.

[53] *See* John J. Donohue III & Peter Siegelman, *The Changing Nature of Employment Discrimination Litigation*, 43 Stan. L. Rev. 983 (1991).

[54] *See* Mariya Aleksynska & Friederike Eberlein, *Coverage of Employment Protection Legislation*, ILO (2016), at 5, https://perma.cc/KBP3-WLJD.

[55] For recent calls for protections against unjustified dismissal, *see* Benjamin Sachs & Sharon Block, *Clean Slate for Worker Power: Building a Just Economy and Democracy*, Harv. L. Sch. Lab. & Worklife Program (Jan. 23, 2020), 46–50, https://perma.cc/G3JG-SCDE; Alexander Hertel-Fernandez, *American Workers' Experiences with Power, Information, and Rights on the Job: A Roadmap for Reform*, Roosevelt Inst. (2020), at 10, 34, https://perma.cc/L5NU-ZDAW. *See also* Ugo Okere et al., *Secure Jobs, Safe Workplaces, and Stable Communities: Ending At-Will Employment in Illinois*, Nat'l Emp. L. Project (Apr. 2021), https://perma.cc/2HSC-AL5P. For an illuminating philosophical take on employment at will, *see* Elizabeth Anderson, Private Government (2017).

[56] *See, e.g.*, Richard Freeman & Joel Rogers, What Workers Want 118–122 (1999); Paul Weiler, Governing the Workplace (1990); Cynthia Estlund, *How Wrong Are Employees about Their Rights, and Why Does It Matter?* 77 N.Y.U. L. Rev. 6 (2002); Pauline T. Kim, *Bargaining with Imperfect Information: A Study of Worker Perceptions of Legal Protection in an*

longer means – as it did a century ago – that employees can be fired for any reason at all. Many reasons for dismissal, including age discrimination, are now illegal, and that probably discourages many unjustified dismissals.[57] But prohibiting discrimination is a far cry from requiring just cause for dismissal, for the former puts the burden of proof of unlawful motive on the employee, and such proof can be very hard to come by. Moreover, some workers pose little risk of litigation, such as low-wage workers in high-turnover jobs (or the growing number of workers bound by mandatory arbitration agreements).[58]

Overturning employment at will and mandating job security would bolster all of workers' rights on the job and would better enable workers to demand overtime pay, complain of discrimination or harassment, or support unionization.[59] It would also promote both economic security and stability within workplace communities, with a range of individual and social benefits. And it would enable older workers to keep their jobs longer. The likely necessity of longer working lives is one more argument in favor of joining the rest of the developed world and protecting job security.

Importantly, employment protections might facilitate longer working lives not just by inhibiting dismissals but also by boosting workers' productivity. How so? By encouraging employers to invest in incumbent workers' skills rather than replacing them with newly credentialed new hires (or machines).[60] That might help to explain recent findings on the economic impact of employment protection laws (EPLs) – those regulating dismissals and layoffs and use of temporary workers.

The conventional economic wisdom, long touted by the World Bank, held that EPL discouraged hiring by taxing dismissals, to the detriment of economic dynamism and workers' overall welfare.[61] But that conventional wisdom has met mounting contrary evidence. A major Cambridge University-based study of 117 countries over several decades found that EPL stringency has modest but mostly positive long-term effects on national economic performance, including slightly lower unemployment and a higher labor share of national income.[62] (Even the World Bank has now acknowledged that "employment regulations are unquestionably necessary" and "benefit both workers and firms."[63]) One explanation for these

At-Will World, 83 Cornell L. Rev. 105 (1997); Cass R. Sunstein, *Switching the Default Rule*, 77 N.Y.U. L. Rev. 106 (2002).

57 *See* Cynthia Estlund, *Wrongful Discharge Protections in an At-Will World*, 74 Tex. L. Rev. 1655 (1996).

58 *See* Cynthia Estlund, *The Black Hole of Mandatory Arbitration*, 96 N.C. L. Rev. 679 (2018).

59 *See* Estlund, *supra* note 57.

60 *See* Simon Deakin et al., *How Do Labour Laws Affect Unemployment and the Labour Share of National Income? The Experience of Six OECD Countries, 1970–2010*, 154 Int'l Lab. Rev. 1, 5–6 (2014).

61 These views on employment protections are summarized in Zoe Adams et al., *The Economic Significance of Laws Relating to Employment Protection and Different Forms of Employment: Analysis of a Panel of 117 Countries, 1990–2013*, 158 Int'l Lab. Rev. 1, 3–4 (2019).

62 *Id.*

63 *Id.*

somewhat-surprising results is that investments in worker training – which make sense in a world of job security – appear to complement employment protections. That includes public spending on "active labor market policies," including vocational training as well as employer investments in on-the-job training, all of which are much greater in most OECD countries than in the US.[64] Those investments should modestly slow the technological displacement of incumbent workers and better enable older workers to hang onto their jobs, extend their working lives, and build up their retirement assets.

One might worry, of course, that job security protects older incumbent workers to the detriment of younger entrants to the labor market. While some studies have linked more stringent EPL with higher youth unemployment,[65] the latest word, based on the aforementioned Cambridge studies, finds no long-term adverse impact on youth employment.[66] Concerns about youth employment should find their solution not in weaker employment protections but in dedicated investments in young people's education and employment prospects and in strengthening the foundations for longer and more varied work lives.

Longer working lives will also be more feasible if the demands of work are less intensive. Technology could contribute on that score not only by taking over physically demanding work tasks, as noted above, but also by allowing for shorter working hours. A more automated economy might augur a future of too little or no work for many workers, but it could be steered in the direction of less work for nearly all – that is, fewer hours per week or fewer weeks per year or both, with guaranteed rights to take extra time off or work shorter schedules as needed. As Anne Alstott has recognized, older workers in particular would value the ability to scale back working hours as they age.[67] Elsewhere I propose a range of strategies for reducing overall hours of work for those with too much of it and for spreading work to those with too little.[68] Those include guaranteed paid vacations and family and sick leaves, guaranteed access to part-time schedules, wider eligibility for overtime pay and other deterrents to excessive and intrusive work demands, and eventually a shorter standard work week. Together, those strategies would help to meet the challenge of a future of less work, promote a better work–life balance for individuals, and facilitate longer working lives by reducing the cumulative toll of decades of work and by accommodating the distinctive toll aging can exact on physical and mental stamina.

[64] *See* Org. for Econ. Co-operation & Dev., *Public Expenditure and Participant Stocks on LMP: Public Expenditure of LMP by Main Categories 2018*, https://perma.cc/R76D-CACQ.

[65] Michael Gebel & Johannes Giesecke, *Does Deregulation Help? The Impact of Employment Protection Reforms on Youths' Unemployment and Temporary Employment Risks in Europe*, 32 Euro. Sociological Rev. 486 (2016), https://doi.org/10.1093/esr/jcw022 (citing numerous studies).

[66] Prabirjit Sarkar, *Does Labor Regulation Reduce Total and Youth Employment?* 52 Structural Change & Econ. Dynamics 374 (2020).

[67] Alstott, *supra* note 27, at 136–137.

[68] *See* Estlund, *supra* note 21, at 125–140.

5.4 CONCLUSION

When we ponder the many and daunting challenges that longer working lives will pose for both individuals and the society, we might ask: Wouldn't it be more sensible – both more humane and more efficient – to maintain the current normal retirement age and find ways to publicly fund longer periods of retirement, at least for those who can't afford to do so themselves, through taxes and transfers? In particular, why compound the challenge posed by automation and a future of less work by extending working lives and increasing the supply of older workers? These are more than fair questions (even if their empirical premises are still debated). But they suggest other questions.

First, if we can muster the political will for that much taxing and spending, how much of it should we direct to the support of retirees? There is no shortage of compelling demands on those societal resources – the needs of the poor and especially poor children, including severe housing insecurity; underfunded educational institutions at every level; unmet healthcare needs, which will rise in an aging society; climate change and its associated costs; and a societal debt from centuries of racial injustice. With all those needs in mind, could it possibly make sense to direct a large share of social resources to supporting seniors, many of whom might be capable of supporting themselves through remunerative work for many years to come?

Second, what are the implications of most people spending the last three to four decades of their lives outside of the nexus of paid work? If the question were simply about individual preferences – when would most people choose to retire if they expected to live to 100? – the answer would obviously vary widely. Many tenured academics, for example, are already choosing to delay retirement, so that "between 2000 and 2010 the proportion of all professors 65 and older nearly doubled, and the median age of the professorate now surpasses all other occupational groups."[69] Most jobs are much less rewarding and more draining, physically and psychically, than ours. Even so, many people have mixed feelings about leaving the workforce when they still have energy and skills to contribute.[70]

Consider also the social and political implications of longer retirements versus longer working lives. If most people continued to retire from work in their mid to late sixties even as life expectancies climb toward a century, retirees would soon make up a quarter or more of the population and a larger share of the electorate. The workplace is not only a source of economic sustenance, status, and identity; it is also our society's single greatest cauldron of cooperation and integration, especially

[69] TIAA-CREF, *Financial Services: An Age of Opportunity* (2012), at 2, https://perma.cc/ZUQ2-JV9P.

[70] *See* Jeffrey M. Jones, *More in U.S. Retiring, or Planning to Retire, Later*, GALLUP (July 22, 2022), https://news.gallup.com/poll/394943/retiring-planning-retire-later.aspx.

across lines of social division.[71] Most people's social circles grow much smaller and less diverse once they retire. As that group swells, the political and social distance between seniors and others will become wider and more consequential, and the potential for intergenerational political conflict will grow.

Ours will be a more vibrant, fair, and cohesive polity and society if we instead find ways to make work less draining and more fulfilling, to spread work from those with too much of it to those with too little, and to enable people to work for more years but fewer hours per year and per week, especially as they grow older.

[71] *See* Cynthia Estlund, Working Together: How Workplace Bonds Strengthen a Diverse Democracy (2003).

PART II

Protecting Rights and Preparing for the Future

6

The New Old Civil Rights

Kenji Yoshino

As the authors of *The 100-Year Life*[1] inform us, a child born today in the West has a 50 percent likelihood of living to be a centenarian. This longevity revolution has been described as "the most important phenomenon of our time in the world, more than the bomb, the Pill, or the Internet."[2] The groundswell of individuals in older-age cohorts – whom I will call the "new old" – could activate a world-historical social movement. To fulfill its potential, however, that movement must resist the temptation to advance age-based civil rights solely within shopworn frameworks established by race or sex. The "new old" should seek instead to fashion an innovative antidiscrimination paradigm that honors distinctive age-related concerns.

In Section 6.1, I describe how legislation and doctrine create the temptation to build "like race" or "like sex" paradigms for age. In Section 6.2, I argue that advocates should resist this temptation for both empirical and strategic reasons. In Section 6.3, I show how unmooring the age discrimination paradigm from traditional civil rights models allows us to apprehend it better by considering the distinctive fears older individuals conjure about our own mortality. In Section 6.4, I consider how such insights might be incorporated into antidiscrimination law and politics.

6.1 UNDERSTANDING THE ANALOGY

Courts interpreting the Age Discrimination in Employment Act (ADEA) and the Equal Protection Clause have traditionally parsed age discrimination through analogy to race or sex discrimination. When courts or legislatures accept this analogy, they afford age discrimination plaintiffs more relief. When such bodies reject that analogy, they look less kindly on those plaintiffs. This pattern presses advocates of older individuals to cast age as analogous to race and sex.

[1] Lynda Gratton & Andrew J. Scott, The 100-Year Life: Living and Working in the Age of Longevity 2 (2016).

[2] Ashton Applewhite, This Chair Rocks: A Manifesto against Ageism 22 (2016) (quoting unnamed journalist at 2012 Age Boom seminar).

6.1.1 *ADEA's Genesis in Analogy and Disanalogy*

Congress fashioned the Age Discrimination in Employment Act of 1967[3] on the premise that age discrimination differed from other forms of discrimination. Congress considered and rejected the proposal to add age[4] to the other classifications protected under Title VII of the Civil Rights Act of 1964 – race, color, religion, sex, and national origin.[5] Instead, the 1964 Act commissioned the secretary of labor "to make a full and complete study of the factors which might tend to result in discrimination in employment because of age."[6]

In 1965, Secretary W. Willard Wirtz submitted *The Older American Worker: Age Discrimination in Employment.*[7] Because the Wirtz Report spurred the enactment of the ADEA, courts rely on it as legislative history.[8] The report began by describing the consensus "that people's ability and usefulness is unrelated to the facts of their race, or color, or religion, or sex, or the geography of their birth."[9] "Having accepted this truth," the report continued, "the easy thing to do would be simply to extend the conclusions derived from it to the problem of discrimination in employment based on aging."[10] The report then dropped the hammer: "This would be easy – and wrong."[11]

Adopting a more nuanced approach, the Wirtz Report sketched how age discrimination converged with and diverged from the discrimination addressed by Title VII. On the one hand, the report observed that age, like other classifications, sometimes triggered "arbitrary discrimination" based on "assumptions about the effect of age … when there is in fact no basis for these assumptions."[12] The report argued that such discrimination "can and should be stopped."[13]

On the other hand, the report underscored some critical differences between age and other classifications. It noted that while no legitimate discrimination existed

[3] 29 U.S.C. §§ 621–634.

[4] *General Dynamics Land Systems, Inc. v. Cline*, 540 U.S. 581, 586–587 (2004) ("Congress chose not to include age within discrimination forbidden by Title VII of the Civil Rights Act of 1964, being aware that there were legitimate reasons as well as invidious ones for making employment decisions on age.").

[5] 42 U.S.C. § 2000e-2(a)(1) (deeming it unlawful for a covered employer "to fail or refuse to hire or to discharge any individual … with respect to his compensation, terms, conditions, or privileges of employment, because of such individual's race, color, religion, sex, or national origin").

[6] 42 U.S.C. § 2000e-14.

[7] W. Willard Wirtz, Report of Sec'y of Labor: The Older American Worker – Age Discrimination in Employment (June 30, 1965) [hereinafter "Wirtz Report"].

[8] *See, e.g., Smith v. City of Jackson*, 544 U.S. 228, 232 (2005); *Cline*, 540 U.S., at 587, 590; *Western Air Lines v. Criswell*, 472 U.S. 400, 409 (1985).

[9] Wirtz Report, *supra* note 7, at 4.

[10] *Id.* at 4–5.

[11] *Id.* at 5.

[12] *Id.* (emphasis omitted).

[13] *Id.* at 31.

where "race or religious discrimination are concerned," such justified discrimination "clearly does exist so far as the age question."[14] Specifically, the Wirtz Report alluded to two distinctive features of age. First, it noted what I call the "universality" argument that "the process of aging is inescapable, affecting everyone who lives long enough."[15] Second, it credited what I call the "real difference" argument that "there is in fact a relationship between [an individual's age] and his ability to perform the job."[16]

In rehearsing these themes, the report strongly implied that the more age was like race or sex, the more protection it deserved. That implication has cast a long shadow over subsequent legislation and doctrine.

6.1.2 *Age Discrimination Plaintiffs Win When Courts Accept the Analogy*

Courts interpreting the ADEA favor age discrimination plaintiffs when they deem their claims analogous to race or sex discrimination. In the 1985 case of *Western Air Lines v. Criswell*,[17] the Court considered an airline policy that required flight engineers to retire at age sixty. The ADEA generally prohibits mandatory retirement, but allows for a bona fide occupational qualification (BFOQ) defense.[18] This defense permits the employer to take "any action otherwise prohibited" where age is a "bona fide occupational qualification reasonably necessary to the normal operation of the particular business."[19] The airline asserted that it had a BFOQ defense because of the increased safety risk posed by older flight engineers.[20]

The BFOQ defense originated in Title VII, which permits the defense in cases alleging discrimination on the basis of religion, sex, and national origin.[21] Title VII affords no BFOQ defense against race discrimination.[22] Even where Title VII permits the defense, courts have construed it narrowly.[23] Seeking to escape that narrow construction, the employer in *Criswell* argued that the ADEA only required employers to show their policy was "reasonable."[24] In rejecting that claim, the Court observed that the ADEA had taken "a concept and statutory language from Title

14 *Id.*
15 *Id.* at 9.
16 *Id.* at 5.
17 472 U.S. 400 (1985).
18 *Id.* at 402–403.
19 29 U.S.C. § 623(f)(1).
20 *Criswell*, 472 U.S., at 403.
21 42 U.S.C. § 2000e-2(e)(1).
22 *Id.*; *see also Malhotra v. Cotter & Co.* 885 F.2d 1305, 1308 (7th Cir. 1989).
23 *See*, e.g., *Dothard v. Rawlinson*, 433 U.S. 321, 334 (1977) ("We are persuaded by the restrictive language of § 703(e), the relevant legislative history, and the consistent interpretation of the Equal Employment Opportunity Commission that the BFOQ exception was in fact meant to be an extremely narrow exception to the general prohibition on the basis of sex.").
24 *Id.* at 419.

VII."[25] It further pointed out that the BFOQ standard in the ADEA "is one of 'reasonable necessity,' not reasonableness."[26] Applying the "reasonable necessity" standard, the Court unanimously ruled against the employer.[27]

Two decades later, the Court again relied on an analogy to Title VII to establish disparate impact liability in *Smith v. City of Jackson*.[28] Since 1971, Title VII has allowed for a "disparate impact" cause of action.[29] Under this theory, a plaintiff can prevail against an employer even in the absence of discriminatory intent so long as the employer's policies have a disparate impact on a protected class.[30] Because discriminatory intent is often difficult to prove, this cause of action is a vital weapon in a plaintiff's arsenal.

In *City of Jackson*, a group of police and public safety officers brought suit against Jackson, Mississippi. Their disparate impact claim alleged that when the City of Jackson gave raises to all such officials, it gave less generous ones to officers over forty.[31] The Fifth Circuit ruled against the plaintiffs, stating that the ADEA never contemplated disparate impact claims.[32] In an opinion by Justice Stevens, a majority of the Court reversed, holding that the ADEA cognized such claims.[33] While the majority splintered on the rationale, five justices underscored the importance of textual similarities between Title VII and the ADEA.[34]

In an opinion disagreeing on this point, Justice O'Connor emphasized how age differed from race and gender. She noted that the Wirtz Report – "the blueprint for the ADEA" – stressed "that age discrimination is qualitatively different from the types of discrimination prohibited by Title VII."[35] Specifically, Justice O'Connor invoked the report's assertion that "there is in fact a relationship between [an individual's] age and his ability to perform his job."[36]

[25] *Id.* at 412.
[26] *Id.* at 419.
[27] *Id.* at 423.
[28] 544 U.S. 228 (2005).
[29] *Griggs v. Duke Power Co.*, 401 U.S. 424 (1971).
[30] *Id.* at 432–433.
[31] *City of Jackson*, 544 U.S. at 230.
[32] *Id.* at 231.
[33] *Id.* at 232.
[34] A four-justice plurality rested its conclusion in part on the ground that "*Griggs*, which interpreted the identical text at issue here, thus strongly suggests that a disparate-impact theory should be cognizable under the ADEA." *Id.* at 236. Justice Scalia, writing separately, observed that while he agreed with the Court's reasoning, he did not find it dispositive. *Id.* at 243. Instead, he found the textual similarity to be a basis to defer to the reasonable view of the EEOC, which he found supported the viability of a disparate impact claim.
[35] *Id.* at 254 (O'Connor, J., concurring). As discussed later, the majority in *City of Jackson* found that while the plaintiffs could assert a disparate impact claim, they had failed to prove one in this case. *Id.* at 243. For this reason, Justice O'Connor's opinion was a concurrence rather than a dissent.
[36] *Id.* at 255 (O'Connor, J., concurring) (quoting Wirtz Report, *supra* note 7, at 5).

6.1.3 *Age Discrimination Plaintiffs Often Lose When Courts Reject the Analogy*

As Justice O'Connor's opinion intimated, courts can be less sympathetic to ADEA plaintiffs when they distinguish age from race and gender. The Court reinforced that point in a different portion of *City of Jackson*. After recognizing disparate impact causes of action under the ADEA, the Court nevertheless held that differences between the ADEA and Title VII conscribed the city's liability.[37]

In this part of its analysis, the *City of Jackson* majority focused on the so-called reasonable factor other than age (RFOA) defense. The ADEA permits an employer to engage in "otherwise prohibited" action "where the differentiation is based on reasonable factors other than age."[38] The RFOA defense is generally applicable to disparate impact claims, while the BFOQ defense is generally applicable to disparate treatment claims. Unlike the BFOQ defense, the RFOA defense has no counterpart in Title VII.[39] The Court deemed the RFOA to be a more lenient version of the "business necessity" defense employers can mount against disparate impact claims under Title VII.[40]

The city asserted an RFOA defense by noting that it had to "raise the salaries of junior officers to make them competitive with comparable positions in the market."[41] The Court acknowledged that the city could have achieved those goals in other ways, suggesting that the rationale was not a "business necessity."[42] Yet because the RFOA only required "reasonableness," the Court ruled for the city. In pinpointing this difference between the ADEA and Title VII, the Court relied on the Wirtz Report to claim that "certain circumstances … unquestionably affect older workers more strongly, as a group, than they do younger workers."[43] It observed that "Congress's decision to limit the coverage of the ADEA by including the RFOA provision is consistent with the fact that age, unlike race or other classifications protected by Title VII, not uncommonly has relevance to an individual's capacity to engage in certain types of employment."[44]

More recently, the Court in 2009 determined that different standards of proof applied under the two statutes. In *Gross v. FBL Financial Services*,[45] the Court grappled with whether the ADEA required the plaintiff to show that age was a "but for" factor or merely a "motivating factor" to prove liability.[46] Under Title VII, the

[37] *Id.* at 240.
[38] 29 U.S.C. § 623(a)(2).
[39] *City of Jackson*, 544 U.S., at 233.
[40] *Id.* at 243.
[41] *Id.* at 242.
[42] *Id.* at 243.
[43] *Id.* at 240–241.
[44] *Id.* at 240.
[45] 557 U.S. 167 (2009).
[46] *Id.* at 180.

plaintiff only needed to show that age was a motivating factor, at which point the burden of production shifted to the employer to show that it would have made the same decision regardless of race.[47] Even though Title VII permitted either cause of action, the Court held that the ADEA required age to be a "but for" factor.[48] It observed that Congress amended Title VII in 1991 to permit the more easily proved "motivating factor" liability. Congress did not, however, amend the ADEA.[49] Justice Stevens, writing for a four-member dissent, noted that the ADEA should require the same burden of proof as Title VII because the operative provisions were the same.[50] The 1991 Amendment was not to the contrary as it simply codified the judicial understanding of Title VII at the time.[51]

To this point, I have only discussed the ADEA, leaving the Equal Protection Clause to one side. This choice may seem quixotic, as the clause is the home of the equality principle in the US Constitution. Yet the Equal Protection Clause is much less relevant because the Court has rendered it close to toothless with regard to age discrimination. It has done so by rejecting the analogy between age, on the one hand, and race and sex, on the other.

The constitutional analysis differs from the statutory one insofar as the clause enumerates no classifications. Instead, it broadly bars states from denying "any person within its jurisdiction the equal protection of the laws."[52] Over the past eight decades, however, the Court has established a framework that affords greater judicial protection to five "suspect" classifications. Three of these – race,[53] national origin,[54] and alienage[55] – receive strict scrutiny. Two others – sex[56] and nonmarital parentage[57] – receive intermediate scrutiny. The Court accords all other classifications so-called rational-basis review. To complicate matters slightly, rational-basis review can take a relatively stringent form – known as "rational basis with bite"[58] – or a highly

47 *Id.*
48 *Id.*
49 *Id.* at 174.
50 *Id.* at 180.
51 *Id.* at 186–187.
52 U.S. Const. Amend. XIV, section 1.
53 *Loving v. Virginia*, 388 U.S. 1 (1967); *McLaughlin v. Florida*, 379 U.S. 184 (1964).
54 *Oyama v. California*, 332 U.S. 633 (1948).
55 *Graham v. Richardson*, 403 U.S. 365 (1971). The heightened scrutiny accorded to alienage has been watered down in ways not relevant for these purposes.
56 *Craig v. Boren*, 429 U.S. 190 (1976).
57 *Trimble v. Gordon*, 430 U.S. 762 (1977).
58 *Romer v. Evans*, 517 U.S. 620 (1996); *Cleburne v. Cleburne Living Center*, 473 U.S. 432 (1985); *Eisenstadt v. Baird*, 405 U.S. 438 (1972). *See* Katie R. Eyer, *The Canon of Rational Basis Review*, 93 Notre Dame L. Rev. 1317, 1319 (2018) ("For example, the modern canon also acknowledges that so-called 'animus' doctrine, or 'rational basis with bite,' can involve a deviation from this exceptionally deferential version of rational basis review.") (internal citations omitted).

deferential form – known as "ordinary rational basis."[59] If state action draws anything other than ordinary rational basis, courts will almost invariably invalidate it.[60] If state action draws only ordinary rational basis, courts will almost invariably uphold it.[61]

How does a classification acquire heightened scrutiny? The Court has not relied on a single theory. It has, however, repeatedly stated that the judiciary should intervene to correct failures in the political process. Drawing on a famous footnote in the case of *United States v. Carolene Products*,[62] the Court has expressed its solicitude for "discrete and insular minorities" in need of protection from the prejudices of the majority.

In the 1976 case of *Massachusetts Board of Retirement v. Murgia*,[63] the Court confronted an equal protection challenge to a state statute requiring police officers to retire at fifty. Applying only ordinary rational-basis review to age-based classifications, the Court upheld the statute.[64] The Court acknowledged that "the treatment of the aged in this Nation has not been wholly free of discrimination."[65] Nevertheless, it found that older individuals had not faced a history of discrimination or stereotyping like "those who have been discriminated against because of race or national origin."[66] It elaborated that "old age does not define a 'discrete and insular' group, in need of 'extraordinary protection from the majoritarian political process.'"[67] To the contrary, the Court remarked, "[I]t marks a stage that each of us will reach if we live out our normal span."[68] This passage is the most prominent example of the "universality" argument in the case law.

The Court later expanded on these themes. In the 1979 case of *Vance v. Bradley*,[69] the Court considered an equal protection challenge to a mandatory retirement age of sixty for foreign service officers. It upheld the policy based on the universality and real-difference rationales. In a succinct – if world-weary –

59 *United States Railroad Retirement Board v. Fritz*, 449 U.S. 166 (1980); *Williamson v. Lee Optical*, 348 U.S. 483 (1955). *See* Eyer, *supra* note 58, at 1318–1319 ("Rational basis review is a form of review that is 'almost empty,' 'enormously deferential,' and 'meaningless.'") (internal citations omitted).

60 Susannah W. Pollvogt, *Beyond Suspect Classifications*, 16 U. PA. J. CONST. L. 739, 744 (2014) ("The term 'heightened scrutiny' refers to both strict scrutiny and intermediate scrutiny, with strict scrutiny being the more demanding of the two standards . . . Minor semantic distinctions aside, the two forms of heightened scrutiny are more alike than different in that a plaintiff's chances of prevailing are much greater under either of these forms of heightened review, as compared to deferential rational basis review.") (internal citations omitted).

61 Susannah W. Pollvogt, *Unconstitutional Animus*, 81 FORDHAM L. REV. 887, 889 (2012) ("Under rational basis review, the plaintiff almost invariably loses.").

62 *United States v. Carolene Products Co.*, 304 U.S. 144, 152–153 n.4 (1938).

63 427 U.S. 307 (1976).

64 *Id.* at 312.

65 *Id.* at 313.

66 *Id.*

67 *Id.* (quoting *Carolene Products*, 304 U.S. at 152–153 n.4).

68 *Id.* at 313–314.

69 440 U.S. 93 (1979).

encapsulation of both ideas, the *Vance* Court referred to "the common-sense proposition that aging – almost by definition – inevitably wears us all down."[70] Similarly, in 1991, the Court in *Gregory v. Ashcroft*[71] sustained a mandatory retirement age of seventy for state judges against an equal protection challenge. The Court observed that the provision was reasonable given that "[i]t is an unfortunate fact of life that physical and mental capacity sometimes diminish with age."[72]

In both the ADEA and equal protection jurisprudence, courts appear to protect age when it is like race or sex, and not to protect it when it is unlike race or sex. Looking only at such cases, advocates would rightly perceive a massive incentive to force age discrimination onto the Procrustean bed of race or sex discrimination. To borrow from the Wirtz Report, succumbing to that impulse would be "easy – and wrong."[73]

6.2 REJECTING THE ANALOGY

The problem here is a specific form of a general pathology in antidiscrimination discourse. Two decades ago, Janet Halley wrote an essay on how LGBT rights advocates felt impelled to make analogies between sexual orientation, on the one hand, and race and gender, on the other.[74] "Particularly when they argue to judges, who are formally if not actually constrained by precedent, and even when they make more general political appeals, advocates are opportunists looking for a simile," she observed. She mimed the advocate addressing the Court: "Your honor, this is just like a race discrimination case; this is just like a sex discrimination case."[75]

Halley advanced an urbane critique of this strategy. She entertained no illusions that this strategy would disappear. She acknowledged that "analogies are probably an inescapable mode of human inquiry and are certainly so deeply ingrained in the logics of American adjudication that any proposal to do without them altogether would be boldly utopian."[76] Nevertheless, she alerted advocates for LGBT rights to the costs of conformity to the regnant paradigms of civil rights – costs that centrally included the misrepresentation of the minority itself. She argued that the analogy faltered on empirical grounds[77] and, less intuitively, on strategic grounds.[78]

70 *Id.* at 111–112.
71 501 U.S. 452 (1991).
72 *Id.* at 472.
73 WIRTZ REPORT, *supra* note 7, at 5.
74 Janet E. Halley, *Like Race*, *in* WHAT'S LEFT OF THEORY, 40–74 (Judith Butler, Tom Guillory & Kendall Thomas eds., 2000).
75 *Id.* at 40.
76 *Id.* at 46.
77 *Id.* at 52 (noting the rise of the argument that sexual orientation, like race, is a biologically immutable characteristic).
78 *Id.* (noting the strategic uses of the analogy between sexual orientation and race, even assuming the analogy is not entirely accurate).

Halley's analysis illuminates age discrimination jurisprudence. Courts insist that age is different because it is (1) universal and (2) creates a real difference. Because of the incentives described earlier, advocates for older individuals seek to elide these differences. Their arguments, however, can be challenged on both empirical and strategic grounds.

6.2.1 *Empirical Argument against the Analogy*

Consider a 2018 report by EEOC Acting Head Commissioner Victoria Lipnic titled *The State of Age Discrimination and Older Workers in the U.S.: 50 Years after the Age Discrimination in Employment Act of 1967*.[79] Written on the fiftieth anniversary of the ADEA's date of enforcement, it reviewed changes and continuity since the promulgation of the ADEA. The Lipnic report decried "a central premise of the Wirtz Report . . . that age discrimination is different than other forms of discrimination," a notion that "continues to seep into ADEA jurisprudence today."[80] "When examined through today's understanding of how discrimination operates," the Lipnic report declared, "age discrimination is more like, than different from, other forms of discrimination."[81]

In making that case, the report addressed both the universality argument and the real-difference argument. With regard to universality, the Lipnic report cited a judge questioning a plaintiff in an age discrimination case: "No, age is different because we are all going to get old . . . but when you're talking about gender or race or ethnicity those are immutable characteristics as the Supreme Court has said."[82] The report responded that "[a]lthough the notion of immutability is irrelevant to protections under Title VII of the ADEA, age is 'immutable' in the sense that it is a characteristic the person has not chosen and cannot change."[83]

The Lipnic report's rejoinder sidestepped the true force of the universality argument by focusing on immutability. The judge's point – like the *Murgia* Court's point – was not really about immutability but about the universality of aging. The argument was that age – unlike race or gender – was not as likely to result in empathy failure because everyone would move from the in-group to the out-group. This peculiarity of age distinguishes it from any other classification, whether immutable or not. The immutability of race means that individuals will not shift from being white to being racial minorities. Yet even mutable characteristics like

79 Victoria A. Lipnic, *The State of Age Discrimination and Older Workers in the U.S. 50 Years after the Age Discrimination in Employment Act (ADEA)*, US Equal Employment Opportunity Commission (June 2018).

80 *Id.* at 13.

81 *Id.*

82 *Id.* at 13 (quoting *Waters v. Logistics Management Institute*, 2018 U.S. App. Lexis 3122, *11 (4th Cir. 2018), audio of oral argument at http://coop.ca4.uscourts.gov/OAarchive/mp3/16-2353-20180123.mp3).

83 *Id.* at 45.

religion do not inevitably entail movement from, say, being Christian to being Muslim. The *Murgia* argument can be rebutted, as we will see below, but not on the ground that age is indistinguishable from race or gender.

With regard to the real-difference argument, the Lipnic report pointed out that "race discrimination also derives from negative views and stereotypes about the abilities of workers of a particular race, like age discrimination does."[84] It also saw "important similarities" between age and sex discrimination, citing "substantial evidence that in the 1960s, people believed that one's gender determined one's abilities, interests and qualifications, just like age."[85]

The Lipnic report's point that race discrimination involved stereotypes may reflect "today's understanding," but it reflected yesterday's understanding as well. The Wirtz report squarely compared race discrimination to "arbitrary discrimination" on the basis of age.[86] The Wirtz report deviated from this commonplace only in noting that race discrimination, unlike age discrimination, was never justified.[87]

This notion – that there are justified and unjustified forms of age discrimination – renders the analogy between age and gender the better one. The Lipnic report is certainly correct to state that gender was unfairly used to limit women's opportunities. Yet the report fails to acknowledge that the courts have allowed discrimination on the basis of gender so long as the distinction is based on a "real difference" between the sexes.[88] In *Nguyen v. Immigration and Naturalization Services*,[89] the Court upheld a facially discriminatory statute that allowed a mother, but not a father, to pass their citizenship automatically to a nonmarital child born in a foreign nation.[90] The Court defended the statute on the ground that mothers were present at the birth of their children, and therefore would be more likely to establish a relationship between the child and the US.[91] "The difference between men and women in relation to the birth process is a real one," it stated, "and the principle of equal protection does not forbid Congress to address the problem at hand in a

84 *Id.* at 14.
85 *Id.*
86 Wirtz Report, *supra* note 7, at 5.
87 *Id.* (noting that justifiable discrimination "clearly does exist so far as the age question, but does not exist so far as, for example, racial or religious discrimination are concerned").
88 While the gender-based real difference doctrine comes up most explicitly in the context of constitutional equal protection doctrine, it has cognates in Title VII as well. The cognized forms of the BFOQ defense, for instance, often turn on "real differences" between the sexes. Arthur Larson & Lex K. Larson, Employment Discrimination (2d ed. 2005), § 43.02, at 43–44 ("The clearest [BFOQ case] is that in which a physical feature unique to one sex is essential to the performance of the job" such as a "wet nurse"), cited in Russell K. Robinson, *Casting and Caste-ing: Reconciling Artistic Freedom and Antidiscrimination Norms*, 95 Cal. L. Rev. 1, 34 n.164 (2007). Moreover, the absence of a BFOQ defense for race suggests that Congress was unwilling to deem any difference "real" in that domain.
89 533 U.S. 53 (2001).
90 *Id.* at 73.
91 *Id.* at 65.

manner specific to each gender."[92] In the Court's view, the differential treatment was based on biology, not bigotry.

Like sex discrimination, age discrimination involves some stereotypical thinking about older individuals, but also some justifiable distinctions based on the "real difference" between individuals of different ages. Indeed, the argument for "real differences" in the age context seems vastly stronger than the analogous argument in the gender context. The Court has only upheld legislation under a real-difference rationale with a majority opinion once in the equal protection context. In stark contrast, it has repeatedly upheld age-based legislation under that rationale.[93] And even Justice Marshall, the greatest champion of age discrimination plaintiffs to sit on the Court, acknowledged that "age, unlike sex, is at some point likely to bear a relationship to ability."[94]

As the genesis of the ADEA suggests, age can easily be distinguished from race. While age may be closer to sex, the similarity disfavors age discrimination plaintiffs. Moreover, the similarity is not that great, as age presents much more of a "real difference" in the workplace than sex does. In the end, the attempts to efface these differences seem so implausible that they suggest some other agenda.

6.2.2 *Strategic Argument against the Analogy*

That agenda is, of course, a strategic one. Halley archly described the advocate's posture: "'It doesn't matter that the simile is a little inaccurate,' they would say; 'judges fall for it, and once we secure some legal rights no one will remember the rhetoric we used to obtain them.'"[95] In fairness, advocates for age discrimination plaintiffs do sometimes prevail by papering over the distinctions between age and other classifications. Nonetheless, they also fail, as we see in *Gross*, *City of Jackson*, *Murgia*, *Vance*, and *Gregory*.

Just as importantly – and much more hopefully – the Court has at times engaged in progressive interpretations of age discrimination precisely because it deems age to be different. In *General Dynamics Land Systems, Inc. v. Cline*,[96] the Court confronted the question of whether the ADEA, which clearly "forbids discriminatory preference for the young over the old," also "prohibits favoring the old over the young."[97] The Court held that it did not. To arrive at that conclusion, it had to join a classic debate within antidiscrimination law between classes and classifications. In this debate, scholars have questioned whether equality principles forbid

[92] *Id.* at 73.

[93] *See, e.g., Gregory v. Ashcroft*, 501 U.S. 452 (1991); *Vance v. Bradley*, 440 U.S. 93 (1979); *Massachusetts Board of Retirement v. Murgia*, 427 U.S. 307 (1976).

[94] *Vance v. Bradley*, 440 U.S. 93, 121 (Marshall, J., dissenting).

[95] Halley, *supra* note 74, at 52.

[96] 540 U.S. 581 (2004).

[97] *Id.* at 584.

government use of a classification (such as race or age) or forbid the subordination of a particular class (such as Blacks or older individuals) within the classification.[98] Generally speaking, progressives tend to favor the class-based antisubordination view.[99] In contrast to the Court's analysis in other domains,[100] the *Cline* Court embraced that view.

Importantly, the *Cline* Court arrived at this conclusion by emphasizing the ways in which age was *not* like race or sex. The Court acknowledged that "age" could be interpreted either to mean "any number of years lived, or as a common shorthand for the longer span and concurrent aches that make youth look good."[101] In adopting the latter view, it noted that "the term 'age' employed by the ADEA is not ... comparable to the terms 'race' or 'sex' employed by Title VII."[102] The Court said that while race was not commonly understood "to refer only to the black race," nor sex "to refer only to the female," age was generally understood to mean only "old age."[103]

Cline does not stand alone. In the 1996 case of *O'Connor v. Consolidated Coin*,[104] the Court considered the age discrimination claim of a fifty-six-year-old plaintiff, James O'Connor, who had been replaced by a forty-year-old employee.[105] The Fourth Circuit rejected the plaintiff's claim by applying a framework developed in the Title VII context. In the lower court's view, the plaintiff had to show that he "was replaced by someone of comparable qualifications outside the protected class."[106] Given that the ADEA protects individuals forty and over, O'Connor failed that requirement.[107]

The Supreme Court unanimously reversed the lower court. In an opinion by Justice Scalia, the Court found that "there can be no greater inference of *age* discrimination ... when a 40-year-old is replaced by a 39-year-old than when a

98 *See* Kenji Yoshino, *Assimilationist Bias in Equal Protection: The Visibility Presumption and the Case of "Don't Ask, Don't Tell,"* 108 Yale L.J. 487 (1998) ("A classification-based view of equal protection seeks to treat all classes created by a classification the same, while a class-based view privileges the disadvantaged class(es) created by a classification. [A classification-view] tends to ignore differences between the classes created by a classification.").

99 *See*, e.g., Reva B. Siegel, *Why Equal Protection No Longer Protects: The Evolving Forms of Status-Enforcing State Action*, 49 Stan. L. Rev. 1111, 1142 (1997) (describing essay's standpoint, "which does not equate discrimination with 'classification,' but begins instead from the premise that status-enforcing state action is mutable in form").

100 As the *Cline* dissent pointed out, the Court has adopted the anticlassification view for Title VII classifications. *See Cline*, 540 U.S., at 611 (Thomas, J., dissenting) (noting that the Court has interpreted Title VII to protect whites as well as racial minorities).

101 *Id.* at 596.

102 *Id.* at 597.

103 *Id.* at 598.

104 517 U.S. 308 (1996).

105 *Id.* at 309–310.

106 *Id.* at 310.

107 *Id.*

56-year-old is replaced by a 40-year-old."[108] Again, the plaintiff prevailed through disanalogy.

6.3 TRANSCENDING THE ANALOGY

I have argued that distinguishing age from other classifications opens space for alternative progressive interpretations of age discrimination. Thus far, I have relied on doctrinal examples. I now cut deeper by turning to a distinctive feature of age that has not yet surfaced directly in the age discrimination jurisprudence. Social scientists have analyzed age discrimination under a "terror management theory" that suggests that age discrimination arises in part out of a fear of our own mortality – a fear without direct analogues in other realms of antidiscrimination law.

6.3.1 *The Nature of Terror Management Theory*

Terror management theory dates back to the work of cultural anthropologist Ernest Becker, who published his Pulitzer Prize-winning book *The Denial of Death* in 1973.[109] In that work, Becker argued that human beings are distinctive in their capacity to apprehend their own mortality.[110] Given this awareness, much of human activity occurs to manage the panic induced by that threat.[111] As developed by subsequent scholars, terror management theory posits that human beings respond to their consciousness of death by investing in beliefs in literal or symbolic immortality[112] or, perhaps less intuitively, by fortifying their self-esteem.[113]

The point about self-esteem is important for our purposes because it leads to particular views about in-groups and out-groups. As psychologists Jeff Greenberg, Sheldon Solomon, and Tom Pyszczynski demonstrated through a series of experiments, individuals who were primed with their own mortality more strongly favored in-group members and more strongly disfavored out-group members.[114] For instance, one experiment with judges had some of them take a survey about what they believed would happen after their own deaths.[115] All the judges were then asked to sentence a hypothetical sex worker. The judges in the control group imposed, on

[108] *Id.* at 312 (emphasis in original).
[109] Ernest Becker, The Denial of Death (1973).
[110] *Id.* at 69.
[111] *Id.* at 15.
[112] Eva Jonas & Peter Fischer, *Terror Management and Religion: Evidence that Intrinsic Religiousness Mitigates Worldview Defense Following Mortality Salience*, 91 J. of Personality & Soc. Psychol. 553 (2006).
[113] Brandon J. Schmeichel et al., *Terror Management Theory and Self-Esteem Revisited*, 96 J. of Personality & Soc. Psychol. 1077 (2009).
[114] Jeff Greenberg, Sheldon Solomon & Tom Pyszczynski, The Worm at the Core: On the Role of Death in Life (2015).
[115] *Id.* at 12.

average, a bond of $50.[116] The judges who had been primed with their own mortality imposed "a far more punitive bond – on average $455, more than nine times the typical tab."[117]

Multiple studies have corroborated that priming individuals with their mortality leads to harsher assessments of out-groups. In a 2005 article, psychologists Andy Martens, Jamie L. Goldenberg, and Jeff Greenberg focused on how terror management theory affected ageism.[118] Their analysis illuminates both the universality argument and the real-difference argument.

6.3.2 *Terror Management Theory and the Universality Argument*

Terror management theory shows us why the universality argument is flawed. As we observed, the courts repeatedly adduced the universality of aging as a reason for why we should not be particularly concerned about age discrimination. Recall that the *Murgia* Court opined that discrimination against older individuals was less likely, because old age "marks a stage that each of us will reach if we live out our normal span."[119]

The rejoinders to the universality argument tend to paper over the difference that universality makes. As we have seen, the Lipnic report deflected the discussion from universality to immutability. Justice Marshall similarly tried to minimize the impact of "universality." He acknowledged that the class of older individuals "is not 'discrete and insular' because all of us may someday belong to it, and voters may be reluctant to impose deprivations that they themselves could eventually have to bear."[120] Nevertheless, he pointed out that "the time lag between when the deprivations are imposed and when their effects are felt may diminish the efficacy of this political safeguard."[121]

Such rebuttals are too anemic. Applying terror management theory to ageism, the Martens article began with the *Murgia*-like question: "[W]hy should individuals exhibit prejudice toward elderly people, if indeed they represent the best-case scenario for the future?"[122] The authors answered that "ageism exists precisely because elderly people represent our future in which death is certain."[123] They asserted "that negative attitudes and behaviors directed toward elderly people can be explained in large part by people's own fears about aging and death."[124]

116 *Id.*
117 *Id.*
118 Andy Martens, Jamie Goldenberg & Jeff Greenberg, A *Terror Management Perspective on Ageism*, 61 J. of Social Issues 223 (2005).
119 *Massachusetts Board of Retirement v. Murgia*, 427 U.S. 307 (1976).
120 *Vance v. Bradley*, 440 U.S. 93, 113–114 n.1 (1979) (Marshall, J., dissenting).
121 *Id.* at 114 n.1.
122 Martens et al., *supra* note 118, at 223.
123 *Id.*
124 *Id.* at 223–224.

The issue of universality should not be addressed by sidestepping or minimizing it. Rather we should cheerfully concur that universality distinguishes age from all other classifications. We should then note that this distinction is not a reason why the courts should care less about ageism. It is the reason they should care more.

6.3.3 *Terror Management Theory and the Real-Difference Argument*

Terror management theory also casts the "real-differences" argument in a new light. Let us take for granted that some age-based generalizations are "real differences" and that some are "unreal differences" – that is, stereotypes. These "real differences" make age discrimination more like sex discrimination than race discrimination.

The existence of real age-related differences helps explain some features of ageism. As Becca Levy and Mahzarin Banaji have noted,[125] several aspects of age discrimination are distinctive. First, "[t]here are no hate groups that target the elderly as there are hate groups that target members of religious and racial and ethnic groups."[126] This is presumably what the Wirtz report meant when it noted "no significant evidence" of discrimination based on "dislike or intolerance that sometimes exists in the case of race, color, religion, or national origin."[127] Yet, on the other hand, the authors stressed the "widespread occurrence of socially acceptable expressions of negativity toward the elderly."[128] Finally, older individuals are distinctive in internalizing that negative view of themselves – "members of all groups tested to date – other than the aged – invariably show more positive implicit attitudes toward their own group compared to non-group members."[129] Older individuals were the only stigmatized group that felt as negatively about themselves as nongroup members did.

While they might seem to be in tension, all these features can be explained through "real differences." As the Wirtz report noted, there are some forms of age discrimination that are entirely justified – indeed, the report agonized over whether to even call this "discrimination."[130] And if age distinctions track real differences, it makes sense that there would be little hatred of older individuals, that we could rationally treat them more poorly, and that they would internalize society's negative views of old age.

Unlike the gender context, however, the "real difference" between older and younger individuals is a source of terror. If we have "death panic" in the context of

[125] Becca R. Levy & Mahzarin R. Banaji, *Implicit Ageism*, *in* Ageism: Stereotyping and Prejudice against Older Persons (T. D. Nelson ed., 2002).

[126] *Id.* at 50.

[127] Wirtz Report, *supra* note 7, at 8.

[128] Levy & Banaji, *supra* note 125, at 50.

[129] *Id.* at 55.

[130] Wirtz Report, *supra* note 7, at 5 (noting that this "type of discrimination . . . should perhaps be called something else entirely").

age, we are less likely to be able to sort through what is a fair and what is an unfair distinction. We are much more likely to overascribe traits and behaviors to biology than to bigotry.

6.3.4 *An Exact Inversion*

I close this portion of the analysis with a deliberately provocative point. The civil rights paradigm in the US has been built on the foundation of race discrimination, to which age discrimination is a belated addition. Yet if we regard civil rights through a terror management perspective, we could invert that analysis.

Take philosopher Martha Nussbaum's analysis of age discrimination in her 2017 work *Aging Thoughtfully*.[131] While Nussbaum spoke in terms of disgust rather than terror management, her thinking can be easily assimilated into the terror management framework. She observed that the prejudice toward aging bodies was largely fueled by a particular form of disgust. "With aging the truth is front and center: it really is for oneself that one fears,"[132] she contended. "Stigma learned early and toward others gradually becomes self-stigma and self-exclusion, as one's own aging body is seen as a site of decay and future death – by oneself as well as by others."[133]

Nussbaum maintained that other forms of discrimination could be driven by this fear of mortality. She contended that "[p]eople seek to create a buffer zone between themselves and their own animality, by identifying a group (usually a powerless minority) who can be targeted as the quasi-animals and projecting onto that group various animal characteristics."[134] She elaborated that "[t]he so-called thinking seems to be: if those quasi-animal humans stand between us and our own animal stench and decay, we are that much further from being animal and mortal ourselves."[135]

Under this view, we see an exact inversion of age discrimination and race discrimination. Age discrimination is no mere adjunct to the paradigm case of race discrimination. Rather, age discrimination is the central category, as it most directly engages this fear of death. Other forms of discrimination displace that terror – or disgust – onto other groups.

In saying this, I do not contest the primacy of race-based civil rights – it is this country's original sin. Rather, I am attempting to dislodge the view that age-based discrimination is the peripheral category we often view it to be.

[131] Martha C. Nussbaum & Saul Levmore, Aging Thoughtfully: Conversations about Retirement, Romance, Wrinkles, & Regret (2017).

[132] *Id.* at 114.

[133] *Id.*

[134] *Id.* at 110.

[135] *Id.* at 111.

6.4 DOCTRINAL AND POLITICAL REFORMS

My primary goal here is not to advance legislative or doctrinal reform. Yet because it is easier to dispose than propose, I make some reconstructive gestures as a token of good faith. To respect the difference that age makes is to transform the law and culture of aging.

6.4.1 *Legal Reforms*

As a matter of constitutional law, my analysis means that *Murgia*[136] must be revisited. Luckily the change required here is doctrinally modest. In its equal protection jurisprudence, the Court has moved away from anointing new classifications as suspect.[137] Instead, it has expanded the "rational basis with bite" category to engage in more searching review under that standard. For this reason, a subsequent Court need not overrule *Murgia* with regard to its adoption of rational-basis review. It need only clarify that the rationality standard there has bite, in the same way it had bite in the contexts of sexual orientation,[138] disability,[139] or marital status.[140]

This analysis would also have implications in the legislative domain. Some advocates for older individuals have argued that Congress should amend Title VII to include age.[141] By doing so, one advocate maintains, Congress could obliterate "some of the U.S. Supreme Court's ill-conceived, pro-business opinions that deny equal protection to older workers."[142] I disagree. Given the cogency of the "real-difference" argument, age is sufficiently distinct that it should remain under its own statutory rubric.

At the same time, the existence of real differences will often blind courts to stereotypical thinking.[143] It seems unlikely that the Court will whittle away at the "real-differences" rationale here as they have done in the gender context. Unlike the gender context, the age context deals with more plausible and salient real differences

[136] *Murgia*, 427 U.S., at 307.

[137] Kenji Yoshino, *The New Equal Protection*, 124 HARV. L. REV. 747, 757 (2011) (noting that "the last classification accorded heightened scrutiny by the Supreme Court was that based on nonmarital parentage in 1977").

[138] *United States v. Windsor*, 570 U.S. 744 (2013); *Romer*, 517 U.S., at 620.

[139] *Cleburne*, 473 U.S., at 432.

[140] *Eisenstadt*, 405 U.S., at 438.

[141] *See*, e.g., PATRICIA G. BARNES, BETRAYED: THE LEGALIZATION OF AGE DISCRIMINATION IN THE WORKPLACE 220–221 (2014) ("Congress must do what it should have done in 1964 – make age a protected class under Title VII.").

[142] *Id.* at 221.

[143] The dissenters in *Nguyen v. Immigration and Naturalization Services*, 533 U.S. 53 (2001) criticized the majority for confusing biology and bigotry. Justice O'Connor observed that "the idea that a mother's presence at birth supplies adequate assurance of an opportunity to develop a relationship while a father's presence at birth does not would appear to rest only on an overbroad sex-based generalization." *Id.* at 86 (O'Connor, J., dissenting).

among cohorts. Moreover, "death panic" means that the line between reality and stereotype may be even more blurred. This point suggests that the real wrong turn in the ADEA occurred in *Gross*,[144] where the Court declined to embrace a "mixed motive" analysis that would require an employer to justify its decision if age was seen as a "motivating" factor. Any time a court recognizes that the employer has used age as a factor, it should adopt a hermeneutics of skepticism.

6.4.2 *Social Reforms*

All of these legal reforms will be for naught unless we change broader social views about older individuals. Again, this is a vast topic, so I will here do no more than identifying one worrisome and one promising solution in Gratton and Scott's *100-Year Life*.

I am pessimistic about Gratton and Scott's endorsement of greater contact as a solution. Gratton and Scott noted their belief that "age segregation is closely connected to ageism, since it sets up sharp distinctions between 'us' and 'them,' and leads to stereotyping and associated prejudices."[145] They noted that as the three stages of life (education, work, and retirement) perforce become "multiple stages," "people from different ages have a chance to engage in similar experiences."[146] Gratton and Scott believed this engagement would have salutary effects on intergroup attitudes. To support that view, they cited Gordon Allport's "classic study" outlining contact hypothesis – the view that stereotypes decrease as contact between groups increases.[147]

Allport's work itself, however, suggests that contact alone will not be enough. Allport underscored that certain conditions need to be met for intergroup contact to diminish prejudice. The groups, for instance, must meet on the terms of relative equality.[148] If that condition does not obtain, contact is not likely to make much of a difference. We see this in the case of gender, where contact between men and women did not, per se, lead to a diminution of stereotyping of women. Indeed, because women were assigned particular roles, this close contact arguably kept those stereotypes in place. So contact alone does not seem to be a sufficient answer.

Gratton and Scott offered a more promising avenue when they discussed a study about how individuals invested differently when they saw their digitally aged avatars.[149] The point of this study was to show that when individuals were shown

[144] *Gross v. FBL Financial Services*, 557 U.S. 167 (2009).

[145] Gratton & Scott, *supra* note 1, at 328.

[146] *Id.*

[147] *Id.* (citing Gordon Allport, The Nature of Prejudice (1954)).

[148] *See, e.g.*, Allport, *supra* note 147, at 281 ("Prejudice (unless deeply rooted in the character structure of the individual) may be reduced by equal status contact between majority and minority groups in pursuit of common goals.").

[149] *Id.* at 257–258 (citing Hal E. Hirshfield et al., *Increasing Saving Behavior through Age-Progressed Renderings of the Future Self*, 48 J. of Marketing Research 23 (2019)).

their projected older selves, they tended to save more for their retirement.[150] Yet this project might not just incentivize greater savings by younger individuals but also push to overcome their denial about the aging process. Confronting one's older self could be the first step in having empathy for that self.

The terror management theory might appear to cast ageism as practically ineradicable. After all, it casts ageism as rooted in a fear of death, which cannot be staved off forever. Yet we do know that some cultures view both death and older individuals with less terror.[151] Thus it is not utopian to posit that we could have a different attitude toward death and, therefore, a different attitude toward old age. Comparative study may be particularly useful here.

6.5 CONCLUSION

Ageism is a problem that cries out for an urgent solution in a period of radically lengthened lifespans. It is all very well to say that individuals should begin their second careers at age sixty-five, but this will be impossible if employers will not hire them at that age. As the problem grows ever more urgent, and the constituency affected becomes ever more numerous, we seem due for a tipping point. I predict that the movement for older individuals will soon have a major mobilizing "moment," much as other groups did with Black Lives Matter or #MeToo.

I have attempted to suggest some ways for older individuals to use their power when the revolution comes. The traditional way of recognizing a new social movement is to bring discrimination against the group within the pale of the traditional antidiscrimination canon. I argue that this is a mistake (indeed a particular iteration of a more general mistake). If age is truly to be protected, we should not force the "new old" into old paradigms. The opposite of "old" is not only "young"; it is also "new."

[150] Hirshfield et al., *supra* note 149.

[151] Jill M. Chonody & Barbara Teater, *Why Do I Dread Looking Old? A Test of Social Identity Theory, Terror Management Theory, and the Double Standard of Ageing*, 28 J. of Women & Ageing 112 (2016) (noting that while the findings are complex, there are transnational differences with regard to ageism and death panic).

7

Age, Inequality, and Political Representation

Ganesh Sitaraman

We live in an age of widening inequality.[1] In the mid twentieth century, income and wealth inequality was declining, leading to an era of comparative economic equality and a large middle class. But since the early 1980s, income and wealth inequality has been on the rise. *The 100-Year Life* describes how increasing life expectancy could transform the course of individual lives in detail – but how does this trend intersect with our age of inequality? And what does it mean for law and policymaking more generally?

The dark side of rising life expectancy is that it is unequally shared. In Section 7.1, I briefly discuss how age and inequality are connected – that is, that not everyone shares in rising life expectancy equally and that those who are living longer share many common attributes. Section 7.2 considers the possible impact of the skew in rising life expectancy on representative government. A wide literature in political science shows how inequality skews politics to favor the wealthy; inequality by age will likely do the same, but with some additional twists. The fundamental problem is that power is held unequally in most societies. Addressing this issue has been one of the central questions of political theory, constitutional law, and institutional design – particularly for those interested in representative democracy. Section 7.3, on age and institutional design, outlines some ways in which political structures might be crafted to account for age-related differences.[2]

[1] Thomas Piketty, Capital in the Twenty-First Century (Arthur Goldhammer trans., Belknap Press of Harvard University Press 2014) (2013).

[2] Throughout this chapter, I do not take on the question of *future generations*, only differences in generations and age of those currently alive. The former topic is one that is much discussed in law and philosophy. *See*, e.g., John Rawls, A Theory of Justice 284–293 (1971) (Chapter: "The Problem of Justice between Generations"); Bruce Ackerman, Social Justice in the Liberal State 101–227 (1980) (Chapter: "Justice over Time"); Richard A. Epstein, *Justice across the Generations*, 67 Tex. L. Rev. 1465 (1989). There are also some proposals for how to design political systems to represent the interests of future generations. *See*, e.g., Matthew W. Wolfe, *The Shadows of Future Generations*, 57 Duke L.J. 1897, 1914–1918 (2008) (describing proposals).

7.1 INEQUALITY AND RISING LIFE EXPECTANCY

Rising life expectancy often comes with optimism and celebrations of progress.[3] But rising life expectancy isn't experienced by everyone equally in society. In fact, the data show a wide range of disparities in life expectancy. Women live longer than men on average, and that disparity is projected to continue into the future.[4] White people live longer than Black people, on average, but Hispanic and Latino Americans live longer than either.[5]

Life expectancy is also tied to a range of social factors like wealth, education, and geography. Perhaps unsurprisingly, the wealthy live longer than the poor.[6] But the difference is striking. The top 1 percent of men in America by income have a life expectancy that is fifteen years longer than the bottom 1 percent.[7] Those with college degrees live longer than those without,[8] and studies show that life expectancy has been *declining* for those without – even as it increases among those with – college degrees.[9] Where Americans live is also tied to life expectancy. People living in metropolitan areas and on the coasts live longer than those in the middle of the country,[10] and people living outside metro areas in the south or in Appalachia have lower life expectancies than much of the rest of the country.[11] Deaths often come

[3] Lynda Gratton & Andrew Scott, The 100-Year Life (2016).

[4] Lauren Medina et al., *Living Longer: Historical and Projected Life Expectancy in the United States, 1960 to 2060* (2020), 1, US Dep't of Com., US Census Bureau, https://www.census.gov/content/dam/Census/library/publications/2020/demo/p25-1145.pdf.

[5] *Id.*, at 7; Elizabeth Arias & Jiaquan Xu, *United States Life Tables, 2017*, 68 Nat'l Vital Stat. Reps. 3 (June 24, 2019), https://www.cdc.gov/nchs/data/nvsr/nvsr68/nvsr68_07-508.pdf.

[6] Cong. Rsch. Serv., R44846, *The Growing Gap in Life Expectancy by Income: Recent Evidence and Implications for the Social Security Retirement Age* (2021), 1, https://fas.org/sgp/crs/misc/R44846.pdf; Sabrina Tavernise, *Disparity in Life Spans of the Rich and the Poor Is Growing*, N.Y. Times (Feb. 12, 2016), https://www.nytimes.com/2016/02/13/health/disparity-in-life-spans-of-the-rich-and-the-poor-is-growing.html.

[7] Raj Chetty et al., *The Association between Income and Life Expectancy in the United States, 2001–2014*, 315 J. Am. Med. Ass'n 1750 (2016), https://jamanetwork.com/journals/jama/article-abstract/2513561; Neil Irwin & Quoctrung Bui, *The Rich Live Longer Everywhere. For the Poor, Geography Matters*, N.Y. Times (Apr. 11, 2016), https://www.nytimes.com/interactive/2016/04/11/upshot/for-the-poor-geography-is-life-and-death.html.

[8] Org. for Econ. Coop. & Dev., *Life Expectancy by Sex and Education Level* (Nov. 10, 2017), https://www.oecd-ilibrary.org/sites/health_glance-2017-7-en/index.html?itemId = /content/component/health_glance-2017-7-en.

[9] Anne Case & Angus Deaton, Deaths of Despair and the Future of Capitalism (2020); Isaac Sasson & Mark D. Hayward, *Association between Educational Attainment and Causes of Death among White and Black US Adults, 2010–2017*, 322 J. Am. Med. Ass'n 756 (2019), https://jamanetwork.com/journals/jama/fullarticle/2748794.

[10] Yana C. Vierboom & Samuel H. Preston, *Life beyond 65: Changing Spatial Patterns of Survival at Older Ages in the United States, 2000–2016*, 75 J. Gerontology: Soc. Sci. 1093 (2020), https://academic.oup.com/psychsocgerontology/article/75/5/1093/5717464.

[11] Yana C. Vierboom et al., *Rising Geographic Inequality in Mortality in the United States*, 9 SSM–Population Health 1 (2019), https://www.ncbi.nlm.nih.gov/pmc/articles/PMC6804490/pdf/main.pdf.

from suicide and drug overdoses,[12] and life expectancy is tied to the prevalence of smoking.[13] In some cases, geography matters even more than poverty. The life expectancy of the poorest 5 percent in Detroit, for example, is more than ten years lower than their counterparts in New York.[14]

It is worth noting that economic inequality persists even *within* age cohorts as well.[15] The Black–white wealth gap, for example, is significant within older age cohorts.[16] White Americans in their thirties, on average, have three times as much wealth as Blacks (about $147,000). By their sixties, the gap has expanded to seven times as much (or about $1.1 million).[17] This is partly a function of the cumulative effects of compounding economic inequality over a lifetime.[18]

There may also be significant period effects in inequality by age.[19] That is, the period of time in which one grew up might shape an entire cohort's economic opportunities. The generation that grew up in the comparative equality of the mid to late twentieth century will have different economic outcomes than a generation that grew up in the more recent age of wide inequality. Studies show, for example, that the ratio of wealth for older and younger cohorts has changed over time. A Deloitte analysis notes that in 1992 the ratio of median family net worth for households older than seventy-five compared to those less than thirty-five years was 9.4. That ratio had jumped to 24.1 by 2016.[20] The median family net worth for those under thirty-five actually declined during this period.[21] Pew's research has led to similar data. In 2009, the median net worth of households headed by adults over sixty-five was 42 percent higher than their counterparts in 1984. But households headed by adults under thirty-five saw a 68 percent decrease in their median net worth compared to their

[12] Anne Case & Angus Deaton, *Rising Morbidity and Mortality among White Non-Hispanic Americans in the 21st Century*, 112 PNAS 15078 (2015), https://www.pnas.org/content/112/49/15078.

[13] Vierboom et al., *supra* note 11, at 7; Vierboom & Preston, *supra* note 10.

[14] Irwin & Bui, *supra* note 7.

[15] Angela M. O'Rand & John C. Henretta, Age and Inequality: Diverse Pathways through Later Life 31 (1999).

[16] Kriston McIntosh et al., *Examining the Black–White Wealth Gap*, Brookings Inst. (Feb. 27, 2020), fig. 2, https://www.brookings.edu/blog/up-front/2020/02/27/examining-the-black-white-wealth-gap/.

[17] Urban Inst., *Nine Charts about Wealth Inequality in America*, https://apps.urban.org/features/wealth-inequality-charts (updated Oct. 5, 2017).

[18] Fed. Rsrv., *Distribution of Household Wealth in the U.S. since 1989*, https://www.federalreserve.gov/releases/z1/dataviz/dfa/distribute/chart/#quarter:122;series:Net%20worth;demographic:age;population:all;units:levels (accessed May 23, 2023).

[19] O'Rand & Henretta, *supra* note 15, at 16.

[20] Patricia Buckley & Akrur Barua, *Are We Headed for a Poorer United States? Growing Wealth Inequality by Age Puts Younger Households Behind*, Deloitte Insights (Mar. 12, 2018), https://www2.deloitte.com/us/en/insights/economy/issues-by-the-numbers/march-2018/us-average-wealth-inequality-by-age.html.

[21] *Id.*

counterparts a generation earlier.[22] Over the past few decades, incomes have increased at a greater rate for older people; poverty is declining for those above sixty-five, but rising for those under thirty-five; and younger people suffered more from the Great Recession than older people.[23]

In sum, what the data show is that rising life expectancy is not experienced equally – and will not be experienced equally in the future. Rather, those who live longer – successive cohorts of older Americans – are more likely to be wealthier, white or Hispanic, better educated, and live in metro areas, particularly on the coasts. Within the cohorts of older Americans, inequalities will persist based on race, geography, period effects, and other factors as well.

7.2 GERONTOCRACY AND ITS DISCONTENTS

Systematic, persistent disparities in age are a problem for representative democracies. The American constitutional system, for example, was designed on a theory that interests – what James Madison calls factions – would be so fragmented that no single faction would be able to dominate politics.[24] Instead, the clashes between groups would lead to the election of leaders who would advance the public good, rather than the preferences of any one group.[25] At the same time, the separation of powers was meant to divide *institutions*, not factions, unlike earlier mixed-government regimes that explicitly saw the primary divides in society as rich versus poor and built those divisions into the constitutional structure.[26] In recent years, many constitutional scholars have shown the limitations of Madison's theory. Some have argued that in an ideologically polarized system, political parties and party identity are the central divide in society, and so a system of checks and balances should focus on the "separation of parties, not powers."[27] Others have noted that policy preferences overlap with wealth and class, and that the political system is dominated by the wealthy and interest groups; those cleavages, not institutional separations, are primary drivers in politics.[28] In both cases, the worry is that the Madisonian system will not function as intended because of acute social cleavages.

[22] Pew Rsch. Ctr., *The Rising Age Gap in Economic Well-Being* (Nov. 7, 2011), 1, https://www.pewresearch.org/wp-content/uploads/sites/3/2011/11/WealthReportFINAL.pdf.

[23] *Id.*

[24] The Federalist No. 10, at 77–78 (James Madison) (Clinton Rossiter ed., 1961).

[25] Book Note, *The Relevance and Irrelevance of the Founders*, 120 Harv. L. Rev. 619, 624–625 (2006).

[26] Ganesh Sitaraman, The Crisis of the Middle-Class Constitution 21–111 (2018).

[27] Daryl J. Levinson & Richard H. Pildes, *Separation of Parties, Not Powers*, 119 Harv. L. Rev. 2312 (2006).

[28] Ganesh Sitaraman, *The Puzzling Absence of Economic Power in Constitutional Theory*, 101 Cornell L. Rev. 1445 (2016); Kate Andrias, *Separations of Wealth: Inequality and the Erosion of Checks and Balances*, 18 U. Pa. J. Con. L. 419 (2015).

Age may offer another example of this problem. According to the Interparliamentary Union, only 2.6 percent of legislators around the world are under the age of thirty, despite that age group comprising nearly 50 percent of the world's population.[29] Only about 17.5 percent are under forty, and 30 percent are under forty-five.[30] Outside of elected officeholding, there are age disparities in voter registration, voting, and political acts from writing letters to making campaign donations.[31] Political scientists have also shown that there are clear life-cycle effects in terms of political participation. Activity in politics is low in youth, increases in middle age, and has a short trail-off at extreme age.[32] As life expectancy grows, we should expect life-cycle effects on the older end to stretch – with older people remaining active for longer. The result of this data is that there is a massive imbalance in representation of the young and an imbalance that will likely expand with rising life expectancy. If, as political scientists have argued, representative democracy is not a system that aggregates the views of individual voters or responds to deliberation, but rather a process by which groups wield power, then the young have and will continue to have comparatively less power and influence than their elders.[33]

The overlap of age and economic inequality only magnifies this problem. Older people (and those with rising life expectancies) are wealthier than younger people. Political scientists have demonstrated that the poor and middle class are not well represented in government, either through elected officials who come from a blue-collar background[34] or through participation in contacting representatives, volunteering, donating, voting, or lobbying (personally or through representatives in Washington).[35] It is perhaps no surprise, therefore, that study after study has concluded that policy outcomes reflect the preferences of the wealthy.[36] Indeed, when the vast majority of Americans' views diverge with those of the wealthy, the wealthy's views tend to control policy outcomes.[37]

The data on age and wealth inequality, and on rising life expectancy, raises the prospect of gerontocracy – a regime defined by the rule of the elderly. If the elderly participate more in politics, serve more in government, and are systematically wealthier than younger people, the elderly will have disproportionately more

29 Interparliamentary Union, *Youth Participation in National Parliaments* (2021), 7, 9.

30 *Id.*

31 Kay L. Schlozman et al., The Unheavenly Chorus 216–218 (2012).

32 *Id.* at 200, 230.

33 Christopher H. Achen & Larry M. Bartels, Democracy for Realists (2016).

34 Nicholas Carnes, White-Collar Government: The Hidden Role of Class in Economic Policy Making (2013).

35 Schlozman et al., *supra* note 31.

36 *See, e.g.*, Larry M. Bartels, Unequal Democracy (2d ed. 2016); Martin Gilens & Benjamin I. Page, *Testing Theories of American Politics: Elites, Interest Groups, and Average Citizens*, 12 Persps. on Pol. 564 (2014).

37 Gilens & Page, *supra* note 36.

political power and influence than younger people. Moreover, political influence, like wealth, can compound over time. Decades of donating to political leaders can build close relationships; decades in office can build political power – in the form of favors done, former staff spread throughout the system, and skills and relationships. It may be, as we approach the unequal 100-year life, that we will have an increasingly unequal system in which wealthy, older people have more and more political power – a gerontocracy.

The specter of gerontocracy might not matter if the elderly's views are similar to those of younger people. But surveys show that different generations have different attitudes toward policy. According to Pew Research, millennials are the most supportive of same-sex marriage, with older generations – Gen X, Boomers, and Silent – exhibiting descending levels of support (the study omitted Gen Z).[38] Views on whether racial discrimination is the primary barrier for why Black people in America "can't get ahead" also diverge by generation, and over time the gap has widened even as attitudes changed. Indeed, younger people's attitudes have shifted further than other generations on whether racial discrimination is a major problem.[39] This gap in age cohorts persists even if comparing only white millennials to white members of older generations.[40] On other questions too, there are serious divides based on age: Do immigrants strengthen the country? Younger generations say yes.[41] Should the US rely more on diplomacy or the military to ensure peace? Younger generations focus on diplomacy.[42] Should the US government be bigger and offer more services? Younger generations say yes.[43] Is it the government's responsibility to provide healthcare coverage to everyone? Younger generations say yes.[44]

Age differences in policy preferences and political participation create a variety of problems. We might call the first the entrenchment problem. Longer life expectancy may mean that people remain in positions of power longer. Commentators regularly note that Presidents Trump and Biden are older than their predecessors, that some congressional leaders are older than is conventional, and that Supreme Court justices regularly serve into their eighties. If older generations remain entrenched firmly in power for longer, that keeps younger generations from gaining power until they too are far older. The result could be a systematic phase shift in the age of political leadership – and continued lack of representation among those who are younger and less wealthy.

[38] Pew Rsch. Ctr., *The Generation Gap in American Politics* (Mar. 1, 2018), 30, https://www.pewresearch.org/politics/wp-content/uploads/sites/4/2018/03/03-01-18-Generations-release2.pdf.

[39] *Id.* at 26–27.

[40] *Id.*

[41] *Id.* at 28.

[42] *Id.* at 19–20.

[43] *Id.* at 13–14.

[44] *Id.* at 15.

A second problem is what we might think of as the increasing imbalance between the wisdom of the ancients and the wisdom of the young. One of the primary arguments for a political system that operates slowly, with many veto-gates, checks, and balances, is that it recognizes the wisdom of past generations. Those who came before were not fools, and their considered decisions should be given great weight before they are displaced by new ideas and new policies. Similarly, societies revere the elderly for their accumulated wisdom and knowledge. A lifetime of successes, failures, and lessons learned may lead to a just and wise gerontocracy. But the problem is that an equal and opposite principle is at play too: the wisdom of the young. As technologies, innovations, and society change, the elderly may not update their technical knowledge or social views as swiftly as they should, particularly in comparison to younger generations who grow up natively familiar with a new context. The wisdom of youth welcomes the future, is more willing to experiment, and charts new frontiers. The young may also think with a longer time horizon, because they must live with policy decisions for many decades to come.[45] As life expectancy rises and if older people remain in positions of power longer, we should expect a political system that is already designed to move slowly to move even more slowly, to adapt less well to social and technological changes, and to be less innovative. The balance between the conservativism of age and the experimentalism of youth will likely lean further toward the former.

A third problem is in the design of public policies. Political scientist Paul Peterson has observed that federal government policies that help children are systematically different from those helping the elderly across a range of dimensions. Programs for children tend to have state-determined eligibility requirements, rather than federal; they tend to have intergovernmental administration, rather than national; they tend to be complex, rather than simple; and they tend to offer substitutable benefits, rather than supplemental benefits.[46] Peterson argues that the dynamics of program design are a function of the political power that the elderly have, compared to the young. Their power enables them to push for programs that bring more benefits, with greater consistency and simplicity.[47]

These three problems may lead to a fourth – an increasing gap between the rulers and the radicalized. If policies systematically lag behind changing trends, if programs are better for those who are older and richer than the overall population, and if political leadership is increasingly entrenched in power, we might expect increasing frustration with politics and increasing radicalization among younger cohorts. Younger cohorts may see themselves shut out of direct political representation and

[45] Juliana Bidadanure, *Six Reasons Why the UK Parliament Should Have Youth Quotas*, OPENDEMOCRACY (June 15, 2015), https://www.opendemocracy.net/en/opendemocracyuk/six-reasons-why-uk-parliament-should-have-youth-quotas/.

[46] Paul E. Peterson, *An Immodest Proposal*, 121 DAEDALUS 151, 161–165 (Fall 1992).

[47] *Id.*

their policy preferences advancing far more slowly than they would like. Overlap with economic inequality means that these dynamics could become acute for many with respect to their basic livelihoods.

Looking globally, some commentators have suggested that a "youth bulge" in a country – a large population of young people without sufficient economic opportunities – can contribute to political radicalization and even destabilize governments.[48] It is possible that rising life expectancy, and the political dynamics it unleashes, might be similar. While some young people may choose to remain in the political system and wait their turn, many others may not. Rising hopelessness and distrust in government's ability to address their concerns might push them to exit the political process and exercise their voice through protest.[49] It is possible that such frustrations could lead, over time, to a greater radicalization of politics, particularly among younger cohorts. In a gerontocracy, the slow pace of reform may lead to calls for revolution.[50]

7.3 AGE AND POLITICAL REPRESENTATION

What can be done about the possibility of gerontocracy? The first option is simply to do nothing. Many social and identity cleavages are not specifically accounted for in political representation – tall people, blondes, fans of crime novels, runners. None of those groups get representation in politics, and few would think they need representation. That intuition likely stems from the view that nothing about their group identity is essential to public affairs or linked to systematic differences in policy preferences. But as noted earlier, this is not true of age. There are significant divergences in policy preferences by age – even among copartisans. Younger conservatives have significantly different views than their elderly counterparts on a variety of policy issues.

Another possibility is that the young are represented, virtually, through their elders. While there is a long tradition of political thinkers who believed representatives should "be in miniature an exact portrait of the people at large,"[51] there is also a long tradition of those who believed representatives would carry the views of their constituents to politics, even if they did not "mirror" the population precisely.[52] For

[48] Lionel Beehner, *The Effects of "Youth Bulge" on Civil Conflicts*, Council on Foreign Rels. (Apr. 13, 2007), https://www.cfr.org/backgrounder/effects-youth-bulge-civil-conflicts.

[49] *See* Albert O. Hirschman, Exit, Voice, and Loyalty (1972).

[50] *Cf.* Sitaraman, *supra* note 26, at 21–55 (describing fears that inequality could lead to revolution); *see also* Daniel Ziblatt, Conservative Parties and the Birth of Democracy (2017) (arguing that conservatives enabled reform in part due to fears of revolution).

[51] John Adams, *Thoughts on Government (1776)*, Nat'l Const. Ctr., https://constitutioncenter.org/the-constitution/historic-document-library/detail/john-adams-thoughts-on-government-1776 (accessed May 25, 2023).

[52] For a discussion of this and other theories of representation, *see generally* Hanna Pitkin, The Concept of Representation (1967).

example, older members of legislatures have children and grandchildren and may consider those younger generations' interests when making political decisions. They may also listen to their constituents and represent those views faithfully, for fear of losing an election. Still, political scientists have shown that actual representation matters. Women in office act differently than men; people of color act differently than whites, and people from blue-collar backgrounds act differently than those from white-collar backgrounds.[53]

A second option, which accounts for policy or other changes, is for the political system to informally consider age as a factor in representation. To some extent, this is currently what happens. Some candidates for office run explicitly on generational change, promising fresh ideas and a new approach compared to the tired politics of the past. Their opponents emphasize their experience and entrenched power after decades in office. For appointed roles, leaders may choose to pick people from different age brackets, in part to ensure age diversity. It is not as obvious that leaders take age diversity into account, especially when compared to gender and racial diversity, but they certainly could. Still, with rising life expectancy in the political class, it is possible that the "younger generation" in politics may not actually be so young.

A third option is to grant specific representation by age. This should not be as outlandish as it might first seem. It is worth noting that constitutional theorists have long considered *some* groups worthy of specific representation. The mixed-government tradition that persisted from ancient times until the American Revolution divided society into classes, giving specific representation to the wealthy and the ordinary people. In comparative politics, the field of consociationalism outlines strategies to give representation to divided societies – decentralization and regional control; power-sharing agreements; and quotas for ethnic group representation at the cabinet or senior level. In societies deeply divided by religion, language, and ethnicity, many have thought to build representation for each faction directly into the political system.

The question, of course, is whether age fits into the same category. People may come to different conclusions on this point, but as noted earlier, there are not only direct correlations between age and wealth but also systematically different policy preferences by age cohort. As life expectancy increases, it is likely that generational divides will increase as well because older generations will be represented for longer. If age is likely to be a more and more significant cleavage over time, it may be worth considering as a factor in institutional design. Let us, therefore,

[53] Clair C. Miller, *Women Actually Do Govern Differently*, N.Y. Times (Nov. 10, 2016), https://www.nytimes.com/2016/11/10/upshot/women-actually-do-govern-differently.html; Robert R. Preuhs & Rodney E. Hero, *A Different Kind of Representation: Black and Latino Descriptive Representation and the Role of Ideological Cuing*, Pol. Rsch. Q. 157 (2011); Carnes, *supra* note 34.

consider a few thought experiments in how age might be incorporated into institutional design.[54]

7.3.1 *Age Minimums – and Maximums*

The US Constitution considers age in representation, through provisions that set age *minimums* for federal elected office. Members of the House of Representatives must be twenty-five years of age. Members of the Senate, thirty years of age. And the president must be at least thirty-five years old. Age minimums are a proxy for maturity and experience, and each office was designed with that in mind.

But if age minimums are conventional and uncontroversial, why not also age maximums? Age maximums for service in office would ensure that different generations are represented in the political process. They would proxy new ideas, energy, and changing social norms. They would also prevent entrenchment in office by long-serving political leaders and preemptively ensure the retirement of leaders whose mental acuity may have begun to decline.

How could age maximums be designed? At the legislative level, one could imagine building overlapping age categories, with minimums and maximums, into the qualifications for officeholding. Service in the House of Representatives, for example, could require a person to be between the ages of twenty-five and fifty-five, and in the Senate might require an age between thirty and seventy. It is possible that all members of both branches would still be on the older side of those ranges, but the House would likely always be younger, given the dramatically younger age maximum.

Alternatively, one could imagine designing a legislature without overlap between the two houses – a House with members age twenty-five to forty, and a Senate with members age forty to seventy. Guaranteeing stark differences in age as a qualification for service would ensure generational representation, akin to classical mixed-government strategies that reserved one House for the wealthy and another for commoners.

One challenge, of course, is what happens to the young who are aged out of their position. The answer is that many will likely seek another role – a spot as governor – or might challenge an incumbent in their older-age body. A legislature designed along these lines could therefore potentially increase electoral competition among credible candidates. It might, however, also lead young members to become

[54] I exclude technocratic policy options, such as setting the discount rate within cost–benefit analysis, to value the interests of future generations more highly. This topic not only has been discussed extensively in the literature but also has a more limited scope than the structural questions of political representation I consider here. For a discussion, *see* David A. Weisbach & Cass R. Sunstein, *Introduction to Symposium on Intergenerational Equity and Discounting*, 74 U. Chi. L. Rev. 1 (2007); Cass R. Sunstein & Arden Rowell, *On Discounting Regulatory Benefits: Risk, Money, and Intergenerational Equity*, 74 U. Chi. L. Rev. 171 (2007).

interest-group lobbyists, drawing on their experience to pressure their former members (and perhaps even mentees) to serve private interests instead of the public good. Post-employment restrictions would therefore probably be necessary for such a system to work.

One could also imagine prescribing an age range on the presidency. A presidential age range would functionally preclude any person from running for that office who would be unable to serve a full four-year term prior to hitting the age maximum and, because party members might want someone who will not be a lame duck from day one, might even prevent most people from winning a nomination to that office if they cannot serve a full two terms. Such a rule would serve as a proxy that presidents have the energy and stamina to handle perhaps the most stressful and consequential job in the world – just as the age minimum proxies a level of life experience needed for the position.

It is also worth noting that there may be value to reducing the age minimums for service in elected office, even without maximums. In response to the disparities in policy designs for children versus the elderly, Paul Peterson has proposed, mostly in jest, allowing children to vote.[55] Whatever one thinks of his provocation, age qualifications for legislative roles could be reduced from current levels. Some countries have dropped age qualifications to eighteen, and at least one study finds this is an effective tactic for increasing youth representation.[56]

7.3.2 *Term Limits*

Another possibility is term limits. Term limits do not directly ensure age-based representation, but they may indirectly help. Legal rules for lifetime service (as with federal judges) and incumbency advantages (even without lifetime service rules) mean that officials can often serve in their same position for decades – perhaps even for life. Term limits would mandate departure from office, ending formal or informal incumbency entrenchment. But it is worth noting that this is an indirect way to get at age: There is no reason why newly elected or selected persons, after a term expires, will not be from the same age cohort – or even an older one – than the previous occupant of the office.

But it is also worth recognizing the severe downsides of term limits. First, for legislative positions, term limits bring a risk of heightened interest-group capture. The reason is that most newly elected members of Congress know very little about the subject areas of law and policy they are legislating or overseeing.[57] Over time, they develop expertise as they see more issues, focus on particular topics, and go into

55 Peterson, *supra* note 46, at 170.

56 Daniel Stockemer & Aksel Sundstrom, *Age Representation in Parliaments: Can Institutions Pave the Way for the Young?* 10 Eur. Pol. Sci. Rev. 467, 486 (2018).

57 *See*, e.g., Nelson W. Polsby, *Some Arguments against Congressional Term Limitations*, 16 Harv. J. L. & Pub. Pol'y 101, 105 (1993) (observing that experience leads to policy knowledge and that

greater depth through committee assignments. In contrast, lobbyists and interest groups have considerable information and expertise – albeit conflicted, and usually deployed to serve their parochial interests. This mismatch in expertise means that overworked, busy members who are constantly running for reelection and do not have much expertise will be more likely to rely on interest-group experts than those who have over many years developed some expertise of their own.[58]

Second, passing significant legislation is often a multi-year and sometimes multi-decade effort. Members sometimes spend years pushing for a particular bill or policy, or at least amassing general expertise on a topic. When the opportunity arises or when a crisis occurs and major legislation is demanded, they have amassed significant expertise to navigate the complex process of passing legislation.[59] If term limits are too short – say, along the lines of eight years – they may simply ensure that *no* members of Congress have sufficient expertise and longevity to pass major legislation. Longer term limits, such as twenty years, might not have this downside.

A third problem is that term limits might lead to greater capture in the form of the revolving door. Members of Congress, for example, may depart their positions and make many times more in salary by decamping to lobbying firms. There they can use their contacts and relationships with former colleagues to push forward the interests of whatever group for whom they lobby. Shorter term limits would exacerbate this problem, creating more and more former members and likely, therefore, more well-connected lobbyists.

All of these problems are less of an issue when considering term limits for leadership offices, such as committee chairs or House and Senate leadership. For these positions, term limits will increase turnover among persons in those positions, without significantly decreasing the experience and expertise of the body itself. Members can still spend years pushing causes and will bring expertise to a crisis. But leaders will rotate, preventing the accumulation of power, and possibly ensuring that younger members have an opportunity to exercise their leadership and pursue their agenda – at least for a time.

7.3.3 *Intergenerational Judiciary*

In recent years, there has been increased interest in reforming the Supreme Court. Proposals have included expanding the size of the Court, rotating judges from lower courts onto the Court, creating partisan balance requirements for the Court, and also establishing term limits for justices. Some who support term limits for Supreme

term limits would reduce knowledge of members of Congress, thereby indirectly empowering lobbyists and others in the political system with more knowledge).

58 *Id.*

59 *See, e.g.*, Robert G. Kaiser, Act of Congress (2014) (describing the expertise of Barney Frank after decades in Congress, passing the Dodd-Frank Act after the 2008 financial crisis).

Court justices have done so explicitly as a way to prevent gerontocracy.[60] They worry that a Court of seventy- and eighty-year-olds is ill-equipped to address many of the innovative issues of the time. Others support the proposal because they worry about too many *young* people being appointed to the federal courts.[61] In recent years, Republicans have nominated and confirmed many judges in their thirties for lifetime appointments, seemingly in order to retain their hold on those judgeships for the extra decade before middle age. Term limits might reduce the pressure to do so.

From the perspective of age-based representation, the judiciary is an interesting case. Both parties appoint federal judges between the ages of forty and sixty-five with great frequency, but Republicans tend to appoint more judges than Democrats at the lower end of the age spectrum (including some in their thirties) and Democrats more than Republicans at the highest end of the age spectrum.[62] One consequence is that there is *some* intergenerational diversity on the courts – judges in their forties, fifties, sixties, and seventies, and a smaller number in their thirties and eighties. While the balance skews conservative at the younger end, there is *some* age cohort representation even into the thirties. But over time, the thirty-something and forty-something judges will get older. And when others retire or pass away, creating new openings on the bench, there is no guarantee they will be replaced by new judges in their thirties or forties. Indeed, if Democrats continue their pattern of largely nominating comparatively older judges, it is likely that there will be a systematic skew over time – youth representation will exist during Republican presidencies from newly minted conservative judges, but not during Democratic presidencies.

With respect to the courts, term limits could create revolving-door problems, with judges departing to become lobbyists, appellate lawyers, or even using the bench as a springboard for a run for office. This dynamic is troubling as it might corrupt their decision-making process as judges. Some might also think that judges should have considerable experience in law and life prior to becoming a judge, as both expertise in the law and the exercise of judgment take time to develop. This might suggest a substantive reason for age representation to skew older for judges than for legislators.

[60] Stephen Calebresi & James Lindgren, *Term Limits for the Supreme Court: Life Tenure Reconsidered*, 29 Harv. J.L. & Pub. Pol'y 769 (2006); Stephen Calebresi & James Lindgren, *Supreme Gerontocracy*, Wall St. J. (Apr. 8, 2005), https://www.wsj.com/articles/SB111292087188301557.

[61] Kermit Roosevelt III & Ruth-Helen Vassilas, *Coming to Terms with Term Limits: Fixing the Downward Spiral of Supreme Court Appointments*, Am. Const. Soc'y (June 2017), https://www.acslaw.org/wp-content/uploads/2017/06/Coming_to_Terms.pdf; Rosalind Dixon, *Why the Supreme Court Needs (Short) Term Limits*, N.Y. Times (Dec. 31, 2021), https://www.nytimes.com/2021/12/31/opinion/supreme-court-term-limits.html.

[62] Moiz Syed, *Charting the Long-Term Impact of Trump's Judicial Appointments*, ProPublica (Oct. 30, 2020), https://projects.propublica.org/trump-young-judges/.

Age minimums could potentially be useful to address that issue, though they would not enhance intergenerational representation.

7.3.4 *Parliamentary Systems, Party Lists, Proportional Representation, and Age Quotas*

Some countries' electoral systems ensure age diversity in legislative representation through quotas for young people. After the Arab Spring protests, Egypt, Morocco, and Tunisia adopted youth quotas for parliamentary service, and after years of domestic conflict, Uganda, Kenya, and Rwanda did as well.[63] These reforms appear to have been a response to a large, disaffected population of young people.[64] Bringing young people into politics might give them a voice, rather than leaving them outside the process to protest.

Research on the efficacy of youth quotas is limited, but one study suggests that proportional representation and dropping age qualifications for officeholding to eighteen may be superior tactics.[65] Youth quotas have thus far tended to be "too low and too selectively applied."[66] In addition, proportional representation systems require party elites to develop a slate of candidates, creating an incentive to appeal to different groups of people, and this may push them to have youth representation.[67] When one party acts in a proportional representation system, there may be a contagion effect pushing others to follow.[68] The advantages of incumbency are also less significant in proportional representation systems than in first-past-the-post systems.[69] In parliamentary systems, and particularly for those with proportional representation, adopting slates with young people may therefore be a promising tactic.

7.4 CONCLUSION

In representative democracies, public policy depends on who has political power and who uses it. Political power turns not simply on the institutional structures of government but on background social conditions such as wealth, ideology, geography, and race. With rising life expectancy pointing toward a 100-year life, age may become an increasingly important feature in determining political power. Older political leaders may become entrenched in office, and older people tend to be

[63] Jana Belschner, *The Adoption of Youth Quotas after the Arab Uprisings*, 9 POL., GRPS., & IDENTITIES 151, 153 (2018).
[64] *Id.*
[65] Stockemer & Sundstrom, *supra* note 56.
[66] *Id.* at 468.
[67] *Id.* at 473.
[68] *Id.*
[69] *Id.* at 473–474.

wealthier – another important aspect of political power. The consequence of gerontocracy could over time be radicalization of the young who feel poorly represented. Addressing this problem will be important to ensuring representative government, and there are a number of formal strategies governments can take, from age qualifications for office to term limits to youth quotas, in addition to informal strategies like candidate recruitment. But whatever the approach, as people live longer – and do so unequally – the policy consequences will be significant.

8

Age-Based Classifications in an Age of Centenarians

Nina A. Kohn

With the number of older adults increasing worldwide[1] – and the ranks of the very old rising especially sharply[2] – countries are confronted with the question of how to respond to their expanding elderly populations. Historically, countries have responded to the "problem" of old age by creating special policies for older adults, such as pension programs for those of "retirement age."

This chapter considers the role of such age-based law and legal entitlements in a world in which people routinely live to be 100 years old. It asks: In such a world, what should be the legal significance of advanced chronological age? Should an adult's chronological age affect his or her legal status or entitlements? It posits that the rise of the 100-year life should prompt a shift away from age-based policy. Specifically, it shows why, as life expectancy increases, chronological age will become an increasingly poor proxy for other characteristics, and that, therefore, using chronological age to establish eligibility for legal entitlements will result in increasingly poorly targeted policy interventions. It also explains how the use of age-based classifications will become increasingly inequitable and regressive.

The chapter calls for a wholesale reconsideration of the use of age-based criteria. It argues that social welfare policies should increasingly reject age-based classifications in favor of approaches that target interventions to populations based on their actual vulnerability to the particular problems the policies aim to address. It explains that although this alternative approach may be more challenging to administer, it is increasingly necessary to ensure efficient and equitable distributions of resources.

1 U.N. Dep't of Econ. & Soc. Aff., *World Population Aging: Highlights* (2017), 8, https://www.un.org/en/development/desa/population/publications/pdf/ageing/WPA2017_Highlights.pdf.

2 *Id.*; Jean-Marie Robine & Sarah Cubaynes, *Worldwide Demography of Centenarians*, 165 Mechanisms Ageing & Dev. 59 (2017).

8.1 THE ROLE OF AGE-BASED CLASSIFICATIONS

Age-based legal classifications are ubiquitous. Across time and across cultures, jurisdictions have used chronological age as a mechanism for establishing rights and responsibilities.

Today, chronological age classifications occur in a variety of legal contexts. Chronological age is used to establish legal duties. In both criminal and civil cases, minors are typically held to a lower standard of care than are adults.[3] Similarly, certain behaviors may be required of individuals at one age, and not at another. For example, states may require education for minors, or special tests for older adults seeking drivers' licenses.[4] Chronological age can also determine eligibility for benefits. Although states have generally abandoned age as a basis for imposing guardianship or conservatorship, eligibility for public health insurance in the US largely depends on chronological age. Not only is Medicare coverage largely limited to those over sixty-five years of age, but older adults and children can more readily qualify for Medicaid than can younger adults. In addition, chronological age can determine the level of protection the law provides against actions by others. For example, the US Age Discrimination in Employment Act (ADEA) provides protection against age discrimination in employment to those aged forty and over, but no protection to those under the age of forty.[5]

The ubiquity of age-based legal classifications, in part, reflects their utility. In some contexts, chronological age is a meaningful predictor of individuals' needs or abilities, and, therefore, using age-based classifications can help efficiently target policy interventions and resources. Compulsory education requirements for minors, for example, largely reflect the distinct needs and abilities of youngsters, whose cognitive abilities generally develop in predictable ways corresponding with their chronological age.

The ubiquity of such classifications also, however, reflects their substantial administrative appeal. Chronological age classifications are easy to administer because chronological age can be readily determined without any need for discretionary judgment. Thus, policymakers are understandably likely to use age as a proxy for a wide range of other less-readily-ascertained characteristics. Indeed, age-based legal classifications are frequently used as proxies for more-difficult-to-measure attributes such as maturity, disability, or financial insecurity.

[3] *See* Dan B. Dobbs et al., The Law of Torts, §§ 134–137 (2d ed. 2019) (discussing the standard of care for minors in US tort law); Am. L. Inst., Model Penal Code § 4.10 (2018) (describing a general policy against convicting persons who were under the age of sixteen at the time an offense was committed).

[4] *See, e.g.*, Fla. Stat. Ann. § 322.18(5) (2021).

[5] 29 U.S.C. § 631(a) (2021).

Consistent with these advantages, chronological age-based classifications are particularly prevalent in policies designed to respond to the risks associated with aging. Indeed, age-based classifications are a core feature of US laws and policies designed to address the needs of older adults. The major entitlement programs in the US – Social Security, Medicare, and Medicaid – have rules that preference individuals for benefits based on advanced chronological age. Most Americans will only become eligible for government-provided health insurance because they become older.

Age-based classifications are also common in policies designed to address concerns about the safety of older adults. Indeed, the use of age-based classifications has increased in recent decades as the US has sought to respond to the problem of elder abuse and neglect. States are embracing elder-specific social service interventions. Almost all states have adopted mandatory elder abuse reporting.[6] Many of these require third parties to report otherwise confidential information if the suspected victim is above a certain age. For example, Rhode Island requires "any person who has reasonable cause to believe that any person sixty years of age or older has been abused, neglected, or exploited or is self-neglecting" to "immediately" report it to the state.[7] Others require reporting of suspected abuse when the victim is above a certain age and has a requisite level of disability.[8]

States have also created new crimes that exclusively apply to behavior directed at older adults.[9] Some states have criminalized certain types of otherwise consensual sexual relationships where the "victim" is an older adult. For example, Washington prohibits sexual relations between disabled persons aged sixty and over and those who provide them with paid transportation.[10] Similarly, some states have adopted statutes that create criminal liability for certain types of financial transactions if those transactions involve a person of advanced age.[11] And Maine allows for certain transactions to be voided if they were the result of undue influence exerted on a person aged sixty or older.[12]

6 Nina A. Kohn, *Outliving Civil Rights*, 86 Wash. U. L. Rev. 1053 (2009).

7 R.I. Gen. Laws § 42-66-8 (2021).

8 *See*, e.g., Mo. Rev. Stat. §§ 192.2400, 192.2405 (2000).

9 *See* Nina A. Kohn, *Elder (In)Justice: A Critique of the Criminalization of Elder Abuse*, 49 Amer. Crim. L. Rev. 1, 8–13 (2012).

10 *See* Wash. Rev. Code § 9A.44.100(1)(f), § 9A.44.010(16) (2020) (criminalizing sexual conduct with a "frail elder or vulnerable adult" defined as "a person sixty years of age or older who has the functional, mental, or physical inability to care for himself or herself"); Wash. Rev. Code § 9A.44.100 (2020) (making it a felony for a paid transportation provider to knowingly cause a disabled person age sixty or older, other than his or her spouse, "to have sexual contact with him or her or another" even if the contact is consensual).

11 *See*, e.g., 720 Ill. Comp. Stat. Ann. 5/17-56(a), (c) (2020).

12 33 Maine Rev. Stat. Ann. § 1021 et seq. (2020).

8.2 IMPACT OF EXPANDED LIFE EXPECTANCY: RECALIBRATION

Expanded life expectancy, and the growing ranks of the extremely old, should trigger recalibration – or, at least, a consideration of whether recalibration is in order – of age-based legal classifications that differentiate among adults.

Recalibration could help to better allocate scarce resources. As the population ages, entitlement programs for older adults will become substantially more costly without recalibration. This has been well recognized in the context of the Social Security system. Scholars and policymakers have long been in conversation about increasing the Social Security retirement age (either the early retirement age, normal retirement age, or both) to maintain the program's financial solvency. Anne Alstott, for example, has suggested that raising the retirement age for higher-income workers is appropriate both to address the program's solvency and to further fairness across the life cycle.[13] Similar suggestions have been made, although with less political support, about raising the Medicare eligibility age in response to changing demographics.[14]

Recalibration could also improve the fit between age-based criteria and the underlying characteristics being targeted. Age-based criteria are often used in policy as a proxy for disability and frailty, but old age is actually a poor predictor of either, especially when it is defined broadly (such as sixty or sixty-five and older, as is common in US policy). At higher age thresholds, by contrast, there is a stronger correlation between chronological age and disability and frailty. For example, although dementia is often thought of as a common ailment in old age, less than 5 percent of those in their seventies have dementia, but over a third of those age ninety and older do.[15]

Thus, ratcheting up age-based eligibility criteria is likely to result in more tailored policy interventions because chronological age is a more accurate predictor of incidence of physical and cognitive disabilities for the very oldest of the old than for older adults who are younger (i.e., the "old-old" and "young-old"). The older the age classification used, the more likely the individuals covered by that classification will have predictable physical and cognitive vulnerabilities and thus the more likely the classification will be a reasonable proxy for such traits.

Recalibration may also impact the experience of growing older, potentially in positive ways for some. Age-based legal classifications help shape the social meaning of chronological age. For example, turning sixty-five is perceived as an entrance into

[13] Anne L. Alstott, New Deal for Old Age: Toward a Progressive Retirement (2017); Anne L. Alstott, *A New Deal for Old Age*, 97 B.U. L. Rev. 1933 (2017).

[14] *See* Kaiser Family Found., Raising the Age of Medicare Eligibility (2013), https://www.kff.org/wp-content/uploads/2013/01/8169.pdf.

[15] B. L. Plassman et al., *Prevalence of Dementia in the United States: The Aging, Demographics, and Memory Study*, 29 Neuroepidemiology 128 (2007), http://www.ncbi.nlm.nih.gov/pmc/articles/PMC2705925/.

old age and a major milestone for Americans because it has been deemed "retirement age" for Medicare (and previously was "normal retirement age" for Social Security benefits). As one blogger wrote: "Turning 65 years old is one of those life passages – like college hazing and infantry basic training – many men would rather avoid contemplating until it's upon us … Nobody wants to think about becoming an elder."[16] Thus, increasing the minimum age criteria for policies designed to address the needs of older adults may prolong the perceived experience of middle age.

On the other hand, recalibration in the form of simply raising the eligibility age for benefits (e.g., Social Security, Medicare, access to retirement accounts without penalty) will come with substantial costs and often inequitable results. As eligibility ages are raised, we can expect people to remain in the workforce longer, potentially crowding out younger workers and workers with lower wages.

Increased inequities can be expected because although people's chronological age increases at parallel rates, their biological ages do not. Biological age, which may be estimated based on biomarkers and other indicia of health, occurs at different rates in different people. In addition to genetic contributors, socioeconomic status, lifestyle, and environmental factors, including exposure to pollution, may impact the rate of biological aging.[17] Thus, responding to increases in longevity by increasing eligibility thresholds – without accompanying those changes with new supports that meet the needs of those of advanced biological age – will tend to be increasingly regressive: disproportionately disadvantaging already disadvantaged and marginalized groups.

In short, the rise of the 100-year life should not simply cause recalibration of age-based classifications; it should trigger reconsideration of their use in the first place.

8.3 THE IMPACT OF EXPANDED LIFE EXPECTANCY: RECONSIDERATION

The rise of the 100-year life should revive and reenergize the classic debate[18] over what role (if any) chronological age should play in determining rights or establishing eligibility for benefits. That is, it should seriously call into question not only *what* age-based classifications are used but also *whether* such classifications should be used at all.

[16] Suddenly Senior, *Turning 65 Years Old: Scream about It* (Mar. 26, 2018), https://www.suddenlysenior.com/turn-65-and-scream-about-getting-old/.

[17] Tze Pin Ng et al., *Socio-environmental, Lifestyle, Behavioural, and Psychological Determinants of Biological Ageing: The Singapore Longitudinal Ageing Study*, 66 Gerontology 603 (2020).

[18] *See* Age or Need? Public Policies for Older People (Bernice Neugarten ed., 1982) (discussing the modern debate over age-based classification – considered the seminal book on the topic).

One reason that expanding life expectancy should also prompt reexamination of the use of age-based legal classifications is that chronological age is likely to be an increasingly poor proxy for underlying characteristics that policymakers wish to target (e.g., functional abilities or needs).

As life expectancy increases, we can expect increased heterogeneity in the experiences and life trajectories of people born in the same year. This is because aging fosters heterogeneity. As a generational cohort grows older, its members become more diverse in their functional abilities and health status. Heterogeneity in health-related characteristics is particularly pronounced in early older age.[19] Consistent with this general pattern, a recent study of older adults in Canada, which considered thirty-four health-related characteristics, found that, overall, health heterogeneity peaks around seventy years of age[20] but continues to increase for certain characteristics – including functional performance – into at least the eighties.[21]

The increased heterogeneity among age peers reflects, at least in part, the effect of cumulative advantage and disadvantage over the life course. In particular, those with lower socioeconomic status and lower levels of education, on average, experience poor health and more functional limitations than those with higher socioeconomic status and levels of education.[22]

A second more fundamental reason why expanding life expectancy should prompt reexamination of the use of age-based classifications is equity. The expansion of the ranks of centenarians, and the oldest-of-the-old more broadly, is not evenly distributed in society. Although it is often said that everyone grows old, this is simply untrue. Old age is not an inevitable experience. Not everyone will reach older age. Illness, accidents, and violence mean that many will die in their youth or younger adulthood. As of 2021, life expectancy at birth for non-Hispanic Black Americans was six years less than for non-Hispanic white Americans, and more than seven years less than that for Hispanic Americans.[23]

Very old age is even less certain. As of 2018, less than 10 percent of Americans born alive lived to the age of ninety, and under 2 percent lived to be 100. Incidence of very old age varies by race and ethnicity. For example, as of 2018, Hispanic Americans were nearly twice as likely to live to age 100 as non-Hispanic Black Americans, and nearly 2.5 times as likely to live to age 100 than non-Hispanic white Americans.[24]

[19] Quoc Dinh Nguyen, *Health Heterogeneity in Older Adults: Exploration in the Canadian Longitudinal Study on Aging*, 69 J. Amer. Geriatric Soc. 678 (2021).

[20] *Id.*

[21] *Id.*

[22] David J. Lowsky et al., *Heterogeneity in Healthy Aging*, 69 J. Gerontology Series A. Bio. Sci. & Med. Sci. 607 (2014).

[23] Ctrs. for Disease Control, *Vital Statistics Rapid Release, Provisional Life Expectancy Estimate for January through June 2020* (2021), https://www.cdc.gov/nchs/data/nvsr/nvsr69/nvsr69-12-508.pdf.

[24] Ctrs. for Disease Control, *National Vital Statistics Reports, United States Life Tables, 2018* (2020), https://www.cdc.gov/nchs/data/nvsr/nvsr69/nvsr69-12-508.pdf.

The likelihood of reaching very old age also varies substantially by socioeconomic status. In fact, in the US, educational attainment level is one of the strongest predictors of adults' health and mortality. Notably, the gap in life expectancy by socioeconomic status is widening in many parts of the country. A recent study of disparities in mortality found that the gap between those with higher levels of education and those with lower levels of education has widened in many states (especially those in the South and Midwest) since the mid 1980s.[25]

Even if all Americans had an equal chance of surviving to very old age, however, the rise of the 100-year life would create new equity concerns about policies that disproportionately allocate resources to the very old. This is because such policies may create an inequity from a lifespan perspective. When compared with younger adults, older adults appear vulnerable. However, when compared to others of their own birth cohort, older adults are resilient – they are the survivors and privileged relative to others born at the same time who did not live to old age. Thus, policies that target older adults for special assistance may further entrench inequities by reducing the overall share of resources spent on groups that disproportionately die at younger ages (a group disproportionately composed of those with lower educational attainment, the poor, individuals with disabilities, and Black Americans).

In short, the effect of differences in life expectancy means that the use of age-based classifications is likely to increasingly result in an inequitable distribution of resources. As gaps in longevity increasingly accrue to some socioeconomic groups and not others, policies that differentiate among adults based on chronological age will increasingly serve to compound disadvantage or advantage.

Radical reconsideration of age-based criteria may have some advantages for older adults. Age-based classifications are typically thought of as benign with regard to older adults. Yet, this is increasingly untrue as states adopt legislation that – in the name of protecting older adults from abuse and exploitation – selectively burdens the rights of older adults.[26]

Moreover, reconsideration may benefit older adults even when it involves reconsidering policies that in fact provide for a preferential treatment of older adults. Chronological age criteria that are used to establish eligibility for benefits or to set legal duties, but which are not highly correlated with need or do not reflect meaningful differences in capabilities, may perpetuate stereotypes about age. This in turn can fuel ageism (i.e., stereotyping and discrimination based on age). Policies that provide special benefits to older adults or try to limit or punish certain types of arrangements if they involve older adults (e.g., certain types of sexual relationships or financial transactions) may promote stereotypes about older adults as helpless, frail,

[25] Jennifer Karas Montez et al., *Education Disparities in Adult Mortality across U.S. States: How Do They Differ, and Have They Changed since the Mid-1980s?* 56 Demography 621 (2019).

[26] For further discussion of this phenomenon, *see* Kohn, *supra* note 6 and Kohn, *supra* note 9.

or unable to make decisions. Such ageist stereotypes are not merely distasteful; they may increase risk of elder abuse. Although the empirical evidence of the link between ageism and elder abuse is still emerging and more is needed to show that ageism in fact causes elder abuse, there is some suggestive evidence that points to a likely causal connection.[27] As Edman Palmore has argued, "stereotypes of the old as helpless, worthless, and repulsive" may promote elder abuse by encouraging "people to vent their frustrations on elders or to see them as vulnerable targets for exploitation."[28]

A move away from age-based criteria has precedent. It would be, for example, consistent with a shift in the law's approach to court-appointed guardians and conservators. Historically US states have authorized the appointment of a guardian or conservator to make decisions for people whom a court determined had a particular status, such as old age and a disability associated with old age, or a particular medical diagnosis. Influenced by the Uniform Probate Code's alternative approach, states have largely moved away from such status and age-based criteria. Today most states only permit the appointment of a guardian or conservator – and the corresponding removal of rights from the person for whom one is appointed – if a court finds that individual has functional limitations that result in a need for such an arrangement.

8.4 AN ALTERNATIVE FRAMEWORK

A reconsideration of age-based classifications should lead to a move away from using chronological age as a proxy for other ascertainable characteristics – such as disability, health status, or financial insecurity – in favor of more direct approaches. In a world where chronological age is likely to be an increasingly poor indicator of functional ability or need, and where socioeconomic gaps in life expectancy are substantial, it will be increasingly indefensible to use chronological age to differentiate among adults.

Chronological age should not be seen as a reasonable criterion for targeting public policy interventions simply because it is convenient or perceived to be a proxy for need, health status, or vulnerability. Instead, polities should seek to find alternative targeting mechanisms. To do so, polities should consider the growing literature on how "vulnerability" can be a basis for the allocation of resources. This school of thought builds on Martha Fineman's "vulnerability theory," which proposes that vulnerability is inherent to the human condition, and that governments therefore have a duty to respond by ensuring that all people have equal access to

[27] Karl Pillemer, David Burnes & Andie MacNeil, *Investigating the Connection between Ageism and Elder Mistreatment*, Nature Aging 159 (2021).

[28] *See* Erdman B. Palmore, Ageism: Negative & Positive 138 (1999).

societal institutions that distribute resources.[29] The approach has captured the imagination of some elder law scholars already.[30] For example, in the context of old-age policy, Swedish scholars Titti Mattsson and Lottie Giertz look to Fineman to argue that states should move away from allocating social services based on group-based identities like age or diagnosis; instead, they propose, the state should focus on vulnerability – which they describe as allowing for more individualistic interventions.[31]

The vulnerability approach is a promising alternative to group identity (e.g., race, gender, poverty) as a basis for targeting social welfare policy. However, as I have discussed at length elsewhere,[32] policies cannot respond to vulnerability merely as a universal characteristic of human beings. Thus, using a vulnerability approach to target policy interventions requires a contextual approach that defines vulnerability relative to the threat being addressed and targets people based on their vulnerability to a specific problem. This would be consistent with a conceptualization of vulnerability being a product of the relationship between individuals and their environment.

By way of example, imagine a state wished to address the problem of financial exploitation. Adopting a vulnerability approach would suggest that states should resist the urge to create age-specific crimes (like "elder abuse" or "exploitation of an elderly adult"). Instead, the state should identify factors that make people susceptible to such exploitation or its impacts and allocate resources with a view to supporting conditions that increase resilience to financial exploitation. Thus, states might support interventions that target conditions associated with the risk of exploitation, such as social isolation, lack of long-term care supports, limited financial literacy, and lack of access to civil legal services for those who experience exploitation.

While vulnerability will increasingly be a superior basis for distributing resources, it would be a mistake to demand an end to all age-based classifications. Even with demographic shifts, polities could reasonably use age-based criteria where their underlying policy goal is specifically related to chronological age. A polity could decide – as a matter of public policy – that it considers age to be an appropriate and ethical basis for allocating resources (e.g., health care, basic income) or assigning duties (e.g., participation in compulsory education). Similarly, a polity might reasonably choose to allocate resources in a way that explicitly favors older adults to express appreciation for older adults or reward them for the contributions they made

29 Martha A. Fineman, *The Vulnerable Subject: Anchoring Equality in the Human Condition*, 20 Yale J.L. & Feminism 1, 9–15 (2008) (originating the theory).

30 *See*, e.g., Alexander A. Boni-Saenz, *Age, Equality, & Vulnerability*, 21 Theoretical Inquiries L. 161 (2019).

31 Titti Mattsson & Lottie Giertz, *Vulnerability, Law, and Dementia: An Interdisciplinary Discussion of Legislation and Practice*, 21 Theoretical Inquiries L. 139 (2020).

32 Nina A. Kohn, *Vulnerability Theory and the Role of Government*, 26 Yale J.L. & Feminism 1 (2014).

during their lifetimes. There are times where policymakers may wish to use age-based legal classifications not as a proxy for other characteristics but because policymakers think chronological age itself matters. For example, schemes that provide pension payments to older adults (such as the US Old Age Survivor's and Disability Insurance program – commonly referred to as Social Security) may also function as a way for society to express appreciation for older adults or reward them for the contributions they made during their lifetimes. Favoring older adults for public benefits may compensate for disadvantages associated with older age. And the prospect of future benefits may help all people by reducing the fear of aging.

Likewise, increased longevity does not call into question distinctions between minors and adults. It remains reasonable for polities to continue to distinguish between adults and minors in a host of situations. Among children, chronological age remains a reasonably robust proxy for the stage of development. Moreover, a polity will frequently have compelling justifications for treating children differently from adults. For example, it might reasonably decide to provide public education to children but not adults on the grounds that children can make best use of that resource because of their development stage or because they will (on average) have more years of life to benefit from that public investment.

In addition, whether abandoning age-based criteria will actually further efficiency and equity depends on politics. Efforts to replace age-based eligibility criteria in critical social safety net programs, such as Social Security and Medicare, risk unleashing political forces that would dismantle the programs.

Thus, those seeking to replace age-based classifications with targeting based on vulnerability will need to be mindful of the potential political consequences of their actions, as well as the additional administrative costs associated with the use of what are likely to be more complex classification systems. But in a world where age-based classifications are becoming more inefficient and inequitable, the benefits of abandoning age-based classifications will likely increasingly outweigh the costs.

8.5 CONCLUSION

This chapter has examined how the law should respond to the challenge posed by old age when old age itself is changing. It has suggested that, as life expectancy increases, the use of age-based classifications will become less efficient and more regressive. Accordingly, not only will age-based criteria need to be recalibrated to ensure that scarce resources can be allocated efficiently, but the use of such criteria should be reconsidered altogether. A promising alternative to reliance on age-based criteria is to use a vulnerability-based approach: targeting social welfare interventions to populations based on the population's vulnerability to the particular concern the intervention aims to address. While this approach may lack the alluring convenience of age-based criteria, it has the potential to more equitably and efficiently allocate resources in an aging world.

9

Working to Death

Labor Law and Collective Voice in the 100-Year Life

Kate Andrias

The premise of this volume – that human beings will soon regularly live to be well over 100 years old – seemed quite plausible just a few years ago. But in the time since Linda Gratton and Andrew J. Scott published *The 100-Year Life* in 2016, the unprecedented COVID-19 pandemic ravaged the globe, increased morbidity, and, for a period of time, significantly reduced human lifespans. Even assuming we have emerged from this public health debacle with the 100-year life once again a possibility, the pandemic has exposed the extent to which any promise of extended life is likely to be defined by deep inequities. Working-class people, and workers of color in particular, are the least likely to enjoy extended lifespans. And if they do live longer, they are unlikely to enjoy a leisurely retirement in which they decide how they spend their extra years. Instead, they are likely to face more toil and precarity.

This chapter imagines a different future. It asks: What would the 100-year life look like if working people had a greater hand in shaping it? What would a legal regime look like that gave working people power to affect decisions about how work is structured and how resources are distributed in the era of the 100-year life? How might we reimagine labor law for a more just and equitable 100-year life?

9.1 WORKING TO DEATH

For many Americans, work is characterized by low wages, long hours, little autonomy, and deep precarity. The pandemic also made work life-threatening. While highly paid professionals retreated to computer screens and home offices, low-wage service workers risked their lives, with few rewards. Those who were in unions were able to negotiate greater protective equipment, safety precautions, hazard pay, and leaves of absence for individuals most at risk. Yet the vast majority of US workers lacked such collective representation. And the vast majority were employed at will, subject to dismissal for any reason or no reason at all (save legally proscribed reasons like discrimination). Against this background, most workers were fearful of reporting violations of workplace safety and health standards that put them, their coworkers, and their communities at risk of infection.[1] Indeed, when workers requested protective equipment like masks and gloves, some employers retaliated, even barring workers from speaking out about weak COVID-19 workplace safety standards.[2] For older workers, for whom the risks of COVID-19 were vastly increased, the lack of a collective organization and resulting lack of power to negotiate were particularly consequential. Some quit their jobs; others risked their lives. Racial inequities intertwined with these class and age inequities: Working-class Black and Latino males faced the largest decrease in life expectancy as a result of the pandemic, while workers of color were hit the hardest by rising unemployment. These dynamics meant that millions of workers, already on the brink, faced eviction, food shortages, and mental health crises.[3]

Even after the pandemic began to subside, age, gender, and racial inequalities in the labor market persisted. As the job market recovered, older workers had more difficulty reentering the labor market than their younger counterparts; women, too, failed to reenter the job market at the same rate as similarly educated men.[4] The pandemic highlighted and increased the amount of care work that people, particularly women, performed without compensation or acknowledgment. And although the unemployment rate for people of color bounced back to prepandemic levels, the racial unemployment and wage gaps remained "high and widespread."[5]

In short, the pandemic and its aftermath left little doubt that, if our political economy remains unchanged, the 100-year life, if not elusive, will bring only more years of arduous work for the vast majority of workers, particularly low-income workers, workers of color, and women workers.

1 *See* Kate Andrias & Alexander Hertel-Fernandez, *Ending At-Will Employment: A Guide for Just Cause Reform*, Roosevelt Institute (Jan. 19, 2021), https://rooseveltinstitute.org/publications/ending-at-will-employment-a-guide-for-just-cause-reform/.

2 Josh Eidelson, *COVID Gag Rules at U.S. Companies Are Putting Everyone at Risk*, Bloomberg (Aug. 27, 2020), https://www.bloomberg.com/news/features/2020-08-27/covid-pandemic-u-s-businesses-issue-gag-rules-to-stop-workers-from-talking.

3 Center on Budget and Policy Priorities, *Tracking the COVID-19 Economy's Effects on Food, Housing, and Employment Hardships* (2021), https://www.cbpp.org/research/poverty-and-inequality/tracking-the-covid-19-recessions-effects-on-food-housing-and.

4 Richard B. Freeman, *Planning for the "Expected Unexpected:" Work and Retirement in the United States after the COVID-19 Pandemic Shock*, *in* Overtime: America's Aging Workforce and the Future of Working Longer 91, 100 (Lisa F. Berkman & Beth C. Truesdale eds., 2022); Richard Fry, *Some Gender Disparities Widened in the U.S. Workforce during the Pandemic*, Pew Rsch. Ctr. (Jan. 14, 2022), https://www.pewresearch.org/fact-tank/2022/01/14/some-gender-disparities-widened-in-the-u-s-workforce-during-the-pandemic/.

5 Christian Weller, *A Hot Labor Market Is Not Enough for Racial Equality*, Forbes (Sep. 12, 2022), https://www.forbes.com/sites/christianweller/2022/09/12/a-hot-labor-market-is-not-enough-for-racial-equality/.

9.2 THE NEED FOR WORKER POWER

How, then, to think about reforming workplace law in the event of the 100-year life? Two other chapters in this volume focus on employment law. Professor Kenji Yoshino considers the pressing problem of how the law can effectively protect against age discrimination in an era in which workers live longer. He argues for unmooring the age discrimination paradigm from the traditional civil rights model, and for the law to take into account the distinctive fears that older individuals conjure about their own mortality. Professor Cynthia Estlund's chapter tackles a related problem: ensuring workers' retirement security over the course of longer lifespans – a problem made more challenging by the fact that most workers already lack adequate pensions and retirement savings. Estlund concludes that it will be necessary to extend work in order to approach a sustainable ratio of workers to retirees, and of work years to retirement years. She also considers how to address the problems of intergenerational competition and integration at work in a world with transformative new technologies and longer lifespans. Noting that a longer life could increase employers' tendency to dismiss or refuse to hire aging workers, she renews calls not only to strengthen antidiscrimination protections but also to limit American law's adherence to employment at will. In an earlier work, Professor Anne Alstott argued for enhancing and revising the Social Security program and delinking benefits from paid work to increase portability and part-time feasibility.[6]

Alstott, Estlund, and Yoshino are all correct that finding new ways to fund retirement, delinking social benefits from employment, rethinking age discrimination law, and protecting workers from unjust termination are all critical policy reforms in an era of extended lifespans. But those reforms are unlikely to be achieved or sustained in ways that address the fundamental inequities that will characterize work in the 100-year life without also addressing the problem of collective voice among workers. That is, if workers are to enjoy longer lifespans and a more dignified and remunerated work life during their expanding lifespans, the law must also include a framework that gives them greater *power* over decisions about the shape of work and the political economy.

9.3 THE DECLINE OF UNIONS – AND THE FAILURE OF US LABOR LAW

In the aftermath of the New Deal and World War II, more than a third of US employees belonged to unions. With workers able to exercise collective power in the workplace, the economy, and the halls of government, inequality was at an all-time low. Labor unions not only fought for higher wages and better working conditions but also backed early state efforts to establish social insurance programs, lobbied for a

[6] Anne Alstott, *Law and the Hundred-Year Life*, 26 ELDER L.J. 132, 142–144 (2018).

comprehensive federal retirement bill, and supported the eventual Social Security Act of 1935.[7] Social Security, in particular, proved to be a crucially important program, lifting millions of seniors out of poverty.

But the goal of an enduring collective voice for working-class people in the US was not achieved. From the outset, at the insistence of southern legislators, millions of workers, primarily African Americans, were explicitly excluded from labor law – as domestic workers and agricultural workers – or worked in sectors and regions of the country that were, in practice, largely unorganized. And unions soon came under significant attack. The 1947 Taft-Hartley Act curtailed numerous labor rights and excluded yet more workers from coverage. Moreover, although the left-leaning industrial unions in the 1930s and 1940s pushed for a social democratic system of universal health care and other social benefits delinked from employment, by the 1950s they had lost this fight. Retirement benefits, as well as health insurance, became closely tied to employment, and unions themselves became more bureaucratic and inward-facing.[8]

By the 1970s, US companies had adopted a position of intense resistance to unions: They globalized and fissured their employment relationships, eliminating union jobs while ramping up their antiunion practices against new organizing efforts. Meanwhile, the Supreme Court interpreted the National Labor Relations Act (NLRA) in ways that limited the ability of workers to bargain and strike in the changing economy.[9] Union membership declined precipitously. Today, while the rate of unionization is on the rise, it stands at about 6 percent among workers in the private sector and only about 10 percent among workers overall.[10]

Economic inequality is now at its highest point since the Gilded Age, when unionization rates were similarly low.[11] And as workers have lost economic power, they have also lost political power. Wealthy individuals and corporations spend vast sums to influence elections and legislative and administrative processes, while workers have largely lost their collective organizations that enable them to engage effectively in politics. Not surprisingly, studies suggest that elected officials are almost entirely unresponsive to the concerns of the poor and working class – at least when their preferences diverge from those of the wealthy.[12]

[7] David Montgomery, *Labor and the Political Leadership of New Deal America*, 39 Int'l Rev. Soc. Hist. 335, 347–349 (1994).

[8] Nelson Lichtenstein, *From Corporatism to Collective Bargaining: Organized Labor and the Eclipse of Social Democracy in the Postwar Era, in* The Rise and Fall of the New Deal Order, 1930–1980 122 (Steve Fraser & Gary Gerstle eds., 1989).

[9] *See, e.g.*, Kate Andrias, *The New Labor Law*, 126 Yale L.J. 2, 25–27 (2016).

[10] Bureau of Labor and Statistics, *Press Release: Union Members – 2024* (Jan. 28, 2025), https://www.bls.gov/news.release/pdf/union2.pdf.

[11] Thomas Piketty, Capital in the Twenty-First Century 31 (2014).

[12] *See, e.g.*, Larry M. Bartels, Unequal Democracy: The Political Economy of the New Gilded Age 2, 285 (2008); Martin Gilens, Affluence and Influence: Economic Inequality and Political Power in America 73–85 (2012).

Meanwhile, although state and federal employment laws, which proliferated in the 1960s, provide a host of protections to workers as individuals, many rights go unenforced or underenforced. Wage theft, health and safety violations, and sexual harassment are rampant in many workplaces.[13] Individual workers, lacking bargaining power, are frequently forced to sign away their rights to go to court and even to proceed collectively in arbitration.[14] Unlike most advanced industrial democracies, the U.S. does not guarantee workers health insurance; nor do most workers receive compensation for the important labor they perform caring for their children or their elderly relatives. Retirement security is, for many, elusive: Just 15 percent of private sector workers had access to a defined benefit plan in 2020,[15] while Social Security benefit cuts are still being implemented from reforms in 1983.[16]

Meanwhile, millions of the most vulnerable workers, predominantly people of color, remain excluded altogether from both collective labor law and individual employment law as independent contractors, domestic workers, or agricultural laborers. These exclusions are particularly relevant for seniors who are more likely to work as independent contractors than younger workers.[17] And one in five workers in their fifties and early sixties work in jobs that lack health or retirement benefits, making it much harder to prepare for retirement.[18] In fact, seniors often take on these jobs specifically to supplement inadequate retirement savings.[19] And while workers in nontraditional jobs are vulnerable due to these statutory exclusions, the ability to work longer to finance a comfortable retirement is already stratified by income: Higher-income workers tend to retire later than lower-income workers, who are more likely to exit the labor market at a younger age due to health issues, caregiving responsibilities, or job loss.[20]

13 Annette Bernhardt et al., *Broken Laws, Unprotected Workers: Violations of Employment and Labor Laws in America's Cities*, NAT'L EMP. L. PROJECT (2009), https://s27147.pcdn.co/wp-content/uploads/2015/03/BrokenLawsReport2009.pdf.

14 *See* Epic Sys. Corp. v. Lewis, 138 S. Ct. 1612, 1621–1622 (2018); Samuel R. Bagenstos, *Consent, Coercion, and Employment Law*, 55 HARV. C.R.-C.L. L. REV. 409, 414; Alexander J. S. Colvin, *The Growing Use of Mandatory Arbitration*, ECON. POL'Y INST. (Sep. 27, 2017), https://www.epi.org/publication/the-growing-use-of-mandatory-arbitration/.

15 US Bureau of Lab. Stat., 67 *Percent of Private Industry Workers Had Access to Retirement Plans in* 2020 (Mar. 1, 2021), https://www.bls.gov/opub/ted/2021/67-percent-of-private-industry-workers-had-access-to-retirement-plans-in-2020.htm.

16 Eric Kingson & Monique Morrissey, *Can Workers Offset Social Security Cuts by Working Longer?* ECON. POL'Y INST. (May 30, 2012), https://www.epi.org/publication/bp343-social-security-retirement-age/.

17 Katharine G. Abraham, Brad Hershbein & Susan N. Houseman, *Contract Work at Older Ages*, 20 J. PENSION ECON. & FIN. 426, 432, 444–446 (2020).

18 Alicia H. Munnell, Geoffrey T. Sanzenbacher & Abigail N. Walters, *How Do Older Workers Use Nontraditional Jobs?* CENTER FOR RETIREMENT RESEARCH: BOSTON COLLEGE (Oct. 4, 2019), https://crr.bc.edu/working-papers/how-do-older-workers-use-nontraditional-jobs/.

19 Caroline Bruckner & Jonathan B. Forman, *Women, Retirement and the Growing Gig Economy Workforce*, 38 GA. ST. U. L. REV. 259, 265 (2022).

20 Jacob S. Hacker & Paul Pierson, *The Biased Politics of "Working Longer,"* in OVERTIME: AMERICA'S AGING WORKFORCE, *supra* note 4, at 276, 280.

On the positive side, a host of recent organizing efforts among workers, from Amazon warehouse workers to healthcare workers, from Uber and Lyft drivers to journalists, have drawn attention to these problems. These workers seek tangible improvements in their jobs; they also seek basic dignity at work. As one Amazon worker involved in a unionization campaign observed, "You're running at a consistent, fast pace … You ain't got time to look around. You get treated like a number. You don't get treated like a person. They work you like a robot."[21]

Meanwhile, seniors have remained organized and politically engaged on issues related to retirement. Notwithstanding the national decline in membership in unions and other civic organizations, the AARP – an organization devoted to organizing and advocating for retirees – maintains a membership of nearly 40 million. The AARP has played a key role in opposing various efforts to erode retirement benefits. For example, in 2021, the AARP lobbied against the TRUST Act, which would empower congressional "rescue committees" to make changes to Social Security and Medicare. While Republican legislators have recently floated both the idea of "sunsetting" the Social Security Act and a federal budget plan that would cut benefits, AARP's political power suggests that these efforts will not go very far.

Though the problems that workers will confront in any future 100-year life are palpable and the interest in organizing to solve such problems is significant, the existing legal frameworks are of little utility. About 70 percent of Americans approve of unions, yet obstacles to achieving unionization among workers even in the traditional labor force are substantial.[22] The law permits employers to engage in a wide range of efforts to persuade workers not to organize while excluding union organizers from the workplace. Moreover, when employers resort to illegal tactics such as threatening or firing workers for organizing, they incur virtually no penalties. Meanwhile, the law does not only exclude independent contractors, agricultural, and domestic workers, but it altogether lacks a framework for retirees and unemployed workers to organize into unions or for unions to bargain to address many problems facing retirees. That is, the law mandates only that employers negotiate with unionized employees about wages, benefits, and working conditions at a single workplace. It does not set up a system for sectorwide bargaining in order to raise wages and benefits throughout the industry, nor does it create a system for bargaining about broader social programs.

[21] Steven Greenhouse, *"We Deserve More:" An Amazon Warehouse's High-Stakes Union Drive*, GUARDIAN (Feb. 23, 2021), https://www.theguardian.com/technology/2021/feb/23/amazon-bessemer-alabama-union.

[22] Justin McCarthy, *U.S. Approval of Labor Unions at Highest Point since 1965*, GALLUP (Aug. 30, 2022), https://news.gallup.com/poll/398303/approval-labor-unions-highest-point-1965.aspx. On obstacles to organizing *see*, e.g., Andrias, *supra* note 9, at 44; Paul Weiler, *Striking a New Balance: Freedom of Contract and the Prospects for Union Representation*, 98 HARV. L. REV. 351, 362–363 (1984).

One proposed legislative reform – the Protecting the Right to Organize (PRO) Act – would better protect traditional workers in the process of organizing, bargaining, and striking, including by increasing penalties when employers attempt to coerce or retaliate against employees for unionizing.[23] The PRO Act would also extend employee status to many workers now classified as independent contractors, like gig workers, FedEx drivers, and many more. These reforms could prove extremely helpful in enabling workers to exercise more voice at work.

However, even with these important reforms, US labor and employment law would not be well designed to give workers a voice in how to structure work and the broader political economy during the 100-year life. This is because even the improved law would lack a framework for retirees and unemployed workers to organize (while still excluding domestic and agricultural workers), and it would lack a system for sectoral or social bargaining. That is, even if the PRO Act passed, US labor law would continue to channel organizing and bargaining to individual worksites, between traditional employees and single firms, without giving worker organizations power to negotiate sectoral standards or broader social benefits. Yet, in a world in which employees, over the course of a lifetime, work for many different firms, move in and out of the workforce over a longer lifespan, spend more years working a reduced load as they age, or spend more years in retirement or caregiving, a labor law system organized solely around worksite-by-worksite bargaining for private benefits makes little sense.

9.4 ALTERNATIVE APPROACHES TO WORKER VOICE AND POWER

The US approach sharply differs from many European systems that are better positioned to enable worker voice over the course of an extended lifespan, though their systems too face significant limitations. For example, in Germany, the union federations participate in basic decisions concerning national wage policy and policies relating to employment, economic growth, and social insurance.[24] Meanwhile, collective bargaining occurs on a regional basis to set wage scales that cover all workers, at least in manufacturing sectors; those agreements then provide a floor above which local bargaining may occur.[25] Many German workers also have a voice at their worksite through statutorily guaranteed works councils.[26] Such works

[23] Protecting the Right to Organize Act of 2021, H.R. 842, 117th Cong. (2021).

[24] *See* Clyde W. Summers, *Worker Participation in the U.S. and West Germany: A Comparative Study from an American Perspective*, 28 Am. J. Compar. L. 367, 385–388 (1980); Steven J. Silvia, Holding the Shop Together: German Industrial Relations in the Postwar Era 38–41 (2013).

[25] Kathleen Thelen, Varieties of Liberalization and the New Politics of Social Solidarity 58 (2014).

[26] Michael Oberfinchtner & Claus Schnabel, *The German Model of Industrial Relations: (Where) Does It Still Exist?* 239 J. Econ. & Stat. 5, 10, 21 (2019). (While workers at companies

councils are granted codetermination rights on topics such as health and safety and working hours.[27] They also are entitled to information and consultation rights on topics such as the introduction of new work methods and technologies – an especially important right in a time of rapid technological change. Additionally, workers at large companies have an automatic voice through representation on corporate boards.[28]

In Denmark, unions have played an even more active role in negotiating social policy. Unions and employers have, for example, collectively negotiated national policies on worker training and parental leave. Moreover, union bargaining in Denmark often builds on statutory entitlements. For example, while older workers and workers with disabilities had statutory protections against age discrimination, social partners expanded these protections through collective bargaining such that workers now have the right to be placed in "light jobs" if they are unable to perform their positions.[29]

And in Norway, unions, employers, and the state have joined together to bargain for policies that improve working conditions so that older workers can remain in the workplace.[30] This bargaining produced the Inclusive Workplace Agreement, which aims to reduce the use of sick and disability leave, extend workers' working lives, and recruit more workers with disabilities and other vulnerable groups.[31] The social partners also serve on the board of the government-funded Centre for Senior Policy, which performs research regarding senior workers and works with companies to improve their policies.[32]

In France, the political organization of unions enables them to mobilize on issues regarding retirement. For example, in 2023, in response to President Emmanuel Macron's proposal to reform the pension system by raising the legal age of retirement from sixty-two to sixty-four, France's eight largest labor unions coordinated nationwide strikes across multiple sectors, including transportation, education, and energy.

with five or more employees can form works councils, they are predominantly found at larger companies.).

27 Eur. Trade Union Inst., *National Industrial Relations: Germany*, http://www.worker-participation.eu/National-Industrial-Relations/Countries/Germany (accessed Mar. 12, 2021).

28 *Id.*

29 Thelen, *supra* note 25, at 65–67.

30 Toms Feifs et al., *Role of Governments and Social Partners in Keeping Older Workers in the Labour Market*, Eurofound (2013), https://www.eurofound.europa.eu/system/files/2021-05/EF13231EN.pdf.

31 Tore Langeland, *Impact of the More Inclusive Working Life Agreement*, Eurofound (Nov. 13, 2011), https://www.eurofound.europa.eu/publications/article/2011/impact-of-the-more-inclusive-working-life-agreement.

32 Bjorn Halvorsen & Asmund Lunde, *Policy Measures to Support Older Workers in Norway*, Norwegian Ministry of Labour and Social Affairs (2015), https://ec.europa.eu/social/BlobServlet?docId=14785&langId=en.

These systems are by no means perfect. Workers' power in these countries has also declined in the face of globalization and neoliberalism.[33] However, a viable framework exists to set fair standards for all workers and to enable senior workers and retirees to exercise their collective voice.

The US lacks any comparable framework. To be sure, the law does facilitate workers' political voice in important ways. Section 7 of the NLRA has been interpreted to protect workers' concerted activity that occurs through political channels – even for nonunion workers, as long as such activity relates to employment issues.[34] In addition, unions, like other organizations, may engage in electoral politics and lobby government officials. Many unions spend a great deal of energy and money on political activity, with significant effect. They have helped enact legislation that protects all workers, from the Fair Labor Standards Act and the Occupational Safety and Health Act to the Family and Medical Leave Act and the Affordable Care Act. But US law does little to facilitate a voice for working people in the various decisions that affect senior workers or that will be posed by the putative 100-year life.

9.5 A NEW LABOR LAW FOR THE 100-YEAR LIFE

What might a different system look like, one that builds on the current regime but gives workers – who may soon enjoy longer lifespans and many different stages of work – greater power over decisions about the shape of work and the political economy?

First, as in the industrial democracies discussed earlier, the law should provide for sectoral bargaining so that collective bargaining agreements apply to workers throughout a region or sector, effectively forming the basis for employment policy in those sectors, while at the same time providing for worker voice at the worksite and firm level through works councils, local unions, and corporate board representation.[35] Such a model would enable workers to move between firms more easily over time and limit risks of leaving and entering the workforce. More generally, research suggests that where sectoral bargaining is combined with worksite

33 Todd E. Vachon et al., *Union Decline in a Neoliberal Age: Globalization, Financialization, European Integration, and Union Density in 18 Affluent Democracies*, 2 SOCIUS (July 2016), at 1, 13–14.

34 Eastex, Inc. v. Nat'l Lab. Rels. Bd., 437 U.S. 556, 564 (1978).

35 Kate Andrias & Brishen Rogers, *Rebuilding Worker Voice in Today's Economy*, ROOSEVELT INST. (2018), https://rooseveltinstitute.org/wp-content/uploads/2020/07/RI-Rebuilding-Worker-Voice-201808.pdf; Sharon Block & Benjamin Sachs, *Clean Slate for Worker Power: Building a Just Economy and Democracy*, https://clje.law.harvard.edu/clean-slate-for-worker-power-building-a-just-economy-and-democracy/ (accessed Oct. 1, 2023); Mark Barenberg, *Widening the Scope of Working Organizing*, ROOSEVELT INST. (2015), https://rooseveltinstitute.org/publications/widening-the-scope-of-worker-organizing/.

organization, racial and gender wage gaps decrease and unions can exercise more economic and political power.[36]

Second, the law should also give organizations of workers a formal role in developing social benefits and policies that will be critical for expanding lifespans, for example, through administrative processes at the local, state, and/or federal levels of government.[37] Beyond simply permitting group participation, as notice-and-comment rule-making currently does, the law could give worker organizations a formal seat at the table in negotiating retirement, disability, family leave, and childcare benefits, and, perhaps, eventually job guarantees, basic income, and more.

Third, to make such social bargaining effective for workers at every stage in the 100-year life, the law should encourage or facilitate new forms of worker organizations that encompass a broader range of working-class people, including those unemployed, engaged in paid and unpaid caregiving, and retired.[38] Examples of such nontraditional worker organizations exist within our own system, past and present. For example, following the Great Depression, unemployed workers organized in large numbers.[39] The movement of the unemployed originated in local communities, with protests and marches demanding – and sometimes winning – public relief funding from local and state governments. Members of unemployed worker groups also banded together and entered relief offices demanding immediate relief for individuals denied aid. A national federation called the Workers Alliance was later formed, consisting of most of the large organizations of unemployed workers. This federation prioritized lobbying for national relief programs over direct action in localities; ultimately, it was unable to win passage of its prioritized legislation for expanded direct relief, higher pay on federal Works Progress Administration projects, and a permanent public works program, and its local organizing diminished as well. Still it provided an important voice for unemployed workers through a critical period.

Welfare organizing of the 1960s provides another example of a nontraditional working-class organizing effort. During this period, welfare recipients, the majority of them Black women, began to organize to change local welfare policies, overturn

36 *See*, e.g., Jonas Pontusson & David Rueda, *Comparative Political Economy of Wage Distribution: The Role of Partisanship and Labour Market Institutions*, 32 British J. Pol. Sci. 381, 289–290, 301 (2002); Andrias, *supra* note 9, at 94; Guy Mundlak, *We Create Spots from Which We Shine to Others*, 38 Compar. Lab. L & Pol'y J. 301 (2017).

37 For existing and historical examples of such administrative initiatives, *see* Kate Andrias, *An American Approach to Social Democracy: The Forgotten Promise of the Fair Labor Standards Act*, 128 Yale L.J. 616 (2019); K. Sabeel Rahman, *Policymaking as Power-Building*, 27 S. Cal. Interdisc. L.J. 315, 340–350 (2017).

38 Kate Andrias & Benjamin I. Sachs, *Constructing Countervailing Power: Law and Organizing in an Era of Political Inequality*, 130 Yale L.J. 546 (2021).

39 Frances Fox Piven & Richard A. Cloward, Poor People's Movements: Why They Succeed and How They Fail 41, 50–60, 68–91 (1978).

benefit denials for members, and win special grants for welfare recipients to cover household furnishings and clothing.[40]

Numerous examples of organizations engaging workers in nontraditional employment exist in the contemporary landscape. For example, home-care organizing has engaged hundreds of thousands of low-wage, formerly isolated workers in collective organization, even without the existence of a central worksite or single employer, helping raise wages and improve funding for caregiving.[41] The Freelancers Union represents independent workers, offering insurance benefits and other resources to various types of freelancers and advocating for legislative protections on their behalf. The Domestic Workers Alliance has succeeded in winning domestic workers' bills of rights in numerous states; the bills provide employment protections such as paid time off and overtime rights. Many Hollywood writers work independently, but through their membership in the Writers Guild of America, they are guaranteed minimum pay levels, residuals, and retirement and health coverage. And community-based worker centers across the nation have organized to combat wage theft, co-enforce workplace protections with state and local governments, and advocate for increased pay and protections.

In a different vein, several organizations already organize retirees. AARP provides individual benefits to members and advocates on behalf of older and retired Americans. The Alliance for Retired Americans is sponsored by unions and aims to mobilize retired union members, seniors, and community activists to advocate for various political causes such as Social Security expansion and reducing prescription drug prices. Several unions also have their own retiree chapters and organizations.

More examples exist abroad. As Professor Katherine Stone has detailed, Japan has seen an explosion of nontraditional forms of labor organizations: City unions have pressured employers in an entire metropolitan area around work-related concerns; women's unions have organized to further the interests of women workers; and ethnically specific unions have asserted pressure on behalf of ethnic groups.[42] In Europe's most progressive social democracies, not only are traditional unions engaged in defining social programs that benefit all workers, but nontraditional worker and retiree organizations exist as well, working to advance policy concerning issues such as social security, pensions, and health treatment among retirees.[43]

40 Premilla Nadasen, *Expanding the Boundaries of the Women's Movement: Black Feminism and the Struggle for Welfare Rights*, 28 Feminist Stud. 271, 275–277 (2002); Piven & Cloward, *supra* note 39, 286–287, 297–300.

41 For a history of care worker organizing, *see generally* Eileen Boris & Jennifer Klein, Caring for America: Home Health Workers in the Shadow of the Welfare State (2015).

42 Katherine Van Wezel Stone, *Green Shoots in the Labor Market: A Cornucopia of Social Experiments*, 36 Compar. Lab. L. & Pol'y J. 293, 319–320 (2015).

43 Ferpa, *The History of Ferpa*, https://ferpa.org/history-of-ferpa/ (accessed Mar. 5, 2021); *see also* Eurofound, *Retirement*, https://www.eurofound.europa.eu/topic/retirement (accessed Mar. 5, 2021); AGE, *About AGE*, https://www.age-platform.eu/about-age (accessed Mar. 5, 2020).

These kinds of nontraditional but democratic organizations can be nurtured and expanded with supportive legal frameworks.[44] For example, law can facilitate the growth of organizations by enabling the aggregation of resources, by allowing access to workers, information, and free spaces to organize, and by effectively protecting workers from retaliation for organizing and engaging in concerted action. In addition, by granting organizations a role in negotiating social benefits in administrative processes, as discussed earlier, the law can give the organizations greater legitimacy, aiding their organizing efforts. Government programs can also partner with democratic membership organizations that represent underrepresented constituencies, giving them grants to provide and administer benefits. For example, under the Ghent system, unions operate unemployment insurance funds and provide benefits to unemployed workers.[45] US policymakers could extend this model to provide portable benefits, training, and increased workplace enforcement to workers across the span of the 100-year life.[46]

9.6 CONCLUSION

As Anne Alstott has written, the predicted "leap in longevity is likely to challenge many of our expectations about work" and could "revolutionize" many of our relationships.[47] But without a fundamental change in the way work is organized, the leap in longevity will also augment and extend existing power dynamics that define the lives of many workers in America, making inequalities and indignities even more acute. To avoid that result, workers – of all kinds and backgrounds – must have a voice in the decisions about what work looks like over the course of the 100-year life.

Of course, one might worry that the reforms suggested above are fanciful or impossible to achieve. Indeed, past experience highlights the difficulty of labor law reform, even in times of unified democratic control of government.[48] Yet the obstacles have been overcome in the past and can be overcome again.[49] COVID-19 made the economic plight of poor and working-class Americans politically salient, as illustrated by the massive, redistributive economic stimulus enacted in March of 2021 and subsequent legislation like the Infrastructure Investment and Jobs Act of

[44] *See* Andrias & Sachs, *supra* note 38, at 555.

[45] Matthew Dimick, *Labor Law, New Governance, and the Ghent System*, 90 N.C. L. REV. 319, 329–336 (2012); Jochen Clasen & Elke Viebrock, *Voluntary Unemployment Insurance and Trade Union Membership*, 37 J. SOC. POL'Y 433, 437–438 (2008).

[46] David Madland & Malkie Wall, *American Ghent: Designing Programs to Strengthen Unions and Improve Government Services*, CTR. FOR AM. PROGRESS (2019), https://www.americanprogress.org/issues/economy/reports/2019/09/18/474690/american-ghent/.

[47] Alstott, *supra* note 6, at 147, 148.

[48] Cynthia L. Estlund, *The Ossification of American Labor Law*, 102 COLUM. L. REV. 1527, 1530–1531 (2002).

[49] *See* Andrias & Sachs, *supra* note 38, at 631–637.

2021 and the Inflation Reduction Act of 2022. The resurgence of organizing among workers, tenants, and debtors that has occurred in the wake of the pandemic has only increased this salience. Meanwhile, the federal structure of our government creates openings for legislative change at the state and local levels, even when federal change is impossible. Ultimately, even if the more ambitious reforms discussed earlier are not possible in the near term, incremental, achievable reforms can get us closer to a world in which workers are not working to death but rather have a collective voice in the 100-year life.

10

The Savings Mirage

Sara Sternberg Greene

Walk into any bookstore's self-help section and you will find a wall of books that were written with one goal: to help Americans figure out how to save money. Saving money is widely considered the cornerstone of how to have a successful life and, perhaps most of all, a relaxing and successful retirement. The titles say it all: "Saving for Retirement Made Easy,"[1] "Winning at Retirement,"[2] "How to Retire Debt-Free & Wealthy,"[3] and so on. The message is clear: It is possible to retire with abundant savings – you just have to learn more and be strategic.

The reality, however, is that retirement savings are an insurmountable aspiration for many Americans, particularly low-wage workers. Indeed, almost one in four Americans has less than $400 in savings.[4] One-third of Black households have zero or negative net worth.[5] But much like the self-help books in the corner of the bookstore, the government's response to this overall lack of savings has been to emphasize the need for individuals to save.[6] Policy initiatives have focused primarily on consumer financial education and nudging people in the "right" direction.

Yet, despite the emphasis on saving for retirement, as Anne Alstott and others have discussed in depth, elderly Americans whose incomes are at the low end of the

[1] Guillermo Bermudez, Saving for Retirement Made Easy (2020).

[2] Patrick Foley & Kristin Hillsley, Winning at Retirement: A Guide to Health, Wealth & Purpose in the Best Years of Your Life (2018).

[3] Christine Ibbotson, How to Retire Debt-Free and Wealthy: A Finance Coach Reveals the Secrets, Tips, and Techniques of How Clients Become Millionaires (2020).

[4] *See*, e.g., Alicia Lloro et al., *Economic Well-Being of U.S. Households in 2022*, Bd. of Governors of the Fed. Reserve Sys. (2023), at 31, https://www.federalreserve.gov/publications/files/2022-report-economic-well-being-us-households-202305.pdf.

[5] Economic Policy Institute, *The State of Working America*, http://www.stateofworkingamerica.org/index.html%3Fp=4173.html. Among Black families with children, 57.5 percent are net-worth-poor. *See* Christina Gibson-Davis, Lisa A. Keister & Lisa A. Gennetian, *Net Worth Poverty in Child Households by Race and Ethnicity, 1989–2019*, J. Marriage & Fam. 1, 1 (2020).

[6] Pamela Foohey & Sara S. Greene, *How Government Rules Prevent Poor Americans from Saving*, Politico (Sep. 3, 2020), https://www.politico.com/news/agenda/2020/09/03/how-government-keeps-poor-from-saving-407839.

income distribution are increasingly worse off than their higher-income counterparts.[7] They enter old age with little or no savings, medical problems without adequate coverage, a necessity to work in order to eat and have a place to live, and, unsurprisingly, increasing rates of bankruptcy filings.[8]

In the past, retirement years were limited in duration for most Americans, as a brief jaunt of post-work life was soon met with death.[9] Indeed, between 1650 and 1850, elderly Americans were less than 2 percent of the population.[10] Yet, as life expectancies have increased,[11] we are faced with the prospect of elderly Americans living in poverty for decades on end. In other words, in the past the problem of no savings, and thus elderly poverty, was simply less of a problem since Americans, on average, spent fewer years in retirement. This, in turn, meant the financial struggle of the retirement years would also be relatively short. But with the 100-year life becoming a reality for more Americans, an elderly poverty crisis looms.[12]

In this chapter, I unpack the contradiction in the message embedded in our cultural narrative about the moral worth of self-sufficiency and savings against the backdrop of the realities of our existing poverty laws. I show how this is a central and unresolved incongruity in US policy toward the poor and near poor. The government does not provide a solid financial foundation for older Americans who were making poverty- and near-poverty-level wages during their preretirement years, yet the government also does not allow those making low wages (low enough to not even provide for basic necessities such as housing, food, and clothing despite full-time work) to build a nest-egg for retirement. This antisavings policy – enforced through asset limitations for basic safety net programs such as the Supplement Nutrition Assistance Program (SNAP, commonly referred to as "food stamps"), Temporary Assistance for Needy Families (TANF, commonly referred to as "cash welfare"), and Social Security Disability Insurance (SSDI, commonly referred to as "disability") – essentially guarantees that those who are poor will continue to be poor

7 Anne L. Alstott, A New Deal for Old Age 1–2 (2016); Anne Alstott, *Law and the Hundred-Year Life*, 26 Elder L. J. 131, 137–138 (2018). *See also* Deborah Thorne, Pamela Foohey, Robert M. Lawless & Katherine M. Porter, *Graying of U.S. Bankruptcy: Fallout from Life in a Risk Society*, 90 Soc. Inquiry 681, 684–685 (2020).

8 Thorne et al., *supra* note 7, at 685.

9 Alstott, A New Deal, *supra* note 7, at 18, 20; Alstott, *Law and the Hundred-Year Life*, *supra* note 7 at 131, 132; Lynda Gratton & Andrew Scott, The 100-Year Life 1 (2016).

10 Kevin C. Fleming, Jonathan M. Evans & Darryl S. Chutka, *A Cultural and Economic History of Old Age in America*, 78 Mayo Clin. Proc. 914, 914 (2003).

11 Gratton & Scott, *supra* note 9, at 1–4.

12 Anne Alstott provides a fascinating and important discussion of inequality in longevity. People who are poor have significantly lower life expectancies than those who are rich. Thus, there is no doubt that it will take longer for those who are poor to reach the 100-year life benchmark than those who are rich. Nonetheless, the upward trend in longevity holds for all groups. Alstott, A New Deal, *supra* note 7, at 20–21.

and without savings throughout their extended old age.[13] Therein lies the savings mirage.

I argue that as a society we have to get our story straight. Are we committed to a country in which we require people to save for themselves in order to avoid an old age of hunger and financial instability? If so, we need to implement policies that make it easier to save, not only for those who are middle or upper class but also for those who are low-income throughout their working years. On the other hand, if we are committed to restricting the savings of low-income workers because of our devotion to the notion that public benefits should only go to those who have otherwise stripped themselves of savings, then we need to develop a plan to provide in retirement for those who struggled through their working years, unable to save in part because of strict government policy. But we can't have it both ways. If we continue with the crash course we are on, an elderly poverty epidemic is bound to emerge. New safety net policies show some promise, but this central contradiction in message and policy needs to be recognized in order to promote substantial policy change.

10.1 A SAVINGS SOCIETY

The history of responsibility for the elderly in the US is an evolving one. Life was short in the mid 1800s, with the life expectancy of most white Americans only thirty-nine years.[14] But those who did live into old age and were poor were usually out of luck. The elderly were generally considered a "burden on the local taxes," and many were either sent to poorhouses, which were "dreary, vermin-infested, and laden with human waste," or auctioned off as farm labor.[15] By the late nineteenth and early twentieth centuries, "the status of seniors had reached its nadir," a time when old age was thought of as a disease in and of itself.[16]

After the Great Depression, life expectancies were increasing as were the percentage of elderly Americans living in poverty – by 1935, 50 percent of elderly Americans were poor, and by 1940, almost two-thirds were poor.[17] These staggering numbers, along with the realities of the Great Depression, led to President Franklin D. Roosevelt signing the Social Security Act of 1935 into law.[18] This was the beginning of a significant shift, where American values transformed and the

[13] *See* Foohey & Greene, *supra* note 6. And obtaining a job available to low-wage workers when one is elderly, even if physically able, is elusive as there are almost always younger people in need, ready and willing to work. Research shows that employers prefer (and hire) these younger workers. So, the elderly are left poor and with few options.

[14] Thorne et al., *supra* note 7, at 681, 682.

[15] *Id.*

[16] Fleming et al., *supra* note 10, at 914, 915; Thorne et al., *supra* note 7, at 681, 682.

[17] Fleming et al., *supra* note 10, at 914, 917.

[18] *Id.*

government began investing in elderly economic security.[19] Indeed, in 1965, Lyndon B. Johnson's administration furthered the goals of Roosevelt by enacting Medicare and Medicaid. At the same time, following World War II, employers began to expand retirement benefits for their full-time employees, providing them with defined benefit pensions and other important benefits for old age. Taking all of these changes together, Americans could in general depend on economic security in their old age.[20]

In the late 1970s and early 1980s, however, the concepts of individualism and self-sufficiency began to pervade US culture and politics.[21] A weakening of the safety net for Americans, including older Americans, followed. Employers began to replace mandatory pension plans with optional higher-risk 401(k) plans that do not guarantee a certain income during retirement, social security payments were reduced, and many more jobs did not provide any avenue at all for retirement savings.[22] Jacob Hacker refers to this as the "Great Risk Shift," one where "a myriad of risks that were once managed and pooled by government and private corporations shifted onto individuals and families."[23]

But people are still getting old, and life expectancies are continuing to increase, with the 100-year life in sight for many Americans. In response to increased longevity, there has been a renewed sense of urgency by the government in setting expectations – expectations that Americans must save for their own retirements. We have transformed into a country that says "take care of yourself" – even when you are old. In 2000, then Treasury Secretary Lawrence Summers gave remarks focusing on the need to encourage Americans to save more.[24] He said that it was critical not only "to our economic health" but also for families "because it influences their capacity to manage what is new in the New Economy: not least, the fact that people are living much longer than before."[25] He went on to discuss the (increased) chances of people living to ninety years old, then concluded that "as people are retiring earlier and living longer, retirement spans for many individuals are approaching half or more of their working lives."[26] Summers acknowledged the challenges that come with longer lifespans and then summarized his goals for the speech as follows:

[19] Thorne et al., *supra* note 7, at 681, 683.

[20] Fleming et al., *supra* note 10, at 914, 917.

[21] Sara Sternberg Greene, *The Broken Safety Net: A Study of Earned Income Tax Credit Recipients and a Proposal for Repair*, 88 N.Y.U. L. Rev. 515, 533 (2013).

[22] Thorne et al., *supra* note 7, at 681, 684.

[23] Jacob Hacker, The Great Risk Shift: The Assault on American Jobs, Families, Health Care, and Retirement and How You Can Fight Back (2006).

[24] Lawrence H. Summers, *Helping America to Save More*, US Dep't of the Treasury (Apr. 4, 2000), https://www.treasury.gov/press-center/press-releases/Pages/ls524.aspx.

[25] *Id.*

[26] *Id.*

1. First, discuss why increasing saving is so crucial both for the American economy as a whole and for the economies of individual American families.
2. Second, discuss our approach to increasing saving based on improving financial literacy and promoting financial access. Recent economic research demonstrates that saving is like any other form of consumer behavior: It is governed by habit, is responsive to social signals, and it can be promoted.
3. Third, discuss the growing problem of borrowing, or negative saving.
4. And fourth, discuss specific legislation that goes beyond existing incentives to further promote savings among Americans who have not had the opportunity to avail themselves of existing incentives.[27]

The government's recent policies and rhetoric indicate that Summers's vision lives on – we must teach Americans how to save and provide behavioral nudges and incentives for doing so.[28] Indeed, in 2015, the Treasury Department released a treasury note entitled "Helping More Americans Save" in part to mark "America Saves Week, an annual opportunity to encourage all Americans to save and a chance for individuals and families to take stock of their financial health and preparedness."[29] The notice, released by J. Mark Iwry, then Senior Advisor to the Secretary of Treasury for Retirement and Health Policy and the Deputy Assistant Secretary for Tax Policy, noted that "[s]avings for retirement is one of the best ways to prepare for a secure financial future."[30] And further, the Treasury Department was "ensuring that more Americans have the knowledge and tools to manage money and credit responsibility because educated and financially capable consumers can better attain their own financial goals and contribute to the strength of our overall county."[31]

There are moralist and paternalistic overtones to both of these releases. The idea is fairly simple: Some Americans are not financially educated and need help "learning" how to save, so the government will do the work to improve "habits,"[32] as Secretary Summers put it. The lesson seems to be that if we create opportunities to save, change habits, and increase social pressure, we will see a difference. There

27 *Id.*

28 *See*, e.g., US Dep't of Lab., *Top 10 Ways to Prepare for Retirement* (Sep. 2021), https://files.eric.ed.gov/fulltext/ED496720.pdf; Fin. Literacy & Educ. Comm'n, Taking Ownership of the Future: The National Strategy for Financial Literacy 1–9, 19–28 (2006), https://www.treasury.gov/about/organizational-structure/offices/Domestic-Finance/Documents/Strategyeng.pdf.

29 J. Mark Iwry, *Helping More Americans Save*, US Dep't of the Treasury (Feb. 26, 2015), https://www.treasury.gov/connect/blog/Pages/Helping-More-Americans-Save.aspx.

30 *Id.*

31 *Id.*

32 Summers, *supra* note 24.

was little discussion in either release (or others like them)[33] of the structural conditions that make it difficult for Americans to save.

The federal government and federal laws certainly incentivize savings and wealth accumulation. But as others have documented in detail, most of these programs primarily benefit middle- to upper-income white citizens. For instance, our tax code has written into it several savings incentives, but low-income people rarely benefit from these incentives.[34] There are some other programs that are more inclusive, but in general they are small in scale and come and go. For example, Treasury created the "myRA" retirement savings program, which was designed to be a starter retirement savings program. It was supposed to help low-income workers who didn't have access to retirement savings plans through their jobs, but the take-up rate was low, and it was eventually shut down after Treasury found it not to be cost-effective.[35] Other Treasury programs sought to work with employers to create simple retirement plans for workers not covered by existing plans.

Ultimately the social construct of savings as moral, trainable, and the right thing to do pervades the culture in the US. And existing research shows that low-income Americans have adopted this ethic and in fact desperately *want* to save – they even work the existing savings-unfriendly systems to try to force themselves to save.[36] However, their efforts are often in vain, in part because of the underappreciated aspects of our laws and policies that make it almost impossible for the working poor to save. In the next section, I discuss these restrictions.

10.2 RESTRICTIONS ON SAVINGS

There are a plethora of reasons why it is difficult for Americans to save. Wage stagnation and rising expenses are significant factors. A 2019 study found that 53 million Americans, accounting for 44 percent of American workers between the ages of eighteen and sixty-four, qualified as "low-wage" earners.[37] The median hourly wage of those low-wage workers was $10.22, with median annual earnings of about $18,000.[38] Further, over half of low-wage earners were either the only workers in their family or lived in families where all workers were low-wage.[39] While wages

33 *See supra* notes 24, 28, and 29.

34 *See* Alstott, A New Deal, *supra* note 7; Dorothy A. Brown, The Whiteness of Wealth (2021).

35 Kate Lobosco, *Treasury Ends the MyRA, Obama's Retirement Savings Program*, CNN (July 28, 2017), https://money.cnn.com/2017/07/28/retirement/treasury-myra-retirement-account/index.html.

36 *See* Greene, *supra* note 21, at 563–564.

37 Martha Ross & Nicole Bateman, *Low-Wage Work Is More Pervasive Than You Think and There Aren't Enough "Good Jobs" to Go Around*, Brookings (Nov. 21, 2019), https://www.brookings.edu/blog/the-avenue/2019/11/21/low-wage-work-is-more-pervasive-than-you-think-and-there-arent-enough-good-jobs-to-go-around/.

38 *Id.*

39 *Id.*

went up a bit in the midst of the pandemic, a recent study found that in 2022 more than 51.9 million workers, or almost 32 percent of the labor force, made less than $15 per hour.[40]

Such low wages leave families vulnerable to economic insecurity – just one small shock, such as missing work due to an illness, a funeral of a family member, or a needed repair for a car used for transportation to work, can send these workers into financial turmoil and create a need to depend on the scant public safety net that is available.[41] In fact, many low-wage workers even working full time and without experiencing economic shocks must depend on Medicaid and food stamps to get by. Numerous studies and reports confirm that large companies pay their workers such low wages that these workers need public assistance, even when working full time.[42]

Even at times when low-wage workers have the opportunity to save – when perhaps they receive an unexpectedly large tax return, they are given extra hours at work, they receive a stimulus payment/credit, or they sell a prized possession for cash – our poverty laws often prevent these workers from accumulating any meaningful savings. How is this possible in a society that so values saving? It happens through asset limitation laws that affect every major public assistance/antipoverty program (outside of the tax system) that provides money or money-like relief to low-income Americans. These limitations impose rigid restrictions on the amount of cash and assets aid recipients can accumulate. Thus, recipients are in a bind. If they attempt to put away meaningful savings when they receive a lump sum in the form of, for instance, a stimulus check or tax credit, they cannot continue to access the programs they need to survive month to month.

Before Ronald Reagan was elected, states set welfare programs' eligibility requirements. President Reagan, however, campaigned in the early 1980s on a promise to reform welfare by cracking down on "welfare queens" (a term he popularized) who, he claimed, abused the public welfare system. During a 1976 stump speech, Reagan described the welfare queen as follows: "She has eighty names, thirty addresses, twelve Social Security cards and is collecting veterans' benefits on four non-existing deceased husbands. And she's collecting Social Security on her cards. She's got Medicaid, getting food stamps and she is collecting welfare under each of her names. Her tax-free cash income is over $150,000."[43] Welfare recipients were

40 Kaitlyn Henderson, The Crisis of Low Wages in the US 3 (2022).

41 *See* Greene, *supra* note 21, at 544–552.

42 U.S. Gov't Accountability Office, *Federal Social Safety New Programs: Millions of Full-Time Workers Rely on Federal Health Care and Food Assistance Programs* (Oct. 2020), https://www.gao.gov/assets/720/710203.pdf.

43 Juliet M. Brodie, Clare Pastore, Ezra Rosser & Jeffrey Selbin, Poverty Law, Policy, and Practice 89 (2014).

portrayed as primarily Black, and the media and other politicians perpetuated this (inaccurate) image.[44]

While Reagan did not succeed in the massive welfare reform he promised, he was able to push through asset restrictions on major welfare programs, which largely remain in place today (though states have regained some control). Reagan did this via the Omnibus Reconciliation Act of 1981, which set asset limits at $1,000 for most welfare programs, a large decrease compared to then-existing state limits. And the federal limits had teeth. A study conducted ten years after Reagan left office showed that low-income single mothers reduced their personal savings by an average of $1,250.[45]

Following Reagan's presidency, the poverty laws in our country moved even further in the direction of building expectations for families to develop and sustain their own safety nets, both during their working years and into their old age. In the mid 1990s, Bill Clinton ran for president on a campaign promise to reform cash welfare (then Aid to Families with Dependent Children – AFDC) into a program that would promote "personal responsibility" and "economic self-sufficiency."[46] When Clinton was elected, welfare reform was indeed passed, transforming AFDC into TANF, stripping away the existing safety net for families, and turning welfare into a bare-bones program with much state control.[47] Further restrictions for eligibility were put on cash welfare, such as more work requirements and a five-year lifetime limit.[48] As part of the changes, states regained control to set asset limits, but only some states made changes.[49]

Asset limitations may seem like small potatoes, but a large percentage of the population is potentially subject to them. Indeed, roughly 20 percent of the US population participates in means-tested government aid programs each month.[50] Generally people move in and out of public assistance programs. Of those who participated in public assistance programs between January 2009 and December 2012, the largest share, 43 percent, stayed in the programs between thirty-seven and

[44] Kathryn J. Edin & H. Luke Schaefer, $2.00 a Day: Living on Almost Nothing in America 15 (2016); Martin Gilens, Why Americans Hate Welfare: Race, Media, and the Politics of Antipoverty Policy 1–32 (2000).

[45] Elizabeth Powers, *Does Means Testing Welfare Discourage Saving? Evidence from a Change in AFDC Policy in the United States*, 68 J. of Pub. Econ. 33, 33–53 (1998).

[46] *See* Vicki Lens, *Public Voices and Public Policy: Changing the Societal Discourse on "Welfare,"* 39 J. Soc. & Soc. Welfare 137, 144–146 (2002).

[47] Sara Sternberg Greene, *The Bootstrap Trap*, 67 Duke L. J. 233, 236–237 (2016).

[48] *Id.*

[49] Leah Hamilton, *The Forgotten 1980s Rule That's Hurting Poor Families Savings*, The Atlantic (Mar. 11, 2015), https://www.theatlantic.com/business/archive/2015/03/the-forgotten-1980s-rule-thats-hurting-poor-families-savings/387373/.

[50] U.S. Dep't of Health and Human Services, *Welfare Indicators and Risk Factors* (Apr. 26, 2022), 33, https://aspe.hhs.gov/sites/default/files/documents/85da9415ece89b2989ad290755d38f7b/welfare-indicators-rtc.pdf.

forty-eight months. Another 31.2 percent of participants stayed in programs between one and twelve months.[51]

Asset limits vary significantly program by program and even state by state. For instance, the Supplemental Security Income (SSI) asset limit, which is controlled at the federal level, is $2,000 for an individual and $3,000 for a couple.[52] Asset limits for SNAP are set by the federal government at $2,750, and $4,250 for households containing a member who is disabled or over sixty.[53] However, states can modify or even eliminate SNAP asset limits through categorical eligibility. TANF limits, now set by states, vary from $1,000 to $10,000 or even no limit, with the average around $1,000–3,000.[54] And Medicaid asset limits again are set by states and most have not increased the dollar limit since 1989.[55] State limitations vary significantly – there are usually none for children, but in about half the states, there are limits for families, usually between $1,000 and $6,000.[56]

For some of these programs, one vehicle (or a certain amount of vehicle value) is excluded from the asset limits, but no more than that. And treatment of retirement savings is "confusing and seemingly arbitrary."[57] When asset tests were first enacted in the 1970s, defined benefit plans such as traditional pensions were common, and asset limitations for some programs (SNAP, for example) did not count such

[51] US Census Bureau, *21.3 Percent of U.S. Population Participates in Government Assistance Programs Each Month* (May 28, 2015), https://www.census.gov/newsroom/press-releases/2015/cb15-97.html.

[52] Kathleen Romig et al., *The Case for Updating SSI Asset Limits*, Center on Budget and Policy Priorities (Sep. 2023), https://www.ssa.gov/ssi#:~:TEXT = SUPPLEMENTAL%20SECURITY%20INCOME%20(SSI)%20IS,OR%20%243%2C000%20FOR%20A%20COUPLE.

[53] US Dep't of Agriculture, Food and Nutrition Services, *SNAP Eligibility for October 1, 2022–September 30, 2023*, https://www.fns.usda.gov/snap/recipient/eligibility (accessed Jan. 7, 2024). Unlike Medicaid, for example, some retirement and pension plans are excluded from SNAP asset limits. However, most low-wage workers do not have jobs that provide employer-sponsored pension or retirement plans. Further, low-wage workers may rationally be hesitant to tie savings up in retirement plans that have penalties for early withdrawal, given the general instability of their financial lives and the potential for a shock to occur, requiring them to use at least some of their savings to recover from the shock. *See* Greene, *supra* note 21, at 533.

[54] Maureen Pirog, Edwin Gerrish & Lindsey Bullinger, *A Report to the Pew Charitable Trusts: TANF and SNAP Asset Limits and the Financial Behavior of Low-Income Households*, https://www.pewtrusts.org/-/media/assets/2017/09/tanf_and_snap_asset_limits_and_the_financial_behavior_of_low_income_households.pdf.

[55] Noelle Cornelio et al., *Increasing Medicaid's Stagnant Asset Test for People Eligible for Medicare and Medicaid Will Help Vulnerable Seniors*, 40 Health Affs. 1943 (Dec. 2021).

[56] The Retirement Security Project, *Removing Barriers to Retirement Saving in Medicaid and Supplemental Security Income* (2016), at 4, https://www.brookings.edu/wp-content/uploads/2016/07/10_removing_barriers.pdf. Many states do count retirement savings in traditional retirement accounts as assets. American Council on Aging, *How Retirement Savings (IRAs, 401Ks or Pensions) Impact Medicaid Long Term Care Eligibility* (updated Nov. 10, 2023), https://www.medicaidplanningassistance.org/medicaid-eligibility-401k-ira/.

[57] The Retirement Security Project, *supra* note 56, at 4.

accounts in the asset calculation. But today, most employees, particularly low-income ones, do *not* have access to traditional pension plans. Instead, if they are part of any plan at all, they tend to be part of defined *contribution* plans, such as 401(k)s.[58] And if a worker is laid off from a job that includes a 401(k), that 401(k) will likely be rolled into an IRA, which then *is* counted. Those accounts are *not* exempt from most asset limitation tests for public benefits.[59]

Asset limitations help ensure that the poor remain poor. Indeed, studies have shown that asset limits create disincentives for low-income families to save. Multiple studies have confirmed that families save more when asset limitations are lower or nonexistent, and save less when asset limits are instituted.[60] Further, to the extent that low-income families may find a work-around by saving money "under their mattress" at home, such practices are counter to the fairly well-accepted goal of trying to move more low-income people to be banked rather than unbanked.[61] But if there is a sense among low-income families that their bank accounts will be surveilled and used against them via asset limit investigations, then they are acting rationally by remaining unbanked and outside mainstream financial institutions.

It is important to understand asset limitations for what they are: a significant, though often overlooked, part of America's structural racism that perpetuates the racial wealth gap and disproportionately leaves poor, Black, elderly Americans struggling. While in absolute numbers whites far outnumber Blacks in their receipt of public benefits, *rates* of participation in public assistance programs are higher among Blacks. According to the US Census Bureau, in 2012, 13 percent of white Americans participated in a public assistance program, compared to 42 percent of Black Americans.[62] Thus, asset limitations perpetuate the racial wealth gap by disproportionately preventing Black Americans from accumulating savings or wealth and, thus, also leave Black Americans particularly vulnerable to experiencing poverty in their old age.

[58] *Id.*

[59] The Retirement Security Project, *Increasing Retirement Savings: Clarifying Food Stamp Asset Test Rules* (2007), at 1, https://www.brookings.edu/wp-content/uploads/2016/07/03_increasing_saving.pdf.

[60] Pirog et al., *supra* note 54; Henry Chen & Robert I. Lerman, *Do Asset Limits in Social Programs Affect the Accumulation of Wealth*, The Urban Institute (2005), https://www.urban.org/research/publication/do-asset-limits-social-programs-affect-accumulation-wealth; Erik Hurst & James P. Ziliak, *Do Welfare Asset Limits Affect Household Saving? Evidence from Welfare Reform*, 41 J. Hum. Resources 46 (2006).

[61] *See* Michael S. Barr, *Banking the Poor: Policies to Bring Low-Income Americans into the Financial Mainstream*, Brookings Inst. (Sep. 2004), https://www.brookings.edu/wp-content/uploads/2016/06/20041001_Banking.pdf; Mehrsa Baradaran, How the Other Half Banks: Exclusion, Exploitation, and the Threat to Democracy (2015).

[62] US Census Bureau, 21.3 *Percent of U.S. Population Participates in Government Assistance Programs Each Month* (May 28, 2015), https://www.census.gov/newsroom/press-releases/2015/cb15-97.html.

10.3 WHERE ARE WE, AND WHERE CAN WE GO FROM HERE?

So where does this leave us? We are at a crossroads, no doubt. While there is a widespread belief that we do in fact take care of our elderly, that Medicare and Social Security cover people in old age, the data show otherwise. The failure of these programs to fully support the poor in old age has been well detailed by others, particularly Anne Alstott in her important book *A New Deal for Old Age*.[63] The data are consistent with Alstott's findings. Being old and poor is not uncommon.[64] One study found that roughly one in three elderly Americans is economically insecure, living at or below 200 percent of the Federal Poverty Line.[65] The data for Black and Latinx elderly Americans are even worse, with half living at or below 200 percent of the Poverty Line.[66] Another study found that 49 percent of older workers and their spouses will experience downward mobility in retirement.[67]

Ultimately, a key problem is that our savings rhetoric largely does not mesh with our law. We pretend that we live in a society that provides structures that enable retirement savings for all, and thus, a policy of "encouraging more low-income Americans to save,"[68] as former Treasury Secretary Lawrence Summers suggested, is a way forward. Encouraging the lowest-paid Americans to save will not cut it, in part because we do not provide realistic structural opportunities for them to do so. Yet we use moralistic overtones around savings to shift responsibility from structures to individuals, all while picking up on Reagan-era tropes about race, potential fraud, and exploitation of government programs in order to support the need for these asset limitation laws.

We must pull out of this false narrative that behavioral interventions are the most promising way forward because savings opportunities are available for low-income workers but often squandered. Once we do so there is much that can be done. Fortunately, the good ideas are abundant, but more attention to this issue is needed. During the height of the COVID pandemic, the Child Tax Credit was improved in multiple ways – increasing the amount per child, broadening the credit's scope, and making it fully refundable. Allocation of the credit was based entirely on income, not assets. The expansion of the Child Tax Credit was not extended, but perhaps as advocates continue to work toward expansion, the ability to save for the long term should be centered in the conversation. The key problem now is that when poor

63 *See* ALSTOTT, A NEW DEAL, *supra* note 7, at 1–2.

64 *See* Alstott, *Law and the Hundred-Year Life*, *supra* note 7, at 141.

65 National Council on Aging, *Get the Facts on Economic Security for Seniors* (Mar. 2021), https://www.ncoa.org/article/get-the-facts-on-economic-security-for-seniors.

66 *Id.*

67 Teresa Ghilarducci, Michael Papadopoulos & Anthony Webb, *40% of Older Workers and Their Spouses Will Experience Downward Mobility in Retirement*, SCHWARTZ CENTER FOR ECONOMIC POLICY ANALYSIS (2018), http://www.economicpolicyresearch.org/images/docs/research/retirement_security/Downward_Mobility_in_Retirement_P_N.pdf.

68 *See* Summers, *supra* note 24.

families gain the opportunity to save, through an expanded social safety net, a promotion at work, or something else, this is a positive change that can help secure their future into old age. But when and if they need to access safety net programs such as SNAP or TANF (or continue receiving help from such programs), the savings will become a burden – something they will have to spend down in order to qualify or continue to qualify.

We can attack the problem in one of two broad categories of change, though the best plan is likely one that pursues both of these avenues. If we want to depend on people to create their own nest-eggs for retirement, then we need to repeal asset limitations and provide benefits and structures, early and often, that allow even our lowest-wage workers to save, and save at a rate that would support them in retirement. Given the very low wages of many Americans, the government would likely have to provide, at a minimum, matching funds, and probably even supplemental funds, in order for such a program to work and make a meaningful difference in retirement savings.

Alternatively, or perhaps in conjunction with an aggressive savings program, reforming social security to truly be progressive can eliminate elderly poverty for many Americans. Such a reform would need to take into account the reality that, at least without change, our structures prohibit many seniors from saving for retirement, and the program would need to provide extensive benefits to these seniors in order to keep them from living an old age of poverty. There are several existing comprehensive plans to reform social security, and an extensive discussion of such plans is not warranted here. However, my broader point is that in order for such plans to gain traction, we need to transform the moralistic narratives around savings that pervade our culture and have been circulating for decades. Indeed, we need to align the national conversation about savings with the realities of the structural systems we have in place – including the laws that prohibit low-income Americans from saving while accessing needed support during their working years.

10.4 CONCLUSION

Ultimately, only when we shift the cultural narrative, peel back the moralistic and judgment-laced rhetoric around poverty, savings, and retirement, and acknowledge existing structural barriers to savings can we then rebuild these structures and circumvent the looming elderly poverty epidemic. If we want the "golden years" to be golden for everyone, it is imperative to attend to this now. As plans and nudges to help Americans save pervade, asset limitations must be addressed in order for these programs to make a meaningful difference in the ability of low-income Americans to save for retirement.

11

Trusts and the 100-Year Life

John Morley

As human lives grow longer, what will happen to the law that governs death? How will a person's property be divided at death, and will we see any changes in the way people make wills, trusts, and plans for the distribution of their estates after they pass away? In this chapter, I argue that the answers to these questions are surprising: As lives grow longer, the law of property distribution at death will become less important. People who expect to live into their second centuries will have less property to pass at death and will feel a greater need to hand it over to their descendants and beneficiaries before they die. The law of trusts and estates will remain a bedrock feature of the legal system, but it will look more and more like a backstop and less and less like a preferred mode for dividing up the bulk of accumulated estates.

11.1 BACKGROUND

The declining importance of the law of decedents' estates promised by the lengthening of human lives will intensify a trend that has already been growing for decades. As John Langbein explained in a seminal law review article in 1988, the law of estates has been diminishing in importance since at least the middle of the twentieth century, and possibly long before.[1] The causes are many. One is the transformation in the character of wealth. Whereas the estates of the old aristocracies prototypically consisted of land, today wealth tends to consist primarily of financial assets, such as securities, savings accounts, and insurance contracts. These forms of financial assets are much easier to transfer than land and, therefore, require less attention from lawyers and judges when they are transferred at death. Similarly, much of the wealth that passes from generation to generation in 2024 consists of investments in human capital that tend not even to register as forms of wealth

[1] John H. Langbein, *The Twentieth-Century Revolution in Family Wealth Transmission*, 86 Mich. L. Rev. 722 (1988).

transfer at all. When a professional family devotes hundreds of thousands of dollars to the private education of its children, no intervention by a probate court is needed.

Still another cause of decline in the law of probate is the growth and now dominance of forms of wealth transfer that self-consciously avoid the law of probate. Life insurance proceeds, bank accounts, retirement accounts, and brokerage accounts can all be crafted to name beneficiaries to take assets in the event of an owner's death. When the day comes, the assets move solely by the actions of these financial institutions, with no need for a will or probate court. Even a family home can be owned jointly with a right of survivorship, so that a spouse's death automatically transfers their share to the spouse who survives, again with no need for probate.

Estate-planning practitioners have cut further into the domain of the probate courts by mastering the so-called "revocable trust." A revocable trust is a trust that its creator – known as a "settlor" – can take back at any time. A revocable trust can work as an excellent substitute for a will because, like a will, it does not become permanent until the settlor's death. The settlor can add and remove assets from it as the settlor pleases during their lifetime, making no final decisions until moments before they pass away. The revocable trust offers many advantages, one of which is to avoid probate. Since, at the time of a settlor's death, the property in a revocable trust formally belongs to the trustee rather than the settlor, the property is not part of the settlor's estate for purposes of probate. The dispositive terms of the trust need not be filed with a probate court, and lifetime transfers to the trustee generally cannot be challenged as part of probate proceedings.

The intentional attempt to avoid probate reflects the reality that probate is often expensive and time-consuming, especially for modest estates that have little need of the benefits probate ostensibly offers. If an estate of modest size can be divided up by a series of financial institutions that merely carry out the orders embedded in financial contracts, the estate can often avoid the costly intervention of lawyers, the potential for dispute, and the occasions for taxation and fee extraction that tend to follow entry into probate.

11.2 LESS WEALTH AT DEATH

The lengthening of human lives will intensify this downward trend in the importance of probate for two reasons. The first is that decedents will have less wealth to pass. For the same reasons that lengthening lives will strain systems of public retirement support, they will also strain private savings. As working years take up a smaller share of human lives, workers will have to spend more years living off of their savings. To support a period of extended retirement and prolonged illness, family homes will have to be liquidated, 401(k) accounts used up, and savings accounts eaten away. All of this will leave fewer assets to be transferred when a person passes away.

Some portion of the burden on private savings might be lightened by lengthening years of work. If people spend some of their extra years working and saving, the financial pressure of those extra years will not be as intense as if people spent all of their extra lifespans on the golf course. But there remains a real possibility that the extra years in income-earning labor will not be enough to compensate for the extra years in retirement and illness. If that happens, the size of probate estates and even nonprobate transfers will decline. A person will have to use their savings to support themselves rather than to provide for the next generation.

11.3 GREATER URGENCY OF LIFETIME TRANSFER

For the fortunate few who have a surplus of wealth even after their extended years of retirement, the lengthening of life will intensify the downward trend in death-time transfers for a second reason: People will feel a greater need to pass their wealth before they die. The trouble is that the age at which people conceive and bear children is not growing as quickly as the age at which people die. Many people can now expect to live past 100, but relatively few will bear children past forty. As a result, the gaps between generations, though growing, are not growing as quickly as human lives, so that as parents die at older and older ages, their children are receiving transfers of wealth at later and later stages in their lives. Think of the difference between Queen Elizabeth II of the United Kingdom, who ascended to the throne at age twenty-five after her father passed away at the age of fifty-six, and Elizabeth's son Charles, who remained a prince into his seventies as his mother continued to occupy the throne well into her nineties. Few families have thrones to pass on to their children. But what about homes, cars, and 401(k) accounts?

This postponement of wealth transfer presents a problem. Money is often most useful when a person is young. This is partly a result of the cycles of human lives and earnings. Income tends to grow over the first five or six decades of life, so that an educated person in their twenties will tend to earn less than they will in their forties or fifties. Help with a down payment for a house is thus more useful when the person is young and has a lifetime of mortgage payments and future earnings still ahead than when they are middle-aged and have a padded savings account and a mortgage that is already half paid off. A related concern about life cycles is that a person's propensity to consume tends to drop later in life. Extra money has little appeal for an infirm elderly person who no longer needs fashionable clothes, comfortable vacations, or extra square footage. A parent with extra resources to spare might therefore feel a greater urgency to subsidize children and grandchildren while they are still relatively young than older children who have established incomes.

Money also tends to be useful when a person is young because money has a time value. The foundation of finance is the conviction that money today is worth more than money tomorrow. All else equal, therefore, a child and his family will prefer to start consuming today than wait for another thirty years while the old family home sits underutilized by parents. Like all rational people, Junior might prefer to spend money now than later. Even if we set aside the concerns about Junior's uneven income over the course of his life, we might still be concerned about the simple time value cost of forcing Junior and his offspring to wait to enjoy the fruits of grandparents' savings. Some of these concerns about time value might be mitigated by the possibility of investment growth. That is, Junior might be rewarded for his patience with compounding returns on the savings and a larger ultimate inheritance upon the death of his parents. But savings may not grow at a rate commensurate with the discount factors of younger generations, especially if the savings consist of assets that are costly to maintain or that might decline in value, such as homes and cars.

A final reason to hasten the transfer of wealth is that wealth sometimes requires active management or even active consumption. Think of a family business in which a founder must transfer control to their children. A son might take over the family restaurant, or a daughter might assume the corner suite of the family investment office. In an age when retirements were short and death came early, the transfer of control over a family business often coincided with death. Junior would take over the day Father was laid to rest. As retirements and lives lengthen, death-time succession will no longer suffice. Later generations have to be given control well before earlier generations pass on. We cannot expect an elderly founder to effectively manage a business into their eighties and nineties, and we cannot expect their children to wait for them to retire when they are in their fifties and sixties.

The need for active management often mixes with a need for active consumption. Though remaining in the family home may be satisfying and comforting to an elderly person who has spent most of their adult life there, the prolonged decades of occupancy may come at a significant financial cost if the home is large enough to be used by (and sold to) a family with children and if it decays through the neglect of maintenance and renovation that often accompanies aging.

The need to shift transfers from death to life will intensify a problem that estate planners have always known and have always struggled with, which is how to balance the need for income in retirement with the need for timely transfer to the next generation. Mother might recognize that it would be good to pass on assets to Junior sooner rather than later, but at eighty-five years old, Mother might not know how many of these assets she will need to support herself for the rest of her life. If she has a million dollars in savings, she might need all of it if she expects to live another twenty years, or she might need just half of it if she expects to be gone in just another ten years. If she knows that Junior and his children could use the money now, how is she supposed to predict how much to give now and how much to hold on to? This is an old problem, and it long predates the growth of the 100-year life. But the greater strain on personal finances and the larger bands of uncertainty introduced by longer lives and retirements will make this needle even harder to thread.

The risk of passing too much too early makes it clear that what we need is not simply to smooth the making of transfers during life but also to allow such transfers to be made flexibly, so that gifts can be made and then taken back if the life and needs of the donor become unexpectedly long and great.

11.4 CHALLENGES

What, then, stands in the way of such a system? What do we need to do to make it possible for long-lived people to pass their property before they die even as they retain enough control to take some of it back to meet the needs of an unexpectedly long life?

Many of the obstacles involve taxation. The system of unified estate and gift taxation we now have in the United States is a major accomplishment, in that it tries to treat life- and death-time transfers as part of a single pool. The details are complicated, but the basic gist is that if I make a gift during my life, I have to file a gift tax return in the year I make it, but I will owe no tax until the total of my life- and death-time gifts together exceeds the value of my exemption from the estate tax. Any excess over the exemption gets taxed only at the time the threshold of exemption is crossed, whether that happens in life or death. This system largely avoids the need to pay taxes on transfers during lifetime for any but the very wealthiest families.

Some obstacles to lifetime transfers remain, however. One is the so-called step-up in income tax basis at death. If a donor takes a piece of property in life and then holds it as it appreciates in value, the income tax basis for the donor is usually the price at which the donor purchased the property minus any depreciation. Were the donor to sell the property during their lifetime, they would owe income tax on the appreciation. But if the donor waits until their death and then transfers the property by will, the basis of the donees will equal the value of the property at the time of the donor's death, appreciation and all. Were the donees to sell the property immediately after the donor's death, they would owe no income tax. Lifetime transfers do not receive the same favor. The donee of a lifetime gift receives the same basis as the donor.

The trouble, of course, is that this system creates profound incentives to hold property until death. If I bought a house in Palo Alto in 1975 and watched it skyrocket in value through 2024, it would be disastrous to sell or donate the house before I passed away. Instead, the tax incentive would be to hang on to the house for all 110 years of my long life and then leave it to my children in my will. A lifetime transfer would be an income tax disaster. A death-time transfer is the only rational strategy.

One can imagine strategies for accelerating the use of the property, but none is fully satisfying. I could rent the house out and make a gift of the income to my children every year. But the income might exceed the annual gift tax exemption. Additionally, I would owe income tax on the rental income, and my children would not have immediate access to the full value of all the capital accumulated in the house.

Another obstacle to flexible and accelerated transferring is the generation-skipping transfer tax. If a 110-year-old donor hesitates to make a gift to their child who is already eighty-five years old, then the donor could achieve greater value for the gift by handing the assets to a grandchild or even great-grandchild who can make better use of the money. If the goal is to support someone who has yet to attend college, a donor can simply select a beneficiary further down the family tree. The donor can wait until death and still see the assets go to a person who is young enough to genuinely need them.

The problem with this strategy is the generation-skipping transfer tax, or GST tax. The tax is designed to ensure that assets subject to the estate tax get taxed at every generation. Congress did not want a person to be able to pass their fortune to their great-grandchildren without making the fortune subject to estate taxation at the deaths of the person's children and grandchildren. To put it a bit crudely, the GST tax imposes the estate tax multiple times, based on the number of generations the donee sits below the donor on the family tree.

Private estate planners have developed strategies for handling the GST tax. One is the creation of a perpetual trust that is funded with assets up to the full amount of the estate tax exemption and then made perpetual so that it can benefit the donor's children, grandchildren, great-grandchildren, and other descendants later on. Since the transfer was made only once, the trust can continue to benefit the donor's descendants across many generations without encountering estate or gift tax.

The perpetual trust has its drawbacks, however, including the obvious governance problems that come with having something exist forever, not to mention the fact that it only works for the estate tax exemption amount, which, though relatively high right now, might easily come down in the future to levels that make life uncomfortable for a greater share of the public.

A further obstacle to lifetime giving is the tax benefits of retirement accounts. A person who contributes to a 401(k), IRA, or similar retirement account owes no income tax on the money contributed at the time of the contribution and continues to owe no income tax as the investments appreciate until the time the person makes a withdrawal. Such accounts can be leveraged to great effect, ensuring that assets appreciate over time without being periodically reduced by capital gains taxation. The effect can be compounded by continuing to hold the account until death and then handing it over to children and letting them continue to enjoy the same benefits until they are forced to make withdrawals of their own. The length of time a child can hold the account was diminished by the tax reforms of 2017, but the possibilities for savings by keeping assets inside the account after a donor's death remain substantial. The benefits available under these retirement accounts thus encourage death-time transfers, because there is no way to hand these assets to spouses or children during the donor's lifetime without undoing the tax benefits.

One might argue with respect to all of these tax issues that convenience and efficiency are not the only policies we must consider in taxation. We have to think about the raising of revenue, redistribution, and so on. Retirement savings, for instance, are supposed to be used to fund retirement, not to accumulate dynastic wealth, and so one might not be troubled by the possibility that lengthening lifespans may complicate the accumulation of dynastic wealth. My point, however, is that whatever our other goals for taxation might be, the lengthening of life will put pressure on them to the extent people come to prefer life over death in the timing of wealth transfers. Tax policy has several goals, but one of them is to avoid distorting people's behavior. And to the extent tax law encourages a person to cling to property they do not need until they pass away at 110 just so their descendants can save money on taxes, it will be shaping people's actions in ways that are not socially optimal.

In addition to posing problems for taxation, a shift toward lifetime giving will raise other challenges for the system of wealth transfer as well. In particular, one wonders about the future of life insurance as a form of wealth transfer. By its nature, a term life insurance policy does not pay out until the insured person dies. So, what if the great length of a person's expected lifespan pushes the person to prefer a transfer before their death? Life insurance will not be a good option. People will continue to use life insurance as a protection against the prospect of an untimely death, but it will cease to be an attractive option for transferring wealth when death comes late.

11.5 CONCLUSION

One might think that as people live longer lives, the system of law that governs the transfer of their property at death would become more important. But the opposite is true. People will have fewer assets to transfer at death and a stronger desire to transfer them during life. People will want flexibility between life and death, and they will want the law to help them achieve it.

12

The Right to Grow Old

Jamal Greene

Americans have no right to grow old. Or so we are told. In 1985, in a case holding that the rights of people with disabilities were to receive no special constitutional protection, Justice Byron White worried in his majority opinion that people with intellectual impairments constituted so broad a class that there would be no "principled" way to distinguish discrimination against them from burdens on "the aging, the (physically) disabled, the mentally ill, and the infirm."[1]

The clear implication was that these other burdens were self-evidently permitted. And so, for the Court, the idea that laws burdening the elderly might be worthy of special attention from judges was not just wrong but also so obviously wrong that it could serve as the lead float, as it were, in a parade of horribles. This chapter is about what US courts find so horrifying about a right to grow old, and whether they are right to be afraid.

It is important first to clear some definitional underbrush. There is, to be sure, a right to grow old in a sense. Deriving from the Fifth and Fourteenth Amendment rights not to be deprived of life without due process of law and the Eighth Amendment right against cruel and unusual punishments, Americans enjoy a right against arbitrary killing at the government's hands.[2] Should the state choose to end your life before you become elderly, it had better have a good reason for doing so. This is the right to grow old in its negative sense, as a right against certain kinds of state action. This negative form is the one US constitutional rights typically take.

Even this negative right has its limits. If the state is not ending life but is merely burdening the elderly in some other way, courts don't take much notice. Age discrimination is barely scrutinized under US constitutional law.[3] The traditional reasons for greater scrutiny, grounded in a group's relative lack of political power, its historical marginalization, or its vulnerability to overbroad and harmful stereotypes, can apply to the elderly with great force. US courts nonetheless tend to consider

1 Cleburne v. Cleburne Living Center, 473 U.S. 432, 445–446 (1985).
2 US Const. Amend. V, Amend. XIV, Amend. VIII.
3 *See* Kimel v. Fla. Board of Regents, 528 U.S. 62 (2000); Gregory v. Ashcroft, 501 U.S. 452 (1991).

discrimination against older people to be obviously rational even when it is sloppy and harmful.[4]

The positive version of the right to grow old, such as it is, is still more limited. In this form, it is not so much the right to life as the right to *live*. It is the right to the support needed to maintain an adequate quality of life up until death. The elderly face predictable challenges that arise less from choices they have made than simply because they are human, and therefore mortal. Our physical dexterity and mental acuity typically lessen as we age, sometimes to a point where they become debilitating in the way of severe physical or mental disabilities. Providing care for older Americans also imposes burdens on the professional lives of family members, and especially women. These challenges require our care, our attention, and our money. The costs of medical care and supervision needed for the elderly to retain their dignity are overwhelming. And even if the morbidity of old age is reduced in the future,[5] we can still expect that as Americans live longer on average, the wages they will have earned in their working lives will be insufficient to cover these costs. They – we, inescapably – will need help.

It might seem as though help is not forthcoming, at least not from constitutional law. Judges accustomed to the American way of thinking seem to resist positive rights. The US Supreme Court has been unusually clear that the Constitution protects individuals against certain state-inflicted harms but generally does not require the state to ensure a minimum quality of life or prevent or deflect the predations of private actors.[6] Of a piece with this narrow rendition of constitutional rights, the Court has also been clear that state actions that reliably burden even protected classes, such as those defined by race, sex, or religion, will be viewed as constitutionally uninteresting unless a victim can show that the state was trying specifically to harm the members of those classes.[7] The US Supreme Court's theory of the Constitution's protections appears to view rights as arising only in those cases in which the government is acting pathologically, not when ordinary governance happens (even knowingly) to spoil some lives along the way. This kind of constitutional austerity sweeps the legs from under any putative right to grow old.

An aging population calls for reconsideration of the constitutional status of the elderly. We can expect *rational* stereotypes about the capacities of older Americans, already troubling, to become ever more outdated and limiting. We can also expect inequality to rise as Americans get older; basic survival skills tend to atrophy with

[4] *See Gregory*, 501 U.S. at 470–471; Vance v. Bradley, 440 U.S. 93, 108–109 (1979).

[5] *See* LYNDA GRATTON & ANDREW SCOTT, THE 100-YEAR LIFE: LIVING AND WORKING IN AN AGE OF LONGEVITY 22–25 (2016).

[6] *See* Castle Rock v. Gonzales, 545 U.S. 748 (2005); DeShaney v. Winnebago County Dep't of Soc. Servs., 489 U.S. 189 (1989); Harris v. McRae, 448 U.S. 297 (1980); San Antonio Indep. Sch. Dist. v. Rodriguez, 411 U.S. 1 (1973); Dandridge v. Williams, 397 U.S. 471 (1970).

[7] *See* Washington v. Davis, 426 U.S. 229 (1976); Personnel Administrator of Mass. v. Feeney, 442 U.S. 256 (1978); Employment Div. v. Smith, 494 U.S. 872 (1990).

age, and there is reason to be skeptical that future Americans will muster the political will to redistribute wealth to make up for it.

Constitutional law can only do so much for a miserly nation, but the prospects for some contribution are less bleak than they might appear. Positive rights are more prevalent in American constitutional law than US courts typically admit. Although courts are, for the foreseeable future, unlikely to create new substantive positive rights out of the cloth of the US Constitution, positive rights are best understood not as new rights but as the positive sides of older ones. And there are US constitutional rights whose protection requires the government to take on affirmative obligations. The Supreme Court's rejection of *overt* protection for positive rights has been deliberate, reflecting less an inherent feature of the US Constitution than a persistent divide in US politics, particularly around issues of race and class. Carving out some constitutional space for a right to grow old would require less a sledgehammer than a scalpel, less a constitutional invention than an exercise of judgment.

12.1 POSITIVE RIGHTS AT THE SUPREME COURT BAR

The Supreme Court has said repeatedly that the constitution protects negative rather than positive rights. Most bracingly, in the 1989 case of *DeShaney v. Winnebago County Department of Social Services*, the Court denied that a boy who had been beaten into a coma by his father had any constitutional rights against the county welfare workers who had negligently kept the boy in the father's care.[8] "Our cases have recognized," Chief Justice Rehnquist wrote, "that the Due Process Clauses generally confer no affirmative right to governmental aid, even where such aid may be necessary to secure life, liberty, or property interests of which the government itself may not deprive the individual."[9]

The refusal to understand the Fourteenth Amendment's rights provisions as conferring a duty on the state to protect citizens from private injuries is consistent with a set of cases that arose in the 1970s, when the constitutional status of the welfare state remained very much in play. Thus, the Court held that a family had no right to have its state welfare benefits increase commensurate with family size,[10] that a woman had no right to a publicly funded abortion, even one that was medically necessary,[11] and that kids in poor neighborhoods had no right to have their public schools funded on par with those in rich neighborhoods.[12]

But as hostile as the Burger Court and its sequelae have been to positive rights, the constraint the Court's body of cases imposes on the recognition of such rights is best understood as one of degree rather than kind. Positive rights are not a question of

[8] *DeShaney*, 489 U.S. 189.
[9] *Id.* at 196.
[10] *See Dandridge*, 397 U.S. 471.
[11] Maher v. Roe, 432 U.S. 464 (1977); *Harris*, 448 U.S. 297.
[12] *Rodriguez*, 411 U.S. 1.

which rights the Constitution protects but rather about what the government is obligated to do in respect of those rights. Rights to food, shelter, education, health care, and other rights often associated with the positive dimension of rights do exist under US constitutional law. The Constitution does not permit the government to take food off American tables or prevent Americans from educating themselves.[13] When courts and commentators say that Americans lack positive rights, what they typically mean, rather, is that the federal Constitution does not obligate the government to provide these entitlements or facilitate access to them. In the language of international human rights law, the government has a duty to respect these rights, but it does not have a corresponding duty to protect or promote them.

This limitation is strict and marks the US as a global outlier, but it is not categorical. The Supreme Court has recognized some instances in which the respect the government must afford to rights extends to positive duties to facilitate their exercise. For example, the constitutional right to counsel is understood not simply as a "negative" right of criminal defendants to bring their own counsel to court but has been read to include a positive right to have the government provide counsel to indigent defendants.[14] The right to vote is not simply a right not to have one's vote unreasonably denied but also imposes obligations upon states to create an effective infrastructure for receiving and counting ballots. The right to marry is not just a right to hold oneself out as married but includes an obligation on the state to solemnify the marriage and, therefore, make married persons eligible for certain state benefits. Even in the US, then, the fact that a right is recognized does not, ipso facto, tell us the degree to which its positive dimensions are constitutionally resonant.

The text of the US Constitution is unhelpful here. Many courts around the world protect the positive dimensions of rights, but the different approach they take to these questions is not, as many believe, because their written constitutions provide for these rights explicitly. Although most of the world's constitutions are indeed longer and more explicit than that of the US, including when it comes to rights often characterized in positive terms, the text of the US Constitution determines neither the substance nor the degree of its rights commitments. As David Strauss has observed, the rights the Constitution protects are surprisingly disconnected from its specific language.[15] The Constitution contains no explicit rights against race or sex discrimination, no right to vote, and no free speech rights against states. The degree to which these or other rights are respected, protected, or fulfilled by US courts depends on acts of construction that could as easily apply to rights to food, health, education, and so forth.

[13] *See* Meyer v. Nebraska, 262 U.S. 390 (1923).

[14] *See* Gideon v. Wainwright, 372 U.S. 335 (1963).

[15] *See* David A. Strauss, *Foreword: Does the Constitution Mean What It Says?* 129 Harv. L. Rev. 1, 3 (2015).

Indeed, US courts nearly accepted this invitation in the 1960s and 1970s. Positive rights relate closely to what American lawyers call the "state action doctrine" and what lawyers in many other parts of the world describe in the language of "horizontal effect:" To what extent does the Constitution require private actors to respect constitutional rights? A constitutional ban on private forms of discrimination is functionally related to a constitutional requirement that the government protect individuals against abuse by private actors. And by the late 1960s, six justices on the Supreme Court were willing to hold that, in at least some senses, the US Constitution could be read to reach such abuse.[16] This posture was manifest in a series of cases that prevented privatization as a means of evading desegregation measures, shielded "sit-in" protesters from state trespass laws, and affirmed Congress's power to guard against private discrimination.[17]

During the same period, in cases concerning the state's obligations toward those it seeks to prosecute criminally, the Court held that the state had to engage in prophylactic acts that lowered the risk of faulty convictions, most famously when it found that the government had to pay for a lawyer for indigent defendants.[18] In extending this last right to the appeal stage, the Court relied not on the Sixth Amendment right to counsel but on the Equal Protection Clause, reasoning that, in the government's refusal to fund appellate counsel for indigent defendants, "an unconstitutional line [had] been drawn between rich and poor."[19] Later, in striking down Virginia's $1.50 poll tax, the Court again relied on the presumptive impermissibility of government distinctions on the basis of wealth.[20] For courts to take seriously the right to be free of the disparate burdens of wealth might, in a practical sense, induce courts to require states to provide certain goods and services to the poor; the only alternative would be to take those goods and services away from the wealthy. An equal protection basis for such holdings could extend them beyond the criminal justice or voting contexts and into other important interests not held to have a specific constitutional basis, such as food, shelter, and health care.

The Court recognized this possibility in later cases placing limits on its incipient wealth discrimination doctrine. Pointedly, in a 1971 decision holding that indigent people can't be denied marital dissolution based on their inability to pay court fees, the Court relied solely on the Constitution's due-process provisions rather than equal protection.[21] Two years later, the Court decided that Texas could tie school funding to local property taxes, plainly disadvantaging students living in poor

[16] *See* United States v. Guest, 383 U.S. 745, 762 (1966) (Clark, J., concurring); *id.* at 774, 777 (Brennan, J., concurring in part and dissenting in part).

[17] *See* Burton v. Wilmington Parking Auth., 365 U.S. 715 (1961); Peterson v. City of Greenville, 373 U.S. 244 (1963); Robinson v. Florida, 378 U.S. 153 (1964); Lombard v. Louisiana, 373 U.S. 267 (1963); *see also* Jones v. Alfred H. Mayer Co., 392 U.S. 409 (1968).

[18] *See Gideon*, 372 U.S. 335.

[19] Douglas v. California, 372 U.S. 353, 357 (1963).

[20] *See* Harper v. Va. Board of Elec., 383 U.S. 663 (1966).

[21] *See* Boddie v. Connecticut, 401 U.S. 371, 380–381 (1971).

neighborhoods.[22] This arrangement did not count as unconstitutional wealth discrimination, Justice Lewis Powell wrote for the 5–4 majority, and the students in poor schools did not suffer so much as to implicate any fundamental right to education.[23]

The San Antonio case was, to be sure, bad news for supporters of positive constitutional rights. Wealth discrimination claims have gotten nowhere since then, and the Court appeared to deny that the Constitution mandated state support for important interests. It is important to linger here, however, because Justice Powell's rejection of a right to education was not total. Because the state did not absolutely deny poor children's right to a public education – they got to go to school, after all – the Court did not reach the question of whether a state had an affirmative obligation to provide a minimum level of public education.[24] And the most significant case to have addressed this question since the San Antonio case, *Plyler v. Doe*,[25] suggests that the state might indeed hold such an obligation.

Plyler arose out of a Texas policy that denied free public education to the children of undocumented immigrants. The Court struck it down. While paying lip service to the *Rodriguez* Court's suggestion that public education is not a constitutional right, "neither," wrote Justice Brennan for the majority, "is it merely some governmental 'benefit' indistinguishable from other forms of social welfare legislation."[26] Justice Brennan singled out "the importance of education in maintaining our basic institutions and the lasting impact of its deprivation on the life of the child."[27]

Taken in tandem, the *Rodriguez* and *Plyler* cases reinforce the idea that judicial recognition of the positive dimensions of rights may be denied at retail, but cannot be denied wholesale. In thinking through how much the crack in the door to positive rights could widen in the case of rights to various forms of support for older Americans, it is necessary to examine the political economy of the right to grow old, especially in relation to rights for which the door has remained closed.

12.2 THE POLITICAL ECONOMY OF POSITIVE RIGHTS

The cases in which US courts stifled the growth of positive rights were not random. They were tied quite directly to race and class and were the products of courts built to produce them. A potential right to grow old involves very different politics.

[22] *See* San Antonio Indep. Sch. Dist. v. Rodriguez, 411 U.S. 1 (1973).
[23] *See id.* at 36–37.
[24] *See id.*
[25] 457 U.S. 202 (1982).
[26] *Id.* at 221.
[27] *Id.*

When Richard Nixon ran for president in 1968 and 1972, his two most significant domestic issue areas were criminal justice and busing.[28] He used these issues and the racialized frame around them as wedges to try to pry working-class whites away from the Democratic Party. Criticism of the Supreme Court's decisions on "law and order" and desegregation made regular appearances in Nixon's stump speeches (as they were, more pointedly, in George Wallace's).[29] At the time of the election, President Lyndon Johnson's nomination of Abe Fortas to replace the retiring Earl Warren was stalled in the Senate, and so the Warren Court was almost literally on the ballot.

The year before, Johnson had made Thurgood Marshall the Court's first African American justice. Marshall was also, of course, the face of desegregation, and the Nixon and Wallace campaigns and their supporters frequently conflated racial integration in schools with crime. "They are afraid of street disorders and crime," the *New York Times* wrote in an article on Wallace's supporters. "They also hate provocative political demonstrators and they resent incursions of Negroes into predominantly white neighborhoods and schools."[30] The militaristic language of *infiltration* was used to describe violent criminals and Black schoolchildren alike. Nixon was vice president when *Brown* was decided, and he publicly supported President Eisenhower's federal interventions in support of integration. Still, especially in light of Wallace's presence in the race, Nixon suggested that the Warren Court's desegregation rulings had been too broad and consistently emphasized themes of federalism and local political control.[31]

These law-and-order and desegregation themes permeated Nixon's judicial selection process. Warren Burger's selection as chief justice and the choice of Harry Blackmun as Nixon's second Supreme Court pick owed in part to the perception that they were "law-and-order" judges.[32] The racial undertones of Nixon's other two selections were undeniable. Lewis Powell had presided over the Richmond School Board during its resistance to desegregation efforts, vowing that he would never favor compulsory integration.[33] As a law clerk to Justice Robert Jackson, William Rehnquist had written a memo supporting *Plessy v. Ferguson*.[34] (Nixon's failed nominations of southerners Clement Haynesworth and Harrold Carswell were widely perceived as efforts to appeal to voters who disapproved of civil rights reforms.)

28 *See* Kevin J. McMahon, Nixon's Court: His Challenge to Judicial Liberalism and Its Political Consequences 7 (2011).

29 *See id.* at 36.

30 *Id.* at 43.

31 *See id.* at 58, 74.

32 *See id.* at 80, 87.

33 *See* John C. Jeffries, Jr., Justice Lewis F. Powell, Jr.: A Biography 40–41 (2001).

34 *See* Brad Snyder & John Q. Barrett, *Rehnquist's Missing Letter: A Former Law Clerk's 1955 Thoughts on Justice Jackson and Brown*, 53 B.C. L. Rev. 631 (2012).

The racial themes of Nixon's campaign against the Warren Court engulfed his stance on government welfare as well. The common association of "welfare" with irresponsible behavior by racial minorities is well established. Nixon's 1968 convention speech played on these themes, accusing government welfare programs of "reap [ing] … an ugly harvest of frustration, violence, and failure."[35] The case rejecting any constitutional right to welfare, *Dandridge v. Williams*,[36] included Chief Justice Warren Burger in its five-justice majority opinion. The cases rejecting the right of Medicaid and state welfare recipients to abortion funding – *Maher v. Roe*[37] and *Harris v. McRae*[38] – both included Burger, Powell, and Rehnquist in their narrow majorities. Race was barely below the surface of the abortion issue. As Justice Marshall wrote in dissent in *Harris*, the abortion rate for nonwhites was about twice what it was for whites, and nonwhites were disproportionately likely to be indigent.[39]

The Court's opinion in the public school funding case, *Rodriguez*, decided two months after *Roe*, had all four of Nixon's appointees in the 5–4 majority, which Powell authored.[40] *Rodriguez* was on its face a case about wealth discrimination, but of course it was also about race, on several levels. *Rodriguez* was a desegregation case. Demetrio Rodriguez brought the lawsuit on behalf of a group of parents of students in schools in Edgewood, a neighborhood whose public schoolchildren, due in large part to housing discrimination, was more than 90 percent Mexican American.[41] More broadly, southern states' massive resistance to the Supreme Court's injunction in *Brown v. Board of Education* that they may not racially segregate their public schools was followed by more passive resistance. Minority-to-majority transfer schemes, whereby students could freely transfer out of schools in which they were a racial minority, were struck down by the Supreme Court in 1963.[42] Closing the public school system to avoid desegregation was ruled invalid in 1964.[43] Freedom of choice plans, which tended to replicate dual school systems, fell in 1968. Most jurisdictions ultimately settled on geographic zoning as the way to assign students to schools. The problem is that geographic zoning is vulnerable to white flight that can reproduce and reinforce racially identified neighborhoods and schools, such as in Edgewood.

The problem of white flight is stubborn enough on its own – as the busing saga demonstrated – but allowing schools to be financed through local property taxes greatly exacerbates the problem by effectively privatizing public schools. Well-financed schools attract more affluent residents, raising property values. The cycle

35 *Id.* at 298 n.53.
36 397 U.S. 471.
37 432 U.S. 464.
38 448 U.S. 297.
39 *Id.* at 343–344 (Marshall, J., dissenting).
40 San Antonio Indep. Sch. Dist. v. Rodriguez, 411 U.S. 1 (1973).
41 *See id.* at 12.
42 *See* Goss v. Knoxville Bd. of Educ., 373 U.S. 683 (1963).
43 *See* Griffin v. Prince Edward County Sch. Bd., 377 U.S. 218 (1964).

then repeats. In this way, formally separate but formally equal schools were replaced by informally separate and formally unequal schools. This inequality, though naked, was ostensibly produced through private market ordering and was therefore invulnerable to constitutional attack.

In nearly every case in which the Burger Court conspicuously limited the respect that needed to be shown to the positive dimensions of constitutional rights – in *Dandridge*, in *Rodriguez*, in *Washington v. Davis*,[44] in *Maher* – those rights were bound up in race and class politics.

The right to grow old is different in this respect because "[a]ll children, except one, grow up."[45] The challenges of aging disproportionately affect the poor and the disadvantaged, of course, but none of us are immune entirely from them. Social Security and Medicare, both of which primarily benefit the elderly, remain two of the most popular government social programs. Research has suggested that media portrayals of these programs tend to be positive and tend to depict white recipients, and indeed that whites with conservative views on race view Social Security more positively than their liberal counterparts.[46] If the positive dimensions of social rights are ever to find favor with US courts, the rights of an aging population are more likely to be recognized than others.

12.3 PUTTING AGE DISCRIMINATION IN CONTEXT

Viewing social obligations toward older Americans as constitutionally enforceable may require a wholesale shift in cultural attitudes about duties toward others, but adopting a different posture toward rights would get some of the way there. American courts faced with rights disputes tend to load the weight of analysis on threshold legal questions, such as whether the Constitution contains particular rights, who is entitled to hold them, and what the standard of review is when those rights are abridged. Identifying rights with particular categories of deference is thought to discipline the inquiry and subject rights to the forms of analysis – interpretation of written texts, historical understandings, and legal precedents – that judges are competent to perform.

These questions are abstractions, deliberately so, and tend toward a style of slippery-slope reasoning familiar to US lawyers. To those socialized into American rights review, declaring a "right to grow old" seems to entail judges attempting to require the government to fund elder care, to make medical and drug payments, to make its buildings and services more accessible to people with physical and intellectual challenges, to impose certain accommodation requirements in workplaces

[44] 426 U.S. 229 (1976).

[45] J. M. Barrie, Peter and Wendy 1 (1911).

[46] *See* Nicholas J. G. Winter, *Beyond Welfare: Framing and the Racialization of White Opinion on Social Security*, 50 Am. J. Pol. Sci. 400 (2006).

population.[53] In both cases, moreover, the objectives behind the policy were legitimate and important. The difference was that, in *Tetreault-Gadoury*, unlike in *McKinney*, the Court believed those objectives could be achieved without burdening the rights of sixty-five-year-olds. There was no evidence that sixty-five-year-olds were any more likely than others to abuse the system by seeking unemployment benefits for which, by not actively looking for work, they were ineligible.[54]

The Supreme Court of Canada differentiated cases on their facts, on the margins, rather than by putting them into separate legal categories. It was able to both recognize and discipline a right against age discrimination without abstracting away from the context of the cases. The next section generalizes this strategy and discusses others that enable courts around the world to do the same.

12.4 STRATEGIES

There are at least five distinct strategies that courts can deploy to discipline a right to grow old without extinguishing it: (1) proportionality, (2) polycentric constitutionalism, (3) a "minimum core" approach, (4) progressive realization, and (5) remedial flexibility. I briefly discuss each strategy below.

12.4.1 *Proportionality*

It is sometimes assumed that what makes courts around the world responsive to positive rights is constitutional enumeration. As I show above, this is not necessarily the case, as US constitutional rights are frequently atextual and sometimes have positive dimensions. What does differentiate the US approach to positive rights from that of many other courts is the all-or-nothing frame that US courts often apply. In cases like *Rodriguez*, courts suggest that positive rights can't be recognized because they can't be maximally enforced.

Proportionality – used nearly all the world over, save the US – is an essential tool for avoiding this dilemma. As the Canadian age discrimination cases show, proportionality analysis tends to divert judicial attention away from interpretive questions, such as whether the constitution recognizes particular rights, and towards questions of application, such as the degree of burden to the rights bearer, what justifications the government is relying on, and what alternatives are available to it. Under proportionality analysis, it becomes possible to treat the positive and negative dimensions of rights in just the same way, because the relevant question is not whether the right is *a right* but rather what the government is obligated to do, or

[53] *See Tetreault-Gadoury*, 2 S.C.R., at 41; *McKinney*, 3 S.C.R., at 279; Andrews v. Law Soc'y of Brit. Col., [1989] 1 S.CR. 143 (Can.).

[54] *See Tetreault-Gadoury*, 2 S.C.R., at 45.

refrain from doing, in virtue of the burdens it is placing on citizens. The answer to that question is neither "nothing" nor "everything." It is, in every case, "it depends."

The landmark Canadian case of *Eldridge v. British Columbia (Attorney General)* provides a striking example.[55] A nonprofit that had been providing sign-language interpretation for hearing-impaired patients in British Columbia hospitals at no cost to the province ceased operation and the province refused to pay for the service to continue. The Supreme Court of Canada held that the province was liable, not because disability rights are especially absolute or subject to some kind of "strict scrutiny" but rather because the ability to communicate with one's healthcare provider is vitally important in a hospital setting and the cost to the province to provide interpretation services was trivial.[56]

The province attempted to defend its actions using US-style slippery-slope arguments to the effect that a holding in favor of the patients in this case meant that the hospital would need to fund a host of language translation services, but Justice La Forest made short work of the claim, calling it "purely speculative" and noting the many relevant differences between people who cannot speak English or French and those who are hearing-impaired.[57] Justice La Forest noted those differences not to say that a different translation case would not arise or would necessarily come out differently but to say that such a claim and its outcome "cannot be predicted in advance."[58] A reluctance to decide hypothetical cases in advance of their concrete facts is a common feature of proportionality, which engages intimately with those facts to reach outcomes.

12.4.2 *Polycentric Constitutionalism*

Rights protection is not solely the province of courts. Indeed, the usual way in which communities protect the rights of their members is by making and enforcing laws in pursuit of public health, safety, and welfare. Whether by providing health care, health insurance, or various forms of assisted living, by promulgating pension or retirement rules, or by crafting other state-provided social insurance programs, legal accommodation of old age should occur primarily through legislation rather than court decisions. It is telling that accommodation and protection for people with disabilities, the closest analogue to a right to grow old, occurs primarily through the Americans with Disabilities Act (ADA),[59] the Rehabilitation Act,[60] the Individuals

55 [1997] 3 S.C.R. 624 (Can.).

56 *See id.* at 676, 686.

57 *Id.* at 687–688.

58 *Id.* at 688.

59 Americans with Disabilities Act of 1990, Pub. L. No. 101–336, 104 Stat. 327 (codified as amended in scattered sections of 29, 42, and 47 U.S.C.).

60 Rehabilitation Act of 1973, Pub. L. No. 93–112, 87 Stat. 355 (codified as amended in scattered sections of 29 U.S.C.).

with Disabilities Education Act (IDEA),[61] and state and local law. What protections federal law offers against age discrimination also occur primarily via statutes: the Age Discrimination in Employment Act (ADEA)[62] and the Age Discrimination Act.[63] Both the negative and – especially – the positive dimensions of the rights these laws advance reflect a constitutional vision enacted through laws, not just litigation.

And yet, these laws need a firmer constitutional foundation. According to the Supreme Court, Congress's power to pass both the ADA and the ADEA stems entirely from its power to regulate interstate commerce rather than from its power to enforce the equality and rights guarantees of the Fourteenth Amendment.[64] The reason for this limitation is that the Court reviews disability and age discrimination under rational-basis review rather than heightened scrutiny. This means that states that discriminate rationally against older people or people with disabilities have not violated the Constitution, which in turn means that Congress cannot premise legislation-holding states to higher standards on its Fourteenth Amendment enforcement power.

Being forced to defend rights-protective statutes as an exercise of the Commerce Clause has significant costs. In the ADA and ADEA contexts, it means that individuals aggrieved under these laws cannot bring damages actions against states.[65] And a chillier wind blows. The Court has declared that the Commerce Clause cannot be used to require Americans to engage in activities, which threaten accommodation requirements.[66]

A right to grow old need not necessarily rely on a heightened scrutiny for individual acts of age discrimination. It could be enough for the Court to recognize the power of Congress to legislate in rights-protective ways even for rights that the Court does not view in the same terms.

12.4.3 *Minimum Core*

International human rights law has grappled with the problem of giving justiciable or administrable content to the positive dimensions of rights. The United Nations Committee on Economic, Social, and Cultural Rights has interpreted the

61 Individuals with Disabilities Education Act (IDEA), Pub. L. No. 101–476, 104 Stat. 1103 (1990) (codified as amended and reauthorized at 20 U.S.C. §§ 1400–1485).

62 Age Discrimination in Employment Act of 1967, Pub. L. No. 90–202, 81 Stat. 602 (codified as amended at 29 U.S.C. §§ 621–634).

63 Age Discrimination Act of 1975, Pub. L. No. 94–135, 89 Stat. 728 (codified as amended at 42 U.S.C. §§ 6101–6107).

64 *See* Bd. of Trustees of Univ. of Ala. v. Garrett, 531 U.S. 356 (2001); Kimel v. Fla. Bd. of Regents, 528 U.S. 62 (2000).

65 *See Kimel*, 528 U.S., at 80.

66 Nat'l Fed'n of Indep. Bus. v. Sebelius, 567 U.S. 519, 550–555 (2012) (opinion of Roberts, J.).

International Covenant on Economic, Social, and Cultural Rights (ICESCR) to protect a "minimum core" of the rights that instrument recognizes, whether to food, health, education, or water.[67] The idea of minimum core obligations counters the concern that positive rights may induce legal decision-makers to try to maximize the provision of services beyond state capacity or the allocative competence of adjudicators by, instead, defining the government's obligations in minimalist terms.

The minimum core idea has held an appeal in international human rights law insofar as it enables the Committee to articulate obligations that must be fully and immediately realized regardless of a country's level of development. Thus, the Committee has offered in its General Comment on the right to health that its minimum core includes the right of nondiscriminatory access to health facilities, goods, and services; basic access to nutritionally adequate and safe food; access to basic shelter, housing, sanitation, and potable water; the provision of "essential drugs;" equitable distribution of health facilities; and adoption and implementation of a national health strategy.[68] Many countries, of course, fall below this minimum core for many of their citizens, but the conceit is that it is nonetheless coherent to label this failure a human rights violation. To apply the same label, for example, to a poor country's failure to provide access to higher standards of care would make the human rights regime (even more) vulnerable to charges of ineffectual idealism.

The minimum core concept has had relatively little traction in national constitutions – it was conspicuously rejected in an early South African Constitutional Court decision[69] – but it is portable between international and domestic law.[70] In the *Rodriguez* case, for example, a minimum core idea would have permitted the court to hold that some but not all discrepancies between rich and poor neighborhood schools were constitutionally tolerable. Perhaps a court could order schools to equalize costs of books and teacher salaries but not necessarily the number of field trips or the food options in the cafeteria. Inequity and injustice would of course remain, but the point of the minimum core in a domestic context is that courts can play a role in mitigating injustice even where institutional constraints prevent them from eradicating it.

In applying this idea to the right to grow old, a court could potentially require, for example, that health insurance for older Americans cover, at least in part, the costs of long-term assisted living, or that the government require, by law, that employers offer

67 *See* U.N. Comm. on Econ., Soc. & Cultural Rights, *Report on the Fifth Session*, Supp. No. 3, Annex III ¶ 10, U.N. Doc. E/1991/23 (1991).

68 U.N. Comm. on Econ., Soc. & Cultural Rights, 22d Sess., *The Right to the Highest Attainable Standard of Health*, U.N. Doc. E/C, Dec. 4, 2000, ICESR General Comment 14 (2000), at ¶ 43.

69 *See* Gov't of the Republic of S. Afr. v. Grootboom & Others, 2001 (1) SA 46 (CC) (S.Afr.).

70 *See* David Landau, *The Promise of a Minimum Core Approach: The Colombian Model for Judicial Review of Austerity Measures*, *in* Economic and Social Rights after the Global Financial Crisis 267 (Aoife Nolan ed., 2014).

employment guarantees for employees who must devote some time to caring for elderly relatives on a long-term basis. At a minimum, a right to grow old could simply mean that the government receives some deference from courts in the choices it makes in structuring programs of this sort.

12.4.4 *Progressive Realization*

The ICESCR obligates states to aim for "progressive realization" of the rights it identifies,[71] in recognition of the fact that, as Katharine Young writes, "[i]n international human rights law, waiting is an accepted part of rights realization."[72] A progressive realization norm generally assumes that "minimum core" is not an adequate global standard – it would, for example, give a pass to the wealthiest countries – but at the same time it concedes that states often lack the material, political, and institutional capacity to respect, protect, and fulfill rights fully and expeditiously. In addition to a variety of international human rights instruments, several domestic constitutions also include the language of progressive realization, and it has been much discussed in the South African constitutional context.[73]

Admittedly "progressive realization" might be a tough sell in the US. It sounds uncomfortably close to "with all deliberate speed," the much-maligned standard the Warren Court deployed in its too-deliberate implementation of *Brown v. Board of Education*.[74] The discomfort is well founded. Permitting a state to delay its implementation of constitutional rights allows it to smuggle political goals – up to and including outright resistance to the right – into claims of administrative necessity.

Still, the failure of the remedy ordered in *Brown* to overcome massive resistance to the implementation of that decision does not mean that progressive realization is never appropriate. That position overstates the capacity of judges to disrupt entrenched racial politics, and, in doing so, it denies courts a tool that may be necessary to the availability of positive rights. Judges don't like to order relief that will reliably be ignored or slow-walked. Without something like a commitment (concession?) to progressive realization, US courts are unlikely to find their way to positive rights.

A right to grow old could benefit from progressive realization through state duties to protect or promote the positive aspects of the right being stated in general terms:

[71] International Covenant on Economic, Social and Cultural Rights, Art. 2(1), Dec. 16, 1966, 993 U.N.T.S. 3.

[72] Katharine G. Young, *Waiting for Rights: Progressive Realization and Lost Time*, *in* THE FUTURE OF ECONOMIC AND SOCIAL RIGHTS 654, 654 (Katharine G. Young ed., 2019).

[73] *See id.* at 661–662; S. AFR. CONST. §§ 26–27; *see also* MALDIVES CONST. § 23; KENYA CONST. §§ 21, 82; S. SUDAN CONST. § 34; ZIMBABWE CONST. §§ 73, 75, 82; FIJI CONST. §§ 31–38; GUYANA CONST. § 154a.

[74] Brown v. Bd. of Educ., 349 U.S. 294, 301 (1955).

for example, a requirement that long-term care be facilitated without specifying exactly how much or through what channels, but by setting benchmarks for evaluation along the experimentalist model identified and championed by scholars such as Charles Sabel and William Simon.[75] Litigants could return to courts at a later date if progress is not forthcoming.

12.4.5 *Remedial Flexibility*

A final piece to the puzzle of respecting, protecting, and fulfilling a right to grow old comes, appropriately, at the end: flexible remedies. In part, the need for flexible remedies is but a restatement of the need for progressive realization. But there is a more specific point that bears mention. US courts tend to view dialogic approaches to remedies as exotic, even threatening to their credibility. Many constitutional courts around the world, including in Canada, Germany, Ireland, Israel, and South Africa, resort routinely to a remedial technique sometimes referred to as a "suspension of invalidity." This is a technique whereby a court issues a ruling on constitutionality but suspends the order for a set period of time to allow the state to structure the remedy as it sees fit. Thus, for example, in a South African case holding that a statute governing the procedure for criminal appeals was unconstitutional, the South African Constitutional Court suspended the validity of its judgment for more than a year to allow Parliament to develop new procedures for the processing of appeals.[76]

This technique is not entirely foreign to US courts. *Brown II* had something of this structure, as noted. Less high-profile but more to the point, in *Northern Pipeline Construction Co. v. Marathon Pipe Line Co.*, the Supreme Court held that bankruptcy courts had been given too much power, but it delayed its judgment by four months to give Congress time "to reconstitute the bankruptcy courts or to adopt other valid means of adjudication."[77] The suspension of invalidity device demonstrates that progressive realization need not involve endless dialogue but is amenable to the adoption of quite specific and coercive benchmarks.

12.5 CONCLUSION

The right to grow old is a tall order in the US, but it is not an impossible one. The inevitability of aging means that such a right likely faces fewer obstacles than other rights that have significant positive dimensions. It does not require the invention of new substantive rights – indeed, it is already constitutionally protected. It does, however, require a recognition of governmental duties of protection and fulfillment

[75] *See* Charles F. Sabel & William H. Simon, *Destabilization Rights: How Public Law Litigation Succeeds*, 117 Harv. L. Rev. 1016 (2004).

[76] State v. Ntuli, 1996 (1) SA 1207 (CC) (S. Afr.).

[77] N. Pipeline Constr. Co. v. Marathon Pipe Line Co., 458 U.S. 50, 88 (1981).

of rights that are not typical (though they do exist) in US constitutional law. The anxiety US courts face about such duties could be soothed by incorporating elements of proportionality analysis, by giving deference to political bodies acting to protect the rights of older Americans, and by availing themselves of some of the tools of incremental or partial rights realization that have become familiar within international human rights law.

PART III

Health, Workforce, and Innovation: The Investments Required for a Healthy Lifespan

13

The 100-Year-Old American and Our Health System

Yaron Covo, Abbe R. Gluck, and Linda P. Fried

There is a consensus among researchers that the US health system is inadequate when it comes to ensuring the health of older adults. Indeed, while many Americans live longer today than several decades ago, they often live those "extra" years in poor health.[1] In fact, Americans are generally less healthy than their counterparts in other high-income nations. For example, they are more likely to experience multiple chronic conditions and have far higher rates of obesity. And this is especially true for certain populations, most notably racial minorities and low-income individuals, who still suffer from structural racism and intergroup disparities in health.[2] This is ironic given that the US spends 4.3 trillion dollars a year on health care, much more than peer countries that enjoy far better health-related outcomes.[3]

In this chapter, we provide some insights into this conundrum, which has become acute due to the aging of the American population. Divided into three sections, this chapter will focus on offering structural interventions and their attendant benefits. Section 13.1 identifies the main goal of a successful health system in the twenty-first century – creating optimal health for a longer life – and the primary conditions needed for accomplishing this goal. These include a public health approach that zeroes in on ex-ante prevention, not just ex-post treatment, and an expanded geriatric healthcare workforce to meet the demands of an aging population. Section 13.2 considers the question of how to finance health care for the older population given the challenges posed by the rise in life expectancy. Section 13.3 imagines the unique opportunities – the so-called third demographic dividend – that may arise if Americans could live long, healthy lives.

[1] *U.S. Health Care from a Global Perspective, 2022: Accelerating Spending, Worsening Outcomes*, Commonwealth Fund (Jan. 31, 2023), https://www.commonwealthfund.org/publications/issue-briefs/2023/jan/us-health-care-global-perspective-2022.

[2] Dayna Bowen Matthew, Just Health: Treating Structural Racism to Heal America 4–13, 33–50 (2022).

[3] *NHE Fact Sheet*, CMS, https://www.cms.gov/research-statistics-data-and-systems/statistics-trends-and-reports/nationalhealthexpenddata/nhe-fact-sheet (accessed Aug. 27, 2023).

13.1 THE GOAL: OPTIMAL HEALTH FOR A LONGER LIFE

One important goal of a successful healthcare system in the twenty-first century is to prolong health span – the average length of healthy life[4] – so that people will be able to live meaningful and purposeful lives well into their nineties and beyond. Achieving this goal is no doubt a difficult task, but it is possible.[5] It requires taking a wide array of measures across several healthcare dimensions, such as physician compensation, insurance, and health professionals' training, as well as focusing on broader issues, including revising the public health system, nutrition, and affordable housing. Space does not permit a comprehensive analysis of all of the steps required to accomplish this goal. Instead, this chapter focuses on two exigent issues: (1) the particular importance, in the context of health span, of investing in public health systems; and (2) reshaping geriatric care. We discuss each of these issues in turn.

13.1.1 *Rebalancing and Aligning Public Health and Healthcare Systems*

Promoting older adults' health requires taking measures during the decades that precede old age. Indeed, as one of us has noted elsewhere, "people who arrive at old age healthy are positioned to remain healthier into the oldest ages."[6] To translate such a "life course" perspective into a practical framework, we need to focus not only on the delivery of health care but also on the conditions necessary for people to be healthy. This means, for example, guaranteeing that all Americans can access healthy food, participate in physical activities, and have opportunities for social engagement. In other words, we need to build a social infrastructure that makes healthy choices easy choices – an approach that has traditionally been associated with a public health framework. To do this, we need to reinvest in the US public health system and mandate it to increase health span for all.

The public health system is responsible for the actions "we, as a society, do collectively to assure the conditions in which people can be healthy,"[7] with particular focus on preventing disease, disability, and injury and on improving the health of the population. It accomplishes this through the work of the Centers for Disease Control and Prevention (CDC) and 3,000 state, local, tribal, and territorial departments, through actions ranging from surveillance to assess health and its drivers to recommending and implementing programs, policies, and practices for improved population health based on scientific evidence.

4 Eileen M. Crimmins, *Lifespan and Healthspan: Past, Present, and Promise*, 55 Gerontologist 901, 901 (2015).

5 National Academy of Medicine, Global Roadmap for Healthy Longevity 1–5, 221–222 (2022) [hereinafter Global Roadmap].

6 Linda P. Fried, *Investing in Health to Create a Third Demographic Dividend*, 56 Gerontologist S167, S171 (2016).

7 Institute of Medicine, The Future of Public Health 1, 19 (1988).

Unfortunately, as the COVID-19 pandemic made evident, the US health system has failed to fully realize a public health infrastructure. One primary reason is that the field of public health has been disinvested over the past sixty years. Responsible for 70 percent of a population's health,[8] it receives less than 3 percent of US health dollars. In the US, the healthcare sector has traditionally focused on *ameliorating or curing* conditions. Despite some progress in recent years, most notably as a result of the passage of the Affordable Care Act (ACA), policymakers have not given enough attention to the role of individualized prevention strategies in promoting health. At the same time, the complementary population-focused perspective of the public health system is critical for success.

In recent decades, the US has only decreased the share of its public health spending vis-à-vis total health spending. One reason has to do with the way federal legislation is scored for budget purposes; it's hard to quantify upfront, as federal law requires, short-term returns on investments in public health infrastructure. Relatedly, the longer timeline for returns on investments in public health often does not sync with election cycles and political arguments. Nevertheless, as a number of researchers have shown, our traditional focus on individualized treatment is often less cost-effective than population-based prevention and health promotion, and individualized care is not sufficient to accomplish prevention.[9] Both are needed, in the right balance.

The US approach is exceptional from a comparative perspective. On average, the Organization for Economic Co-operation and Development (OECD) member countries spend more than double on non-healthcare social investments than they do on health care.[10] And the data unequivocally indicate that the approach taken by other OECD members leads to far better outcomes at lower cost: The US obesity rate is almost double the OECD average and the percentage of people experiencing chronic conditions is also much higher in the US than in other countries. Against this backdrop, the US National Academy of Medicine's recently released "Global Roadmap for Healthy Longevity" called for significantly increased investment in public health system-led prevention.[11]

Promoting a public health perspective has the potential to benefit everyone, but it is particularly important for older adults, who are at greater risk of experiencing chronic conditions such as cancer, hypertension, diabetes, and Alzheimer's. In recent years, there has been growing evidence showing that, despite common

8 J. Michael McGinnis & William H. Foege, *Actual Causes of Death in the United States*, 270 JAMA 2207 (1993); Steven A. Schroeder, *We Can Do Better: Improving the Health of the American People*, N. Eng. J. Med. 1221 (2007).

9 Inst. of Med., For the Public's Health: Investing in a Healthier Future 28 (2012) [hereinafter For the Public's Health].

10 Ano Lobb, *Health Care and Social Spending in OECD Nations*, 99 Am. J. Pub. Health 1542, 1543 (tbl. 1) (2009).

11 Global Roadmap, *supra* note 5, at 14–15, 178–179, 182–191.

beliefs, the emergence of chronic conditions in older ages is not inevitable; rather, it may depend on an array of individual, social, and environmental factors, and reducing such exposures is effective prevention.[12] Thus, we need the public health system to deliver programs for older adults, as well as middle-aged, to prevent heart disease, strokes, falls, diabetes, cognitive impairment, disability and frailty, as well as loneliness. Specific interventions include investing in a range of community-based public health programs aimed at increasing physical activity, eating healthy foods, and not smoking, as well as increasing social connection and engagement. For example, programs involving food labeling and public service announcements have been proven useful in encouraging people to consume healthier products.[13] Allowing older adults to buy affordable bags of vegetables, fruits, and protein from accessible stores serves as another example for an intervention in the area of nutrition. Other public health programs may include, perhaps more ambitiously, controlling air and water pollution and toxins in our environment that both damage children's brains and increase dementia risk.

Loneliness is epidemic among both old and young. The US Surgeon General's report in 2023 advocates public health systems and offices for the aging working together to build expanded opportunities for social connection and engagement in communities to help decrease loneliness.[14] For example, group exercise programs designed for older adults with different health statuses may foster connectivity and increase strength, balance, and fitness among participants.

There is strong evidence that a diversity of population-based programs to increase a community's physical activity levels, to make healthy foods accessible and affordable, and to teach people to prepare nutritious foods are important components of preventing obesity and diabetes, and lowering the risks of these diseases reduces risks of subsequent cardiovascular disease.[15] Moreover, in an oft-cited study conducted in Finland, researchers found that elderly people who were at risk of dementia and had received a two-year, "multidomain" preventive intervention (focusing on dietary changes, physical activity, and cognitive training) experienced a significant improvement in cognitive functions in comparison to their counterparts who only received general health recommendations.[16] This finding is promising in its own right, but it is especially important given that existing medical treatment for Alzheimer's disease,

[12] *Id.* at 26–27, 180.

[13] *Id.* at 184.

[14] Vivek H. Murthy, *Our Epidemic of Loneliness and Isolation: The U.S. Surgeon General's Advisory on the Healing Effects of Social Connection and Community*, US Dep't of Health & Hum. Servs. (2023), https://www.hhs.gov/sites/default/files/surgeon-general-social-connection-advisory.pdf.

[15] Global Roadmap, *supra* note 5, at 180–191.

[16] Tiia Ngandu et al., *A 2 Year Multidomain Intervention of Diet, Exercise, Cognitive Training, and Vascular Risk Monitoring versus Control to Prevent Cognitive Decline in At-Risk Elderly People (FINGER): A Randomised Controlled Trial*, 385 Lancet 2255 (2015).

the most common type of dementia, has yet to prove meaningful, long-term efficacy.[17]

Given the promise of preventive care, why haven't we put more emphasis on public health interventions? One explanation found in the literature has to do with the so-called "prevention paradox," which means that individualized treatment is prioritized over preventive measures because the former (individualized medical care) is perceived as more exigent, even though the latter (preventive measures) may be more cost-effective. However, the data are clear that both are necessary to increase the health span of Americans or any population, and investment in public health needs to be adequate.

To prolong health span, we will need to overcome the prevention paradox. One possible avenue to promote preventive measures is to use tax benefits and reimbursement structures to incentivize healthcare providers to incorporate individualized prevention into the care provided to patients. Professor Lindsay Wiley points to several real-world examples of programs implementing this approach, including the ACA's preventive services mandate (which has recently been subject to legal challenges), tax benefits structures that trigger hospitals' engagement in community needs assessments, and other reimbursement structures that encourage hospitals to offer flu testing and vaccinations to their patients.[18] Yet as Wiley notes, a meaningful alignment of public health and healthcare systems requires more investment on both prevention and collective concerns.

Another avenue is to create a legal infrastructure in which public health departments provide data and monitoring to support healthcare providers. For example, stronger public health–clinical care alignment may allow public health entities to utilize population-level data and assist the medical care delivery system in "identifying ineffective or inappropriate clinical care."[19] This entails recruiting public health practitioners with expertise in health promotion and prevention, with an emphasis on older adults' health.

13.1.2 *Reshaping Geriatric Care*

Even with the needed focus on a healthy life span throughout the ever-longer "old age," older adults often do experience age-related illnesses and decline in physical and cognitive functioning. As a result, older adults are more vulnerable to frailty, falls, disability, and injury or acute illness than their younger counterparts. Further,

[17] Elodie Passeri, *Alzheimer's Disease: Treatment Strategies and Their Limitations*, 23 Int. J. Molecular Sci. 13954 (2022).

[18] Lindsay F. Wiley, *From Patient Rights to Health Justice: Securing the Public's Interest in Affordable, High-Quality Health Care*, 37 Cardozo L. Rev. 833, 867–871 (2016).

[19] For the Public's Health, *supra* note 9, at 21.

approximately 80 percent of people sixty-five and older have one or more chronic conditions, and half have two or more such conditions.[20]

Yet geriatric care in the US remains inadequate, in terms of both workforce size and quality of care, despite the essential expertise that geriatric medicine provides in the care of older adults. However, understanding the physiologic changes with aging and managing older people with multiple chronic conditions and complex needs require that expertise. For example, according to one estimation, there are only 7,500 certified geriatricians in the US[21] – approximately half of the estimated number of practicing urologists (14,000)[22] and less than a fifth of practicing OB-GYNs (50,000).[23] As we describe further below, the low number of geriatric specialists leads to a shortage at a time when there is an increasing demand for geriatric health care.

By way of comparison, consider the way in which the demand for pediatric services created by the mid twentieth-century "baby boom" transformed pediatric care. Between 1938 and 1955, the number of pediatricians in the US tripled,[24] and by the end of the 1960s, the American Association of Pediatricians had almost quadrupled in size compared to 1950.[25] During this period, pediatricians in the US shaped a "new," holistic form of pediatric practice, in part in response to the jump in the number of births after World War II.[26] One would expect the US health system to similarly evolve to meet the needs of the growing population of older adults, but this has not been the case. Indeed, the current number of certified geriatricians reflects only a minuscule increase in comparison to the already small number of certified geriatricians almost two decades ago.[27]

Thus, to adapt to the increasing number of older adults and the ensuing demand for high-quality geriatric services, there is a need to fundamentally invest in geriatric care. In doing so, policymakers should focus on four existing dilemmas: (1) how to

[20] Joelle H. Fong, *Disability Incidence and Functional Decline among Older Adults with Major Chronic Diseases*, 19 BMC GERIATRICS 323 (2019).

[21] *Current Number of Board Certified Geriatricians by State*, AM. GERIATRICS SOC'Y (updated July 2022), https://www.americangeriatrics.org/sites/default/files/inline-files/Current%20Number%20of%20Board%20Certified%20Geriatricians%20by%20State%20%28July%202022%29.pdf.

[22] *Practicing Urologists in the United States 2022*, AM. UROLOGICAL ASS'N 5, 16 (2023), https://www.auanet.org/documents/research/census/State%20Urology%20Workforce%20Practice%20US.pdf.

[23] US DEP'T OF HEALTH & HUM. SERVS., PROJECTIONS OF SUPPLY AND DEMAND FOR WOMEN'S HEALTH SERVICE PROVIDERS: 2018–2030 (2021), at 10, https://bhw.hrsa.gov/sites/default/files/bureau-health-workforce/data-research/projections-supply-demand-2018-2030.pdf.

[24] DOROTHY PAWLUCH, THE NEW PEDIATRICS: A PROFESSION IN TRANSITION 31 (1996).

[25] AM. ACAD. OF PEDIATRICS, 90 YEARS OF CARING FOR CHILDREN, 1930–2020 (2020), at 10–12.

[26] Alexandra Minna Stern & Howard Markel, *Introduction, in* FORMATIVE YEARS: CHILDREN'S HEALTH IN THE UNITED STATES: 1880–2000, 1, 12 (Alexandra Minna Stern & Howard Markel eds., 2002).

[27] INST. OF MED., RETOOLING FOR AN AGING AMERICA: BUILDING THE HEALTH CARE WORKFORCE 125 (2008) [hereinafter RETOOLING FOR AN AGING AMERICA].

attract and retain high-quality geriatric specialists; (2) how to improve training and education; (3) how to design settings and systems in which proper care can be provided; and (4) how to create robust social and digital infrastructure for care and health promotion.

Let us begin with the healthcare workforce. Over the past two decades, an array of reports and studies have consistently shown that the US healthcare system experiences significant shortages of board-certified geriatricians, and this supply–demand gap is projected to increase in the near future.[28] There are several reasons for this deficiency, but one particular factor is compensation: Geriatricians have lower salaries than general internists and family medicine physicians, even though geriatric certification generally requires additional training (most commonly in the form of fellowships) that goes beyond what is required for internal or family medicine certification.[29]

When the relatively low compensation is combined with the perceived lower prestige of the profession and the complex clinical needs associated with some older adults, specializing in geriatric health care may be less appealing. To make things even more complicated, the widespread reliance on the relative value unit (RVU) as a metric to assess clinical productivity for reimbursement purposes fails to adequately account for the time and effort needed to provide high-quality care for older adults with complex healthcare needs.[30] As a result of these structural features of geriatric care, some medical professionals may choose an alternative, higher-income medical specialty. In fact, some physicians cannot even afford to become geriatric specialists. And the problem does not end with certified medical geriatricians: Similar shortages exist across other elder-care professions, from nurses, to pharmacists, to social workers, to other healthcare providers.

To address the workforce problem, policymakers should craft plans to recruit high-quality healthcare professionals with geriatric specialty. In addition to increasing wages, policymakers should use scholarships, loan forgiveness, clinical internships, and other financial incentives to attract qualified geriatricians, as well as to solve reimbursement and financial disincentives.[31]

We do not think that machines can or should replace clinical support workers. A number of scholars have argued that so-called "care robots" – which have been recently introduced to support elder care around the world – can address shortages in skilled labor and may "increasingly play a role in supplementing lower-skilled

[28] *Id.* at 123–126.

[29] John W. Rowe, Terry Fulmer & Linda P. Fried, *Preparing for Better Health and Health Care for an Aging Population*, 316 JAMA 1643, 1643 (2016).

[30] Neil M. Resnick & Nichole Radulovich, *The Relative Value Unit in Academic Geriatrics: Incentive or Impediment?* 62 J. Am. Geriatric Soc. 553 (2014).

[31] Terry Fulmer et al., *Actualizing Better Health and Health Care for Older Adults*, 40 Health Aff. 219, 220 (2021).

work and providing new avenues for patient engagement."[32] Insofar as artificial intelligence (AI) and care robots can assist patients and healthcare workers with performing technical, administrative tasks such as reminding a person to take routine medication, this may ameliorate some of the demands on the geriatric workforce. Nevertheless, the use of care robots also exposes patients to digital devices with far-reaching recording and surveillance capacities, which raises significant concerns about the ability to protect patients' privacy and autonomy. Moreover, we are wary that the use of AI and robots could distract decision-makers from the need to invest in the elder-care workforce. Thus, to the extent robots are being used to provide care, it should be in addition to – not instead of – human physicians and providers.

However, recruitment and retention of a high-quality workforce is not enough; the education and training provided to healthcare professionals, both geriatricians and nongeriatricians, should also be improved. Although people sixty-five and older use various health services – including hospital visits and emergency medical service responses – at much higher rates than the rest of the US population, many healthcare professionals lack the sufficient competency to understand and deal with the challenges associated with age-related frailty and vulnerability. A 2008 Institute of Medicine report pointed to "lack of faculty, lack of funding, lack of time in already-busy curricula, and the lack of recognition of the importance of geriatric training" in medical schools as the primary reasons for this inadequacy.[33]

Another recent report found that the US healthcare system is rife with "neglect, insensitivity, and even abuse" when it comes to treating older adults.[34] The report documents physicians' use of demeaning language directed toward older adults and concludes that the "lives of older patients are seen as less valuable than younger patients."[35] It also finds that elder abuse in nursing homes and other institutional settings results in part from insufficient staff training that could otherwise prevent such disturbing phenomena. These findings reflect the entrenched ageism in the US healthcare system – ageism that was exacerbated during the COVID-19 pandemic, when institutionalized older adults were put at great risk. Although more than 165,000 nursing home residents have died from COVID-19,[36] the conditions that gave rise to the deaths of institutionalized older Americans have still not been addressed postpandemic.

[32] Valarie K. Blake, *Regulating Care Robots*, 92 Temp. L. Rev. 551, 553, 555 (2020).

[33] Retooling for an Aging America, *supra* note 27, at 128.

[34] The Anti-Ageism Taskforce at the International Longevity Center, Ageism in America (2022), at 71, https://aging.columbia.edu/sites/default/files/Ageism_in_America.pdf [hereinafter Ageism in America].

[35] *Id.*

[36] *COVID-19 Nursing Home Data*, Centers for Medicare & Medicaid Services (Sep. 10, 2023), https://data.cms.gov/covid-19/covid-19-nursing-home-data.

To improve the geriatric competence of healthcare workers, researchers have proposed several strategies that pertain to both geriatricians and nongeriatricians. First, with respect to all healthcare workers, both in clinical care and in public health, researchers recommend training such workers in a variety of settings, including nursing homes and older people's homes, as well as incorporating simulations and virtual learning into their training. Adopting this strategy would change the status quo, whereby most of the training of healthcare professionals takes place in hospitals, even though older adults receive large portions of care in nonhospital settings. Second, with respect to providers who pursue a career in geriatrics, researchers suggest conditioning the granting of license and certifications on proof of competence in the care and health promotion of older adults, as well as raising minimum training standards for certain paraprofessionals, including certified nursing assistants and personal care aides. While these proposals address different objectives and target different healthcare and public health professions, they all share the underlying recognition that respectful and effective care for older adults begins at the training stage and requires regulators to take proactive approaches.

As the population ages, healthcare professionals – regardless of whether they specialize in geriatrics – will increasingly need to be attuned to elder mistreatment. Healthcare professionals are often in the best position to recognize the warning signs of elder abuse, neglect, and exploitation. In addition, they may be in a unique position to intervene. Since abusers often isolate their victims, older adults' healthcare providers may be their only meaningful human contact other than their abuser. When healthcare providers do not recognize mistreatment, they not only miss a potentially valuable opportunity to intervene but may end up facilitating the mistreatment. For example, a provider who does not recognize a caregiver's abuse of a patient may implicitly signal to the caregiver or patient that the mistreatment is "normal" and that it can continue with impunity.

Similarly, it will be ever more imperative for healthcare professionals to have a sophisticated understanding of how to support patients with diminished cognitive capacity. For example, healthcare professionals will increasingly need to not only be alert to the possibility that their older patients may be experiencing cognitive decline, but also recognize when additional support or time may be needed for patients to be able to make informed choices.

As for the settings in which care is provided, most older adults in the US live in their homes or in a family member's house.[37] By contrast, 1 million older adults (4 percent of the entire older adult population) live and receive care in nursing homes. While this may seem a relatively small number, it is important to address the consequences of providing care to older adults in nursing homes and other institutional settings. The COVID-19 pandemic exposed the inadequacy of some

[37] Allison K. Hoffman, *Reimagining the Risk of Long-Term Care*, 16 Yale J. Health Pol'y. L. & Ethics 147, 165–171 (2016).

institutional long-term care facilities in the US, including care provided in many nursing homes. The devastating number of COVID-19-related deaths, noted above, alongside long-standing evidence about the poor conditions surrounding many nursing homes across the country, has led to major proposals for designing long-term care in people's homes and other noninstitutional settings. There is also a pressing need to redesign nursing homes to prevent infectious diseases and maintain human contact.

While scholars disagree about whether nursing homes – as a distinct concept – are necessarily part of the problem or potentially part of the solution, all seem to recognize that most US nursing homes are currently underresourced and prone to abuse and neglect. According to a 2022 report, 90 percent of nursing homes suffer from inadequate staffing,[38] and this is particularly the case when it comes to settings with high percentages of Black residents.[39] To address this problem, in April 2024, the US Department of Health and Human Services adopted a final rule setting a minimum staffing threshold for nursing homes that participate in Medicaid and Medicare.[40] Some elder advocates, however, argue that more ambitious standards are necessary to meaningfully improve the conditions in nursing homes.[41]

The US nursing home problem is exacerbated by the fact that (1) Medicare, which provides health insurance to people aged sixty-five and older, covers only peripheral aspects of long-term services, and (2) to be eligible for long-term services under Medicaid, one must first exhaust their own financial resources. Moreover, Medicaid coverage for long-term care is limited and reflects a preference for nursing homes over private homes and community-based settings in that it requires states' programs to provide funding for long-term care in nursing homes while at the same time conditioning the provision of care in people's homes on the availability of discretionary "waiver programs."[42]

To be sure, recent decades have seen a shift in federal policy with the aim of moving people from nursing homes and institutions to community-based settings, a shift that was initially bolstered by the Supreme Court 1999 decision in *Olmstead v. L.C. ex rel. Zimring*,[43] which held that undue institutionalization constitutes disability discrimination. But the Court also considered states' budgetary constraints,

38 Ageism in America, *supra* note 34, at 9.

39 Global Roadmap, *supra* note 5, at 205.

40 89 Fed. Reg. 40876, 40879 (2024); *Biden-Harris Administration Takes Historic Action to Increase Access to Quality Care, and Support to Families and Care Workers*, CMS (Apr. 22, 2024), https://www.cms.gov/newsroom/press-releases/biden-harris-administration-takes-historic-action-increase-access-quality-care-and-support-families.

41 Jordan Rau, *Federal Officials Propose New Nursing Home Standards to Increase Staffing*, N.Y. Times (Sep. 1, 2023), https://www.nytimes.com/2023/09/01/health/nursing-home-staffing-cms.html.

42 Larisa Antonisse, *Strengthening the Right to Medicaid Home and Community-Based Services in the Post-COVID Era*, 121 Colum. L. Rev. 1801 (2021).

43 527 U.S. 581 (1999).

holding that a state could avoid liability if it showed that it had a "working plan" for placing disabled people in community-based settings. The upshot is that, even after *Olmstead*, many states keep long waiting lists for Americans who wish to receive home- and community-based services.[44] Thus, expanding in-home Medicaid coverage would allow more older adults to receive care in their homes – which is where they usually prefer to reside – instead of in nursing homes. The goal should be a coordinated continuum of care rather than discrete systems with lack of care continuity and shared medical records.

The final problem addressed here is that the social, digital, and legal infrastructure in the US is not strong enough to allow all older adults to take advantage of recent technological developments, most notably telehealth. For example, according to estimates, 21–42 million people in the US do not have access to broadband internet,[45] and those who are connected to the internet may lack the digital literacy necessary to receive high-quality telemedicine care. This is ironic, given that older adults in remote and rural places – where it is sometimes hard to find specialists in various medical disciplines – are more likely to benefit from telehealth but are less likely to have access to the digital infrastructure needed for such services. Thus, the unequal access to digital devices and broadband internet may *increase* health disparities across socioeconomic and geographic lines, notwithstanding the promise that telemedicine holds.

In sum, the myriad problems described earlier require an overhaul to the structural and institutional systems that affect the compensation, education, training, and evaluation of geriatricians and other healthcare professionals, as well as the systems and environments in which care is provided.

13.2 FINANCING A TWENTY-FIRST-CENTURY ELDER-CARE SYSTEM

The question of how to finance health care for the older population is particularly challenging given the demographic trend that is the focus of this volume, as well as the sociopolitical situation surrounding the US healthcare system's funding. For example, Medicare is facing "significant financing issues."[46] According to 2023 federal reports, the annual cost of Medicare is projected to increase from 3.9 percent of GDP in 2023 to 6 percent of GDP by 2045. As a result, Medicare's Hospital Insurance trust fund – which covers inpatient hospital care and posthospitalization care in rehabilitation or nursing facilities – is projected to become depleted as early as 2031. The main reason, of course, has to do with the aging population, which

[44] Nina A. Kohn, *Nursing Homes, COVID-19, and the Consequences of Regulatory Failure*, 110 Geo. L.J. Online 1, 11 (2021).

[45] Linda P. Fried, *The Need to Invest in a Public Health System for Older Adults and Longer Lives, Fit for the Next Pandemic*, 9 Frontiers in Pub. Health (2021).

[46] Social Security and Medicare Boards of Trustees, Status of the Social Security and Medicare Programs: A Summary of the 2023 Annual Reports (2023), at 2.

increases the number of beneficiaries and consequently the costs of insurance coverage. Existing proposals to solve this problem include increasing Medicare tax rates, introducing changes into Medicare's funding mechanisms, and increasing the program's enrollment age.

So, what can be done to tackle the financing issue? Let us begin by noting that adopting some of the proposals described in Section 13.1 might actually *save* money for the US health system. In an ideal world, that money, in turn, could be used to finance additional services and programs aimed at prolonging Americans' health span. The problem is that federal spending is often siloed; money saved in Medicare isn't given to the CDC for public health infrastructure investment, for example. And the way federal budget scoring occurs, long-term investments in public health are often scored as deficits on the books, if the expected benefits occur outside a ten-year budget window.[47]

Nevertheless, there is robust evidence that increasing public health investments is likely to reduce healthcare costs associated with treating disease and injury by advancing prevention at the population level. One study, for example, estimated that ex-ante interventions aimed at preventing obesity, diabetes, and hypertension would accrue considerable health-related benefits at reduced costs compared to the costs associated with ex-post clinical treatment.[48] In fact, the decrease in cardiovascular disease and other causes of ill health reduces healthcare costs, with a fourteenfold return on investment.[49] However, America's health has been worsening,[50] with rising infant and maternal mortality, obesity, diabetes, homicides and suicides, loneliness, worsening mental health, and drug addiction. In combination, these contribute to rising healthcare costs.

There is also evidence that providing care in homes and community-based settings is not more expensive – and may even be cheaper per individual – than institutional settings and nursing homes. One study examined data pertaining to the expansion of home- and community-based services in Ohio over a twenty-year period and found that the expansion did not result in a significant increase in expenditures.[51] Another study, which analyzed data from the vast majority of US

47 This might result in sequestration under PAYGO ("pay-as-you-go") rules, which require that new legislation involving mandatory spending "must not increase projected deficits." *The Statutory Pay-As-You-Go Act of 2010: A Description*, White House Off. of Mgmt. & Budget, https://obamawhitehouse.archives.gov/omb/paygo_description/#:~:text=2010%3A%20A%20Description-,The%20Statutory%20Pay%2DAs%2DYou%2DGo%20Act%20of%202010,must%20not%20increase%20projected%20deficits (accessed Sep. 26, 2023).

48 Dana P. Goldman et al., *The Benefits of Risk Factor Prevention in Americans Aged 51 Years and Older*, 99 Rsch. & Practice 2096 (2009).

49 Matt McKillop & Dara Alpert Lieberman, The Impact of Chronic Underfunding on America's Public Health System: Trends, Risks, and Recommendations (2021), at 8.

50 Inst. of Med., U.S. Health in International Perspective: Shorter Lives, Poorer Health 1–4 (2013).

51 Diane Berish et al., *Is There a Woodwork Effect? Addressing a 200-Year Debate on the Impacts of Expanding Community-Based Services*, 31 J. Aging & Soc. Policy 85, 94–96 (2019).

jurisdictions, estimated that the provision of home- and community-based services actually saved money in comparison to the costs associated with the provision of care in nursing facilities.[52] All of this is to say that the US healthcare system can do more to improve older adults' health with the money already spent on health-related measures.

But even if creating a health system with well-balanced investments in public health and medical care would entail an additional investment of public funds, such an investment is essential. An aging population that is unhealthy in large part will bring new financial stresses, not to mention increasing stress on family caregivers. In 1965, when Medicare was enacted, President Lyndon Johnson declared that older Americans would no longer "be denied the healing miracle of modern medicine."[53] He referred to Medicare protection as "the hand of justice" that is offered to older adults who themselves had given "a lifetime of service and wisdom and labor to the progress" of the US.[54] As these statements make clear, federal legislation concerning healthcare funding for the elderly has been inextricably linked to norms about caring for older adults.

Long-term care is one of the areas where investment of public funds is most needed. Although the Community Living Assistance Services and Supports Act (CLASS) established a social insurance program aimed at addressing this issue, the program has never been activated because of its sole reliance on participants' premiums (with no additional tax dollars), which was insufficient to ensure solvency. Given the limited coverage offered by Medicaid and Medicare, as described earlier, and the fact that the vast majority of Americans do not have private insurance coverage for long-term care, it is imperative to increase funding for such care – either under Medicaid or a potential universal social insurance policy – to allow Americans to receive care in the setting they prefer and to relieve some of the burden on older adults' caregivers.[55]

Indeed, the failure to ensure adequate funding for long-term care has been detrimental not only to the older adults who need such care but also to their formal and informal caregivers. With respect to formal caregivers, federal labor laws in the US have historically provided insufficient wage and work-hour protections to direct-care workers who provide older adults with clinical services, emotional support, and assistance with bathing, dressing, and other everyday activities. This state of affairs has resulted, at least in part, from concerns that improving labor standards for such

[52] Charliene Harrington, N. G. Terence & Martin Kitchener, *Do Medicaid Home and Community Based Service Waivers Save Money?* 30 Home Health Care Services Q. 198 (2011).

[53] Lyndon B. Johnson, *Remarks with President Truman at the Signing in Independence of the Medicare Bill* (July 30, 1965), https://www.presidency.ucsb.edu/documents/remarks-with-president-truman-the-signing-independence-the-medicare-bill.

[54] *Id.*

[55] Rachel M. Werner, Allison K. Hoffman & Norma B. Coe, *Long-Term Care Policy after COVID-19: Solving the Nursing Home Crisis*, 383 N. Eng. J. Med. 903 (2020).

workers would increase the costs of long-term care and ultimately force older adults to receive fewer services.[56] While some progress has been made in this regard (most notably by extending Fair Labor Standards Act protections to home-care workers in 2013), many home-care workers – who are disproportionally women and people of color – are still underpaid and often unable to gain overtime payments.[57] Moreover, poor working conditions for direct-care workers may lead to high turnover rates and low motivation among these workers, which run counter to the interests of older adults themselves.

The lack of a social insurance policy for long-term care also affects informal caregivers, who are disproportionately women and often have to reduce their own household or workforce productivity to care for elderly family members. In fact, family members and friends frequently have no choice but to fill the caregiving vacuum, resulting in tremendous monetary and emotional costs.[58] As Professor Allison Hoffman has demonstrated, these costs are currently not accounted for under existing policies.[59] And taking them into consideration, Hoffman notes, helpfully "redefines the scale of the problem of long-term care."[60] Addressing the problem will require a multidimensional solution, but one thing seems clear: Part of the solution should involve increased state and federal funding. As the final section will illustrate, investing in the health of older adults may actually have unexpected benefits for society at large.

13.3 IMAGINING HEALTHY LONGEVITY: UNLEASHING A THIRD DEMOGRAPHIC DIVIDEND

Our contention is that the measures proposed in this chapter to improve Americans' health span could unleash a "*third* demographic dividend" whereby society reaps the benefits – both economic and noneconomic – of having a healthy and engaged older population.[61]

According to the conventional narrative, a first demographic dividend occurs when children survive and age into employability.[62] A second demographic dividend results from labor supply then exceeding the share of the population that is

56 Lisa I. Lezzoni, Naomi Gallopyn & Kezia Scales, *Historical Mismatch between Home-Based Care Policies and Laws Governing Home Care Workers*, 38 Health Aff. 973, 976–977 (2019).

57 Pamela J. Doty, Marie R. Squillace & Edward Kako, *Analysis of State Efforts to Comply with Fair Labor Standards Act Protections to Home Care Workers*, US Dep't Health & Hum. Services (Dec. 2019), at 2–3, https://aspe.hhs.gov/sites/default/files/migrated_legacy_files//193336/FLSAimpl.pdf.

58 Hoffman, *supra* note 37.

59 *Id.*

60 *Id.* at 156.

61 Fried, *supra* note 6.

62 David E. Bloom, David Canning & Jaypee Sevilla, The Demographic Dividend 39 (2003).

below working age. As a result of this shift in labor supply, society experiences an increase in production and benefits from a stronger workforce, strengthening the economy and investments that further increase longevity. As people live longer, they are more likely to save money and prepare for retirement. With more productivity and national wealth, increased life expectancy creates opportunities and incentives to invest in education and human capital.

Longevity, however, has more to offer US society. If we develop the proper public health, social, and legal infrastructure, our society can extend health span and enable older adults' social capital to confer generative impact through more paid employment, national or local service, volunteering, and social and political activism. This, in turn, could give rise to a third demographic dividend in which society can thrive due to both healthy longevity and transformations to a society that enables the opportunities of our longer lives to support all ages flourishing.[63]

To have a sense of what such a society might look like, consider the education arena. As students in the US try to fill the educational gaps that resulted from the COVID-19 pandemic, the American education system could benefit from older volunteers assisting students in various academic and social tasks. Such a mentoring and tutoring program – the "Experience Corps" – is already operating in twenty cities across the country, connecting senior adults with students in public elementary schools who need assistance in reading and other aspects of academic performance. The senior volunteers benefit not only from the human interaction and generative impact that the program facilitates[64] but also from improved cognition, mental health, and physical strength.[65] Similar programs can address other social goals. For example, during public health emergencies such as the COVID-19 pandemic, older adults could take on community roles aimed at supporting their neighbors, sharing advice, and building resilience. As a different kind of example, many retired health professionals were called back into service to fill work shortages during the pandemic.[66] Here again, such programs would not only contribute to the public's health but also reduce older adults' loneliness and promote their self-esteem and sense of belonging.

Other examples pertain to the potential contribution of older adults to labor and consumer markets. Many of today's jobs do not entail physically strenuous work and could be fulfilled by older adults. Requiring employers to provide reasonable accommodations for aging workers regardless of disability status may

63 Global Roadmap, *supra* note 5, at 51–81.

64 *Id.* at 72–73.

65 Linda P. Fried et al., *Experience Corps: A Dual Trial to Promote the Health of Older Adults and Children's Academic Success*, 36 Contemp. Clin. Trials 1 (2013).

66 Chris Farrell, *Retired Doctors Return to Work for COVID-19*, Next Avenue (Mar. 27, 2020), https://www.nextavenue.org/retired-doctors-return-to-work-for-covid-19/.

allow more older adults to retain their jobs.[67] Further, employers are increasingly recognizing that intergenerational teams are more proactive and innovative. They are developing flexible approaches to retirement and time commitments, which ultimately benefit adults of all ages. To incentivize employers to hire older adult workers, Fried and her colleagues suggest using subsidies that would help to reduce employers' costs associated with employing older adults, for example, by ensuring that Medicare would serve as a primary payer for health insurance for such employees.[68] Another way to increase work opportunities among older adults is retraining programs that allow people to develop new expertise and careers.[69]

As people live and work longer, more age-friendly products will be needed to fit their needs. That, in turn, is likely to give rise to the involvement of older adults in the development and design processes of such products. A new market that relies upon the contribution of older adults as expert designers and customers may emerge – and with it, expanded jobs for all ages.

To be sure, healthy longevity alone is not sufficient for creating a society in which older adults are active participants in every aspect of social life; we also need to find the ways to counteract ageism and establish the social institutions that would allow such participation. But ensuring the health of older adults – through public health investments and a healthcare system better prepared for this specific and growing population – is necessary for unleashing the third demographic dividend. Indeed, research suggests that one of the major factors hindering the emergence of large-scale programs, such as the Experience Corps, is older adults' chronic conditions and disability.[70] Thus, if we want to enable the unique and valuable social capital of older adults in an aging population, we first need to make sure they have the conditions to stay healthy.

13.4 CONCLUSION

This chapter has explored some ways in which the US health system has to change to accommodate the 100-year-old American. It identifies the creation of optimal health for a longer life as the health system's primary goal, and points to two primary avenues to achieve this goal: (1) investing in a public health system that can increase health span for the whole population and (2) improving geriatric care and health

[67] Michael Ashley Stein et al., *Accommodating Every Body*, 81 U. Chi. L. Rev. 689, 755 (2014).

[68] Linda P. Fried, *A Prescription for the Next Fifty Years of Medicare*, 39 Generations 180 (2015).

[69] Ramsey Alwin & Lona Choi-Allum, *Career Changes Are Becoming More Common with Increased Longevity*, AARP Rsch. (Apr. 23, 2020), https://www.aarp.org/pri/topics/work-finances-retirement/employers-workforce/adults-career-journeys.html.

[70] Linda P. Fried, *Older Women: Health Status, Knowledge, and Behavior*, *in* Women's Health, The Commonwealth Fund Survey, 175, 177–181, 188–190 (Marilyn M. Falik & Karen Scott Collins eds., 1996).

systems. As for the first avenue, we argue that implementing population-based preventive measures under the auspices of the public health system could reduce chromic conditions among older adults and lead to better health outcomes in the long term. As for the second avenue, we argue that the provision of high-quality and age-friendly care requires a more robust and well-trained geriatric workforce, focusing on providing a coordinated continuum of geriatrically informed systems of care and using emerging technologies to make health care more accessible for everyone. Further, enabling engagement that older adults seek will improve health in aging while supporting societal flourishing.

As this chapter has shown, the sharp increase in the share of older adults in the US population poses significant challenges for the American healthcare system. This is particularly true with respect to funding, the subject of the chapter's second section. We argue that even though there are no easy solutions for the financing dilemma, some of our reform proposals could actually save money in the long term.

Ultimately, the constant increase in life expectancy not only poses challenges but also creates unique opportunities: If we find the ways to incorporate health into older adults' so-called extra years, older adults will be able to use their experience and expertise to contribute to society by engaging in work, volunteering, leadership, and advocacy activities. Perceived this way, longevity can have ripple effects that have the potential to create a long-lived society in which all ages can thrive.

14

Making the Best of Long-Term Care for Seniors

Katherine Pratt

The 100-Year Life explores the opportunities longer life will provide, assuming individuals have sufficient financial resources to fund their longer lives. Many people save too little for their retirement, but the federal government's two largest social insurance programs – Social Security and Medicare – keep millions of seniors out of poverty. The Social Security old-age benefit partially replaces lost wages, using a statutory retirement age as a proxy for being unable to work.[1] The federal Medicare program provides health insurance at subsidized rates to beneficiaries based on age, starting at age sixty-five.[2] In addition, the federal government provides grants to states for state-run Medicaid programs, which provide health insurance to impoverished Medicaid-eligible persons, including seniors.

This chapter addresses a frequently overlooked retirement expense – the cost of nonmedical custodial care. Most individuals aged sixty-five or older will require custodial care – Long-Term Care (LTC), also known as Long-Term Services and Supports (LTSS). LTC includes assistance with activities of daily living (ADLs), such as eating, bathing, dressing, getting in and out of a chair, walking, toileting, and continence; and instrumental activities of daily living (IADLs), such as grocery shopping, banking, bill paying, and filling prescriptions.

Most LTC is unpaid family care because most seniors and their families cannot afford the cost of paid LTC. Paid LTC is very expensive. For example, in 2021, the average annual cost of a year of LTC was:

- $108,408 for a nursing home private room;
- $94,896 for a nursing home semi-private room;

1 When the Social Security program was enacted in the 1930s, life expectancy was not many years beyond the age to qualify for old-age benefits. As life expectancy increased, Social Security old-age benefit payments also increased, both in total amount and duration. On average, Social Security old-age beneficiaries now expect to receive Social Security benefits for twenty years.

2 The Medicare program includes hospitalization insurance ("Part A"), medical insurance ("Part B"), and prescription drug insurance ("Part D").

- $54,000 for a one-bedroom apartment in an assisted living facility; and
- $59,484 for forty-four hours per week of LTC in the senior's home.[3]

Medicare generally does not cover LTC, although many people assume it does.[4] State-run Medicaid programs provide significant LTC funding – but only to Medicaid-eligible persons with low income and almost no savings. Access to paid LTC currently is a patchwork crazy-quilt of public (federal, state, and local) and private funding mechanisms.

This chapter first explores the implications – for current and future seniors and their caregivers – of increased longevity and other trends on *unpaid family* LTC and on *publicly funded* and *privately funded paid* LTC. Second, this chapter surveys alternative means of accessing and funding LTC. Third, this chapter notes LTC trends, innovations, legal developments, and proposals that might improve the LTC outlook for seniors and their families.

14.1 UNPAID FAMILY LTC

Ninety percent of seniors who need LTC receive unpaid care from members of their "family," defined broadly.[5] Two-thirds rely *exclusively* on unpaid family care, and another quarter combine unpaid family care and paid care. In 2021, for example, 38 million family caregivers provided 36 *billion* hours of unpaid care.[6] The aggregate economic value of unpaid family LTC is enormous, both in absolute terms – about $600 billion in 2021 – and in relative terms – about 20 percent of US healthcare costs.[7]

Family members often share caregiving duties. Spouses and adult children – generally daughters – provide most unpaid care. Spouses usually provide more hours of care per month than other types of caregivers. Women provide over 60 percent of unpaid care, although men provide more unpaid care today than in the past. Unpaid female caregivers average eighty-one hours per month of caregiving, while unpaid

3 *Cost of Care Survey*, Genworth (June 2, 2022), https://www.genworth.com/aging-and-you/finances/cost-of-care.html.

4 Medicare does not cover LTC generally, but covers up to 100 days of nursing home care after a hospitalization as well as some hospice care and special-needs care.

5 Admin. for Cmty. Living, US Dep't of Health & Hum. Serv., 2022 Nat'l Strategy to Support Family Caregivers 9 (2022), https://acl.gov/CaregiverStrategy (defining family "in the broadest possible sense" to include everyone with whom the person needing LTC has a relationship bond).

6 Susan C. Reinhard et al., AARP Pub. Policy Inst., Valuing the Invaluable 2019 Update: Charting a Path Forward (2019), https://collections.nlm.nih.gov/catalog/nlm:nlmuid-101767885-pdf [hereinafter Valuing the Invaluable 2019].

7 Susan C. Reinhard et al., AARP Pub. Policy Inst., Valuing the Invaluable 2023 Update: Strengthening Supports for Family Caregivers (2023), https://www.aarp.org/ppi/info-2015/valuing-the-invaluable-2015-update.html (noting $600 billion value of LTC provided by 38 million unpaid caregivers); Valuing the Invaluable 2019, *supra* note 6 (estimating that the economic value of unpaid family care was 20 percent of US healthcare costs).

male caregivers average sixty-five hours per month. Seniors who require LTC often have unmet LTC needs if their caregivers' availability to provide care is limited.

Multiple demographic trends may impact the future availability of unpaid family caregivers. The overwhelming majority of female caregivers under age sixty-five also work for pay, and the percentage of women who work outside the home is projected to increase. Also, women are projected to work to older ages in the future. Increasing participation in paid work may reduce the availability of family members for unpaid caregiving. Potentially offsetting these trends, remote work and improved technology might increase the availability of family members for unpaid caregiving.

Women also have increased their educational attainment and delayed having children, which may limit the scheduling flexibility of "sandwich-generation" caregivers (30 percent of family caregivers) to care for both their children and their parents. Also, fertility rates in the US have declined and the large Baby Boomer cohort is aging. By 2035, seniors aged sixty-five and older will outnumber youths aged eighteen and younger in the US for the first time. The caregiver support ratio, which compares adults in the prime caregiving age group (45–64) to seniors in the age group most likely to require LTC (eighty and over), will shrink going forward.[8]

Rates of "gray" divorce have increased, although divorced seniors often find new partners. Among seniors aged seventy-five and older, two-thirds of men have a spouse or partner, compared to just one-third of women.[9] Unmarried seniors, especially unmarried white women, increasingly live alone. The number of "elder orphans" (seniors with no support network) is projected to increase in the future.

Family members are becoming caregivers at younger ages. About one-third of adults aged forty and younger and one-quarter of Millennials already provide unpaid care to family members.[10]

Older Americans and their unpaid family caregivers will be more diverse in the future. Cultural differences in attitudes toward family responsibility and the care of seniors will create divergent patterns of unpaid and paid care. Some cultures have norms of providing unpaid care to seniors in the community. In such cultures, several generations of a family often live together, with younger generations sharing the care of elderly members of the family in the multigenerational home. Other cultures have norms of minimizing the burdens older generations impose on their adult children. Seniors from such cultures are more likely to seek out paid LTC.[11]

8 Brenda C. Spillman et al., Office of the Assistant Sec'y for Planning & Evaluation, US Dep't of Health & Hum. Serv., Informal Caregiver Supply and Demographic Changes: Review of the Literature 18, 22 (2020), https://aspe.hhs.gov/pdf-report/informal-caregiver-supply-and-demographic-changes-review-literature [hereinafter Informal Caregiver Supply].

9 Deborah Carr & Rebecca L. Utz, *Families in Later Life: A Decade in Review*, 82 J. Marriage Fam. 346 (2020).

10 Valuing the Invaluable 2019, *supra* note 6.

11 Informal Caregiver Supply, *supra* note 8.

Seniors of color, in particular Black seniors, are more likely to require LTC – and to require it at an earlier age – than white seniors. Appalling, persistent racial and socioeconomic health disparities, which are evident throughout the lifespan, increase and accelerate disadvantaged seniors' need for LTC. Myriad environmental stressors (e.g., pollution, lead paint, food insecurity) and poverty contribute to such disparities. In addition, research over the past two decades establishes that pervasive, lifelong exposure to social and structural oppression and racism cause premature biological aging – *weathering* – of Black people regardless of their income or wealth.[12] Compared to white seniors, Black seniors are more likely to be disabled, to reside in a nursing home, and to receive substandard care.

Both rates of poverty and the likelihood a senior will need paid LTC increase with age. The need for LTC is highest in the eighty-and-older senior cohort, the fastest growing segment of seniors. Poverty rates for elderly women exceed that for elderly men. In the future, as longevity increases, more seniors are likely to require paid LTC and to qualify for Medicaid-funded LTC.

The potential negative effects of caregiving on *family caregivers* – in particular women – who *provide* unpaid LTC are underappreciated. Unpaid family caregiving entails significant – albeit hidden – costs. To provide care at home, family caregivers with paying jobs often must reduce their work hours and effort, or exit the paid labor market entirely, reducing employer-provided health insurance coverage and retirement plan contributions. These hidden costs "help explain the much higher poverty rates for older women relative to men."[13]

Family caregivers often incur substantial out-of-pocket costs to care for their family members. In 2016, the average annual out-of-pocket expenses for a family caregiver were $7,000 overall and 27 percent of the income of Millennial caregivers.[14] Family members who must pay these costs reduce their own income and retirement savings.

Family caregivers often experience stress and anxiety, especially when a dependent family member's health deteriorates, and care becomes more complex. Seniors with multiple chronic medical conditions or with Alzheimer's disease or related dementias (ADRD) require the most intensive caregiving. Over time, the stresses of caregiving can negatively impact the health of the caregiver. In addition, healthcare providers increasingly delegate to family members medical tasks that go beyond IADLs and ADLs, such as wound care and operating medical equipment

[12] Arline T. Geronimus, Weathering: The Extraordinary Stress of Ordinary Life in an Unjust Society 10–11 (2023).

[13] Sean Fahle & Kathleen McGarry, *Women Working Longer: Labor Market Implications of Providing Family Care, in* Women Working Longer: Increased Employment at Older Ages, 161 (Claudia Goldin & Lawrence F. Katz eds., 2018).

[14] Valuing the Invaluable 2019, *supra* note 6.

(e.g., dialysis equipment).[15] Many caregivers are uncomfortable performing such tasks, yet perform them because no one else is available to help. Also, family caregivers generally receive little guidance about how to provide care. The need to complete frustrating administrative tasks, such as insurance paperwork, often adds to caregivers' stress and anxiety. When seniors' care needs exceed family caregivers' capabilities, *paid* LTC becomes a necessity.

14.2 PAID LTC

Many Americans incorrectly assume that Medicare covers the cost of paid LTC for seniors. Medicare covers "medical" treatment – narrowly and clinically defined – but generally does not cover LTC. Nor does the federal government provide any other universal LTC benefit. State-run Medicaid programs (jointly funded by the federal government and states) provide LTC to seniors living in *poverty*. Strict legal rules, which vary from state to state, limit Medicaid eligibility to individuals with little income and *very* little wealth – in many states, not more than $2,000 of assets.

If a senior has too much wealth to qualify for Medicaid, but not enough to fund LTC, the senior must *spend down* her assets to qualify for Medicaid. The low asset threshold for Medicaid eligibility yokes the beneficial receipt of Medicaid-funded LTC to unintended financial risks created by Medicaid-mandated impoverishment. Notwithstanding the strict Medicaid eligibility requirements, Medicaid pays a significant percentage of aggregate US LTC costs.

The likelihood that a senior will enroll in Medicaid increases with the length of time the person requires paid LTC. The lower a senior's lifetime earnings, the sooner they are likely to enroll in Medicaid. By the fifth year of requiring paid LTC, the vast majority of seniors – including the top 20 percent of all income earners – are enrolled in Medicaid.[16] The duration of needing LTC varies. Patients with ADRD often require many years of LTC. About 18 percent of women and 14 percent of all seniors require five or more years of LTC. On average, women need 3.7 years of LTC and men need 2.2 years of LTC. For seniors "with less education, lifetime earnings, and wealth," both disability and the need for LTC "come earlier and last longer."[17]

[15] Admin. on Aging, Admin. for Cmty. Living, Dep't of Health & Human Serv., FY 2016 Rep. to Congress: Older Americans Act 23–24 (2016).

[16] Richard W. Johnson et al., Office of the Assistant Sec'y for Planning & Evaluation, US Dep't of Health & Hum. Serv., Extended LTSS Utilization Makes Older Adults More Reliant on Medicaid 5 (fig. 2) (2021), https://aspe.hhs.gov/pdf-report/extended-ltss-utilization-makes-older-adults-more-reliant-medicaid-issue-brief.

[17] Melissa M. Favreault, Urban Inst. Health Policy Ctr., & The Commonwealth Fund, Incorporating Long-Term Services and Supports in Health Care Proposals: Cost and Distributional Considerations (2020), https://www.urban.org/research/publication/incorporating-long-term-services-and-supports-health-care-proposals.

14.2.1 *Nursing Homes as the Default Delivery Site for Medicaid-Funded LTC*

Skilled nursing homes always have been the default delivery site for Medicaid-funded LTC. At the creation of Medicare and Medicaid in 1965, both programs "adopted a medicalized model of care, prioritizing the use of licensed providers and institutions," which made caregiving outside of licensed care facilities "invisible" and financially "unsupported."[18] Nursing homes typically are large institutional medical facilities, more suited to deliver skilled medical care than LTC. Patients in nursing homes include post–acute-care (recently hospitalized) patients, for whose skilled nursing care the facility is reimbursed at a high Medicare rate; and LTC patients, for whose custodial care the facility is reimbursed at a low Medicaid rate.

Long-standing shortcomings of providing LTC in nursing homes include (1) poor infection control; (2) high staff turnover and chronic worker shortages; (3) neglect of patient needs and low quality of care, often due to understaffing; and (4) patients' loss of privacy, agency, and control over their environment. The COVID-19 pandemic exacerbated these shortcomings.

The pandemic increased the chronic shortage of care workers and high staff turnover in nursing homes, both of which are associated with lower-quality patient care. This shortage has many causes. Nursing home-care workers (other than nurses) earn very low wages and often juggle jobs at multiple nursing homes, which increases infection risks. Care work in nursing homes was always a dangerous profession, due to infection risk and the physical demands of the job. COVID turned it into one of the most dangerous jobs in America. In addition, entrenched racial hierarchies are common in nursing homes. Managers generally are white, but care workers disproportionately are Black women and other women of color. Care workers express the feeling they are working on "the plantation,"[19] invoking the long history in our country of relegating Black workers to low-wage, dirty, domestic servant work.[20]

Improving working conditions for care workers is essential as a matter of racial justice and to reduce the acute shortage of LTC workers. Reversing systemic racism in LTC work will require nursing homes and other healthcare organizations to provide higher pay and employee benefits to care workers; to promote Black

[18] Rachel M. Werner et al., *Long-Term Care Policy after COVID-19: Solving the Nursing Home Crisis*, 383 N. Eng. J. Med. 903 (2020).

[19] Robyn I. Stone, *LTSS: A Microcosm of Systemic Racism*, Leading Age LTSS Center @UMass Boston (Dec. 15, 2020), https://www.ltsscenter.org/ltss-a-microcosm-of-systemic-racism (noting that low pay, physically demanding work, and racial hierarchies in nursing homes make LTC workers of color "subservient," "leading many workers to tell me over the years that they feel as if they are working 'on the plantation'").

[20] *See* Isabel Wilkerson, Caste: The Origins of Our Discontent 132–133 (noting African Americans throughout US history "were relegated to the dirtiest, most demeaning and least desirable jobs ... and well into the twentieth century, they were primarily restricted to the role of sharecroppers and servants – domestics").

frontline care workers and other workers of color to management and board positions; to recruit Black students for internships and management positions; and to empower care workers to direct more of their own care work.

Black care workers and other care workers of color also can organize their own LTC businesses. Bronx-based Cooperative Home Care Associates (CHCA) provides an example of a successful LTC business managed and owned by Black women and other women of color. Founded in 1985 by twelve care workers, CHCA now employs 2,300 care workers. It offers its employees free training, health insurance, a pension plan, union membership, regular work hours, and an hourly wage of $16. Employees also can elect to buy a share of stock in the business for $1,000, by paying $50 one time and $3.65 per week for five years. About half of CHCA employees own stock in the company. By improving working conditions and promoting its employees' agency and economic dignity, CHCA achieved much lower employee turnover than most home-care providers. Lower turnover translates to better patient care. CHCA is a model for other minority-owned LTC businesses.

The pandemic also reinvigorated long-standing policy critiques of legal rules that make institutional nursing homes the default setting for Medicaid-funded LTC. In a 1992 case, *Olmstead v. L.C.*, the US Supreme Court held that federal disability law prohibited states from forcing persons with mental illness to live in segregated, congregate-care facilities to receive medical treatment, if the care of the patients could be less intrusively integrated into their home community.[21] *Olmstead* supports an argument that persons who need LTC should not be forced into segregated, congregate nursing homes – the Medicaid default setting – but instead should have access to home- and community-based services (HCBS) if their care needs do not require them to be in a nursing home.

14.2.2 *Growth of HCBS as an Alternative to Nursing Home LTC*

Years before the pandemic, concerns about poor infection control, chronic staffing shortages, and poor quality of care in many nursing homes led states to *gradually* begin offering HCBS as an alternative to nursing home LTC.[22] The default Medicaid setting for LTC continued to be nursing homes, but states applied for federal waivers that allowed them to experiment with offering HCBS to some, but not all, state Medicaid patients. HCBS is provided to seniors at "home" in a wide range of residential settings, including a single-family home or apartment and assisted living apartments.[23]

[21] Olmstead v. L. C., 527 U.S. 581 (1999).

[22] Federal funding for state HCBS programs includes Medicaid grants and grants under the Older Americans Act. 42 U.S. Code § 3030(d).

[23] *See What Medicare Covers, What Part A Covers, What Are My Other Long Term Care Choices?* MEDICARE, https://www.medicare.gov/what-medicare-covers/what-part-a-covers/what-are-my-other-long-term-care-choices#collapse-4912.

Infection risks are lower in the HCBS setting, and seniors strongly prefer HCBS to nursing home care. As of 2020, patient demand for HCBS was so great that around 700,000 patients were on waiting lists to receive HCBS. The average wait time to receive HCBS was thirty months, although wait times varied widely between states. After the pandemic highlighted the need for additional HCBS, states and the federal government increased funding for HCBS. Proposed legislation would further increase funding for HCBS.

To date, however, state Medicaid HCBS programs are still operating under federal Medicaid waivers, meaning HCBS is not a universal mandatory Medicaid benefit. The hesitancy to make HCBS a universal Medicaid benefit stems from the immense cost of such an expansion. The cost *per patient* of providing LTC generally is lower in the home than in the nursing home setting.[24] The aggregate public cost of HCBS ultimately may be higher than that of nursing home LTC, however, because *more patients want HCBS than nursing home LTC*. As HCBS expands, patients only receiving unpaid family LTC may enroll for paid LTC through the HCBS program – converting some unpaid LTC into *new* government-funded paid LTC. LTC experts observe that the chief difficulty with expanding access to HCBS is containing public costs by structuring the benefits around the senior population that would go into a nursing home absent the provision of HCBS.[25]

14.2.3 *Programs of All-Inclusive Care for the Elderly*

Over the past decade, various demonstration projects have shown promise to provide HCBS, while containing costs and providing noninstitutional LTC. For example, Programs of All-Inclusive Care for the Elderly (PACE) allow seniors who want to stay in their "home" (broadly construed) to combine traditional Medicare benefits and LTC in a managed care plan, using a team-care approach and a capitated (per enrollee) payment structure instead of a fee-for-service structure.[26] In addition to providing medical care, PACE "centers" provide adult day care, nutritious food, and recreational activities to seniors, along with transportation from the senior's home to the center and back. PACE enrollees must be nursing home-eligible and live near a PACE center. Seniors who are eligible for both Medicare and Medicaid (dual-eligible) qualify for enrollment in PACE. Seniors who are enrolled in Medicare but ineligible for Medicaid can pay a premium to enroll in a PACE program. About

[24] The LTC cost comparison omits seniors' housing costs. If a senior does not have access to housing options other than a nursing home, HCBS is not an option.

[25] David C. Grabowski, *The Cost-Effectiveness of Noninstitutional Long-Term Care Services: Review and Synthesis of the Most Recent Evidence*, 63 Med. Care Res. & Rev. 1, 6 (2006).

[26] *See generally Program of All-Inclusive Care for the Elderly*, Medicare, https://www.medicaid.gov/medicaid/long-term-services-supports/program-all-inclusive-care-elderly/index.html.

90 percent of PACE enrollees are dual-eligible. Over thirty states offer at least one PACE program.

14.2.4 *Naturally Occurring Retirement Communities*

Certain innovative HCBS programs are well suited for particular residential settings. For example, in dense urban areas, large rent-controlled apartment buildings with a high percentage of seniors, referred to as Naturally Occurring Retirement Communities ("NORCs"), can become a focal point for efficient delivery of HCBS. Paid LTC staff working in these buildings can assist seniors on site. Seniors in NORCs are, on average, in the low- to middle-income ranges, and about half are usually also eligible for Medicaid. NORCs are funded by a combination of government funding, philanthropic funding, and contributions from residents.[27]

14.2.5 *Medicare Advantage Plans*

Since 2020, Medicare Advantage (MA) plans have been allowed to offer Special Supplemental Benefits for the Chronically Ill ("SSBCI"), with a *primary* focus on improving social determinants of health. The benefits available to patients with complex chronic conditions include pest control, indoor air quality, nonmedical transportation, meal delivery, produce and grocery delivery, and virtual visits to reduce social isolation.

Expansion of next-generation programs that incorporate LTC – including PACE, NORCs, and MA plans – will facilitate data collection and reviews of their effectiveness and costs. For example, a stunning 2023 study concluded that MA plans received $75 billion in government *overpayments*, prompting calls for reform of the MA fee structure.[28]

14.2.6 *Older Americans Act Programs*

In addition to federal grants to state-run Medicaid programs, the federal Older Americans Act (OAA) provides grants to states for programs supporting Americans aged sixty or older.[29] Seniors qualify for OAA benefits without regard to the

[27] Emily Greenfield et al., *A Tale of Two Community Initiatives for Promoting Aging in Place: Similarities and Differences in the National Implementation of NORC Programs and Villages*, 53 Gerontologist 928 (2013), https://pubmed.ncbi.nlm.nih.gov/23626371.

[28] Steven M. Lieberman et al., *Medicare Advantage Enrolls Lower-Spending People, Leading to Large Overpayments* (Schaeffer Center White Paper Series, June 2023), https://healthpolicy.usc.edu/wp-content/uploads/2023/06/2023.06_Schaeffer_Center_White_Paper_Role_of_Risk_Adjustment_in_Overpaying_Medicare_Advantage_Plans.pdf (estimating $75 billion of government overpayments to MA plans in 2023 and suggesting MA fee structure reform).

[29] The Administration for Community Living (ACL) is a unit of the Administration on Aging (a division of the US Department of Health and Human Services). *See About ACL*, Admin. for

Medicaid income or asset tests. OAA programs include meals delivered to the senior's home (e.g., Meals on Wheels), congregate meals served in the community, caregiver supports, home care, adult day-care services, and assisted transportation. Local Agencies on Aging can provide information about OAA-funded programs offered to seniors in the community.

14.2.7 *Aid and Attendance for Military Veterans and Their Spouses*

A subset of seniors – *military veterans* and their *surviving spouses* – may qualify for another public source of LTC funding, referred to as Aid and Attendance, through the US Department of Veterans Affairs.[30] Veterans and their surviving spouses who qualify for a military pension benefit may be eligible for supplemental pension benefits if they are "medically rated" to require LTC (either "Aid and Attendance" or "housebound" care). Each type of pension and supplemental benefit has specific eligibility requirements (e.g., based on the length of active military service and whether the veteran died while on active duty). The veterans' benefit program has a wealth test but allows much greater wealth than Medicaid.[31]

14.2.8 *Private LTC Insurance*

Another potential LTC funding source – albeit *private* rather than public – is Long-Term Care Insurance ("LTCI").[32] The nontrivial risk of needing catastrophically expensive LTC is exactly the type of risk against which consumers might insure. At the start of the twenty-first century, over 100 insurance companies sold stand-alone LTCI policies to consumers. Consumer purchases of LTCI were modest, however, in part because of the availability of Medicaid as the LTC payer of last resort.[33]

Over time, the LTCI insurance market contracted sharply. Insurers discovered they initially underpriced LTCI premiums. State insurance regulations prevented

Cmty. Living, https://acl.gov/about-acl/organization. Aging and Disability Resource Centers and Area Agencies on Aging provide information on ACL programs for seniors and family caregivers.

30 *See generally* US Dep't of Veterans Affairs, *VA Aid and Attendance Benefits and Housebound Allowance*, https://www.va.gov/pension/aid-attendance-housebound.

31 *See* US Dep't of Veterans Affairs, 2023 *VA Pension Rates for Veterans*, https://www.va.gov/pension/veterans-pension-rates/#:~:text=What's%20the%20net%20worth%20limit,Veterans%20Pension%20benefits%20is%20%24150%2C538 ($150,538 net worth limit in 2023).

32 Eric Nordman et al., Ctr. Ins. Pol'y Res., The State of Long-Term Care Insurance: The Market, Its Challenges and Future Innovations (2016), https://nabip.org/media/2654/study-naic-state-of-ltci-may-2016.pdf.

33 *See, e.g.*, Leonard E. Burman, *The Perverse Public and Private Finances of Long-Term Care, in* Universal Coverage of Long-Term Care in the United States: Can We Get There from Here? 179 (Douglas A. Wolfe & Nancy Folbre eds., 2012).

insurers from prospectively correcting the mistakes through premium increases on existing policies, leading almost all insurers to exit the LTCI market. The few remaining insurers reduced their risks by significantly increasing premiums on new LTCI policies and declining to cover a high percentage of prospective purchasers with underlying health conditions. As the LTCI market contracted, many employers that previously offered LTCI as an employee benefit eliminated it from their employee benefit package. Currently only 7 million LTCI policies are in force in the US. Just 11 percent of seniors own LTCI policies, which paid about 8 percent of LTC costs in the US in 2016.

As the LTCI industry contracted, state insurance commissioners and regulators urged federal and state policymakers to adopt policies that might make LTCI more appealing to consumers and increase private, individual funding of LTC risk. Although state legislatures and the US Congress enacted legislation intended to encourage the purchase of LTCI, such incentives have not been particularly effective. Income tax deductions for LTCI premium payments – available only to a very small percentage of taxpayers – provide one example of an ineffective LTCI subsidy.

Long-Term Care Insurance Partnerships ("LTCIPs") provide another example of legislation intended to increase LTCI purchases. LTCIPs allow state Medicaid eligibility without the usual extreme spend-down of assets if a consumer purchases qualified LTCI. For example, assume Diana purchases a qualified LTCI policy that covers $100,000 of LTC. If Diana later requires LTC, exhausts her $100,000 LTCI benefit, and subsequently applies for Medicaid, the state Medicaid asset limit for Diana is increased by $100,000. The younger and healthier a consumer is when she purchases LTCI, the lower the LTCI premiums will be.

Despite widespread adoption of LTCIP statutes by most states, the early consensus among researchers was that the adoption of LTCIPs failed to significantly increase the purchase of LTCI. A recent study found otherwise, however, partly because "the effect of LTCIP appears over time and the effect is mostly driven by partnerships set up after 2010," which were not considered in earlier studies.[34] The new study concludes that the adoption of an LTCIP "increased the uptake of LTCI coverage by 1.64 percentage points[;] reduced Medicaid uptake by 1.46 percentage points[;]" and reduced federal Medicaid expenditures by $36 for each senior. Notwithstanding the continued availability of Medicaid as a payer of last resort, consumers purchased LTCI to protect their assets and increase their bequests. This study offers some hope for LTCIPs. In addition, LTCIPs could be combined with a mandatory state or federal social insurance program, funded by new taxes, with a tax opt-out for purchasers of LTCI.

[34] Joan Costa-Font & Nilesh Raut, *Long-Term Care Partnership Effects on Medicaid and Private Insurance* (CESifo Working Paper No. 9335, 2021), https://papers.ssrn.com/sol3/papers.cfm?abstract_id=3938648.

Another LTCI development is that insurers have created *hybrid* insurance products that blend LTC coverage with other popular forms of coverage, such as life insurance or annuities. The hybrid products generally do not qualify as LTCI, for purposes of state LTCIP programs.

Policymakers disagree about whether LTC should be privately funded through the individual purchase of LTCI, or publicly funded through premiums or payroll taxes for a state or federal LTC social insurance program. Although the availability of Medicaid-funded LTC discourages the purchase of private LTCI, repealing Medicaid-funded LTC would be deeply unpopular with Americans. In addition, private individual LTCI still would be too costly for millions of Americans. State or federal LTC social insurance proposals, which would reduce the need for Medicaid-funded LTC, seem more politically plausible, but only if the funding mechanism for the proposal does not turn the political tide against it. Allowing an opt-out for purchasers of private LTCI would reduce the public cost of the social insurance program.

14.3 PUBLIC LTC SOCIAL INSURANCE DEVELOPMENTS AND PROPOSALS

14.3.1 *State LTC Social Insurance Program Developments*

Some state legislatures have considered making LTC benefits available to all state residents, including those ineligible for Medicaid. In 2019, the state of Washington enacted the country's first state LTC social insurance program.[35] Washington's Long-Term Services and Supports Trust Program (now called the Washington Cares Fund) is the first universal state social insurance program covering LTC. The Washington program is funded by a new 0.58 percent ($58 per $10,000 of wages) payroll tax on wages, which the state began to collect on July 1, 2023. A payroll tax opt-out is available for those who previously purchased their own private LTCI. The state LTC benefits of up to $36,500 can fund in-home care (including care by family members), home modifications, transportation, food delivery, caregiver training, and respite care. Hawaii also provides LTC to residents but funds the care out of general revenue instead of pairing social insurance LTC benefits with a dedicated tax. Other states also are considering LTC proposals.[36]

[35] Long-Term Services and Supports Trust Program, H.B. 1087, 66th Leg. Reg. Sess. (Wash. 2019).

[36] *See generally* Marc A. Cohen et al., *Learning from New State Initiatives in Financing Long-Term Services and Supports* (2020), https://www.ltsscenter.org/wp-content/uploads/2020/07/State-LTSS-Financing-Full-Report-July-2020.pdf (summarizing proposals and legislation in six states).

14.3.2 *Federal LTC Social Insurance Program Proposals*

Experts in LTC have long argued for a universal *federal* LTC social insurance program, but repeated congressional attempts to create such a program have failed. For example, in 2010, as part of the Affordable Care Act, Congress enacted the Community and Living Assistance Services and Supports (CLASS) Act, a federally subsidized voluntary LTC insurance program with no eligibility exclusions. The CLASS Act was soon repealed, however, due to concerns about the financial viability of the program. The decade since its repeal has been a time of transition for LTC programs. Although traditional Medicare continues to exclude LTC, MA plans and PACE-managed care plans with LTC benefits are available to seniors in some but not all geographic areas.

Senior care experts and policymakers continue to advocate for a universal federal LTC program. Situating an LTC funding program at the federal level would eliminate LTC eligibility variation between states and could relax draconian state asset tests. Expanding LTC eligibility would, in turn, increase the costs of the LTC program.

Health economists have modeled the distributional effects and costs of a new federal social insurance program for LTC. Low- and middle-income Americans would disproportionately benefit. Many seniors and their families would replace *unpaid* family LTC with *new paid*, federally funded LTC. The projected ten-year costs of the new LTC are in the trillions – ranging from 5.7 to 8.1 trillion, depending on how LTC eligibility is defined.

The costs of a new LTC social insurance program could be reduced by making LTC available only to seniors who cannot perform three or more ADLs. Costs also could be lower if medical science discovers ways to reduce or defer the onset of diseases that produce the highest LTC costs. For example, ADRD risk might be reduced through exercise and diet.[37] In addition, just delaying ADRD onset could reduce projected LTC spending significantly.[38] Even with such medical breakthroughs, however, the cost of new federally funded LTC services would be enormous.

From a political perspective, long-simmering concerns about the solvency of the existing Medicare trust fund – much less the funding of new universal LTC benefits – provide a difficult fiscal backdrop for enacting a federal LTC program. On the other hand, the COVID pandemic highlighted the significance of the care economy in the US and created political momentum to improve LTC, increase access to paid LTC at home, and expand public funding for paid LTC.

[37] *See*, e.g., Martha Clare Morris et al., *MIND Diet Associated with Reduced Incidence of Alzheimer's Disease*, 11 ALZHEIMER'S & DEMENTIA 1007 (2015) (Mediterranean diet adherence is associated with 56 percent lower Alzheimer's risk).

[38] Julie Zissimopoulos et al., *The Value of Delaying Alzheimer's Disease Onset*, 18 FORUM HEALTH ECON. & POL'Y 25 (2014) (concluding "5-year delay [in onset of AD] leads to 2.7 additional life years [and] total [net] value of $511,208 per person").

15

Immigration and the 100-Year Life

Eleanor Brown

The quality of a civilization is judged by how well older people are treated.

—Pope Benedict XVI[1]

One of every two babies born today will live until age 100. This chapter is about the immigration-related implications of this remarkable demographic change, which only five decades ago would have seemed inconceivable. Even with medical advances, as our population ages, a larger proportion of the population will be unable to live independently. Immediately the question arises: Who will care for our elderly population? The US will need many more care workers and, overwhelmingly, they will be migrants.

While, in the popular imagination, elder care is typically associated with nursing homes, a report from the Department of Health and Human Services estimates that fewer than 5 percent of seniors reside in institutional settings like nursing homes.[2] The senior population overwhelmingly continues to reside at home. Thus, most care workers will not work in hospitals or nursing homes; rather most care work will be delivered in the home. Much of this home care will not be subsidized by government; the US stands out among rich OECD countries in the relatively paltry sums that it dedicates to long-term care for seniors.[3] Most home care is paid for by a

[1] *Pope: Societies Are Judged by How They Treat Elderly, Who Are an Asset for Young People*, Pime Asia News (Nov. 12, 2012), http://www.asianews.it/news-en/Pope:-Societies-are-judged-by-how-they-treat-the-elderly,-who-are-an-asset-for-young-people-26331.html. (Please note that due to space constraints, this chapter is only lightly footnoted.)

[2] National Library of Medicine, *Providing Healthy and Safe Foods As We Age: Workshop Summary* (2010), https://www.ncbi.nlm.nih.gov/books/NBK51841/#:~:text=Only%204.5%20per cent%20(about%201.5,million)%20live%20in%20the%20community.

[3] OECD, *Spending on Long Term Care* (2020), https://www.oecd.org/health/health-systems/Spending-on-long-term-care-Brief-November-2020.pdf (the US does not figure in this OECD study on long-term care); Celli Hortsman, Evan D. Gumas & Gretchen Jacobson, *U.S. and Global Approaches to Financing Long-Term Care: Understanding the Patchwork*, The Commonwealth Fund (2023), https://www.commonwealthfund.org/publications/issue-briefs/2023/feb/us-global-financing-long-term-care-patchwork#:~:text=How%20U.S.%20Long%2DTerm%20Care,out%2Dof%2Dpocket%20spending (the Commonwealth Fund Study makes

patchwork of financial sources – very occasionally with state aid, but mostly with funds from seniors themselves, their children, and nonfamilial sources, such as nonprofits and churches.[4]

It bears emphasis: Most of this at-home care is *unpaid* and provided by family members. However, *paid* home care has been steadily growing. Twenty-five percent of senior citizens need significant assistance with "ADL" (activities of daily living).[5] With over 55 million people who are senior citizens, the percentage of people who now need paid help is already significant and will surely continue to rise. This is also true because of compositional effects; with lower fertility, a larger portion of the population becomes older. Even if eighty becomes the new sixty, that still means a higher percentage of the total population will be frail, and a lower percentage of the population will be available to help them.

We have long understood the implications of the aging population for health care – this is a primary reason that the growth of jobs in the healthcare sector has long outpaced the growth of jobs in the regular economy. Further, the pace of growth for home-care aides is even more extraordinary. One recent report projected that between now and 2026, jobs in home-care settings will grow by 41 percent.[6] Yet, while the pace of growth of jobs remains high, the salaries are modest. Pay for aides is not much higher than the minimum wage in most states.

Trends are already clear. The home-care sector looks a lot like other sectors in which Americans are typically *not* employed and undocumented migrants dominate. One need only think, for example, of farm work – a field dominated by undocumented labor. This work is difficult, and the pay is low. Moreover, home-care work is particularly well suited to the undocumented population since it is difficult for immigration officials to police work that occurs inside people's homes.

How has the US typically managed the need for a large and steady group of low-skilled workers? There is a large gap between what immigration institutions purport to do and what actually happens. That is, the stated goal of immigration institutions is twofold. First, these institutions seek to ensure that aliens are screened ex-ante (i.e., preentry) for suitability to particular visa types; and second, that they are sanctioned if they do not abide by the terms of their visas. Thus, if the US is looking for a law-abiding temporary elder-care worker, it would screen for a "short-term" type, with caregiving skills and no criminal record.

clear that the US spends a smaller share of its health expenditure on long-term care than other countries).

4 *See* Hortsman et al., *supra* note 3.

5 Howard E. LeWine, *Two-Thirds of Seniors Need Help Doing One or More Daily Activities*, Harvard Medical School (Dec. 13, 2012), https://www.health.harvard.edu/blog/two-thirds-of-seniors-need-help-doing-one-or-more-daily-activities-201312136942#:~:text=We've%20known%20for%20some,of%20daily%20living%20without%20help.

6 Alexia Fernández Campbell, *Home Health Aides for the Elderly: Who Will Care with Them?* Vox (Aug. 21, 2019), https://www.vox.com/the-highlight/2019/8/21/20694768/home-health-aides-elder-care.

With respect to screening and sanctioning, the reality is that this system only works right now for *skilled workers*. If a visa candidate is a computer scientist with a prospective job in Silicon Valley, the candidate is carefully screened ex-ante or preentry – she must submit her academic credentials, her prospective job, and undergo a detailed background check. It should be noted that the visa type for which the computer scientist is eligible (typically H1B) provides a path first to permanent residency, and later to citizenship. This means that the formal system carefully screens for those with the right qualities to not only do skilled work but also become American citizens. Therefore, the potential sanction is clearly implicit. A skilled person who does not abide by their visa terms potentially forfeits their opportunity for American citizenship. Again, here I am describing the system for *skilled* workers. For *unskilled* workers, the outcome, in sharp contrast to the skilled system, involves the de facto permanent residence of 12 million undocumented persons, the overwhelming majority of whom have never been screened or sanctioned.

How did this come to be? Outside of guest worker programs, which are primarily used for seasonal agriculture (H2A) and tourism and other seasonal industries (H2B), there is no equivalent system of comprehensive preentry screening for low-skilled workers. In some countries, such as the anglophone Caribbean Islands, which are the highest source of guest workers on a per-capita basis, the state seeks to reduce unemployment and buttress remittances by sending citizens overseas. Thus, the state works alongside American agricultural and tourism companies to recruit potential low-skilled guest workers to apply for visas. The state then helps these otherwise poorly resourced guest workers to source and submit the required visa application paperwork at the US Embassy.

Thus, if you are a farm worker or tourism worker from Jamaica or Antigua, you may receive help. But as a practical matter, most low-skilled workers who are poor residents of developing countries simply lack the resources to compile the documentation, pay the visa fees, and undergo a screening process. Moreover, many American companies are perfectly willing to hire undocumented persons. Thus, if you are low-skilled and seeking work in the US as a practical matter, your easiest choice is to cross the border without documentation, or to enter on some other sort of easier-to-acquire visa, such as a visitors' visa (B2), knowing fully well that you will work in violation of the visa's terms.

Law Professors Eric Posner and Adam Cox explain how this system has evolved. For the low-skilled portion of the population, as a practical matter, rather than screening all persons (as they are required to do in theory on the basis of their obligations under law to screen ex ante), immigration officials have only pursued those who commit non–immigration-related crimes. Thus, in reality, the system as it relates to low-skilled workers is an ex-post system in which undocumented entrants, who later provide evidence of undesirability (through their contact with the criminal justice system), are screened only after their entry, and then deported.

For low-skilled workers, the system is currently designed to sidestep ex-ante screening and ex-post sanctioning (unless the low-skilled worker commits a non–immigration-related crime).

Difficulties in negotiating compromises on immigration reform reflects that many Americans are unconvinced that policymakers and immigration enforcement officials can design, and enforce, a credible program in which temporary workers will in fact be temporary.[7] To build broad-based political support for a temporary worker elder-care program, policymakers will have to design a program that in fact screens for workers who are competent caregivers, who are seeking temporary work, and who will keep with the terms of their visas and return to their countries of origin. Recognizing that for decades the political climate has been decidedly restrictionist, political actors have long sidestepped hard questions about how to design a program that will admit large numbers of low-skilled migrants who actually comply with the temporary terms of their visas. This is why the 100-year life matters for immigration. Perhaps the aging of the population and the inevitable need for care workers will force policymakers to confront these questions.

A large population of elderly citizens will likely mean that the US will have a large population of temporary workers who have no reasonable prospect of becoming permanent residents. The influential political philosopher Michael Walzer has warned of the dangers of a long-term population of temporary residents without the rights and responsibilities of citizenship in constitutional democracy. His view is that most (if not all) persons admitted should have a path to permanent residency and citizenship. Many law professors (including myself) share his expansionist sentiments. Yet, as law professors, we also need to confront the reality that most Americans do not share our expansionist inclinations. Whatever our inclinations may be, there is a desperate need for an academic focus on institutional design. Specifically the need to focus on how immigration institutions can do what Americans want them to do – screen for migrants who abide by the rules of their visas and sanction those who do not.

I believe that I have a model for how such immigration institutions may be designed. My own region of origin – the Caribbean – currently supplies many home-care aides in two states with disproportionate representation of seniors, Florida and New York. As a scholar of "low-skilled" migration from the Caribbean, in this chapter I consider questions of immigration institutional design in light of lessons learned from how Caribbean home-care aides currently work and travel. In Section 15.1, I provide details of the lives of these undocumented workers to consider how we might incentivize compliance with immigration rules.

In Section 15.2, I contend that Caribbean workers who are working (*ultra vires*) while on "visitors'" (B2) visas have already provided a model that institutional design

[7] Daniel Costa, *Temporary Migrant Workers or Immigrants*, 6 Russell Sage Found. J. of the Soc. Sci. (2020), https://muse.jhu.edu/article/777518.

experts might want to replicate. Caribbean home-care aides on visitors' visas understand that they are not supposed to work. However, since the B2 visa permits a maximum of a six-month stay after entry, they also understand that they are unlikely to be penalized for working as long as they do not stay in the US for longer than six months on any one visit. If they violate this rule, the US is unlikely to renew their visas.

Thus, they have devised a system to comply with the six-month rule – job splitting. This is a pattern whereby home-care aides split their work between two workers, each of whom works for six months per year before turning over the job to a companion care worker for the remaining six months. Thus, each worker is in fact temporary. In any given year, they spend no more than six months in the US, before returning to their country of origin and then coming again the following year. The workers comply with the six-month rule because they feel secure in the knowledge that they will be permitted to come the following year. This pattern typically continues over several years. An upside of job splitting is that it leads to continuity of care, since the elders who they care for have the same two caregivers over several years. This is important; indeed, continuity of care is prioritized in the elder-care literature.

That this system persists not only for "low-skilled" workers who pick tomatoes but also for "low-skilled" workers who care for grandparents speaks volumes about the long-term likelihood of its persistence. But this is unnecessary. In Section 15.3, I argue that most of these workers are in fact "good types," who could have been favorably screened ex-ante for elder-care visas. I propose that we urgently devise a system that permits temporary entry of elder-care workers. If they are permitted long-term temporary visas in which they can work in the US for a few months per year over several years, they have every incentive to comply.

We must confront the reality of a shadow system of undocumented persons in home care and design a system to replace it. Postponing such questions is no longer sustainable in light of the 100-year life.

15.1 A MODEL FOR ELDER CARE: LESSONS FROM CARIBBEAN HOME-CARE AIDES

In the popular imagination during the pandemic, elder care became synonymous with nursing homes. However, most elderly Americans do not live in nursing homes. Nor do scholars of elder care want them to live in nursing homes. There had been an increasing consensus among scholars that we need to prioritize "aging in place," that is, noninstitutional solutions to elder care, with an emphasis on keeping the elderly in their homes and communities.[8] The pandemic has reinforced this sentiment. Based on data, over 23 percent of people who died from COVID

[8] Wei-Duan Porter et al., *Interventions to Prevent or Delay Long-Term Nursing Home Placements for Adults with Impairments: A Systematic Review of Reviews*, 35 J. GEN. INTERN. MED. 2118 (2020) (an excellent summary of the "aging in place" literature).

complications in the US were nursing home residents.[9] The disastrous impact of COVID in institutional settings has underlined the need for more sustainable elder care, particularly in-home elder care. Thus, I begin with a different population, which I believe distinctively illustrates the challenges of redesigning an immigration system to provide sustainable care to an aging population: home-care aides.

I have spent most of my life in a region of the world – the Caribbean – that disproportionately supplies the workers who take care of the American elderly. Although formal data are hard to find (perhaps because so many persons are undocumented), it is inarguable that the Caribbean supplies the majority of home-care aides in at least two regions of the country, namely Florida and New York (the first of which has the second-highest proportion of elderly populations). This chapter is based in part on research into Caribbean migrant workers, many of whom are home-care aides.

Of the migrant workers who have been seriously studied (primarily in agriculture, construction, tourism, and food plants), workers in elder care are undoubtedly the least studied population. Home-care aides are by definition "out of sight." While this population has been insufficiently studied within the US (perhaps because so many of them live in the homes of their elderly employers and are paid in cash), the same is not true in the Caribbean. The home-care aide population regularly sends money to their countries of origin and, in so doing, provides a steady pool of cash to their families and their countries.

Much information can be ascertained from their remittances, which have become indispensable to the foreign exchange reserves of Caribbean central banks. Their sizable earnings provide a clue to the unique importance of this population – not only to their countries of origin but also to elderly Americans. It is not an exaggeration to say that in-home elder care in both Florida and New York would collapse if Caribbean migrant workers disappeared.

How did home-care workers providing services "under the table" become so important? The oft-told narrative is as follows. A New York or Florida family has a parent or grandparent who is no longer able to live independently. The family visits a few nursing homes and finds either the facilities unattractive or the costs prohibitive, despite having access to Medicare since state coverage of nursing home care is paltry in the US (certainly in comparison to other rich OECD countries). Moreover, for many families, nursing home workers seem overextended, raising concerns as to whether their elderly relative would be properly cared for.

Of course, in-home elder care also has its challenges – for example, the provision of care is governed by a patchy network of licensing and regulations (with some

[9] Priya Chidambaram, *Over 200,000 Residents and Staff in Long-Term Care Facilities Have Died from COVID-19*, Kaiser Family Foundation (Feb. 2, 2022), https://www.kff.org/policy-watch/over-200000-residents-and-staff-in-long-term-care-facilities-have-died-from-covid-19/#:~:text=Long%2DTerm%20Care%20Facility%20Residents,of%201%2F30%2F2022.

localities having no licensing requirements or regulatory framework at all) – leading to concerns about the quality of care. Naturally, many families prefer in-home care. Moreover, many discover that they can provide care for their grandparent more cheaply through in-home care, particularly when such care is subsidized by state insurance that may provide an in-home care aide for a few hours each week (typically the state will only subsidize those who are home *healthcare* aides, that is, those who have some basic medical training). However, usually the state will provide only a fraction of the care that the elderly relative needs. Thus, many families supplement their state-subsidized care with lower-cost options; they hire home-care aides who are undocumented and pay them under the table. In the absence of a formal state-supported care infrastructure (such as exists in many other developed countries, including in Western Europe), families create a home-care infrastructure themselves.

In New York and Florida, home-care aides are predominantly Caribbean women[10] who are not licensed[11] even though families are clearly satisfied with their services as evidenced by their multi-year tenure with the same families. How do these women come to be home-care aides? For a Caribbean woman who is not university educated (and thereby ineligible for most skilled work visas in the US), there are basically three options to work in the US. The first is what we typically think of as agricultural guest work – a yearly sojourn (at least pre-COVID) on an H2A visa to work on a US farm for several months. For most women, unfortunately, agricultural visas are not a practical option; their recipients are overwhelmingly men. The second option is to be a documented guest worker in the tourism or other seasonal sector on an H2B visa. This, for example, might involve working in a hotel in Aspen, Colorado. These guest workers unsurprisingly pay taxes. They also incur other expenses, such as living expenses for staying in staff quarters that are deducted from their salaries by the hotels. From a take-home pay perspective, the most desirable option for many Caribbean women is the third option, namely, undocumented care work. I use the word "undocumented" to mean *both* those who are either working without any visa whatsoever (the popular understanding of the term "undocumented") *and* those who have visas that preclude legal work but who work anyways.

[10] Jeanne Batalova, *Immigrant Health-Care Workers in the United States*, Migration Policy Institute (Apr. 7, 2023), https://www.migrationpolicy.org/article/immigrant-health-care-workers-united-states-2021 (the percentage representation of Caribbean people among home healthcare aides would be expected to be higher in both New York and Florida, which are the two highest receiving states for Caribbean migrants. The same report notes that New York and Florida have the highest proportion of home healthcare aides who are immigrants).

[11] Mehgan Gallagher, *The Truth behind Home Health Aid Certifications*, O'Neil Institute for National & Global Health Law: Georgetown Law (Feb. 15, 2018), https://oneill.law.georgetown.edu/the-truth-behind-home-health-aide-certification-requirements ("there is no formal education requirement … to secure a position as an HHA").

Why is care work so popular? Having spoken to Jamaicans who have done tourism work and home-care work, they will explain that they are better off as undocumented home-care aides than as documented guest workers. The money is steady, their living expenses are often covered since many live in their clients' homes, and they avoid tax obligations. Nearly every Jamaican knows of some relative or friend working as a home-care aide in the US. (I say this as a native Jamaican, with only slight exaggeration!)

Some of these home-care aides are "undocumented," in the popular understanding of the term, in that they have typically overstayed their B2 visas (known informally as visitor's visas). I highlight a few of the terms under which visitor's visas are typically issued. First, the visa applicant is expected to provide accurate information about her travel intentions and her historical behavior, that is, including her historical record of abiding with the terms of visas. That is, if she is applying for a visitor's visa, she should really be intending to make a short-term visit. Second, the visa recipient agrees that she will not impose welfare costs on the government. Third, the visa recipient agrees only to visit and not work, as well as to exit the US within the prescribed time period, which for B2 visas is six months after entry. Some Jamaicans who work under the table initially enter on B2 visas that then expire. They then become undocumented in the typical understanding of the term since they no longer have visa documentation.

However, there is a different pool of home-care aides that I would like to highlight for the purposes of this chapter because their work patterns provide important lessons about institutional design. Many Caribbean home-care aides who engage in unauthorized work have come up with unconventional and interesting mechanisms of maintaining their job security. Setting aside the fact that they are working (a clear violation of the terms of their B2 visas), they take pains not to overstay. That is, on every visit, they make sure they stay no more than six months after their initial entry. In so doing, they seek to preserve the possibilities that their visas will be renewed. Thus, the pattern is as follows. Beverly, a hypothetical in-home aide, enters on January 1, Year 1. She leaves on June 30, Year 1. She returns to her country of origin for the rest of the calendar year. In Year 2, she enters on January 1 and leaves on June 30, returning to her country for the rest of the year. And so the pattern continues.

If Beverly is only in the US for six months, is her job surely at risk? Not so. In order to maintain the continuity of her work with elderly clients, she "splits" her job. That is, Beverly is the home-care aide for the first six months. She is then replaced by Janet – a sister, a cousin, or a close friend – who works as the home-care aide for the other six months. I refer to this pattern as job splitting.

15.2 WHY JOB SPLITTING MATTERS

Any competent immigration lawyer would agree that these Jamaican women who work while they are on visitor's visas are not in fact complying with their visa terms.

Yet on further examination, what these women do is in fact quite innovative. What is striking about job splitting is that these women do not "overstay" while simultaneously maintaining their employment for when they return. They have in essence created a type of "de facto" job security. That is, an elder-care worker may only work for six months of the year, but she has done it for the last ten years.

Moreover, for students of the literature on elder care, there is an unanticipated benefit of their efforts to avoid overstaying while maintaining their jobs. Job splitting has the upside of helping to ensure continuity of care for their elderly clients. Continuity of care is a major theme in the elder-care literature. That is, by splitting the job, Janet and Beverley are able to provide elder-care services to one client for ten years. Rather than receiving services from many different home-care aides, the client only receives services from Beverley and Janet.

Researchers have long emphasized that continuity of care matters for patient well-being. Immigration institutional design has clear implications for patient well-being and longevity. Researchers have long emphasized that continuity of care matters for patient well-being, and the COVID pandemic only served to reinforce its importance. Indeed, continuity of care may have life-or-death implications. During the pandemic, elderly persons who were cared for at home by one long-term caregiver were less likely to be exposed to COVID infections, to be hospitalized, or to die than their counterparts in nursing homes. Additionally, one study contends that an elderly person fares better when the worker who takes care of her perceives herself to be the long-term caregiver of that elderly person. Why is this? Persons who believe themselves to be long-term caregivers are more likely to advocate for their clients to receive good health care, or to speak candidly about what they perceive to be in the best interests of their patients.

In support of this theory, I turn to the nursing home context. There appear to be differential outcomes in infection and death rates in those nursing homes with long-term employees with minimal turnover versus those homes where turnover rates are higher.[12] Again, one reason for these differential outcomes is obvious. A high-turnover staff is more likely to introduce infection to a nursing home. But there are other reasons. Where staff turnover was lower, staff were more likely to be invested in providing good care to the nursing home residents and to advocate for COVID prevention protocols to protect the residents.

Surely this is relevant to planning for the 100-year-old citizen. As we prepare for a world where centenarians become the norm, I argue that this is the model that the US should try to emulate when addressing questions of institutional design in immigration – creating incentives for migrants who care for the elderly to invest in the longevity of their jobs. Migrants who invest in the longevity of their jobs are

[12] Lacey Loomer et al., *Association between Nursing Home Staff Turnover and Infection Control Citations*, 57 Health Serv. Res. 322 (2022) (a good summary of the literature on the connection between nursing home staff turnover and infection control).

typically also invested in the longevity of their patients. If they are secure in the knowledge that their visas will be renewed – provided that they abide by the terms and do not overstay – they will be invested in the well-being and good health of their clients, who they will be likely to serve over several years.

15.3 DESIGNING A SYSTEM WITHIN RESTRICTIONIST POLITICAL REALITIES

In a landmark book, Law Professor Hiroshi Motomura calls on Americans to treat lawful immigrants as "Americans in Waiting," largely entitled to the benefits of citizenship. Motomura is concerned primarily with what the larger goals of immigration should be, given the underlying constitutional and moral commitments of American democracy. His work typifies the expansionist flavor of much immigration law scholarship. Scholars typically focus on admitting more migrants, for longer periods, and with a more robust group of rights. Although I am very sympathetic to these expansionist goals, I believe that they are not realistic in light of current political constraints, given that the dominant immigration sentiments appear to be restrictionist.

What do I mean by restrictionist constraints? Most Americans want fewer immigrants who are long-term permanent residents. Moreover, they are skeptical of temporary migrant programs, believing that guest workers will inevitably overstay and become long-term residents. Although restrictionist policies were promoted most passionately by the Trump administration, it is already clear that restrictionist immigration policies have outlived President Trump. One need only consider what appears to be an emerging bipartisan political backlash to the perceived increase in the numbers of persons applying for asylum at the southern border.[13]

A more realistic view of what is possible with restrictionist political realities is articulated by Law Professor Cristina Rodriguez, who quite clearly understands the inevitable trade-off between the number of migrants admitted and the rights they receive upon admission. She termed this trade-off "the admissions-status dynamic." Responding to Motomura's challenge to treat more migrants as "citizens-in-waiting," Rodriguez characterizes the challenge as follows:

> According to the dynamic, more immigration translates into diminished support for immigrants' rights, and more robust immigrants' rights translate into less support for immigrant admission. To put it crudely, if cheap labor is suddenly transformed into expensive citizens in waiting, the doors to immigrants may well close altogether. If we commit to treating immigrants as citizens, we may well erode what support exists for largescale immigration, giving rise to policies that more strictly limit the

[13] Jonathan Weisman & Nicholas Fandos, *G.O.P. Gets the Democratic Border Crisis It Wanted*, N.Y. Times (Sep. 8, 2023), https://www.nytimes.com/2023/09/08/us/politics/gop-migrants-blue-cities.html.

> number of people permitted to enter. Such restrictions would be justified on the ground that we must be highly selective about those we admit given that they will be presumptively entitled to join our political community. In short, a society may be willing to absorb large-scale immigration only if it can maintain tight control over the benefits that accrue to immigrants, reserving for citizens alone the most expensive or most valued goods of citizenship. Trends in immigration law and policy in the United States reflect this trade-off.[14]

Rodriguez's perspective is relevant to any program aimed at admitting elder-care workers. If Rodriguez is right (as I believe she is), realistic immigration proposals will need to assure Americans that the elder-care workers who are being admitted will not be long-term members of the political community, with entitlements to the benefits that come with this status. The US's refusal to design an immigration system that includes these assurances is, in part, responsible for the large undocumented population. Any program designed to recruit guest workers specifically to provide elder care needs to clearly establish that these workers are temporary.

The key in my mind is not only to look for ex-ante signals of temporary intent but also to incentivize compliance. If guest workers are assured that they could come for six months, with a near guarantee of visa renewal if they abided by the terms of their visa requirements, they will take compliance seriously.

Other incentives for compliance could also be built in. For example, a portion of their earnings might be held in escrow to be released when they return to their country of origin. However, these other incentives will pale in importance to the primary incentive – namely an assurance of visa renewal if they comply. These guest workers would be not unlike the aforementioned Caribbean home-care aides, who are "self-enforcing" precisely because they feel secure that their visitors' visas will be renewed as long as they do not stay in the US longer than six months.

Moreover, to ensure continuity of care, one of their visa requirements might be that they provide care services to clients who they have serviced in the past (with a clear exception if the client dies). This would provide an additional incentive to do what the Caribbean home-care aides are already doing. That is, they return to provide care services to their former employers, secure in the knowledge that their jobs will be waiting for them the following year when they return. It is possible to model "de jure" after what Caribbean home-care workers have been doing "de facto."

We already know that most of these workers are in fact "good types" who would likely have been favorably screened. We know this because of the market – these elder-care workers would hardly have been able to maintain employment with the same family over several years if they were not providing competent care services. Moreover, recall Cox and Posner, finding good visa applicants is primarily an

[14] Cristina Rodriguez, *The Citizenship Paradox in a Transnational Age*, 106 Mich. L. Rev. 1111 (2008).

informational problem; a state is seeking to find enough information to ascertain whether a potential entrant matches its type preferences. Notably, the communities of origin for Caribbean elder-care workers are small and tightly knit – if a person has a poor reputation, the word will spread. If someone is an incompetent caregiver, they are unlikely to get referrals or positive recommendations from other care workers (who are always being asked for referrals). Of course, the state cares about matters that families may not care about (e.g., their inclination to comply with their visas), so family approval is not the final word, but it is surely a good sign.

There would of course be other requirements. For example, in conducting visa screening, the US might quite reasonably want to conduct detailed background checks, such as ensuring that the applicant has no history of abuse against the elderly. However, these prospective elder-care workers are not Silicon Valley-bound computer scientists; they cannot present university diplomas or letters from professors and employers in the formal market to serve as testament to their background and character. Yet overcoming the challenges of ex-ante screening in nontraditional populations – whose members may lack access to the resources needed to credibly document their backgrounds – seems particularly possible in the small Caribbean countries from which the elder-care workers that I have described in this chapter originate.

These workers typically originate from small towns and villages – they are known at multiple levels of community life. Indeed, this is precisely how Canada screens its guest workers – relying on Caribbean governments to share information about visa candidates ascertained through cooperation with clubs, churches, and other community organizations. That Spain has been able to implement a similar model in screening guest workers from Morocco – a much larger country with arguably a more challenging risk profile than the Caribbean Islands – is indicative that the utility of this approach of transnational cooperation to augment screening capabilities goes beyond small island countries of origin.

Finally, to maintain certain standards of care, one might also want to institute some sort of licensing regime, in which those who have demonstrated some historical competence in elder care receive a certificate licensing them to provide elder care in the US. If a person has historically been involved in elder care (such as the aforementioned Caribbean women), they should be initially eligible even if they lack formal credentials, while providing them an incentive to pursue additional training to maintain their licenses in the future. Since such licensing is typically provided by the states rather than the federal government, the federal government might simply want to stipulate that visa recipients demonstrate that they have met licensing requirements, to provide an additional incentive for caregivers to become licensed.

15.4 CONCLUSION

What we will end up with is a large population of people who are in essence guest workers in perpetuity – assured of the right to return if they only stay a few months and leave and return to their country of origin every year. This of course is precisely what the political philosopher Michael Walzer has warned against – the presence of a long-term pool of persons who live in perpetual "guest-workerness," with no realistic means of participating in the democratic experiment. Would a great constitutional democracy really tolerate the presence of such a population within its borders?

This of course is an important question for any constitutional democracy to grapple with. But it appears to be a question that Americans have already answered – even if some of us find the answer deeply troubling. For example, Americans already tolerate guest workers in perpetuity in their farm work and tourism worker programs – it bears emphasis that a significant proportion of visa recipients in these programs are multi-year repeat participants. And the huge undocumented population is in essence a de facto population of permanent residents with no political voice of their own – they are typically only able to act politically through their allies. Thus, what Americans are prepared to tolerate is perfectly clear; the question of the "justice" of what they perceive to be tolerable is different. I believe the outline of the guest worker program for elder-care workers is practicable within the aforementioned political constraints. As we approach the era of the 100-year life, this provides a clear model for how we might proceed to design a system that provides a robust pipeline of well-screened migrant workers.

16

Science Fiction, Legal Fiction, Political Fiction, and the 100-Year Life

Daniel J. Hemel

A child born in the West today has a more than 50 per cent chance of living to be over 105 . . . This is not science fiction.[1]

The claim by Lynda Gratton and Andrew Scott that "the 100-year life" will become the norm for cohorts born in the Western world today is startling. It also is, contrary to the authors' characterization, "science fiction." By "science fiction" I do not mean that it is necessarily wrong – science fiction sometimes proves prescient, as with Jules Verne's predictions of electric submarines and space travel. But the claim is "science fiction" within the dictionary definition: a "story featur[ing] hypothetical scientific or technological advances."[2] For Gratton and Scott's claim to come true, biomedicine will need to make advances against aging that – for now – remain hypothetical.

Imagining a 100-year life requires us to engage not only in science fiction but also in legal and political fiction. I do not mean "legal fiction" in Blackstone's sense – a fiction that litigants and judges use to rationalize particular jurisdictional results, such as the fiction that defendants before the King's Bench committed trespass in Middlesex county.[3] And by "political fiction," I do not mean that the 100-year life is a *House of Cards*-style thriller about officeholders in Westminster or Washington. Rather, the journey to a 100-year life will likely require new developments in law and politics that – as with their biomedical counterparts – remain hypothetical. Not only have we failed to achieve the biomedical advances that will allow 100-year lives to become the norm, but we have also failed to build the legal institutions and political coalitions that will foster those biomedical advances. As with Verne's submarines, today's fiction may become reality in the not-so-distant future. But the journey to a

[1] Lynda Gratton & Andrew Scott, The 100-Year Life: Living and Working in an Age of Longevity 2 (2016).

[2] *Science Fiction*, Oxford English Dictionary Online, https://www.oed.com/dictionary/science-fiction_n?tab=meaning_and_use#23960648 (accessed Nov. 27, 2023).

[3] William Blackstone, Commentaries on the Laws of England 28 (Thomas P. Gallanis ed., 2016).

100-year life will require creative solutions in the realm of law and public policy, just as it will require ingenuity in the scientific realm.

While other chapters explore the implications of the 100-year life *for* law and public policy, this chapter explores the role *of* law and policy in achieving century-long lifespans. Section 16.1 argues that for 100-year lives to become the norm within the time frame that Gratton and Scott envision, we will need to make extraordinary progress in reducing old-age mortality. These advances will need to be qualitatively different from the disease-specific innovations that attract the bulk of biomedical investment today.

Section 16.2 considers the role of law and policy in efforts to delay aging and death. It argues that patent law – the most familiar tool in the innovation policy toolkit – is ill fitted for the goal of achieving century-long lives. Many of the most promising longevity-enhancing innovations fall outside the legal and practical limits of patent protection. Even for new pharmaceutical and biologic products that lie closer to patent law's core, the long time frame necessary to establish efficacy through clinical trials leaves few years for firms to monetize their innovations. Section 16.2 goes on to consider other legal mechanisms that can potentially sustain longevity-related research and development – specifically the private foundation and the for-profit corporation, which, unlike patents, can have infinite legal lives. Although nonprofit and corporate law have facilitated significant longevity-related investments in recent years, they have done so for reasons that are more idiosyncratic than systematic – and in ways that highlight the potential pitfalls of a private sector-driven quest for 100-year lifespans.

The chapter concludes by considering the political economy of public sector investment in longevity research. To achieve century-long lives, we will likely need governments – in particular, the US federal government – to commit to a moonshot investment in longevity akin to the Apollo project that brought Neil Armstrong and Buzz Aldrin to the lunar surface. But whereas the Apollo project commanded broad bipartisan support, a longevity moonshot is bound to encounter powerful political resistance. That wall of resistance may prove penetrable, but not easily so. Thus the path to a 100-year life will likely require major breakthroughs not only in the laboratory but also in the legislature.

16.1 A 100-YEAR LIFE EXPECTANCY IS STILL SCIENCE FICTION

Understanding the incredible optimism of Gratton and Scott's predictions requires a brief primer in demographic terminology. Life expectancies are conventionally stated in *period mean* terms. Life expectancy at birth in a given year reflects the average number of life-years remaining for a newborn if age-specific mortality rates remain at that year's levels. For example, life expectancy at birth in the US in 2021 was 76.4 years, meaning that if age-specific mortality rates remain at 2021 levels, the average age at death would be 76.4.[4] Most likely, babies born in the US in 2021 will on average live longer than 76.4 years because age-specific death rates will decline from 2021 levels. (The year 2021 was especially bad for period mean life expectancy because it coincided with the COVID-19 pandemic's peak.) But of course, we don't know how fast death rates will decline because we can't see into the future.

Gratton and Scott offer life expectancy estimates in *cohort median* terms. By their estimates, 50 percent of babies born in the US in 2007 will live to be at least 104, and half of babies born in Japan that year will celebrate their 107th birthdays. Cohort lifespan estimates are in some ways more useful than period life expectancies because cohort estimates, unlike period estimates, apply to identifiable individuals (individuals born in a given country and year). By contrast, period mean life expectancy at birth in a particular year is *not* an estimate of the mean lifespan of individuals born in that year – it is a calculation of the mean lifespan of individuals born in that year under the unrealistic assumption that all age-specific mortality rates remain at that year's levels. A downside of using cohort statistics, though, is that we can't measure the cohort median until half a cohort has died. Barring catastrophe, we won't know the cohort median lifespan for babies born in the US in 2007 until the late twenty-first or possibly early twenty-second century.

Gratton and Scott draw cohort lifespan projections from a 2009 paper in *The Lancet* by Kaare Christensen, Gabriele Doblhammer, Roland Rau, and James Vaupel ("CDRV").[5] CDRV observe that "best practice" period mean life expectancy – the highest period mean life expectancy in any country in any given year – increased almost linearly at an annual rate of 0.25 years from 1840 into the 2000s. (Sweden was the best practice country for much of that period; Hong Kong is now.) CDRV then translate this observation about best practice period mean life expectancy into projections of cohort median life expectancy for eight high-income countries: Canada, Denmark, France, Germany, Italy, Japan, the UK, and the US.

To arrive at these projections, CDRV assume that period mean life expectancy in high-income countries will increase linearly at an annual rate of 0.2 years into the twenty-second century. They also assume that age-specific mortality rates will follow a particular path that generates annual increases of 0.2 years in period mean life expectancy. Mortality rates from age zero to fifty and from 110 on up will remain

[4] Mortality rate and life expectancy data come from the Human Mortality Database, https://mortality.org (accessed July 17, 2023).

[5] Gratton and Scott cite the Human Mortality Database for their cohort median estimates, *see* GRATTON & SCOTT, *supra* note 1, at 24 fig. 1.1, but that database does not include cohort median projections for post-1990 cohorts. Gratton and Scott's numbers align precisely with estimates in another paper – Kaare Christensen, Gabriele Doblhammer, Roland Rau & James W. Vaupel, *Ageing Populations: The Challenges Ahead*, 374 LANCET 1196, 1197 tbl.1 (2009) – and Gratton and Scott cite Vaupel's work elsewhere. *See* GRATTON & SCOTT, *supra* note 1, at 377.

unchanged from 2006 levels, and mortality rates from age 50 to 110 will decline at a rate of 2.2 percent per year.[6]

To recap: When Gratton and Scott say that "a child born in the West today has a more than 50 per cent chance of living to be over 105," what they really mean is this: If cohort median lifespans in advanced economies grow as fast as CDRV project, then there is a 50 percent probability that a member of a high-income country cohort born in the first or second decade of the twenty-first century will reach age 105.

How plausible are CDRV's projections? As CDRV note, previous prognosticators have often underestimated future life expectancy growth. As recently as 1990, an article in *Science* stated that "it seems highly unlikely that life expectancy at birth will exceed the age of 85"[7] – a threshold that Hong Kong surpassed in 2018. But while past projections of life expectancy growth have been unduly pessimistic, the growth rate that CDRV project appears to be extraordinarily optimistic – for at least two reasons.

First, CDRV project that period mean life expectancy in high-income countries will increase at an annual rate of 0.20 years from 2006 onwards, but we already know that – even before COVID-19 – those countries were not keeping up with that pace. The average annual rate of life expectancy growth across the eight countries in CDRV's study from 2006 through 2019 was 0.15 years, and the rate for the US during that stretch was just 0.09 years. At a 0.15-year annual rate of life expectancy growth from 2006 onwards, none of the eight high-income countries in CDRV's study would reach century-long life expectancies by 2120. At a rate of 0.09 years, US life expectancy in 2120 will be 88.1 years. For US life expectancy to reach 100 within a century, we will need to pick up the pace substantially.

Second, not only are CDRV's period mean life expectancy projections quite optimistic relative to recent experience, but their projections for mortality rates are extraordinarily optimistic in light of historical experience. As noted earlier, CDRV project that mortality rates from age 50 to 110 will decline at a rate of 2.2 percent per year from 2006 to 2120. Yet over the entire period of the Human Mortality Database's coverage from 1933 through 2019, the mortality rate for fifty-year-old Americans has declined at an annual rate of only 1.3 percent, or about three-fifths as fast as CDRV project. And the mortality rate for 100-year-old Americans has declined at an annual rate of 0.2 percent – less than a tenth of the rate that CDRV project going forward.

One might ask: How do CDRV arrive at such optimistic predictions if their model simply projects outwards from pre-2006 life expectancy growth? The primary reason is that CDRV's model does not account for the different trajectories of mortality rates at different age levels. The US, like other high-income countries, made huge

6 Author's correspondence with Roland Rau.

7 S. Jay Olshansky, Bruce A. Carnes & Christine Cassel, *In Search of Methuselah: Estimating the Upper Limits to Human Longevity*, 250 SCIENCE 634, 634 (1990).

progress in reducing childhood and midlife mortality over the course of the twentieth century, which fueled similarly large gains in period mean life expectancy. In recent years, progress in reducing childhood and midlife mortality has slowed (and midlife mortality rates have actually increased in the US since 2010), but even if those mortality rate reductions picked up pace, they would have a relatively small impact on overall life expectancy. Indeed, even if we eliminated *all* mortality before age fifty, life expectancy at birth in the US would increase by less than four years. For century-long lifespans to become the norm, the US and other high-income countries will need to make extraordinary improvements in mortality rates at older ages.

Reducing mortality rates at older ages is not necessarily impossible, but it will require interventions different from those that are effective at younger ages. Disease-specific interventions can lead to large reductions in mortality at younger ages because if a younger person does not die of a particular cause (e.g., breast cancer), she is relatively unlikely to die of a competing cause in the near future (e.g., heart disease). By contrast, disease-specific interventions hold less promise for reducing mortality at older ages because if an older person does not die of a particular cause, she remains highly vulnerable to other fatal risks. For example, the Centers for Disease Control and Prevention estimates that a complete cure for Alzheimer's disease – a top-five cause of death among Americans over age sixty-five – would extend overall US life expectancy by only about seven weeks.[8] To achieve the twenty-year life expectancy increase that CDRV project over a century, we will need to do more than play a game of disease-specific whack-a-mole.

This recognition raises two related questions. The first is whether any intervention – a lifestyle change, a miracle drug, a nonpharmacological therapy, or some other innovation, alone or in combination – can generate the all-cause mortality reductions at older ages that would be needed to realize CDRV's forecasts. The second is whether, if there is any such intervention out there, countries can identify it and disseminate it to their populations. The former is, at bottom, a bioscientific question that lies beyond this chapter's scope. The latter is a question of law, economics, and politics – and the question upon which the remainder of this chapter focuses.

16.2 THE LIMITS OF LAW

16.2.1 *Patents and Their Discontents*

Discussions of law and innovation often begin – and too often end – with intellectual property – in particular, patent law. The promise of patent protection can

[8] Elizabeth Arias, Melonie Heron & Betzaida Tejada-Vera, *United States Life Tables Eliminating Certain Causes of Death*, 1999–2001, 61 NAT'L VITAL STATISTICS REPORT, 1, 101–104 tbl. 22 (2013).

encourage profit-seeking firms to undertake costly investments in the development of new technologies. But for most innovations with the potential to bring about century-long lifespans, the incentives generated by patent law are severely underpowered.

Consider, for example, intermittent fasting (fasting for one to two days per week), which – according to a recent article in the *New England Journal of Medicine* – appears to have "broad-spectrum benefits for many health conditions, such as obesity, diabetes mellitus, cardiovascular disease, cancers, and neurologic disorders."[9] While the strength of these findings is a subject of much debate among biomedical researchers, the example of intermittent fasting provides a helpful illustration of patent law's limits. A method for extending human lifespan through intermittent fasting would almost certainly lie outside the scope of patent eligibility under current law.[10] And even if Congress changed the law to permit patents on dietary innovations, it is hard to see how a patent on intermittent fasting could be enforced. A patent holder could not realistically determine whether individuals have gone twenty-four hours without eating and sue them if so. A firm that sponsored a clinical trial successfully showing that intermittent fasting extends lifespan would have little ability to monetize its investment.

Other promising longevity-enhancing interventions relate to drugs that have been off-patent for several years – and there, too, existing legal institutions generate weak incentives for research. Consider metformin – a drug that has been used to treat Type 2 diabetes for decades and that has been off-patent in its tablet formulation in the US since the beginning of the millennium. A 2014 study lifted hopes that daily metformin use might produce significant reductions in all-cause mortality even in nondiabetic patients.[11] But in the decade since that finding grabbed headlines, no pharmaceutical firm has conducted a clinical trial to see whether the results are robust. In 2015, the FDA green-lighted a proposal for a study to test whether metformin could reduce all-cause mortality in elderly patients, but the researchers who designed the trial have failed to attract the necessary funding – roughly $50 million.[12]

Why have for-profit firms proved unwilling to finance a clinical trial of metformin – notwithstanding the potentially massive demand for a drug that reduces the risk of death across the board? In theory, firms can apply for new-use patents

9 Rafael de Cabo & Mark P. Mattson, *Effects of Intermittent Fasting on Health, Aging, and Disease*, 381 New Eng. J. Med. 2541, 2548 (2019).

10 *See In re* Zunshine, 816 Fed. App'x 477 (Fed. Cir. 2020) (affirming Patent and Trademark Office's rejection of patent application for method of calorie restriction).

11 C. A. Bannister et al., *Can People with Type 2 Diabetes Live Longer Than Those Without? A Comparison of Mortality in People Initiated with Metformin or Sulphonylurea Monotherapy and Matched, Non-Diabetic Controls*, 16 Diabetes, Obesity & Metabolism 1165 (2014).

12 Megan Molteni, *As Billionaires Race to Fund Anti-Aging Projects, a Much-Discussed Trial Goes Overlooked*, STAT News (Aug. 9, 2022), https://www.statnews.com/2022/08/09/anti-aging-projects-funding-much-discussed-trial-overlooked.

covering the application of an existing drug to treat a different medical condition – for example, the use of metformin to reduce all-cause mortality in nondiabetic patients. However, enforcing a new-use drug patent is extraordinarily difficult in practice. Typically, a pharmacist who fills a metformin prescription will not know whether the prescribing physician ordered metformin as an antidiabetic medication or an antiaging drug. And in many states, the pharmacist has a legal obligation to fill the prescription with the cheapest medicine available.[13] Thus, even when physicians prescribe a drug for a new use, the revenues are likely to flow to a low-cost generic manufacturer rather than the new-use patentee.

Even for new longevity drugs that are legally eligible for patent protection, long commercialization lags are likely to remain a significant impediment to profit-seeking investment. An analogy from the cancer context sheds light on the scope of the challenge. Eric Budish, Benjamin Roin, and Heidi Williams have shown that private sector firms are less likely to initiate clinical trials for drugs that treat slow-acting cancers than for drugs that target fast-acting cancers.[14] An important reason is that trials for slow-acting cancers last longer, thus taking up a larger chunk of the twenty-year patent life. By the time a pharmaceutical firm can win approval from the Food and Drug Administration (FDA) for an early-stage cancer treatment, the firm has only a short period of exclusivity within which to monetize its investment before generics can enter.

Aging is the ultimate slow-acting disease. Each step of the research process is likely to take longer for antiaging agents than for therapies that target quick killers. The antiaging treatment may require years to show any effect, and even if the effect on aging is immediate, the effect on clinical outcomes – for example, all-cause mortality – may not be detectable until much later. By that point, the patent clock may have run out.

A possible policy solution is to extend the exclusivity period for treatments that slow the aging process. Congress has enacted several other provisions that provide fixed periods of market exclusivity for manufacturers of new drugs, irrespective of whether the patent term has expired. For example, under the Orphan Drug Act of 1983, the manufacturer of a drug that treats a "rare disease" – typically a disease affecting fewer than 200,000 people in the US – can qualify for seven years of market exclusivity starting from the date of FDA approval, even if patent protection has run out. Aging is the polar opposite of a rare disease – it affects us all – but Congress could seek to incentivize the development of antiaging drugs by offering a similar exclusivity period. Such a statute might, for example, make eligibility conditional

[13] Daniel J. Hemel & Lisa Larrimore Ouellette, *The Generic Drug Trilemma*, 2 Entrepreneurship & Innovation Policy & the Economy 41, 47–48 (2023).

[14] Eric Budish, Benjamin N. Roin & Heidi Williams, *Do Firms Underinvest in Long-Term Research? Evidence from Cancer Clinical Trials*, 105 Am. Econ. Rev. 2044 (2015).

upon the manufacturer demonstrating a statistically significant reduction in all-cause mortality among the general population.

Exclusivity, however, is a double-edged sword. Market exclusivity incentivizes investment because it allows firms to charge higher prices for their products. Those higher prices tend to place products out of the reach of some consumers. Exclusivity thus implicates a trade-off between innovation and access, potentially resulting in the development of more antiaging interventions but not necessarily ensuring that those interventions reach more patients.

Another way for policymakers to encourage pharmaceutical firms to invest in the development of antiaging drugs would be for the FDA to confirm that a drug that reduces all-cause mortality – even if it does not target any specific disease – could achieve agency approval. Traditionally, the FDA has oriented its approval process around a "one disease, one drug" model, raising doubts that a drug that extends lifespan but does not target a specific recognized disease could be approved for sale in the world's most lucrative pharmaceutical market. The FDA through regulatory guidance – or Congress through legislative action – could lay that concern to rest.

But even with the promise of market exclusivity beyond the end of the twenty-year patent life, and even with assurance that the FDA would approve an effective antiaging drug, large pharmaceutical companies still may balk at R&D efforts that won't affect quarterly earnings in the short to medium term. Likewise, biotech startups may steer away from projects that won't come to fruition before venture capital funding runs out. These concerns about short-termism motivate a search for institutions beyond the pharmaceutical and biotech sectors that might facilitate investment in longevity research.

16.2.2 *Nonprofits and Pet Projects*

The first stop on that search is an institution with a long history of financing ambitious public health investments: the philanthropic foundation. Millionaire and billionaire philanthropists who fund foundations would seem to have more of an incentive to invest in longevity research than in solving most other public health problems. After all, while many global public health challenges (e.g., malaria and tuberculosis) are unlikely to affect millionaires and billionaires, extreme wealth is no cure for aging. Foundations, moreover, can operate on a longer time frame than publicly traded corporations that must report quarterly earnings, or startups burning through their venture capital funding. Longevity research, with its high risks and long timelines, would seem to be exactly the sort of area in which foundations can play a productive role.

Some foundations have indeed emerged as major funders of longevity research. One of the most famous cases in the law of philanthropy – mentioned in almost every nonprofit law casebook – even has a longevity twist. *In re Estate of Buck*, described at the time as the "Super Bowl of probate,"[15] involved the will of Beryl Buck, a long-time resident of wealthy Marin County outside San Francisco. Buck's will established a charitable trust – a private foundation for tax purposes – that was to be used entirely for nonprofit activities in Marin. Buck funded the trust with oil company stock that traded for less than $10 million at the time of her death but ballooned in value to more than $250 million a few years later.

Reasoning that Buck's largesse exceeded Marin County's needs, the San Francisco Foundation – Buck's designated trustee – sought permission from a California probate court to distribute trust income across the Bay Area. The court rebuffed the foundation's request, ordering instead that funds be allocated to Marin-based projects with the potential to benefit "all of humankind." One of these, in northern Marin County, is now named the Buck Institute for Research on Aging and provides a home to a world-class faculty of academic scientists searching for cures to age-related diseases.

Yet foundations like the Buck Trust are unlikely to fill the void left by industry underinvestment in longevity research. Foundation funding is often contingent upon the whims of millionaires and billionaires whose moneymaking skills in one sector – or whose luck in the birth lottery – may not necessarily qualify them as biomedical grantmakers. While perpetual trusts like Buck's may provide sustained support, other foundations – especially those with living donors – can be more mercurial. A case in point is the Ellison Medical Foundation, financed by Oracle cofounder Larry Ellison, which spent more than $300 million on antiaging research before Ellison abruptly halted further funding in 2013.[16] Moreover, the aggregate amount of foundation funding for biomedical research remains just a drop in the bucket relative to industry and public sector sources – only around 1 percent of total US biomedical research spending, compared to 66 percent from industry and 25 percent from the federal government.[17]

In recent years, another private sector source has emerged as a much more significant funder of longevity research – at least in dollar terms – than any philanthropic foundation: Alphabet, the parent company of Google. Since 2014, Alphabet has committed $1.75 billion to Calico Life Sciences, an internal laboratory focused on longevity. This is a startling sum for a for-profit company to spend on R&D unrelated to its core business. Yet it represents less than 0.1 percent of Alphabet's market capitalization as of this writing.

[15] *In re* Estate of Buck, No. 23259 (Cal. Super. Ct. 1986), reprinted in 21 U.S.F. L. Rev. 691 (1987); *see* Douglas Bartholomew, *The Battle for the Buck*, L.A. Times (Dec. 21, 1986), https://www.latimes.com/archives/la-xpm-1986-12-21-tm-3738-story.html.

[16] Tad Friend, *Silicon Valley's Quest to Live Forever*, New Yorker (Mar. 27, 2017), https://www.newyorker.com/magazine/2017/04/03/silicon-valleys-quest-to-live-forever.

[17] Research! America, *U.S. Investments in Medical and Health Research and Development, 2016–2020* (2022), https://www.researchamerica.org/wp-content/uploads/2022/09/ResearchAmerica-Investment-Report.Final_.January-2022-1.pdf.

Alphabet has faced criticism for pursuing what seems like a distraction from its profit-generating activities.[18] But Alphabet's dual-class corporate structure shields the company from investor pressure. Cofounders Larry Page and Sergey Brin control more than 50 percent of Alphabet's voting power, even though they own only a little more than one-tenth of the corporation's stock by value. This dual-class structure would seem to encourage pet projects like Calico, because the cofounders who effectively decide whether to pursue the projects bear only a fraction of the cost.

Nevertheless, mega-corporations like Alphabet are no more likely than philanthropic foundations to bring about century-long lives. For one thing, laboratories inside mega-corporations are vulnerable to their own pathologies. Biomedical researchers outside Calico have described Alphabet's longevity lab as "hyper secretive" – a clandestinity consistent with the competitive corporate culture of Silicon Valley but at odds with the values of academic science.[19] For another, Alphabet's $1.75 billion commitment – though beyond the means of all but the wealthiest private foundations – still pales in comparison to the more than $100 billion that the biopharmaceutical industry spends on R&D each year. Alphabet no doubt has the resources to up its commitment, but at some point – notwithstanding the insulation provided by a dual-class share structure – forces inside and outside the corporation (e.g., independent directors and institutional shareholders) would likely push back if Alphabet allocated substantially more money to a research effort so far afield from the company's core competencies.

Thus, even in a "second Gilded Age" of billionaire philanthropy and trillion-dollar mega-corporations, we cannot rely exclusively on the private sector to lead us down the path to century-long lives. By far, the entity with the greatest ability to finance longevity research – perhaps the only hope for investment on the requisite scale – remains the US federal government. The prospects for the 100-year life thus depend, in large part, on the political economy of public sector investment in longevity. Encouragingly, the US has a history of financing large-scale R&D efforts – the Apollo project being the most famous example. But as this chapter's final section highlights, the political landscape for the 100-year life is far less inviting than it was for the original moonshot.

16.3 THE POLITICAL ECONOMY OF THE 100-YEAR LIFE

Each year Congress plows tens of billions of dollars into biomedical research – with $47.5 billion budgeted for the National Institutes of Health (NIH) in fiscal year 2023.

[18] *See* Leonid Bershidsky, *Google's Main Business Could Use Some Moonshots*, BLOOMBERG (May 8, 2021), https://www.bloomberg.com/opinion/articles/2021-05-08/google-s-other-bets-should-focus-on-its-main-business.

[19] Julia Belluz, *Google Is Super Secretive about Its Anti-Aging Research. No One Knows Why*, VOX (Apr. 28, 2017), https://www.vox.com/science-and-health/2017/4/27/15409672/google-calico-secretive-aging-mortality-research.

Yet only a tiny sliver of that sum – $405 million – goes toward the Division of Aging Biology (DAB), the unit within NIH's National Institute on Aging that studies interventions that might slow the aging process.[20] (The bulk of the National Institute on Aging budget goes toward Alzheimer's disease and related dementias.) To put the DAB figure in perspective, NIH now spends more each year on research related to brain cancer than the DAB's entire budget, even though brain cancer affects 0.1 percent of the population while aging ultimately affects everyone.[21]

In recent years, several scientists and public health advocates have argued for a dramatic increase in federal funding for longevity research – a "longevity moonshot."[22] They argue that sustained federal investment – on the order of $3 billion annually – will produce long-lasting health and economic gains that compensate for the cost many times over. As the DAB funding figures illustrate, this argument has yet to win over congressional appropriators. Why not?

A partial answer is that the push for a longevity moonshot defies the logic of collective action. As economist Mancur Olson famously observed, small groups with well-defined memberships enjoy political advantages vis-à-vis larger and more diffuse groups: they are better able to forge common identities and less vulnerable to free-riding.[23] The success of rare-disease patient groups in securing federal funding for orphan drug research is arguably an illustration of the Olsonian logic: Relatively small groups of rare-disease patients have large individual stakes in finding a treatment or cure – and often strong group identities borne out of a shared experience. By contrast, individuals experiencing the aging process are the ultimate large group: Everyone is included.

Beyond the large-group problem, proponents of a moonshot investment in delayed aging face a fiscal challenge. Although the $3 billion-per-year outlay proposed by moonshot advocates would have only a trivial effect on the federal government's fiscal position, the effort would – if successful in lengthening lifespans – lead to a significant increase in the number of people eligible for old-age entitlement programs such as Social Security and Medicare. Some of the corresponding fiscal burden could be offset by additional tax revenues from older workers who remain in the labor force for longer, as well as from a reduction in per-capita Medicare costs among healthier seniors. Yet economist Dana Goldman and coauthors have projected that even with those offsets, an increase in life expectancy of 2.2

[20] US Dep't Health and Human Services, Congressional Justification FY 2024 (2023), at 18–19, https://www.nia.nih.gov/sites/default/files/2023-03/nia_congressional-justification_fy2024.pdf.

[21] *Estimates of Funding for Various Research, Condition, and Disease Categories*, Nat'l Institutes Health (Mar. 31, 2023), https://report.nih.gov/funding/categorical-spending#.

[22] S. Jay Olshansky et al., *The Longevity Dividend*, The Scientist (Mar. 2006), https://www.the-scientist.com/uncategorized/the-longevity-dividend-47757; Bonnie Kavoussi, *The Case for a Longevity Moonshot*, Foundation for Am. Innovation (July 27, 2021), https://www.thefai.org/posts/the-case-for-a-longevity-moonshot.

[23] Mancur Olson, The Logic of Collective Action (1965).

years due to delayed aging would add nearly $420 billion to the federal entitlement deficit by 2060.[24] The life expectancy gains envisioned by CDRV – twenty years over the course of a century – would place an even greater burden on Social Security and Medicare.

Economically the US could very likely bear the additional fiscal weight of an older but healthier population. For example, Goldman and coauthors estimate that raising the Social Security normal retirement age and the Medicare eligibility age to sixty-eight would more than offset the additional entitlement program costs of delayed aging. But as demonstrated by the recent experience in France – where President Emmanuel Macron's increase in the retirement age from sixty-two to sixty-four sparked nationwide strikes – retirement age changes remain "the third rail" of politics across the high-income world. An alternative way to offset rising entitlement program costs would be to raise taxes, but both major political parties in the US have soured on broad-based tax hikes in recent years. Most Republican lawmakers have pledged not to vote for any net tax increase, while Democratic President Joe Biden has promised not to raise taxes on any household earning less than $400,000 annually – a promise that puts three-quarters of the income tax base beyond reach.

To be sure, the entitlement spending effects of longer lifespans will accrete slowly, with most of the expenditures lying decades down the road. By then, most of today's elected officials will have long since retired, died, or been ousted by voters. In that respect, political short-termism – unlike corporate short-termism – may be complementary to longer lifespans: Lawmakers can appropriate more funds to a longevity moonshot while externalizing the difficult fiscal choices to their successors.

But even if the extra entitlement spending triggered by longer lifespans won't come due for decades, government debt markets may transform those future liabilities into near-term costs. As the US proceeds down a fiscally unsustainable path, investors are likely to demand higher interest rates on Treasury bonds. For that reason, today's lawmakers may be reluctant to commit to a longevity moonshot that – without unpopular entitlement reforms or tax hikes – will force the federal government to face higher near-term debt service expenses.

This is where the science fiction and the political fiction of the 100-year life converge. The Olsonian logic of collective action is not an iron law: Advocates for programs with diffuse benefits sometimes prevail in the hurly burly of distributional politics. But to do so, proponents of a longevity moonshot will need to weave a narrative that motivates legislators to allocate funds toward longevity research. In other words, the biomedical advances needed to normalize century-long lifespans will likely depend on political developments that require storytelling and imagination.

This political-fiction framing flips Gratton and Scott's script. Gratton and Scott tell us that the 100-year life is coming, and they argue that policy needs to adapt to

[24] Dana P. Goldman et al., *Substantial Health and Economic Returns from Delayed Aging May Warrant a New Focus for Medical Research*, 32 Health Affs. 1698 (2013).

that reality. But whether the 100-year life becomes a reality depends in large part on whether longevity moonshot advocates can convince lawmakers and voters that century-long lifespans are worth pursuing. That persuasion effort involves many of the same elements as Gratton and Scott's adaptation effort: thinking about how different elements of law and society might respond to century-long lifespans and considering whether those responses would leave us better off or worse. But at the end of the day, whether we proceed down the path to a 100-year life remains a political choice, not a fait accompli.

The science fiction and political fiction aspects of the 100-year life merge in another respect: Mapping out the plausible biomedical pathways to century-long lifespans will help us understand what collateral benefits a longevity moonshot might bring. The original moonshot and other NASA space exploration efforts have generated a long list of spinoff technologies ranging from the programmable cardiac pacemaker to the modern cochlear implant. A longevity moonshot may likewise yield collateral biomedical benefits. For example, research on intermittent fasting may yield glycemic control benefits for Type 2 diabetes patients.[25] Senolytic therapies that delay or reverse aging may help address frailty among childhood cancer survivors.[26] By highlighting these and other potential payoffs, longevity moonshot proponents may be able to forge political alliances with advocates for disease-specific research, who – for Olsonian reasons – tend to be better organized and more easily mobilized.

In short, understanding the 100-year life as an aspiration rather than an inevitability may make the outcome more realistic. Our legal and political institutions can help to provide the support that makes scientific breakthroughs more likely, but first, advocates will need to convince lawmakers that a longevity moonshot justifies the financial and political costs. Thus, to say that the 100-year life is a work of science fiction, legal fiction, and political fiction is not to write off the possibility of century-long lifespans. Rather, it is to say that in order to achieve the 100-year life, we need to imagine it first. In that sense, the enterprise that Gratton and Scott ask us to engage in is worthwhile even though – indeed, precisely because – century-long lifespans cannot be taken for granted.

[25] Sharayah Carter, Peter M. Clifton & Jennifer B. Keogh, *Effect of Intermittent Compared with Continuous Energy Restricted Diet on Glycemic Control in Patients with Type 2 Diabetes: A Randomized Noninferiority Trial*, 1 JAMA Network Open e180756 (2018).

[26] J. L. Kirkland & T. Tchkonia, *Senolytic Drugs: From Discovery to Translation*, 288 J. Internal Med. 518 (2020).

17

Bioethics, Reproduction, and Extending Life

I. Glenn Cohen

This chapter considers where law and bioethics intersect as to the 100-year life. It tackles two different issues. The first is an exploration of the bioethics of life extension and whether such extension is something that should be pursued. The second considers attempts to extend reproduction into the late period of life and the ethics thereof.

17.1 THE BIOETHICS OF LIFE EXTENSION: SHOULD WE DO IT?

In bioethics it is commonplace, albeit not without its critics, to distinguish treatment from enhancement. Treatments – whether curative (e.g., antibiotics for a bacteria), ameliorative (albuterol for asthmatic episodes), palliative (e.g., morphine for someone in pain in their final days before death), or preventative (vaccination for mumps) – are fully and uncontroversially consistent with the ends of medicine. Enhancements, by contrast, are viewed by some with more suspicion as either things to be prohibited or at least not subsidized by the state.

The political philosopher Norman Daniels is one of the most cogent defenders of the line, which he demarcates around the idea of "species-typical" functioning – that is, an enhancement is what boosts our capabilities *beyond* a species-typical level of normal functioning, while a treatment corrects for a disease, which is defined as a function of our biology or psychology that reduces an individual *below* a level of normal functioning.[1]

The pursuit of the 100-year-old life and beyond, especially one that seeks to increase not only the lifespan but also the wellspan and enables longevity and excellent functioning, puts pressure on the treatment enhancement distinction's attractiveness as a guide either for what individuals should be allowed to pursue on their own (i.e., what should not be prohibited by a society), or what we are owed by

[1] NORMAN DANIELS, JUST HEALTH: MEETING HEALTH NEEDS FAIRLY 149 (2008); Einer Elhauge, *I'm Not Quite Dead Yet – and Other Health Care Observations*, 49 TULSA L. REV. 607, 617 (2014).

the state (the way Daniels primarily employs the distinction). Put simply, living beyond 100 today at the wellness and functioning level of, say, a sixty-year-old is highly species-*a*typical – experienced by very few, if any. As such, under the Daniels definition it would clearly be an enhancement not a treatment. For some, that would be a reason to prohibit it (such as prohibiting attempts to improve IQ) or exclude it from the health care a society is obliged to provide (or at least unless and until it has met the needs for treatments of disease fully, it is a sort of "bonus").

That perspective is in tension with many authors of this book and, I would suspect, the majority of the polity, who think pursuing excellent health past 100 is not only permissible but also desirable (possibly even obligatory) for the state to invest in. How to explain this divergence? An "error theory" approach would suggest either that it is a mistake to pursue the 100-year life as all-things-considered justified *or* that it is the enhancement treatment distinction as a guide for wise public policy that is the error.

In my view, the latter holds. The enhancement treatment distinction seems problematic at least as applied to lifespan and wellspan extension. The distinction seems to trade on a "baseline problem" that confuses is and ought. Consider the way the human lifespan and wellspan have varied dramatically across time. If 200 years ago someone proposed medical interventions to extend our lives by decades to their *present* length and wellness, would we have been right to resist those interventions as enhancements?

One might retort that there is a distinction between raising more people to the highest level attainable by our species and going beyond that level.[2] If we pursued lifespans of 200 years, for example, we would cease being human and become something quite different. At best, the objection is making a problematically undefended appeal to the natural (in this case, what is natural for a human person). Even if we can agree that some things are natural and some are not, there is "no factual reason to suppose that what is natural is good (or at least better) and what is unnatural is bad (or at least worse)."[3] As Frances Kamm puts it:

> The assumption behind [this view] is that nature is sacred and should be honored. But why should we believe this? Cancer cells, AIDS, tornadoes, and poisons are all parts of nature. Are they sacred and to be honored? The natural and the good are distinct conceptual categories and the two can diverge: the natural can fail to be good and the good can be unnatural (e.g., art, dams, etc.). Suppose nature was sacred and to be honored. We would clearly be overriding its dictates by making people able to resist (by immunization) illnesses that they could not naturally resist. Is doing this impermissible because it does not honor nature? Surely not.[4]

[2] I. Glenn Cohen, *What (If Anything) Is Wrong with Human Enhancement? What (If Anything) Is Right with It?* 49 Tulsa L. Rev. 645, 650 (2014).

[3] Julian Baggini, Making Sense: Philosophy Behind the Headlines 181–182 (2002).

[4] Frances M. Kamm, *Is There a Problem with Enhancement?* 5 Am. J. Bioethics 5, 8–9 (2005).

Of course, rejecting the treatment enhancement line or appeals to the natural does not guarantee that a *particular* "enhancement" (if you must use that word) is unobjectionable. But increasing the number of years of healthy life escapes many of the stock objections to "enhancements."

Additional healthy years are more absolute than positional goods,[5] and as such we are less worried about individuals pursuing them to produce private benefit at externalized costs.[6] If the project aims at reducing the gap between wellspan and lifespan, there is a plausible argument that it generates significant positive externalities in healthcare spending rates given the fact that healthcare spending currently increases substantially with age.[7] By contrast, increasing lifespan *without* correspondingly increasing the wellspan would produce significant cost externalities in terms of healthcare spending.[8]

Some object to enhancements done on children or others as violating a "right to an open future" – that children should be "permitted to reach maturity with as many open options, opportunities, and advantages as possible."[9] Even if you are persuaded in general by this objection,[10] when lifespan and wellspan expand in tandem it is hard to see the extension as deeply limiting rights to an open future. If anything, the number of "futures" one might pursue seem to expand in that one could imagine fourth or fifth careers, marriages, and so on, with a long-enough healthy life.

A different objection is about the irreversibility of some enhancements – especially when imposed on those who do not yet exist but, because of irreversibility, are stuck with them.[11] There is a sensitive question about when life extension counts as "irreversible." One could seek to end one's life, and there is an argument that in a world of longer life spans there would be an obligation to also provide more end-of-life options. But ending one's life is not a "reversal" of healthy longevity. It is the cessation of a life of a being who has been enhanced to live much longer. A "natural death" (whatever that means) becomes available only if one "sticks it out" – can we

5 Cohen, *supra* note 2, at 651.

6 Elhauge, *supra* note 1, at 613.

7 *E.g.*, Ctrs. for Medicare & Medicaid Servs., *National Health Expenditure Data* (updated Mar. 24, 2020), https://www.cms.gov/Research-Statistics-Data-and-Systems/Statistics-Trends-and-Reports/NationalHealthExpendData/NHE-Fact-Sheet.

8 The caveat of "healthcare spending" is essential because the all-things-considered level of positive or negative externalities is much more complicated to calculate and also more contested on what "counts." For example, would effects on delayed entry to the job market for younger individuals because of people working longer count? Changes toward different numbers of offspring? What about additional years of grandparenthood and potential help in rearing?

9 Joel Feinberg, *The Child's Right to an Open Future*, *in* Whose Child? Children's Rights, Parental Authority, and State Power, 126, 130 (William Aiken & Hugh LaFollette eds., 1980).

10 *See* Cohen, *supra* note 2, 672–673; Dov Fox, *The Illiberality of "Liberal Eugenics,"* 20 Ratio 1, 20–21 (2007).

11 Cohen, *supra* note 2, at 672–673.

consider that a kind of injury that cannot be reversed? Without resort to a problematic baseline or undefended appeals to the natural it may be hard to characterize this as a deep problem with life extension; if *this* is a problem to impose on our children, so is our imposition of disease-free (or disease-reduced) lives for our children right now – they too cannot easily be "reversed."

A different objection is what I have elsewhere called "The Coercion of Voluntary Enhancements (not Oxymoronic!)."[12] Imagine the extension of lifespan and wellspan were completely optional – individuals could choose it or not without state penalty. Let's further assume the extension is completely state-subsidized or otherwise costless (see below regarding the effect of relaxing this assumption). While this seems like a victory, as with all voluntary enhancements, there is a concern that it will result in "a new equilibrium where everyone enhances, or at least many choose to enhance who would not choose to enhance but-for the need to compete with the enhanced in a zero-sum distribution, and those who fail to enhance will suffer in terms of the distribution."[13]

With increased lifespan and wellspan it is easy to see how this will work. Why should law school only last three years, or medical school four? Why shouldn't a thirty-year mortgage be extended by years or decades given longer life? Even if we imagine that each of these changes are, on balance, good, there is a distributional effect: Those who do not extend their lives face more life plans to which they are shut out (or at least delayed entry, with fewer years to experience them) as against a world where the extensions never happen. The end result is that many people who, but for this dynamic, would not choose to extend their (or their child's) life will now do so. Furthermore, the "exit" options of ending one's life will not solve the problem since the dynamic produces a "delayed start" in access to life plans.

I am fully convinced this is a real dynamic we would see if wellspan and lifespan are extended. But is it a moral *problem*? One answer is to say it is a problem, but not a problem *for* the "enhancement." That is, we should strive to have our cake and eat it too – enabling life extension while seeking to correct this dynamic through other means such as labor law, antidiscrimination law (which must now protect the young more than in the past), forced retirements, and so on. Alternately, we could disagree that this is a problem, or at least a serious one. In prior work I have explored this with a hypothetical about a safe and costless drug that would improve the safety of airplane pilots and wondered whether we should be sympathetic to a pilot who argues "I have a right not to enhance and improve the safety of passengers, and the fact that it makes me a worse pilot and makes it more likely that my plane will crash, should not count against me in competing for this job."[14]

[12] *Id.* at 658.
[13] *Id.* at 659.
[14] *Id.*

The pilot case – like all cases – has a mix of absolute and positional benefits skewing toward the absolute. Is the same true of life extension? Moreover, part of the "intuition pump" of this example is set up by assuming that the drug is safe and improves pilot performance significantly. This suggests that one may not make a judgment about life extension and the "voluntary coercion" effect *as a whole* but, instead, one might need to go institution by institution to determine whether requiring more experience as a condition of entry in a particular case is "credential inflation" without offsetting benefit or not.

One final relevant objection to enhancements is that when an enhancement becomes available it causes us to lose solidarity with those who choose not to avail themselves of it, including by shifting responsibility to them for bad health states. As framed by Michael Sandel, the more we come to view our lives as chance not choice, the more reason we have to share our fate with others, including through public financial support. However, all that might wither with enhancement.[15] Those who live for a very long time might come to view those with normal (as of 2023) lifespans and wellspans as poor unfortunate souls, the human equivalent of mayflies (who live for only a day), or perhaps as something quite different from ourselves, to whom we stand in the same distant relationship as to an unknown "beggar in Spain," to borrow Nancy Kress's novel's title.[16] It is possible to contest the descriptive claim – to note that extending wellspan, in particular, might open more resources to all; to carve out the cases of failure to enhance children as one where the dynamic is least likely to hold; or to contest that our obligations to help others meet their health needs ought not to be premised on responsibility-based arguments.[17] One might also choose to "bite the bullet" and argue that, at least regarding wellspan extension, we *ought* to heap scorn or otherwise pressure others to engage in enhancement.[18] Still the possibility that life and wellspan extensions might create a genetic overclass and underclass is worrying and a reason why it is essential for the state, if possible, to try to equalize access to this extra time lest it become one more way of achieving hierarchy – especially dynastic.[19]

Resources, though, are not infinite. Is it appropriate for the state to spend resources (such as grant funding) on extending the lifespan of those who already live fairly healthily into their seventies and eighties given how many people fail to live even that long or whose shorter lifespan is plagued by illness? One's commitment to particular theories of distribution will shape the reply; utilitarianism, prioritarianism, and sufficientarianism offer well-established answers regarding what

[15] Michael J. Sandel, The Case against Perfection: Ethics in the Age of Genetic Engineering 87–92 (2007).

[16] Nancy Kress, Beggars in Spain (1993).

[17] Cohen, *supra* note 2, at 662–665; Kamm, *supra* note 4, at 13.

[18] *See* Cohen, *supra* note 2, at 664 (arguing).

[19] *Cf.* In Time (2011). Of course, given what we know about social determinants of health, it is entirely possible to view our current society as already structured along similar lines.

counts as a just distribution. Each of these theories can be applied to allocating "life years" or "health life years" and will provide different answers to when it is appropriate for the state to make the "rich" (in terms of years or health life) richer as opposed to focusing (or at least first focusing) efforts on the "poor." There is also well-developed, if perhaps not resolved, literature in the space of rationing scarce medical goods (such as organs, vaccines, ICU beds) debating when it is appropriate to engage in "age weighting" – giving priority to younger over older claimants all else being equal, with one of the central arguments being the need to give everyone "fair innings" – a requisite number of life years to enable a particular kind of life.[20] Many of the same concepts are applicable if we were allocating life extension directly rather than having it as an output of one of these other scarce goods. To the extent the relevant resources (e.g., research funding) were fungible, on many plausible theories the state would only be justified in pursuing or promoting life extension once it had already satisfied its duties toward those who currently receive lives that are unfairly short.

17.2 FERTILE OCTOGENARIANS ABOUND! REPRODUCING LATE IN EXTENDED LIVES

As some may remember dimly from their property law class (or – in my case – studying for the bar) there is a funny pitfall in the application of the classic Rule Against Perpetuities to trusts that goes by the name of the "fertile octogenarian" rule, stemming from "a conclusive presumption of lifetime fertility."[21] While at one point reproducing in one's eighties – for women at least – was a fanciful law school hypothetical, in fact it is very possible today. What would it mean to reproduce late in the 100-year life?

The oldest reported successful *pregnancy* I know was of a seventy-three- or seventy-four-year-old woman (depending on the report) in India, who gave birth to twins by caesarean section.[22] But, of course, in "collaborative" or "third-party" reproduction the person seeking to produce a child to rear need not carry the child to term and may instead use a gestational surrogate. Many couples fertilize additional embryos as part of in vitro fertilization (IVF) and cryopreserve (i.e., "freeze") them for a potential future use. In 2017, it was estimated that about 1 million

[20] E.g., Alan Williams, *Intergenerational Equity, an Exploration of the "Fair Innings" Argument*, 6 HEALTH ECON. 117 (1997); Samuel Kerstein & Greg Bognar, *Complete Lives in the Balance*, 10 AM. J. BIOETHICS 37 (2010).

[21] Jonathan R. Macey, *Private Trusts for the Provision of Private Goods*, 37 EMORY L.J. 295, 307 (1988).

[22] Joshua Bote, *A 74-Year-Old Woman Reportedly Gave Birth to Twins, May Be the Oldest Ever to Give Birth*, USA TODAY (Sep. 6, 2019), https://www.usatoday.com/story/life/parenting/2019/09/06/oldest-woman-to-ever-give-birth-has-twins-at-74-years-old/2231598001/.

embryos were housed in subzero facilities in the US alone.[23] One could imagine a case where a couple fertilizes seven embryos at age thirty and implants them one at the time, leading to a successful pregnancy and the birth of a boy. Fifty years later they decide they want another child and then find a surrogate willing to assist. After paying her and thawing and transferring one of their cryopreserved embryos, there is a successful pregnancy and the birth of a girl. This girl would be fifty years younger than her full genetic brother in terms of her chronological age, but, if viewed from the moment of fertilization, she would be the exact same age as that brother – a strange incongruence.

This thought experiment is not that fanciful: in 2020 a child was born from a donated embryo frozen on October 14, 1992 and thawed for implantation in February 2020.[24] The embryo was successfully transferred to and carried by Tina Gibson, who would serve as its legal and rearing mother – she herself was two years old when the embryo was first created.[25] At twenty-seven years this is the current record for freezing and thawing, but there is no reason to think it could not go longer.

There are many other ways that reproduction so late in life could occur – frozen eggs, posthumously retrieved sperm, or perhaps most simply for older men with younger female partners. For example, James Doohan, who played "Scotty" on the original *Star Trek*, apparently had a daughter when he was aged eighty with his forty-four-year-old wife without intending to conceive.[26]

New technologies might provide still further extension of our reproductive periods. Mitochondrial replacement technique (MRT, sometimes called "three-parent IVF" by the lay press) is one "that involves removing an intended mother's [nuclear] DNA from her oocyte [egg] or zygote, which contains mutated [mitochondrial] DNA, and transferring it into a female provider's oocyte or zygote, which contains nonpathogenic [mitochondrial] DNA and from which the [nuclear] DNA has been removed."[27] While MRT's primary use, and the use to which it has been authorized in the UK and a few other countries, has been to avoid transmitting mutant mitochondrial DNA to offspring while maintaining a mother's genetic tie to

[23] *E.g.*, Judith Daar, I. Glenn Cohen, Seema Mohapatra & Sonia M. Suter, Reproductive Technologies and the Law 636 (3rd ed. 2022).

[24] Maria Cramer, *Girl Is Born in Tennessee from Embryo Frozen for 27 Years*, N.Y. Times (Dec. 3, 2020).

[25] *Id.*

[26] *Actor Doohan to Be Dad at 80*, AP (Feb. 4, 2000), https://apnews.com/article/e427be362e2d89caca6e08dcab335d50.

[27] Committee on the Ethical and Social Policy Considerations of Novel Techniques for Prevention of Maternal Transmission of Mitochondrial DNA Diseases, National Academies of Science, Engineering, and Medicine, Mitochondrial Replacement Techniques: Ethical, Social, and Policy Considerations 1 (Anne Claiborne et al. eds., 2016).

the child,[28] there have also been discussions of using it as a way to "rejuvenate" the eggs of older mothers.[29] In vitro gametogenesis (IVG) in lay terms refers to deriving sperm or egg from a human's adult cells – for example, skin cells.[30] While the technique has thus far only been used to produce offspring in nonhuman animals, there is significant interest in many human applications of IVG, including as a way of enabling older women to produce eggs for reproduction.[31]

Becoming a biological parent so late in life raises a host of interesting issues that stretch across many private and public law areas, including trust and estates, family law, insurance law, and public benefits law. I will not do any of it justice in this short space, but instead want to connect "reproducing so late in life" to two more general debates about the ethics of reproduction that I have written on: the rights claim to reproduce (especially as to state support for reproduction), which I will discuss in some depth, and claims of harm to offspring, which I will touch on only briefly.

In a recent paper on uterus transplants (currently used for women with uterine factor infertility, but in the future potentially for those assigned male at birth), I drew a distinction between the "first wave" of reproductive technologies "encompassing everything from Artificial Insemination to In Vitro Fertilization (IVF), Surrogacy, and Preimplantation Genetic Diagnosis (PGD)" and a new wave that encompasses uterus transplants, MRT, IVG, and potentially egg-freezing.[32] The first wave "focused on restoring or enabling the kind of reproductive options available to fertile, heterosexual, couples, a focus on what I call 'mimicking'" and thus "largely expanded access to that which could be achieved by traditional reproduction."[33] The new wave, by contrast, is "more focused on 'extending' reproduction beyond what is possible through sexual reproduction."[34] The mimic extender distinction is interrelated to distinctions others have drawn in the literature:

> [Lisa Ikemoto distinguishes] between fertile, medically infertile, and "dysfertile" individuals. Ikemoto defines the dysfertile as "those rendered childless by their

[28] *See* I. Glenn Cohen, Eli Y. Adashi & Sara Gerke, *The Regulation of Mitochondrial Replacement Techniques around the World*, 21 Ann. Rev. Genomics & Hum. Gen. 565 (2020).

[29] Cristina Rodríguez-Varela, Sonia Herraiz & Elena Labarta, *Mitochondrial Enrichment in Infertile Patients: A Review of Different Mitochondrial Replacement Therapies*, 15 Ther. Adv. Reprod. Health. (2021).

[30] E.g., Mitinori Saitou & Katsuhiko Hayashi, *Mammalian In Vitro Gametogenesis*, 374 Science 47 (2021). For a discussion of its legal and ethical issues, *see*, e.g., Daar et al., *supra* note 23, at 1049–1100; Henry T. Greely, The End of Sex and the Future of Human Reproduction (2016).

[31] *See*, e.g., Sonia M. Suter, *In Vitro Gametogenesis: Just Another Way to Have a Baby?* 3 J. L. & Biosci. 87, 99–100 (2016); Emily Witt, *The Future of Fertility*, New Yorker (Apr. 17, 2023) (discussing company seeking approval for clinical human use).

[32] I. Glenn Cohen, *Borrowed Wombs: On Uterus Transplants and the "Right to Experience Pregnancy,"* 2022 U. Chi. L. F. 127, 134–135 (2023).

[33] *Id.* at 136.

[34] *Id.*

> failure to fit the definition of infertile, because they are unmarried and/or lesbian or gay." I would expand the category slightly to include all individuals who have no medical limitation to their fertility but instead face an obstacle towards their reproduction.[35]

The rights claim of a hypothetical ninety-year-old woman who wants to use one or more of the technologies discussed above to reproduce so late in life seems to be an extension, and not mimic use. The extension-mimic line seems normatively attractive in part because it mirrors the distinction between treatment versus enhancement discussed earlier.

> Those defending such a line claim the state has an obligation to permit (and perhaps fund) medical interventions that seek to restore individuals into the range of species-typical normal functioning (treatment), whereas there is no obligation to permit (and certainly no obligation to fund) that which allows individuals to exceed that range (enhancement). This is connected . . . to a conception of health and why the state has a role in promoting it, namely, as a way of furthering the larger goal of ensuring that all have access to the "normal opportunity range" that is "the array of life plans reasonable persons are likely to develop for themselves." Extenders are seeking things that are clearly species *a*typical, and the case of men using uterus transplants is a good illustration of that.[36]

The same might apply to our hypothetical ninety-year-old woman: She is asking for something species-*a*typical. While that fact may not justify a negative liberty restriction – I return to harm-based arguments that would be more common reasons for such restrictions later – does it defeat her rights claim to positive liberty state support for such reproduction?[37]

One response to this suggestion is to reject a keying of the treatment enhancement line to the conception of species-typical normal functioning, but then one needs another way to distinguish claims to assistance for health needs (with the moral urgency we normally assign to it) from nonhealth needs. A more radical approach would be to reject views that assign a special importance to health in favor of more consequentialist theories that

> may discard "health" as an intermediate concept to some extent; that is, it does not matter whether [the intervention] advances "health" or a nonhealth interest of the individual. What matters is how much it advances that welfare interest and at what cost . . . On such views, if we ask, "Yes, but is it a health care intervention?" we ask that question not because it matters as a first-order matter, but because we have

35 *Id.* at 137 (discussing Lisa C. Ikemoto, *The In/Fertile, the Too Fertile, and the Dysfertile*, 47 Hastings L.J. 1007, 1033 (1996)).

36 Cohen, *supra* note 32, at 138–139.

37 To be sure, in the US, at least as compared to a country like Israel, we have relatively little state-mandated support for even simple IVF.

ministerially divided the world of what the government pays for into buckets, and we are asking whether this should come out of the health care bucket.[38]

A third response is from *within* the species-typical normal functioning approach and suggests we may be too quick to assume that a woman's reproduction at ninety is *not* species-typical. It is, after all, species-typical for men to be able to reproduce quite late in life like *Star Trek*'s Scotty did. Why is the right "comparator" group for species typicality the "female of the species" and not "the species, sex unspecified"?[39]

Another possible rejoinder is that while reproduction so late in life is species-atypical for a kind of organism that lives till eighty, it would *not* be atypical for a species that lived so much longer than that. For someone likely to live to age 200 reproducing at age ninety is roughly at the same point in one's lifespan as it would be for someone likely to live to eighty to reproduce at age thirty-six – and we would view that as quite normal. Why not view the species-typical question in terms of proportions of a life-span – that is, it remains "species typical" to reproduce in the first third to half of one's life span, with a third or a half being much longer with life extension?

For me there is a bit of a bootstrap "hat on a hat" quality to this argument: It suggests that once we have permitted the enhancement that enables individuals to live a much longer life (see Part I), our expectation of what is species-typical would reset – thus treating reproduction so much later in life *as* typical. On the other hand, when our range of lifespan or wellspan extends so much longer, why should our idea of a normatively tinged "normal opportunity range" not extend commensurately?

This move might generate the following countermove: There is an old maxim in the law of equity that "equity aids the vigilant, not those who slumber on their rights."[40] Those making a rights claim to use reproductive technologies at age ninety have, like Rip Van Winkle, slept an awful long time on their reproductive capacities. Does that suggest their claim to state assistance is forfeit or at least much diminished? Is it discriminatory against older individuals to deny them state support for opportunities not because they are older or is the fault theirs in failing to take advantage of an opportunity available to them when they were younger? Some might find that such a framing of formal equality misses the point. After all, one might use the same logic as to state support for women given our current lifespans: that the state can justifiably deny women past age thirty-eight state support for IVF in that they too slept on their rights – a right to reproduce earlier without the need of such technology. This feels like a *reductio ad absurdum*, especially when one considers how a society that refuses to support reproduction after age thirty-eight fosters a widening gap of sex inequality since it is women whose health and professional lives are most burdened by pregnancy.

[38] Cohen, *supra* note 2, at 148–149.

[39] *Cf.* Suter, *supra* note 31, at 99 ("If men can reproduce late into life, why should women be limited simply because biology precludes them from doing so at a younger age than men, particularly when men have a shorter life expectancy than women?").

[40] John N. Pomeroy, A Treatise on Equity Jurisprudence §§418–419 (5th ed. 1941).

On the flipside, though, state support of reproduction quite late in life might lead to a different kind of inequality through the dynamic of "voluntary coercion" of enhancements discussed earlier. Those who decide to extend their lives and have the resources to do so might feel the need to delay their reproduction to give themselves or their child the best start in life from a resource perspective. Some will simply not be able to afford the technologies needed to delay reproduction. Others who can afford it but would rather not reproduce so late may feel pressure to do so for their children to compete in a zero-sum society.

From the admitted (science fiction) armchair, it is a little hard to predict if this dynamic would take hold. So long as our ability to extend life or wellspan has a stopping point, one might argue that the pressure to delay reproduction is countered by the reality that every year of delay is one fewer year to spend with the child one produces. The equilibrium that results from trade-offs between enjoying one's life without children, furthering one's own non–child-rearing goals, building resources to give one's children an excellent life, the number of years of life people would prefer to share with their children (and countless other factors) is hard to predict. So much seems likely to be mediated by culture that it seems like a shot in the dark to guess people's first-order preferences.

While we started with the mimic-extension line, we have found both normative uncertainties about the moral force of species typicality and its underlying architecture of the normal opportunity range to this question, as well as difficulty predicting how extending lifespan would affect individuals' reproductive choices if reproducing much later in life was also possible. One seemingly potential way out might be – in the positive liberty and even the negative liberty sense – to set policy based on the idea that reproduction so late in light is harmful to children.

The problem is twofold. One part is descriptive – how sure are we that reproduction late in life is bad for offspring? Over the past couple of decades, several jurisdictions – including France, Greece, Italy, Japan, and some Australian states – have at various points had in place prohibitions on IVF for women above a certain age premised on concern for the welfare of offspring.[41] It is important to distinguish risk to offspring from risk to pregnant persons (including the risk of losing the pregnancy). A recent review article summarized the existing state of the literature:

> Advanced maternal age is associated with a wide range of risks for adverse perinatal outcomes, although the magnitude of risk for most outcomes is small. The risks are strongest for early miscarriage, late miscarriage and chromosomal abnormalities. There are weaker associations with stillbirth, FGR, PTB, pre-eclampsia, GDM and CS, not all of which rise to the level of clinical significance.[42]

[41] *See* I. Glenn Cohen, *Regulating Reproduction: The Problem with Best Interests*, 96 Minn. L. Rev. 423, 451–452 (2011).

[42] Alexander P. Frick, *Advanced Maternal Age and Adverse Pregnancy Outcomes*, 70 Best. Pract. Res. Clin. Obstet. Gynaecol. 92 (2021).

Whether these problems would become worse, improve, or stay the same in individuals whose life was radically extended will certainly depend on how life extension is achieved. But it seems plausible that some but not all of those risks might be mitigated by permitting *reproduction* but not *pregnancy* very late in life. Such a strategy would require increased use of gestational surrogacy, which for some may be a normative reason to oppose it. But the normative justification of prohibition on this basis would be explicitly paternalistic (harm to self) rather than offspring-focused (harm to others), the latter being a more common basis for reproductive regulation.[43]

What about risk to offspring in a possible future where individuals (especially women) can produce gametes much later in life than they currently can? In our current technological attainment, advanced maternal and paternal age has been associated (among other things) with autism spectrum disorders in children – with the most frequently cited hypothesized mechanisms on the paternal side being "increased rates of de novo mutations and epigenetic alternations associated with increasing age," and on the maternal side being "higher rates of chromosomal abnormalities, perinatal and obstetric complications, and potential genomic and/or epigenetic alterations induced by cumulative exposure to environmental toxins."[44] If these trends persist with radical life extension and reproduction even late in life, are these the kinds of deficits that should matter to that state? Or does such an intervention impermissibly favor the neurotypical over the neurodiverse in a way that should be intolerable from a disability rights perspective? A different set of arguments surrounds the harm to a child from being born to parents who will be deceased early on in that child's life – in fact, this is an area where life extension might be a solution rather than part of the problem.

But even if one resolves these kinds of questions in favor of the view that the risks to offspring are so great that they would justify prohibition on reproduction late in life, there is a second more conceptual problem associated with Derek Parfit's non-identity problem:[45] We cannot justify prohibiting an act of reproduction on the basis of harm to the offspring that would result (what I have called "best interests of the resulting child" justifications) if we provide the child a life worth living, because that child's existence is not worse than a counterfactual of not existing at all. As I wrote more than a decade ago:

> The easiest version of the problem to see involves regulation of whether individuals reproduce, for example, the denials of access to reproductive technology to gay,

[43] *See* Cohen, *supra* note 2, at 431.

[44] Yu Gao, Yongfu Yu & Jingyuan Xiao, *Association of Grandparental and Parental Age at Childbirth with Autism Spectrum Disorder in Children*, 3 JAMA Network Open e202868 (2020). There is some evidence of transgenerational risk transmission based on studies of autism prevalence in grandchildren based on advanced grandparental age at the time of conceiving the grandchild's parent. *Id.*

[45] Derek Parfit, Reasons and Persons 358–359 (rev. ed. 1987). *See also*, e.g., John A. Robertson, *Procreative Liberty and Harm to Offspring in Assisted Reproduction*, 30 Am. J.L. & Med. 7 (2004).

> aged, or single parents. Imagine that sixty-year-old Ethel wants to have a baby through reproductive technology and assume arguendo that this child, Maxwell, will be worse off (physiologically, psychologically, etc.) than would the average child born to a woman in her twenties. We cannot say that a state law preventing Ethel's access to reproductive technology at her age furthers the welfare of Maxwell, because if the State blocks that access Maxwell will never exist and, so long as he has a life worth living, coming into existence does not harm him.[46]

My claim remains controversial among both philosophers and legal scholars.[47] Even if accepted, this does not rule other arguments for prohibiting reproduction by aged parents for which the welfare states of offspring may be relevant: arguments premised on non–person-affecting principles, wronging without harming, reproductive externalities, virtue ethics – or arguments premised on legal moralism, or justified paternalism, and perhaps other arguments might still be available.[48] But to justify age-based regulation of reproduction on one of these grounds is more fraught, normatively speaking, than relying on the much simpler harm principle-type argument I believe is illusory in this space. These alternative arguments often have premises or entailments that some will find problematic and require us to step outside of the more comfortable liberal commitment to child welfare as a north star.[49]

[46] Cohen, *supra* note 2, at 437–438.

[47] *See, e.g.*, I. Glenn Cohen, *Sperm and Egg Donor Anonymity: Legal and Ethical Issues, in* The Oxford Handbook of Reproductive Ethics, 499, 515–524 (Leslie Francis ed., 2015–2016); Helen M. Alvaré, *A Response to Professor I. Glenn Cohen's Regulating Reproduction: The Problem with Best Interests*, 96 Minn. L. Rev. Headnotes 8 (2012); Kimberly M. Mutcherson, *In Defense of Future Children: A Response to Cohen's Beyond Best Interests*, 96 Minn. L. Rev. Headnotes 46 (2012).

[48] *See generally* Cohen, *supra* note 2; I. Glenn Cohen, *Beyond Best Interests*, 96 Minn. L. Rev. 1187 (2012).

[49] *See generally* Cohen, *supra* note 48.

PART IV

The 100-Year Life and Our Broader Environment

18

Weathering the 100-Year Life

Eugene Rusyn and Douglas A. Kysar

Climate change is reshaping how and where we grow old, as well as the likelihood of growing old. The 100-year life will play out against this backdrop, with almost no aspect of aging left untouched. Retirement savings will be strained by the costs of disaster recovery. Aging in place might become impossible in many parts of the country as homes and communities are lost to floods or wildfires. Access to health care may be disrupted due to evacuations and lengthy dislocations. All while existing inequities will be amplified and the hardships that define old age for many – from poverty to illness – deepened.

Law and policy can help protect older Americans from climate harms. This chapter suggests how. It begins by describing the climate vulnerabilities older Americans face. It then considers relevant adaptation policies, focusing on programs that help people relocate from at-risk areas, as well as suggesting additional reforms to support those who are dislocated. The chapter closes by discussing how older people could help disrupt climate policy inertia through litigation – seeking to compel government action through claims that center the elderly's distinct dependency on a stable climate.

18.1 CLIMATE AND AN AGING NATION

The US faces widespread climate impacts. Rolling heatwaves blanket vast swathes of the country; increasingly severe wildfires race across the West; more powerful hurricanes lace the eastern seaboard. The toll is severe. In 2023 alone, twenty-eight disasters claimed 492 lives and resulted in losses exceeding $1 billion each.[1] Where "billion-dollar disasters" happened once every four months in the 1980s, they now occur once every three weeks on average.[2] Many losses are unquantified or unquantifiable – whether the disruption of indigenous cultural practices by rising

[1] Adam B. Smith, *2023: A Historic Year of U.S. Billion-Dollar Weather and Climate Disasters*, Beyond the Data (Jan. 8, 2024), https://www.climate.gov/news-features/blogs/beyond-data/2023-historic-year-us-billion-dollar-weather-and-climate-disasters.

[2] US Glob. Change Research Program, *Fifth National Climate Assessment: Overview* (2023), https://nca2023.globalchange.gov/#overview.

seas, or the mounting burdens of respiratory illness worsened by wildfire smoke or mold from flooded homes.

Climate change intersects with an aging America. More than half of older Americans live in just nine states, areas that face a high risk of hurricanes, flooding, wildfires, or extreme heat: California, Florida, Texas, New York, Pennsylvania, Illinois, Ohio, Michigan, and North Carolina.[3] If older Americans' current preferences regarding where to live as they age extend into the future, more will move to the southeast and southwest, along the Atlantic and Gulf coasts, and into Northeastern and Midwestern cities – all subject to extreme weather risks.

18.1.1 *Vulnerabilities*

Older people are among the most vulnerable to the effects of climate change. Vulnerability varies based on many often-intersecting factors, including age, race, gender, socioeconomic status, education, level of disability or special needs, social isolation and the presence of community and family support, mobility, and proximity to health services.

Older Americans might not remain vulnerable in the same ways over time – changes tied to birth cohort are expected. For instance, the percentage of older Americans possessing at least a high school degree is increasing. Less education is adversely linked to climate vulnerability. Meanwhile, there is a growing prevalence of elder orphans, defined by one study as "older adults living in the community who lack caregivers or surrogates."[4] This can deepen social isolation, a risk factor in assessing climate vulnerability.

Place – where older Americans live – also matters. Housing intersects with socioeconomic status and race. A higher concentration of low-income older adults live in areas at risk of severe climate-related events.[5] Those with limited means have fewer options about where to live and are less able to move should their homes become damaged or uninhabitable by catastrophic events. Communities near hazardous industrial facilities – disproportionately home to BIPOC and low-wealth inhabitants – face a heightened risk of chemical, industrial, and other disasters *after* a severe weather event. Approximately 70 percent of Superfund sites are within 1 mile of federally assisted housing, whose residents are disproportionately people of color.[6]

[3] Emma Rubin, *Elderly Population in U.S. by State*, Consumer Affairs (Jan. 19, 2023), https://www.consumeraffairs.com/homeowners/elderly-population-by-state.html.

[4] Regina Roofeh, Dylan M. Smith, and Sean A. P. Clouston, *Estimated Prevalence of Elder Orphans Using National Health and Aging Trends Study*, J. Aging Health 1443 (2020).

[5] Janet L. Gamble et al., *Climate Change and Older Americans: State of the Science*, Env. Health Perspect. 15–22 (2013).

[6] Emily Coffey et al., Poisonous Homes: The Fight for Environmental Justice in Federally Assisted Housing (2020).

Illness shapes climate vulnerabilities and can be exacerbated by severe weather events. Disasters have been linked to worse outcomes for older adult cancer patients, with researchers citing disruptions to timely treatment and continuity of care.[7] Mental health burdens from extreme weather events manifest long after the immediate impact of a storm and may be more pronounced among older people.[8] One study found that adults over sixty-five had higher stress levels relative to younger adults three years after Hurricane Katrina.[9] A meta-analysis of studies addressing the psychological effects of natural disasters found that older adults were 2.11 times more likely to develop posttraumatic stress disorder and 1.73 times more likely to develop adjustment disorders relative to younger adults.[10]

A growing number of older Americans suffer from cognitive impairments that can impede their ability to prepare for a disaster and accept assistance. Nearly 5.8 million Americans currently live with Alzheimer's disease – a common type of dementia. This number is expected to rise to 14 million by 2050, with evacuations posing a unique risk. A study found that nursing home residents with severe dementia who were evacuated during Hurricane Gustav in 2008 experienced increased mortality risk thirty to ninety days after evacuation.[11]

Vulnerabilities overlap and compound. A 2014 study found that older Americans with less education, lower incomes, or physical disabilities had worse overall preparedness for disasters.[12]

18.1.2 *Impacts*

Climate harms adversely impact older people – threatening to transform the later stages of the 100-year life into a period of risk and uncertainty for some while robbing others of old age entirely.

The year 2023 was the warmest year on record by a wide margin. From June through December of that year, global temperatures shattered records from the past century and a half. When compared with geological evidence reflecting a deeper

[7] Kathleen A. Lynch & Alexis A. Merdjanoff, *Impact of Disasters on Older Adult Cancer Outcomes: A Scoping Review*, JCO Glob Oncol. (2023).

[8] James M. Shultz et al., *Public Health and Mental Health Implications of Environmentally Induced Forced Migration*, Disaster Med. & Pub. Health Prep. 116 (2019).

[9] Francis O. Adeola & J. Steven Picou, *Social Capital and the Mental Health Impacts of Hurricane Katrina: Assessing Long-Term Patterns of Psychosocial Distress*, Int'l J. Mass Emerg. & Disasters 121 (2014).

[10] Georgina Parker et al., *Mental Health Implications for Older Adults after Natural Disasters: A Systematic Review and Meta-analysis*, Int'l Psychogeriatrics 11 (2015).

[11] Lisa M. Brown et al., *The Effects of Evacuation on Nursing Home Residents with Dementia*, Am. J. Alzheimer's Dis. Other Demen. 406 (2012).

[12] Tala M. Al-Rousan, Linda M. Rubenstein & Robert B. Wallace, *Preparedness for Natural Disasters among Older U.S. Adults: A Nationwide Survey*, Am. J. Pub. Health 506 (2014).

history, 2023 appears to be among the warmest in at least 100,000 years,[13] an unsurprising finding given that atmospheric carbon dioxide concentrations have risen to a level unequalled in at least 4 million years.[14] Heatwaves put older people at an increased risk of hospitalization and death. One study found that summer heatwaves in Europe in 2022 led to the death of over 61,000 – with women over eighty facing a particularly high mortality burden.[15] In Japan, the first nation where more than 20 percent of the population is sixty-five or older, an average of 1,295 heatstroke-linked deaths were reported between 2018 and 2022 – compared to 201 between 1995 and 1999. Over 80 percent of those who died from heat-related causes were sixty-five or older.[16]

Similar trends are playing out in the US. Some older Americans are not habituated to using air conditioning. The Pacific Northwest, which traditionally experienced cooler summers, offers a bracing example. This region experienced a punishing "heat dome" in 2021 – an event that scientists found to be "virtually impossible" in the absence of human contributions to global warming[17] – that claimed an excess 600 deaths during one June week in Oregon and Washington alone, according to an analysis of preliminary mortality data.[18] Cooling shelters may be of little help to those who are socially isolated or with limited mobility. And retirees living on fixed incomes in a time of surging energy prices may not be able to afford the expense of buying, running, or repairing air-conditioning units. As elsewhere, the impact of heat falls disproportionately on communities of color, women, and those with limited means. One study found that formerly redlined neighborhoods in cities across the country experienced temperatures nearly 13 °F hotter than wealthier districts mere blocks away.[19]

13 Raymond Zhong & Ketih Collins, *See How 2023 Shattered Records to Become the Hottest Year*, N.Y. Times (Jan. 9, 2024), https://www.nytimes.com/2024/01/09/climate/2023-warmest-year-record.html.

14 *Carbon Dioxide Now More Than 50% Higher Than Pre-industrial Levels*, National Oceanic and Atmospheric Administration (June 3, 2022), https://www.noaa.gov/news-release/carbon-dioxide-now-more-than-50-higher-than-pre-industrial-levels.

15 Joan Ballester et al., *Heat-Related Mortality in Europe during the Summer of 2022*, Nat. Med. 1857, 1864 (2023).

16 Tomoko Otake, *In Japan, Extreme Heat and an Aging Population Are a Deadly Mix*, Japan Times (July 30, 2023), https://www.japantimes.co.jp/environment/2023/07/30/climate-change/climate-change-heat-waves-aging-society/#:~:text = Recent%20data%20also%20shows%20over,t%20use%20an%20air%20conditioner.

17 *Western North American Extreme Heat Virtually Impossible without Human-Caused Climate Change*, World Weather Attribution (July 7, 2021), https://www.worldweatherattribution.org/western-north-american-extreme-heat-virtually-impossible-without-human-caused-climate-change/.

18 Nadja Popovich & Winston Choi-Schagrin, *Hidden Toll of the Northwest Heat Wave: Hundreds of Extra Deaths*, N.Y. Times (Aug. 11, 2021), https://www.nytimes.com/interactive/2021/08/11/climate/deaths-pacific-northwest-heat-wave.html.

19 Jeremy S. Hoffman, Vivek Shandas & Nicholas Pendleton, *The Effects of Historical Housing Policies on Resident Exposure to Intra-urban Heat: A Study of 108 U.S. Urban Areas*, Climate 12 (2020).

Extreme weather events, including storms and hurricanes, significantly burden older people. Almost half of those killed during Hurricane Katrina's initial impact were older than seventy-five, while elderly Medicare beneficiaries constituted one-fifth of the displaced population.[20] Similar outcomes mark more recent disasters, including Superstorm Sandy in 2012 (older adults constituted more than half of those who died from the storm, which saw a surge in visits to emergency departments by older people – particularly those at or over eighty-five)[21] and Hurricane Maria in 2017 (people sixty-five and older were found to have the greatest mortality risk).[22]

18.1.3 *Aging Upended*

Taken together, climate change is transforming aging in America – from the viability of retirement to where we grow older.

Paying for old age, already a challenge, will become more difficult. Anne Alstott has noted that many lower earners reach traditional retirement age without sufficient funds to retire, forced to continue working as a result.[23] In this volume, Sara Greene suggests we may face an elderly poverty epidemic without significant reforms to our retirement system. Meanwhile, older Americans face the prospect of exhausting what savings they have as the costs of nursing homes, assisted living facilities, and in-home care rise. Absorbing the financial shocks of losing one's home to disaster and being forced to rebuild or relocate on a fixed income will compound this crisis, especially as insurers abandon high-risk areas like Florida and California.

Those able to afford nursing homes face acute challenges as well. Adults living in nursing homes during a hurricane were found to have a 2.6 percent higher risk of ninety-day mortality.[24] Strained energy infrastructure puts this population at further risk. A 2017 power failure in South Florida following Hurricane Irma left more than 3 million Floridians in the dark, including 160 nursing homes. Eight residents died in one home, ranging in age from seventy-one to ninety-nine.[25]

Receiving medical care is threatened as healthcare networks struggle with climate impacts. Almost 250 California hospitals lost power in 2019 in an intentional power

[20] *Mortality Impacts of Hurricane* Katrina, BULLETIN ON AGING & HEALTH (2018), https://www.nber.org/bah/2018no4/mortality-impacts-hurricane-katrina.

[21] Sidrah Malik et al., *Vulnerability of Older Adults in Disasters: Emergency Department Utilization by Geriatric Patients after Hurricane Sandy*, DISASTER MED. & PUB. HEALTH PREP. 184 (2018).

[22] Raul Cruz-Cano & Erin L. Mead, *Causes of Excess Deaths in Puerto Rico after Hurricane Maria: A Time-Series Estimation*, AM. J. PUB. HEALTH 1050 (2019).

[23] Anne Alstott, *Law and the Hundred-Year Life*, 26 ELDER L. J. 131, 138 (2018).

[24] Lisa M. Brown et al., *The Effects of Evacuation on Nursing Home Residents with Dementia*, AM. J. ALZHEIMER'S DIS. OTHER DEMEN. 406 (2012).

[25] Neil Reisner, Sheri Fink & Vivian Yee, *Eight Dead from Sweltering Nursing Home as Florida Struggles after IRMA*, N.Y. TIMES (Sep. 13, 2017), https://www.nytimes.com/2017/09/13/us/nursing-home-deaths-florida.html.

outage, part of a wildfire prevention effort,[26] while one study found that nearly three-quarters of hospital evacuations between 2000 and 2017 resulted from climate-related events.[27]

Aging in place may become difficult in communities facing extreme weather events. Where homes must be evacuated in the face of wildfires or floods, dislocation itself presents cascading risks. Reduced mobility, social isolation, and limited means may all interfere with receiving and accepting evacuation orders. Furthermore, those dislocated may be vulnerable to abuse – including financial exploitation. Limited studies indicate that older people are subject to theft, contractor fraud, neglect, and abandonment, as well as physical abuse after disasters.[28] All the difficulties that typically attach to reporting these harms – from depending on the abuser for support to fear of retaliation – could be exacerbated by dislocation. Ageism meanwhile can impede older peoples' involvement in disaster preparedness, response, and recovery efforts, resulting in programs insufficiently tailored to their needs.[29]

One climate impact alone – more frequent and severe flooding – is expected to remake the demographics of entire regions. A recent study predicts skewed out-migration from vulnerable areas to safer inland communities, impacting Florida and the coastline communities of Georgia and South Carolina the most.[30] Young people are more likely to relocate than their older neighbors. This core trend – the young leaving while the old remain – could increase the median age in some areas by ten years over the twenty-first century. It could also trigger a downward spiral in vulnerable communities. With fewer young people – and a lower share of working-age adults – in a community, tax revenue and property values may decline. A higher concentration of older residents could also lead to decreased investment in long-term infrastructure and public education, all of which could deter younger potential residents. Termed "demographic amplification," the effects of this cycle on population movement are pronounced. While 1.5 million people are projected to relocate from coastal areas under a scenario where the earth warms by 2 degrees Celsius by 2100, demographic amplification could increase that number to 15 million.

In sum, we face a future where elderly people will endure increasingly severe weather and a growing threat of injury or death. Those who attempt to flee climate

26 Renee N. Salas, *The Climate Crisis and Clinical Practice* N. Eng. J. Med. 589 (2020).

27 Sharon E. Mace & Aishwarya Sharma, *Hospital Evacuations Due to Disasters in the United States in the Twenty-First Century*, Am. J. Disaster Med. 7 (2020).

28 Gloria M. Gutman & Yongjie Yon, *Elder Abuse and Neglect in Disasters: Types, Prevalence and Research Gaps*, Int'l J. Disaster Risk Reduction 38 (2014).

29 Elburg van Boetzelaer et al., *Involving Older People in the Preparedness, Response, and Recovery Phases in Humanitarian Emergencies: A Theoretical Framework on Ageism, Epistemic Injustice, and Participation*, The Lancet: Health Longevity (2024).

30 Mathew Hauer, Sunshine Jacobs & Scott Kulp, *Climate Migration Amplifies Demographic Change and Population Aging*, Sustainability Science (2024).

impacts will often be forced to do so with limited or no resources absent meaningful reform to government assistance programs. Given demographic trends, the number of climate-vulnerable elders in both categories will grow.

This is only a partial account of how climate will shape the 100-year life. Yet even this limited survey underscores how law and policy must adapt to better serve the needs of older people.

18.2 TOWARD AN ELDER CLIMATE LAW

Climate change is a threat multiplier, magnifying flaws in how we support older Americans. Adaptation policy seeks to help individuals and communities adjust to current and projected climate impacts. This section considers how select aspects of adaptation policy – managed retreat and the disaster response system – should evolve to better serve older Americans. These are but two examples of what must become an entire field of elder climate law and policy.

The section closes by discussing how older people might help catalyze this field's development by influencing the political economy of climate law and policy through litigation.

18.2.1 *Managing Managed Retreat*

Facing a high risk of repeat flooding, residents of some frontline communities are relocating through a process known as managed retreat. Usually administered through voluntary[31] buyouts of flood-prone properties by local governments, these programs demolish purchased homes and convert the remaining land to nonresidential and noncommercial uses – such as greenspaces that can help absorb flooding and storm surges.

The need is acute. While the Federal Emergency Management Agency (FEMA) estimates that nearly 13 million Americans live within a floodplain, some researchers argue that more accurate flood maps raise that total to nearly 41 million.[32] The elderly are among those in harm's way. One study found that 28 percent of households in the combined 100- and 500-year floodplain included older adults.[33] And the costs are severe. Since 1980, flood-related damages in the US exceed $2.655 trillion.[34]

[31] The degree to which buyouts are "voluntary" – particularly for lower-income and other vulnerable populations – is contested. *See* Katharine J. Mach & A. R. Siders, *Reframing Strategic, Managed Retreat for Transformative Climate Adaptation*, 372 Sci. 1294, 1298 (2021).

[32] Oliver E. J. Wing et al., *Estimates of Present and Future Flood Risk in the Conterminous United States*, Environ. Res. Lett. (2018).

[33] Caroline Peri et al., NYU Furman Center, *Data Brief: Population in the U.S. Floodplains* (Dec. 2017), https://bit.ly/3P702co.

[34] *See* Smith, *supra* note 1.

The federal government has funded buyouts for decades. Multiple federal agencies are involved, particularly FEMA and the Department of Housing and Urban Development (HUD). These agencies provide localities with funds *after* a presidential disaster declaration has been made – meaning after a disaster takes place. The federal government typically foots 75 percent of the bill. State and local governments make up the rest while administering the buyouts themselves – determining who should receive offers of compensation, usually tied to the predisaster value of their homes. Between 1989 and 2017, FEMA alone funded over 43,000 voluntary buyouts throughout the country, including every state except Hawaii, as well as Puerto Rico, the Virgin Islands, and Guam.[35]

Though increasingly widespread, managed retreat programs do not benefit everyone equally. A recent study found that wealthier, predominantly white urban regions are more likely to gain access to buyouts – though homeowners in marginalized neighborhoods are more likely to accept them.[36] Because homeownership is required to participate, many renters in vulnerable regions are left behind – particularly impacting communities of color. Seventy percent of white households owned their primary residence in 2021, compared to 40 percent of Black and 47 percent of Hispanic households.[37] Renters in vulnerable regions are more likely to be nonwhite, with less access to pre- and postdisaster support, including relocation.[38]

Even when a home is owned, establishing legal title to it may be difficult. Heirs' property – passed down from one generation to the next without a will and absent probate – offers a case in point. It has been estimated that heirs' property accounts for 30–40 percent of Black-owned land in the South.[39] Though FEMA recently introduced reforms meant to make it easier for individuals to prove home ownership, lacking a formal legal title may still make it difficult to access disaster aid, bank loans, and other forms of vital assistance.[40]

The relative wealth of communities influences the likelihood of buyouts. One recent study found that counties with higher incomes and larger populations were

[35] Katharine J. Mach et al., *Managed Retreat through Voluntary Buyouts of Flood-Prone Properties*, Sci. Adv. (2019).

[36] James R. Elliott, Phylicia Lee Brown & Kevin Loughran, *Racial Inequities in the Federal Buyout of Flood-Prone Homes: A Nationwide Assessment of Environmental Adaptation*, 6 Socius 1 (2020).

[37] Rakesh Kochhar & Mohamad Moslimani, *Wealth Surged in the Pandemic, but Debt Endures for Poorer Black and Hispanic Families*, Pew Rsch. Ctr. (Dec. 2023), https://www.pewresearch.org/race-ethnicity/2023/12/04/the-assets-households-own-and-the-debts-they-carry.

[38] Leah A. Dundon & James S. Camp, *Climate Justice and Home-Buyout Programs: Renters as a Forgotten Population in Managed Retreat Actions*, 11 J. of Env't Stud. and Sci. 420, 426 (2021).

[39] Cassandra J. Gaither & Stanley J. Zarnoch, *Unearthing "Dead Capital": Heirs' Property Prediction in Two U.S. Southern Counties*, 67 U.S. Forest Serv. 367, 369 (2017).

[40] Kendall B. Bargeman, *The Heirs' Property Dilemma: How Stronger Federal Policies Can Help Narrow the Racial Wealth Gap*, 27 N.C. Banking Inst. 320 (2023).

more likely to implement buyout programs.[41] Smaller and less well-resourced localities may lack the staff and expertise to secure and administer funds.

The emphasis on *individual* buyouts falls short for those who value preserving their community, especially indigenous groups. Government programs for relocating whole communities have been limited to date. HUD gave a $48 million grant to Isle de Jean Charles in southeastern Louisiana, encouraging its tribal residents to move to safer ground together.[42] In 2022, the Interior Department committed $135 million to help Native American tribes relocate from threatened land – with initial grants extended to five tribes in Alaska and Washington states.[43]

Proactive efforts to move vulnerable people *before* they are impacted are inadequately supported as access to these funds usually becomes available only after a disaster. Skewed incentives between localities and the federal government complicate the picture further. The former stand to lose residents, diminishing their tax base. The federal government meanwhile provides most of the funds for managing the aftermath of a flood or storm – absorbing the costs of potential local inactions – without being able to make critical decisions on zoning and related matters that determine where people live in the first place.

Older people risk social isolation whether they accept or reject buyouts. While most people tend to relocate close to their original homes – a 2023 study found that 58 percent of bought-out homeowners move within a ten-mile drive of their original home, while 74 percent relocate within a twenty-mile drive[44] – older people might find themselves too far removed from family, friends, or caregivers to receive the support they need. Driving can become dangerous if not impossible later in life, with some outliving their ability to drive by ten or more years while living in built environments with limited – if any – public transit. As Gregory Shill notes in this volume, losing the ability to drive (or be driven by nearby friends or family) can cut older people off from necessities like access to food and medical care. Moving to a new neighborhood and potentially being uprooted from existing support networks could exacerbate these challenges.

Those who remain face distinct challenges. With fewer residents constituting a diminished tax base, there are both less resources and political incentives to fulfill government obligations like providing essential services and maintaining infrastructure. As these systems degrade, older residents may become increasingly isolated and have greater difficulty evacuating should the need arise. And even if they find

[41] Mach & Siders, *supra* note 31.

[42] Coral Davenport & Campbell Robertson, *Resettling the First American "Climate Refugees,"* N.Y. TIMES (May 2, 2016), https://www.nytimes.com/2016/05/03/us/resettling-the-first-american-climate-refugees.html.

[43] Christopher Flavelle, *In a First, U.S. Pays Tribes to Move Away from Climate Threats,* N.Y. TIMES (Nov. 4, 2022), https://www.nytimes.com/2022/11/04/climate/native-americans-relocate-climate-change.html.

[44] James R. Elliott & Zheye Wang, *Managed Retreat: A Nationwide Study of the Local, Racially Segmented Resettlement of Homeowners from Rising Flood Risks,* ENV. RESEARCH (2023).

temporary shelter, they might lose their most valued asset – their home. The finances of some older Americans may be especially hard hit, with Black and Hispanic homeowners deriving more of their net worth from home equity than white and Asian homeowners.[45]

The American system of disaster response and adaptation privileges costly recovery over preemptive risk reduction. This echoes our flawed approach to public health, where underfunding prevention contributes to predictable, costly, and often deadly outcomes. The 100-year life offers an opportunity for reform. Updating adaptation policy could help encourage older people to move out of harm's way well before the risk of a flood or hurricane is imminent. Relocating to places more suited to older peoples' needs – whether through better public transport, easier access to health care, or access to housing conducive to aging – should be prioritized. Communities should be encouraged to move together, preserving existing social networks that sustain older people. To do so, federal funds should become available to vulnerable regions without waiting for a disaster to strike. Relocation programs should also consider ways to enhance the administrative capacity of underresourced localities, allowing them to navigate the complex process of applying for and carrying out coordinated buyouts.

18.2.2 *Reforming Disaster Recovery*

For those uprooted by extreme weather events, getting help entails navigating a complex web of federal and state agencies. At the federal level alone, disaster recovery plays out across more than thirty agencies and departments. Streamlining assistance should be coupled with expanding aid for older people – especially the most vulnerable among them.

A displaced older person will likely turn to FEMA for help. FEMA financial support for individuals is limited. Each eligible household typically receives grants ranging from $1,000 to $8,000 through FEMA's Individuals and Households Program (IHP).[46] IHP can provide funds up to a cap – $42,500 for 2024.[47] This support is meant to cover temporary housing assistance and housing repair alongside other costs like uninsured medical expenses. FEMA's aim is not to return individuals or homes to their predisaster state; rather, it is to secure habitable housing and

[45] Kochhar & Moslimani, *supra* note 37.

[46] This applies to major disasters over nearly two decades, including Hurricane Katrina and Superstorm Sandy. Chad Calder, *How Much Can You Expect from FEMA? Disaster Grants Sure to Disappoint, Analysis Finds*, The Advocate (Aug. 17, 2016), https://www.theadvocate.com/louisiana_flood_2016/how-much-money-can-you-expect-from-fema-disaster-grants-sure-to-disappoint-analysis-finds/article_22c86fe0-64cd-11e6-9bb2-07f95d36ee28.html#:~:text=Although%20a%20federal%20aid%20program,dozen%20recent%20high%2Dprofile%20disasters.

[47] *Biden–Harris Administration Reforms Disaster Assistance Program to Help Survivors Recover Faster*, Federal Emergency Management Agency (Jan. 19, 2024), https://www.fema.gov/press-release/20240119/biden-harris-administration-reforms-disaster-assistance-program-help.

help people fill gaps between their savings and insurance (should they have any). Additional funding from other agencies such as HUD can take years to arrive, exacerbating inequities within and between communities.

Recent updates to FEMA's Individual Assistance Program, which went into effect in March 2024, aim to make assistance more accessible. For instance, the program will now automatically provide households affected by a disaster with $750 to address immediate needs. Even with these improvements, however, the needs of displaced older people will remain acute. FEMA's support is unlikely to meet the cost of permanent relocation or even temporary living arrangements in old age. For those on fixed incomes and with limited if any retirement savings, the effect could be ruinous.

Several long-term policy trends converge in the 100-year life, to ill effect for many older Americans. For decades people were encouraged to move to at-risk areas, such as floodplains, by policies that opened them for development, while discriminatory zoning practices left many communities of color with little choice about where to live. This legacy endures, with a higher percentage of homes in formerly redlined areas at an increased risk of flooding today relative to traditionally white neighborhoods.[48] The dangers of living in a vulnerable region were sometimes underwritten by federal flood insurance. Even when homes flooded repeatedly, they were rebuilt – leading to the phenomenon described as "flood, rebuild, repeat." Meanwhile, costs associated with care in older age began climbing precipitously, and the retirement system became increasingly insufficient for supporting a multi-decade period of diminished or no paid work.

A coherent national plan is needed to avoid a 100-year life marked by dislocation and poverty. To begin, we should consider an expanded safety net for climate-vulnerable older people alongside efforts to relocate them before disaster strikes. This could take the form of increased emergency benefits administered through existing disaster recovery programs. Building on Nina Kohn's insights in this volume, such an initiative could be tailored to the vulnerabilities of a given person – providing more support for those in greater need rather than a flat amount based on age or otherwise irrespective of need.

Pending broader reform, creating a service to help at-risk individuals navigate the recovery ecosystem – finding existing benefits while encouraging proactive planning – could help older people prepare, respond to, and recover from disaster. A navigator program for at-risk communities could be piloted within Area Agencies on Aging, which administers programs at the local level under the Older Americans Act, including services and supports such as meal delivery and legal

[48] Lily Katz, *A Racist Past, a Flooded Future: Formerly Redlined Areas Have $107 Billion Worth of Homes Facing High Flood Risk: 25% More Than Non-redlined Areas*, REDFIN (Mar. 14, 2021), https://www.redfin.com/news/redlining-flood-risk.

assistance.[49] Ideally drawn from the local community, navigators could inform older residents about where to turn for everything from local disaster preparedness – including potential buyout programs – through how to respond to losing one's home.

18.2.3 *Litigating Climate Change*

When William Butler Yeats's protagonist went sailing to Byzantium, it was to flee a place that offered "no country" for "dying generations."[50] On current emissions trajectories, the level of warming projected for the remainder of the century threatens to offer "no climate" in addition to "no country" for our older populations. Thus, in addition to adapting to climate change, every effort must be made to limit the amount of warming that does occur. There are few Byzantiums on hothouse earth.[51]

Litigation offers a powerful tool for compelling government climate action, with age playing an increasingly notable role. Several cases involving children and youth have been filed in the US, including *Juliana v. United States* – currently before a federal district court in Oregon – and *Held v. State*, filed in Montana state court. Internationally, a survey conducted by the Sabin Center for Climate Change Law found that approximately thirty-four cases had been brought by and on behalf of children through December 2022.[52]

Litigation by or on behalf of the elderly, however, has been limited despite the unique harms this vulnerable population faces – with a notable exception. In March 2023, the European Court of Human Rights (ECtHR) heard a case brought by an organization representing older Swiss women (the Senior Women for Climate Protection). This group, joined by four additional applicants (all women over eighty), sued the Swiss government alleging a violation of their human rights caused by the government's failure to adequately address climate change.

In doing so, the applicants emphasized the unique harms they face due to their age and gender. They cited an increase in severe climate change-induced heatwaves over the past twenty years and the rise in heat-related deaths among older women. Arguing that their rights to life as well as privacy and family rights are adversely impacted by climate-amplified heatwaves, the applicants noted that worsening harms are foreseeable unless government action is taken commensurate to the threat. Some of the women testified to the hardships they already experience, including living in isolation during periods of crippling heat – unable to leave their

49 Danielle Arigoni, Climate Resilience for an Aging Nation 61 (2023).

50 William Butler Yeats, *Sailing to Byzantium*, *in* The Collected Poems of W.B. Yeats 163 (2008).

51 Chi Xu et al., *Future of the Human Climate Niche*, Proc. Nat'l Acad. Sci. 11350 (2020).

52 Michael Burger & Maria Antonia Tigre, *Global Climate Litigation Report: 2023 Status Review*, Sabin Center for Climate Change Law 40 (2023).

homes for weeks at a time, leading to anxiety and loneliness – as well as losing consciousness and a worsening of preexisting conditions such as cardiovascular illness and asthma.

In a landmark April 2024 ruling, the ECtHR held that the Swiss government breached its duties under the European Convention on Human Rights by failing to develop and effectively implement measures mitigating the effects of climate change. In so doing, the Court recognized the convention to include "a right for individuals to effective protection by the State authorities from serious adverse effects of climate change on their life, health, well-being and quality of life."[53]

Litigation involving youth plaintiffs often reflects principles of intergenerational equity, highlighting the disproportionate risks younger people and future generations confront from a worsening climate. Older people face a related if distinct societal harm: They will be the last to remember the world before climate change while being among the most vulnerable to the new world's threats.

18.3 CONCLUSION

Honoring the 100-year life requires mitigating further climate change and adapting to its unavoidable effects – protecting longevity for present and future generations while securing it for our most vulnerable now. If elder law and climate law do not prioritize one another in this manner, Byzantium will become a climate forever lost rather than a home still attainable.

[53] *Klimaseniorinnen Schweiz v. Switzerland*, App. No. 53600/20, ¶ 519 (Apr. 9, 2024), https://hudoc.echr.coe.int/eng?i=001-233206.

19

Local Government Law for the 100-Year Life

Noah M. Kazis

Local government law focuses its gaze on certain fault lines: city and state, urban and suburban, insider and outsider, rich and poor, Black and white. A new fault line deserves increased attention. Local government law has a senior citizen problem. To be crystal-clear, the problem isn't with senior citizens themselves. Older Americans are terrific participants in local government; indeed, they are the foundation of this entire level of government. They vote, they serve, and they volunteer. But therein lies the problem.

Our system of local government, in its very design, privileges older residents' interests even as local government has been assigned responsibility for a set of issues where age is particularly salient. In an aging country, this interplay of structure and function threatens to distort and destabilize the local democratic process.

Local government is an arena where many of the central political issues – most pointedly public education – feature inherent generational conflict. Education, by far the top-ticket item for local budgets, pits those with children under eighteen against those without. Senior citizens, of course, rarely have school-age children.[1] Other quintessentially local issues, like infrastructure development and land use regulation, likewise center conflict between today's residents and future generations who might need a new road or more housing. Inasmuch as self-interest enters people's calculations, older people calculate that self-interest on a different time horizon.

Now, local government law offers many tools for managing political conflict; such is the nature of democracy. If anything, local government offers additional tools for satisfying heterogeneous preferences compared to higher levels of government. There are more opportunities for dissenters to protect their interests with both voice (through richer forms of public participation) and exit (through voting with one's feet). But conflicts across age groups already strain the efficacy of those tools, as they

[1] Matthew Rae et al., *Millions of Seniors Live in Households with School-Age Children*, KFF (July 16, 2020), https://www.kff.org/coronavirus-covid-19/issue-brief/millions-of-seniors-live-in-households-with-school-age-children (finding that about 6 percent of people aged sixty-five or older live with a school-age child).

are available unequally. For reasons that appear structural, not contingent, seniors vote disproportionately more than nonseniors in local elections and participate more in local community processes.

Putting these features together, seniors are not just another set of citizens in the democratic mix. They are a group whose political power at the local level can far exceed their numbers. This distribution of power offers advantages, to be sure. Long-time residents may bring deeper local knowledge to bear, for example, and such local knowledge is often what justifies otherwise less-expert local governance in the first place. But it brings costs too, and those costs may rise quickly if the demographic predictions of *The 100-Year Life* play out. What is currently a difficult undercurrent of local politics may rush to the fore. This points to the importance of law in mediating, structuring, and restructuring those coming conflicts. This chapter asks whether our current system of local government can adequately and equitably serve an aging nation. In doing so, it focuses on uniquely local functions of service provision rather than on functions shared with states and the federal government, whether those be the exercise of regulatory powers or the administration of Medicaid and public hospital systems.[2]

This is of course a speculative endeavor. Divining just how politics evolve in a future where half of all babies live to be 100 seems a thankless task.[3] Will advances in fertility treatment simultaneously shift the age at which parenthood turns to empty nesting? Will eighty be the new sixty, such that longer lives are spent in active retirement (and most importantly for local politics, as homeowners), or will large populations move to assisted living? Will growing ranks of seniors identify as a coherent group, even as being a senior becomes a more common trait? I would not hazard a guess, especially since this volume makes clear that the answers depend on the legal and policy choices we make along the way. To be conservative, I assume only that a growing share of people will exhibit political behavior approximating that of today's older citizens: those whose children, if they had them, have left the home.

This chapter proceeds in five parts. First, it explains how some of local government's central functions – education and infrastructure, especially – divide voters by age. Second, it describes how the institutions of local democracy – its low-turnout elections and rich participatory processes – disproportionately represent older residents' interests. Third, it reviews the empirical literature on how these features of local government play out on the ground, which confirms the risks of an aging population for investments in the future. Fourth, it highlights the ill effects of local

2 For one broader vision of cities' role in aging, *see* NYC Dep't Aging, *Age-Friendly New York: New Commitments for a City for All Ages* (2017), https://www.nyc.gov/assets/dfta/downloads/pdf/publications/AgeFriendlyNYC2017.pdf.

3 As an urbanist, I am wary of overconfidently predicting the future: it often goes poorly for cities. *Cf.* Le Corbusier, The City of To-Morrow and Its Planning (1929). But demographers may have a better track record.

governments' existing mechanisms for managing age-based conflicts, which rely on (and generate) exclusion and an overly market-based approach to providing public goods. Finally, it schematizes the alternative options for resolving these tensions: aligning voters' preferences, equalizing voters' political power, or reassigning responsibilities away from local governments.

19.1 AGE AND THE FUNCTIONS OF LOCAL GOVERNMENT

Local governments are the country's public service providers. They do much else besides, of course. Local governments are often at the forefront of public policy, innovating on everything from civil rights and employment law to climate change. But what makes local governments truly unique is that they employ the actual people who carry out the work of government. Nearly two-thirds of public employees, not counting the armed forces, work for local governments.[4]

And more than anything else, service provision means public education. There are over 8 million local employees working in elementary and secondary education, almost three-fifths of total local public employment.[5] K–12 education is almost as dominant in local finances as it is in local employment. Elementary and secondary education made up 40 percent of local spending in 2020, far more than anything else.[6] It is an exaggeration, but only a small one, to say that the politics of local taxation *is* the politics of public education.

After education, the next largest categories of local spending relate to health and public welfare, followed by infrastructure. Local health spending overwhelmingly reflects local administration of the state/federal Medicaid program, over which local governments play a distinctly secondary policymaking role. Infrastructure spending, in contrast, is a quintessentially local function, the interstate highway system notwithstanding. State and local governments pay for about 60 percent of capital spending on infrastructure and 90 percent of operational costs; they split these costs roughly evenly, with states taking more responsibility for highways and other regional infrastructure.[7] These investments go toward roads, in particular, but also water, sewer, and solid waste infrastructure and, importantly, debt service on past

[4] Lynn A. Baker et al., Local Government Law: Cases and Materials 59 (6th ed. 2022).

[5] Nicholas Saxon et al., *Survey of Public Employment & Payroll Summary Report: 2022* (2023), https://www.census.gov/content/dam/Census/library/publications/2023/econ/2022_summary_brief.pdf.

[6] Urb. Inst. State & Local Backgrounders, *State and Local Expenditures* (Feb. 24, 2023), https://www.urban.org/policy-centers/cross-center-initiatives/state-and-local-finance-initiative/state-and-local-backgrounders/state-and-local-expenditures.

[7] Cong. Budget Off., *Public Spending on Transportation and Water Infrastructure, 1956 to 2017* (Oct. 2018), at 5, https://www.cbo.gov/system/files/2018-10/54539-Infrastructure.pdf; Urb. Inst. State & Local Backgrounders, *Highway and Road Expenditures* (Feb. 27, 2023), https://www.urban.org/policy-centers/cross-center-initiatives/state-and-local-finance-initiative/state-and-local-backgrounders/highway-and-road-expenditures.

capital expenditures.[8] The centrality of education and infrastructure to local budgets makes age a fault line in local politics. They divide parents from nonparents and pit current spending against long-term investments.

Moreover, unlike at the federal level, age may not be just one fault line among many. Most local governments are substantially more homogeneous than the nation at large: inside a given city's or suburb's limits, there aren't the urban/rural or north/south divides that typify national politics, and persistent segregation makes many localities racially and economically uniform as well. Local governments also deal with a smaller set of issues: There are fewer independent political axes like foreign policy or international trade to cross-pressure voters. Nor can local governments use deficit spending to finesse intergenerational fiscal conflict. Thus, when demographic divides emerge at the local level, they may loom large.

19.2 AGE AND THE GOVERNANCE OF LOCAL GOVERNMENT

Even as the three-tier system of American federalism assigns certain age-related services to local governments,[9] the structures of local democracy dramatically overrepresent older residents. Older residents' voices are elevated through both electoral and participatory channels.

First, while older Americans are generally better voters than younger people, the nature of local elections widens that gap considerably. Local elections often take place off the presidential (or even midterm) cycle. At the same time, they frequently lack political parties or popular media coverage to inform and mobilize voters. This leaves elections shockingly low-turnout, limited to the most dedicated voters and, more importantly, to those connected to local politics through their social networks. This favors long-time residents and those with more time – and therefore seniors.

The age divide in local voting behavior is overwhelming. Political scientist Sarah Anzia calculated that California residents aged sixty-five to ninety registered to vote at rates 17.7 percentage points higher than those aged twenty to forty-five.[10] Of those already unequally registered voters, the older group then voted in city elections at a rate 26.6 percentage points higher than their younger neighbors.[11] That gap in voting rates rises to as high as 46.4 percentage points in the most unusually timed elections.[12] Notably, off-cycle elections empower seniors even more than they do other

[8] Urb. Inst. State & Local Backgrounders, *supra* note 6.

[9] These questions about responsibility for age-inflected *public services* should be juxtaposed with the long literature on the two-tier system of *social welfare benefits* that assigns universal old-age programs to the national level and less-generous means-tested programs – often aimed at protecting children – to states. *Cf.* Jamila Michener, Fragmented Democracy: Medicaid, Federalism, and Unequal Politics 36 (2018).

[10] Sarah F. Anzia, *When Does a Group of Citizens Influence Policy? Evidence from Senior Citizen Participation in City Politics*, 81 J. Pol. 1, 3 (2019).

[11] *Id.*

[12] *Id.*

groups – like unionized teachers – who are thought to benefit from low-turnout elections.[13]

Just as importantly, local politics distinctively centers face-to-face self-government, whether through public hearings or conversations at the grocery store. The ballot box is relatively less central to local democracy – and, in smaller municipalities, sometimes a distinctly peripheral mechanism for years at a time. Again, this gives older Americans a distinct advantage. Deep community roots again matter here, but so does a flexible schedule.

In their path-breaking study of local public participation, political scientists Katherine Einstein, David Glick, and Maxwell Palmer found that 75 percent of those who spoke at public land use meetings in Massachusetts were older than fifty. This is 22 percentage points higher than the share of voters over fifty (and higher still than the share of the general population over fifty).[14] A thirty-year-old, they found, is 20 percent as likely to comment as a seventy-year-old.[15] The volunteer advisory boards so common at the local level display similar bias. Among community board members in Queens, New York, 47 percent are aged sixty or older (compared to 24.7 percent of the population), and 70 percent are fifty or older (compared to 38.4 percent of the population).[16]

Perhaps most strikingly, the median age of a school board member in 2017 was fifty-nine,[17] well past the age when people are likely to have a child in the home.[18] Indeed, this is older than the median age in the US House of Representatives.[19] Yet one imagines school boards to be institutions where parents take a particular interest. If so, the rest of local government likely skews older still.[20]

[13] Vladimir Kogan et al., *Election Timing, Electorate Composition, and Policy Outcomes: Evidence from School Districts*, 62 Am. J. Pol. Sci. 637, 638 (2018).

[14] Katherine Levine Einstein et al., Neighborhood Defenders 101 (2019).

[15] *Id.* at 102.

[16] Donovan Richards Jr., Queens Borough President, Queens Community Board Demographic Report 30 (2022), https://queensbp.org/wp-content/uploads/2022/07/2022-Queens-Community-Board-Report-lores.pdf; US Census Bureau, *American Community Survey 1-Year Estimates Subject Tables, Table S0101, Age and Sex*, 2022, https://data.census.gov/table/ACSST1Y2022.S0101?q=Age+and+Sex&g=050XX00US36081.

[17] Nat'l Sch. Bds. Ass'n, *Today's School Boards & Their Priorities for Tomorrow* 3 (2018), https://cdn-files.nsba.org/s3fs-public/reports/K12_National_Survey.pdf.

[18] The median age at last birth for mothers is thirty-one; for fathers, thirty-four. Karen Benjamin Guzzo & Katherine Graham, *Median Age at Last Birth for Fathers*, Nat'l Ctr. for Fam. & Marriage Rsch. (2022), https://www.bgsu.edu/ncfmr/resources/data/family-profiles/guzzo-graham-median-age-last-birth-fathers-fp-22-05.html.

[19] Carrie Blazina & Drew Desilver, *House Gets Younger, Senate Gets Older: A Look at the Age and Generation of Lawmakers in the 118th Congress*, Pew Rsch. Ctr. (Jan. 30, 2023), https://www.pewresearch.org/short-reads/2023/01/30/house-gets-younger-senate-gets-older-a-look-at-the-age-and-generation-of-lawmakers-in-the-118th-congress/.

[20] Data on the demographic composition of local boards are scarce. *See* Noah M. Kazis, *The Structure of Land Use Administration: A Research Agenda*, *in* A Research Agenda for US Land Use and Planning Law (John Infranca & Sarah Schindler eds., 2023).

Thus, local government features a potentially uncomfortable combination of responsibilities and governance institutions. These first make age especially salient and then make older people especially well represented. The next question, then, is how local government manages this political pressure.

19.3 HOW LOCAL POLITICS RESPONDS TO AN OLDER POPULATION: EMPIRICAL EVIDENCE

Spurred by the property tax revolts of the 1970s, social scientists have worked for decades to discern the actual effects of population age on local political economy.[21] The conventional wisdom is that older residents, all other things equal, demand lower taxes, especially where those taxes fund education. Most empirical research on local education politics supports this conventional wisdom, at least to some extent, though this literature has been notably inconsistent.[22] Political scientist Arnaud Maurel has extended this literature from education spending by school districts to the other programs funded by municipalities. Maurel finds limited effects on total spending, but a dramatic shift away from capital investments and long-term debt – in other words, a shift from spending on the future to spending on the present.[23]

Even taking older voters' opposition to education spending as given, the net effect of an older population on that spending remains ambiguous. While seniors are less supportive of spending on schools or infrastructure, they also consume less in services. Thus, the presence of seniors in a jurisdiction can increase the per-capita resources available for school spending; many jurisdictions chase seniors as a lucrative boon to the tax base. Seniors' immediate effect on the tax base increases per-capita school spending, even as their political behavior can decrease it.[24] Which effect dominates depends on the number of seniors and their political organization.

What is particularly interesting for local government law, though, is not how much age affects political behavior but what legal mechanisms regulate that relationship. The empirical literature identifies two mechanisms as particularly important in mitigating the effects of older residents' opposition to education spending: Tiebout sorting across jurisdictions and the capitalization of services into home prices.

[21] Helen F. Ladd & Julie B. Wilson, *Who Supports Tax Limitations: Evidence from Massachusetts' Proposition 2½*, 2 J. POL'Y ANALYSIS & MGMT. 256 (1983).

[22] Amy Rehder Harris et al., *Education Spending in an Aging America*, 81 J. PUB. ECON. 449, 450–451. Age might not affect support for education spending because older people are more altruistic, more affluent, or more accustomed to higher taxes. James W. Button, *A Sign of Generational Conflict: The Impact of Florida's Aging Voters on Local School and Tax Referenda*, 73 SOC. SCI. Q. 786, 787 (1992).

[23] Arnaud Maurel, *Managing an Aging City: Evidence from Five Decades of Municipal Budgets* (Aug. 14, 2023), at 2, https://papers.ssrn.com/sol3/papers.cfm?abstract_id=4414134.

[24] Dennis Epple et al., *The Intergenerational Conflict over the Provision of Public Education*, 96 J. PUB. ECON. 255, 256 (2012).

First, Tiebout mobility ostensibly lets those with different preferences sort into separate communities, allowing all to better meet their needs. The famous Tiebout model imagines mobile households shopping for bundles of taxes and services by "voting with their feet" and moving to localities whose bundles match their preferences. In theory, those with children can move to higher-tax locations with better schools while the elderly select into retirement havens where education is not prioritized. In reality, of course, there are any number of limitations to Tiebout sorting: households may not want or be able to move, and there may be no jurisdiction offering households the particular package they prefer.

With respect to the elderly, there is some evidence of Tiebout sorting. Some research suggests that when local governments raise property taxes, older residents move to new homes with lower property taxes.[25] More tellingly, this sorting occurs only under certain conditions. In one study, people who moved upon becoming empty nesters generally didn't secure any change in their fiscal bundle.[26] The conditions weren't right. Many empty nesters still worked and were tied to their commute patterns; others lived in regions with school districts too large to easily leave; and still others lived in states where school finance equalization meant that crossing local boundaries still wouldn't get them out of paying for schools. When the researchers narrowed in on those whose conditions were most Tiebout-amenable – retirees in regions with fragmented local governments and no school finance equalization – they found substantial sorting into places with less school spending and lower taxes.[27]

At the same time, capitalization provides residents a self-interested reason to invest in services they don't personally use: the value of their home. A homebuyer purchases not only land and a structure but also the amenities connected to the location of that land, many of which are provided by local governments. They buy access to the neighborhood school and proximity to the neighborhood park. That access is priced into the sale of the house, along with the accompanying taxes. Accordingly, non-parents still care about school quality: Worse schools would mean losses on their largest financial asset. The tighter the link between service quality and home prices, the more those who don't use local services will still work to maintain their quality. This mechanism helps minimize conflict between older and younger residents. Economists have found that the extent of capitalization, as determined by differences in the housing market, mediates whether the elderly support public education.[28]

[25] Hui Shan, *Property Taxes and Elderly Mobility*, 67 J. URB. ECON. 194, 195 (2010). *But see* Maurel, *supra* note 23, at 5 (finding that tax-motivated migration is low because seniors wish to age in place).

[26] Martin Farnham & Purvi Sevak, *State Fiscal Institutions and Empty-Nest Migration: Are Tiebout Voters Hobbled?* 90 J. PUB. ECON. 407, 409–410 (2006).

[27] *Id.* at 425.

[28] Randall Reback, *Buying Their Votes? A Study of Local Tax-Price Discrimination*, 53 ECON. INQUIRY 1451, 1453 (2015); Harris et al., *supra* note 22, at 465.

19.4 THE HIGH COSTS OF EXISTING MECHANISMS FOR MITIGATING AGE-BASED CONFLICT

As mechanisms for navigating the politics of age, Tiebout sorting and capitalization are both rooted in the market for public services purchased through residency. Current political dynamics, therefore, point to two models for managing the local political economy: one based on democratic and participatory mechanisms, and the other based on these markets. In the first, an older populace leverages the mechanisms of local government to reduce investment in the future, potentially well beyond what the median voter might choose. In the second, public investment is preserved by letting people sort into different communities and capitalizing service quality into home prices. For many, this is an unappealing set of options.

First, the market model carries an initial drawback when applied to aging: It relies on mobility when many seniors hope to age in place. Surveys suggest that seniors overwhelmingly prefer to age in place for as long as possible.[29] While some households are excited to move to retirement communities designed for a new phase in life, many more wish to maintain their community roots. Those who need assistance generally rely on informal care from friends and family, which may be harder to obtain after a move. Not all people want to, or ought to, trade those connections for an age-appropriate mix of taxes and services. Society should be careful about using prices to push seniors to move.

The larger issue, though, is that for many those market mechanisms offer a decidedly unattractive vision of local government: if not for senior citizens, then for everyone else. This model treats local government as a product to be consumed by those with the means to pay. As scholars like Gerald Frug and Richard Schragger have argued, this violates basic tenets of distributive justice, allocating fundamentally public services like a child's education based on their parents' wealth.[30] Moreover, this model creates its own self-reinforcing politics, forcing households into a position that is "explicitly defensive and separationist."[31] This market incentivizes local voters to demand homogeneity, to exclude anyone who might need more services than they pay in taxes, and to block any redistribution of local taxes. Even if it protects education from underfunding based on age, it might increase underfunding based on wealth, impeding efforts to fairly fund schools in districts with low property values.[32]

[29] Sewin Chan & Ingrid Gould Ellen, *Housing for an Aging Population*, 7 HOUS. POL'Y DEBATE 167, 167 (2017).

[30] Gerald E. Frug, *City Services*, 73 N.Y.U. L. REV. 23, 30–31 (1998); Richard Schragger, *Consuming Government*, 101 MICH. L. REV. 1824, 1836 (2003).

[31] Schragger, *supra* note 30, at 1836.

[32] William A. Fischel, *Did Serrano Cause Proposition 13?* 42 NAT'L TAX J. 465 (1989).

Leaning into these mechanisms further results in ever-tightening exclusionary zoning as voters strive to maintain exclusivity by any means available.[33] Indeed, this market model relies on walls of exclusion, which must be maintained to divide those who bought public services at the "right price" from those who did not.[34] Neither capitalization nor sorting is possible otherwise. Such exclusionary land use policies, however, come at enormous cost, driving an affordable housing crisis, entrenching racial segregation, costing the economy trillions of dollars, and spurring environmentally disastrous development patterns.[35]

The country's most successful retirement communities paint a picture of this world's highs and lows, as applied to aging. Florida's The Villages, for example, is the country's fastest-growing community, with over 145,000 residents. It has thrived by offering seniors a residential experience designed for them, with everything from social clubs to a golf cart-friendly transportation network. The community has its own hospital, but as a childless community, the only area school serves The Villages' employees rather than its residents. From the perspective of its self-selected residents, this targeted experience provides a vindication of the Tiebout model; 90.8 percent of residents report high satisfaction with The Villages.[36] Sun City, Arizona, the original active retirement community, receives similar raves: "I have some apprehension about dying, because to go to heaven won't be as good as this," reported one resident.[37]

But The Villages, Sun City, and their peers vindicate the Tiebout critics' fears as well. As Lior Strahilevitz has observed, these are some of the most segregated places in the country, not just by age but also by race.[38] Of the country's five largest age-restricted communities, four have a population less than 1 percent Black; the fifth is 2.6 percent Black.[39] Sun City and the other Arizona retirement communities notably rejected the state's referendum to make Martin Luther King Jr. Day a holiday by ratios from 2:1 to 4:1, espousing what close observers called a "fortress

33 Jacob Krimmel, *Reclaiming Local Control: School Finance Reforms and Housing Supply Restrictions* (working paper, Feb. 8, 2022), https://static1.squarespace.com/static/5f75531c54380e4fb4b0f839/t/620320d5ce8b010bca2552af/1644372186832/Krimmel_HousingSupply_SchoolFinance_draft_mostrecent.pdf.

34 *See* Christian A. L. Hilber & Christopher Mayer, *Why Do Households without Children Support Local Public Schools? Linking House Price Capitalization to School Spending*, 65 J. Urb. Econ. 74, 75 (2009) (finding that capitalization generates senior support for school spending only "in locations with limited opportunities for new construction").

35 *See* David Schleicher, *Exclusionary Zoning's Confused Defenders*, Wisc. L. Rev. 1315, 1323–1333 (2021).

36 Lior Jacob Strahilevitz, *Historic Preservation and Its Even Less Authentic Alternative*, *in* Evidence and Innovation in Housing Law and Policy, 108, 113 (Lee Anne Fennell & Benjamin J. Keys eds., 2017).

37 Kevin E. McHugh & Elizabeth M. Larson-Keagy, *These White Walls: The Dialectic of Retirement Communities*, 19 J. Aging Stud. 241, 245 (2005).

38 Strahilevitz, *supra* note 36, at 109.

39 Michael C. Pollack & Lior Jacob Strahilevitz, *Property Law for the Ages*, 63 Wm. & Mary L. Rev. 561, 633 (2021).

mentality" manifest in the communities themselves.[40] These physically and demographically closed-off communities became politically closed-off, as they "feel that they have nothing in common with outsiders and that they and the state owe these outsiders nothing."[41] In creating places limited to people "just like them," developers have offered seniors homogeneity in more ways than one – and perhaps built that segregation into residents' political identity.

These purpose-built communities also blur the line between public and private governance. In The Villages, the developer owns the local newspaper and radio station, spends heavily on local elections, and even had a senior executive serving as a state legislator.[42] Just as the detractors of a Tiebout world predicted, these are places where private values and private power can, even more than usual, invade public policymaking.[43]

Finally, this solution still leaves education and infrastructure spending vulnerable. Sorting residents by age places the full cost of education and other long-term investments on middle-aged families with children. That increases the effective price of these services for those families, presumably requiring them to spend less. Some economists might like this outcome – it moves the property tax toward being a true benefit tax – but it would impose a sudden negative shock to current spending levels. Depending on how jurisdictional lines are drawn – a question of law – the withdrawal of funds might be considerable. Sun City, for example, eventually seceded from the local school district after years of conflict.[44]

Taken as a whole, then, the challenge posed by an aging population appears even starker. Voice and exit are always imperfect tools for informing and constraining government. But to manage local conflicts along the lines of age, they perform especially badly. Voice is distorted by the unrepresentative qualities of local politics. Exit relies on mobility that many seniors lack and requires entrenching some of the more troubling features of local governance.

19.5 THE THREE PATHS TO MANAGING LOCAL AGE-BASED POLITICS

Conceptually the challenges that age poses to the local political economy can only be solved in three ways: reducing the generational gap in political preferences, reducing the generational gap in political influence, or reallocating functions to a

[40] Robert Kastenbaum, *Racism and the Older Voter? Arizona's Rejection of a Paid Holiday to Honor Martin Luther King*, 32 Int'l J. Aging & Human Dev. 199, 203, 207 (1991).

[41] Pollack & Strahilevitz, *supra* note 39, at 641.

[42] Ryan Grim, *The Villages Vendetta: How a Grassroots Revolt in the Iconic Retirement Community Ended with a 72-Year-Old Political Prisoner*, Intercept (Feb. 5, 2023), https://theintercept.com/2023/02/05/ron-desantis-florida-villages-oren-miller.

[43] Future research should evaluate how these dynamics play out in public or nonprofit senior housing. This may help disentangle the relevant mechanisms at play.

[44] McHugh & Larson-Keagy, *supra* note 37, at 251–252.

level of government where politics work differently. The market mechanisms described earlier are examples of the first strategy, albeit costly ones. This section offers an additional example of each strategy to begin mapping what paths forward are available.

First, many places may be attempting to defuse conflict between seniors and nonseniors through targeted property tax relief. As of 2018, twenty states gave seniors a property tax exemption or credit, another ten gave localities the option to extend such exemptions, and thirty-nine states offered at least one program granting seniors property tax deferrals, circuit breakers, or assessment freezes.[45] Such programs remain popular. In 2023, New Jersey cut most seniors' property taxes in half, one of the largest tax cuts in state history.

These benefits are not usually pitched as political interventions. Instead, they are conceptualized as responding to seniors' liquidity constraints. Seniors may be house-rich but income-poor, in which case rising property taxes can strain household budgets and force residents to leave their homes. But, as economist Randall Reback has observed, this tax relief can be understood as price discrimination for the Tiebout marketplace.[46] Seniors are essentially offered a discount on their public services. This strategy manages the risks of both exit and voice. For mobile households, property tax relief offers a more attractive fiscal package. For those likely to stay, it is an inducement – some would say a "bribe" – to keep them from voting down school taxes.[47] Empirical results confirm that property tax limits for seniors significantly reduce the negative effect of age on school funding.[48] Under certain conditions, property tax relief might be a fiscal positive for local governments, if it buys tolerance for spending.

Such relief carries its own risks, of course. Many programs are economically regressive, offering the biggest benefits to those with the most valuable homes. Indeed, if programs are designed to prop up support for spending, this regressivity might be unavoidable. Oversubsidizing seniors also risks incentivizing people to stay in large homes they don't need (and whose maintenance demands or age-unfriendly designs they might not want), freezing the housing market. Moreover, these programs risk intergenerational equity issues. Today's seniors received help paying for schools from their elders but will not pay it forward to the next generation. And if the senior population grows enough, tax exemptions may prove unsustainable: The young will provide too narrow a tax base. But given the empirical uncertainties about the world of the 100-year life, the point is not to evaluate how well tax relief

45 H. Spencer Banzhaf et al., *Age-Based Property Tax Exemptions*, 121 J. Urb. Econ. 103303 (2021), at 1.

46 Reback, *supra* note 28, at 1465.

47 Frug, *supra* note 30, at 28 (quoting Clayton P. Gillette, *Equality and Variety in the Delivery of Municipal Services*, 100 Harv. L. Rev. 946, 961 (1987)).

48 Reback, *supra* note 28, at 1452; Kogan et al., *supra* note 13, at 646.

can smooth frictions over local finances. Rather, these programs show the potential of law to realign voters' preferences.

A second strategy would rebalance local politics to account for younger voices. Moving local elections onto the presidential cycle is probably the lowest-hanging fruit here. At least for contested elections, this alone could help significantly. However, many local elections are not meaningfully contested.[49] For these localities – for smaller jurisdictions in particular – elections are not usually where politics takes place and, therefore, are not a promising lever for reform.

Also important, therefore, is empowering younger residents in the rich participatory processes that occur between elections. This challenge has received some attention in the land use context, but proven tricky to solve. For example, one often-cited obstacle to including parents (and especially lower-income parents) in public hearings is the need for childcare. Thus, the COVID-19-era switch to online meetings hoped to reduce inequalities in participation.[50] But it was a bust. In person, there was a 22.4 percentage point gap between the share of commenters over fifty and the share of voters over fifty. Online, that gap was 22.3 percentage points: identical.[51] Simply reducing barriers to participation appears insufficient. Bringing in diverse voices may require affirmatively soliciting input from residents separately by age and other demographics, a strategy that is effective but labor-intensive, hard to scale, and politically sensitive.[52] Avoiding the domination of unrepresentative voices, then, may require eliminating some participatory forums, especially where the additional process provides little probative value. But how to do so – what is best practice and what is feasible politics – is highly controversial.

If the local politics of age-skewed services cannot be improved, the third option is to avoid local politics altogether. Local responsibility for education and infrastructure emerged in one era. In a demographically different future, local governments might be the wrong stewards of these responsibilities. In state and national politics, older Americans are one interest group among many. Moreover, politics are more ideological, potentially cross-pressuring the effect of age on spending. While local government has many virtues, it may be a bad fit for managing these issues.

49 J. Eric Oliver et al., Local Elections and the Politics of Small-Scale Democracy 120–122 (2012) (describing the prevalence of uncontested elections); Carissa Byrne Hessick et al., *Donating to the District Attorney*, 56 U.C. Davis L. Rev. 1769, 1780, 1829 (2023) (observing that most elections for a local prosecutor are uncontested and suggesting that alternative, nonelectoral forms of oversight are necessary).

50 Katherine Levine Einstein, *Still Muted: The Limited Participatory Democracy of Zoom Public Meetings*, 59 Urb. Affs. Rev. 1279, 1284 (2022).

51 *Id.*

52 Katherine Levine Einstein & Maxwell Palmer, Representation in the Housing Process: Best Practices for Improving Racial Equity 8–13 (2022), https://www.tbf.org/-/media/tbf/reports-and-covers/2022/june/final-representation-in-the-housing-process-report-20220615.pdf.

The effects of such a significant shift, though, are especially unclear. First, it's uncertain whether such a shift would even succeed at protecting spending on long-term investments. William Fischel has argued that when California reduced local control over education spending, the immediate result was the state's property tax revolt. Voters who couldn't ensure that their taxes would be spent locally (and capitalized into their home value) wouldn't let those dollars be spent at all.[53] There is similar age-specific evidence that older households oppose state spending on education far more than they oppose local spending.[54] If these results generalize (including to federal politics), shifting issues to higher levels of government is no solution. Even if that shift worked, it would let localism wither. Take away education, infrastructure, and probably land use as well, and outside big cities, there's not much left for local governments to *do*.[55] Local government could not function as a site for political empowerment, policy innovation, and meeting the disparate demands of a diverse polity. Such a trade-off raises profound questions about the purpose of local government.

19.6 CONCLUSION

As this brief discussion indicates, there are no easy answers here. There is too much uncertainty even about how aging affects the current local political economy, much less how future aging patterns (of a different generation, decades from now) change those politics again. Yet even as reforms addressing the local politics of age seem uncertain to work, they are guaranteed to implicate a host of fraught competing concerns. Age cuts too deeply, across too many core issues of local government, to be treated in isolation.

But, for the same reason, states and cities cannot ignore the aging of their populations. Doing so risks pitched fiscal conflict at best and potentially serious disinvestment in our future. Scholars and practitioners of local government law must, for at least some discussions, add age to race, class, and geography as a lens through which we view our subject. Then, at least, the effects of aging on local politics can be managed and, inevitably, muddled through.

[53] Fischel, *supra* note 32.

[54] Helen F. Ladd AND Sheila E. Murray, *Intergenerational Conflict Reconsidered: County Demographic Structure and the Demand for Public Education*, 20 ECONOMICS OF EDUCATION REVIEW 343, 344 (2001).

[55] For most jurisdictions, criminal justice would be the last big-ticket item. A local politics overwhelmingly oriented around policing and prosecution would involve its own new dynamics, which are hard to predict but not intuitively attractive. *Cf.* Rebecca Goldstein, *Senior Citizens as a Pro-police Interest Group*, 2 J. POL. INSTS. & POL. ECON. 303 (2021) (describing generational politics of local policing).

20

Transportation Policy for the 100-Year Life

Gregory H. Shill

Consider two Americans, one born in 1824 and the other in 1924. Both are fortunate to enjoy a 100-year life[1] in a small or midsize city. Over the course of the first American's lifespan, it is likely that she would see her independence increase on at least one dimension: her practical ability to access valued destinations.[2] The advent of steam locomotives and steamboats made long-distance travel feasible, and horse-cars and rail did the same for local travel. Roads became more common and improved dramatically in connectivity and quality.[3] As the twilight of her life approached, the automobile was becoming a mass-market product that opened up still other avenues of possibility. In her nineties, she likely could not take full advantage of this innovation, but she didn't need to. All the other options still existed. In very old age, she continued to enjoy high levels of independence for as long as she could board a streetcar.

In terms of independence during the golden years, the American born in 1924 isn't so lucky. As she progressed from early adulthood to middle age, cities dismantled their streetcar networks, shrank their sidewalks to widen roads, and routed highways right into the heart of their downtowns, dividing communities and gutting Main Streets in the process. Viewed narrowly, this might not have seemed all bad: In her middle years, it perhaps improved her independence on net, if she was in the fortunate majority able to take advantage of the car's promise in that era even as other forms of transportation languished or were discontinued. But by the time she reached her eighties, when her ability to drive safely was deteriorating, reliable rapid transit no longer existed. In her final two decades, the fulfillment of her basic

1 *See* Lynda Gratton & Andrew Scott, The 100-Year Life: Living and Working in an Age of Longevity (2016).

2 Of independence's many dimensions, this chapter emphasizes the ability to reach valued destinations, a concept known in urban planning as accessibility and detailed in Section 20.2, *infra*.

3 Transportation technology and physical infrastructure are only a few of the determinants of an individual's ability to access valued destinations; others include disability access and safe access for marginalized groups.

needs – buying groceries, accessing medical care, seeing family – became increasingly laborious, expensive, or infeasible. The ability to travel by air did little to offset these daily difficulties. Progress in technology, medicine, civil rights, and the economy left her much better off overall than her counterpart a century earlier, but her independence diminished more in old age than it would have in a different transportation paradigm. The driving life expectancy of Americans – the period during which they are able to drive safely – is about seven to ten years shorter than their life expectancy,[4] and for those who live 100-year lives, this gap is far larger.

In the US, the natural challenges of aging are magnified by a land-use and transportation system that compels reliance on the car. Alongside the rise of mass motoring in the middle third of the twentieth century, regulations that inhibit the growth of population density – zoning, parking requirements, minimum lot sizes, maximum lot coverage ratios, and so forth – came to dominate at the local level across the country. These ensured that different uses of land, like housing, schools, grocery stores, and job centers, were more separated from one another than they had been when their location was dictated by the usual pressures of supply and demand, and that they were arranged along a road network that required a car to navigate. This generates a variety of challenges for society as a whole, ranging from climate change to traffic deaths, as well as for particular groups. Older Americans are one such group: Many cannot operate a vehicle safely but could ride a bus, light rail, or train if a reliable and accessible network existed.

These policies, and the laws that implement them,[5] create two barriers to realizing the promise of the 100-year life. The first is that they shorten Americans' lifespans. Compared to their peers in other high-income countries, the life expectancy of Americans is brief. Paradoxically, however, boosting American longevity would aggravate a second problem: In their golden years, Americans enjoy less independence than their peers. These problems cannot be reduced to a single cause, but they do share a common, vexing, and perhaps unexpected input: a built environment that requires driving as the price of first-class citizenship.

Addressing the bundle of laws and policies that require universal automobility is a colossal undertaking. Viewing these matters through the narrower aperture of the 100-year life, however, suggests cause for optimism: Perhaps more than in any other area, policy governing transportation can both increase life expectancy and broadly enhance quality of life in old age.

Section 20.1 considers the impacts of America's automobile-first transportation system on the US's life expectancy. It urges the adoption of proven, low-cost, and high-value automobile and roadway safety interventions in response. Section 20.2,

[4] *See* Daniel J. Foley et al., *Driving Life Expectancy of Persons Aged 70 Years and Older in the United States*, 92 Am. J. Pub. Health 1284, 1286 (2002).

[5] *See* Gregory H. Shill, *Should Law Subsidize Driving?* 95 N.Y.U. L. Rev. 498 (2020) (describing and analyzing incentives from varied areas of law that increase the level and risk of driving in the US).

which addresses quality of life in the golden years, proposes efforts to catalyze a competitive market to attract older Americans to locations that enhance their independence.

The concept of a competitive locational marketplace is well grounded in urban economics, but its potential as a solution to the challenges of sustaining independence in old age, described in Section 20.2, is relatively underexplored. The basic problem is that those fortunate to enjoy long lifespans can expect to outlive their driving life expectancy – the age when they can no longer drive safely – yet, outside of a handful of costly cities, America's automobile paradigm offers them no viable alternative.[6] Section 20.2 makes the case for differentiated forms of living arrangements in old age that increase independence – the ability to access valued destinations – in diverse ways. Specifically, drawing on the stylized consumer-voter model of residential sorting developed by Charles Tiebout,[7] it observes that local governments can (and to an extent already do) join forces with developers to compete for retiree population share, allowing seniors to sort into communities that foster greater access to valued amenities in their golden years. This decentralized, instrumental approach will not appeal to everyone, but has the potential, through competition, to generate benefits beyond the places where it is embraced directly.

20.1 CAR CRASHES AND LIFE EXPECTANCY

Unintentional injuries – accidents, colloquially – are the leading cause of premature death for Americans aged one to forty-four.[8] In 2021, they accounted for more such deaths than the other top five causes combined.[9] In 2020 – a year when the COVID-19 pandemic caused approximately 350,000 deaths in the US[10] – unintentional injuries, which disproportionately claim young victims, cost more potential *years*

6 *See* Anne Alstott, *Law and the Hundred-Year Life*, 26 ELDER L.J. 131, 141 (2018) ("The suburban model of housing ... tends to immobilize and isolate older people").

7 Charles M. Tiebout, A *Pure Theory of Local Expenditures*, 64 J. POL. ECON. 416 (1956). Legal scholars have applied Tieboutian principles to local government law. *See* Daniel B. Rodriguez & David Schleicher, *The Location Market*, 19 GEO. MASON L. REV. 637 (2012); Clayton P. Gillette, *Regionalization and Interlocal Bargains*, 76 N.Y.U. L. REV. 190 (2001); Richard Briffault, *The Rise of Sublocal Structures in Urban Governance*, 82 MINN. L. REV. 503 (1997).

8 Ctrs. for Disease Control & Prevention, *Injuries and Violence Are Leading Causes of Death: Top Ten Leading Causes of Death in the U.S. for Ages 1–44 from 1981–2021* (Oct. 25, 2023), https://www.cdc.gov/injury/wisqars/animated-leading-causes.html ("Unintentional injuries include opioid overdoses (unintentional poisoning), motor vehicle crashes, and unintentional falls").

9 In 2021, unintentional injuries were the leading cause of death in the US for people aged one to forty-four, accounting for 89,700 such deaths, followed by suicide (23,900), COVID-19 (23,700), homicide (19,900), and heart disease (18,200). *Id.*

10 Meredith S. Shiels et al., *Leading Causes of Death in the US during the COVID-19 Pandemic, March 2020 to October 2021*, 182 JAMA INTERN. MED. 883 (2022) (reporting that COVID-19 accounted for 350,000 deaths in 2020).

of life than any other cause.[11] Among such accidental deaths, traffic fatalities are either the leading or second leading cause of death for all age groups above one year.[12] Because of their intensely negative impact on lifespan, these early-in-life deaths have a disproportionate impact on life expectancy in the US.

20.1.1 *Car-Crash Deaths Reduce US Life Expectancy*

Life expectancy represents a prediction about how many years of life a given person has remaining from a given age (at birth, at age eighteen, etc.).[13] A focus on life expectancy brings out the distinction between, say, drug overdoses and heart attacks: both cut lifespan, but the former cause of death, which skews young, reduces life expectancy more than the latter.

Life expectancy is positively associated with national income: Those who live in high-income countries can generally expect to live longer than those in middle- and low-income countries.[14] However, the US is a partial exception to this rule. While average life expectancy in the US was once comparable to that in Germany and the UK, beginning in the 1990s the US began to lag behind its peers.[15] In 2019, the last full year that excludes the effects of the COVID-19 pandemic, Americans' life expectancy at birth was just shy of seventy-nine years, lower by over three years than a peer group of twenty-one "high-income advanced democracies"[16] despite the fact that the US is far wealthier on all or nearly all economic measures than each of those countries. This gap – long a focus of demographers and public health scholars – both widened notably and garnered increased attention during the pandemic.[17] It has since reverted

[11] Ctrs. for Disease Control & Prevention, *Leading Causes of Death and Injury* (Nov. 8, 2023), https://www.cdc.gov/injury/wisqars/leadingcauses.html ("Unintentional injury contributed to more years of potential life lost than any other cause of death" (footnote omitted)).

[12] Ctrs. for Disease Control & Prevention, *10 Leading Causes of Injury Deaths by Age Group*, https://www.cdc.gov/injury/wisqars/pdf/Leading-Causes-of-Injury-Deaths-by-Age-Group_2020_508.pdf (data for 2020). As a cause of unintentional injury death for babies under one year of age, motor vehicle traffic ranks third. *Id.* Covered fatalities include those of vehicle occupants, pedestrians, cyclists, and others killed by motor vehicles.

[13] *See* Ctrs. for Disease Control & Prevention, *Health, United States, 2020–2021: Life Expectancy* (June 26, 2023), https://www.cdc.gov/nchs/hus/sources-definitions/life-expectancy.htm (defining life expectancy as "the average number of years of life remaining to a person at a particular age and based on a given set of age-specific death rates – generally, the mortality conditions existing in the period mentioned").

[14] *See National Income's Connection to Life Expectancy*, FRED Blog (June 15, 2020), https://fredblog.stlouisfed.org/2020/06/national-incomes-connection-to-life-expectancy.

[15] Derek Thompson, *America Is a Rich Death Trap*, Atlantic (Sep. 7, 2022), https://www.theatlantic.com/newsletters/archive/2022/09/america-mortality-life-expectancy-pandemic/671350.

[16] *See* Steven H. Woolf, Ryan K. Masters & Laudan Y. Aron, *Changes in Life Expectancy between 2019 and 2020 in the US and 21 Peer Countries*, 5 JAMA Network Open (2022), at 4.

[17] *See, e.g.*, Roni Caryn Rabin, *U.S. Life Expectancy Falls Again in "Historic" Setback*, N.Y. Times (Aug. 31, 2022), https://www.nytimes.com/2022/08/31/health/life-expectancy-covid-pandemic.html; Matthew Yglesias, *Tackling America's Weirdly Short Life Expectancy Should Be a Priority*,

somewhat as the virus has waned,[18] but this only returns the US to roughly the same uncompetitive position that it previously occupied.

Explanations for American weakness in life expectancy abound. Commonly identified causes include infant mortality, roadway mortality, gun homicides and suicides, drug overdoses, and cardiac events – all of which are more common or more deadly in the US.[19] Several of these claim young lives disproportionately, causing the US to experience a very high number of potential years of life lost (PYLL)[20] compared to other industrialized countries.[21] Indeed, among members of the Organisation for Economic Co-operation and Development (OECD), plus a few other middle-income countries, the US suffered one of the highest levels of PYLL; only countries that have a far lower national income, such as Mexico and Latvia, perform worse.[22] In Canada and Australia, for example, premature death erases half as much or less early-life potential as compared to the US.[23] Road traffic deaths, as well as gun violence and drug overdoses, contribute substantially to America's distinctively low average life expectancy.

It is worth unpacking why the roadway mortality contribution to US life expectancy is so negative relative to that of America's peers. For starters, a high number of Americans – on average, about 40,000 a year – die on roadways. On a per-population basis, the US has more than twice the number of deaths as the European Union.[24] These deaths are overrepresented at the low end of the age distribution. The situation is deteriorating in the US, especially for certain subgroups; during the 2010s, for example, deaths of pedestrians in peer nations dropped 20 percent on average, while in the US they increased 46 percent.[25]

SLOW BORING (July 25, 2022), https://www.slowboring.com/p/tackling-americas-weirdly-short-life.

[18] Josh Zumbrun, *The (Surprisingly) Good News on Life Expectancy: It's Still Going Up*, WALL ST. J. (Dec. 15, 2023), https://www.wsj.com/health/healthcare/the-surprisingly-good-news-on-life-expectancy-its-still-going-up-239b6252; Emily Anthes & Benjamin Mueller, *U.S. Life Expectancy Creeps Up as Covid Deaths Fall*, N.Y. TIMES (Nov. 29, 2023), https://www.nytimes.com/2023/11/29/health/us-life-expectancy-covid-deaths.html.

[19] *See* Thompson, *supra* note 15.

[20] PYLL represents "a summary measure of premature mortality, providing an explicit way of weighting deaths occurring at younger ages, which may be preventable." Org. for Econ. Coop. & Dev., *OECD Data: Potential Years of Life Lost*, https://data.oecd.org/healthstat/potential-years-of-life-lost.htm#indicator-chart (accessed Dec. 17, 2023).

[21] *See id.*

[22] *Id.* (reporting statistics for PYLL).

[23] *Id.* (reporting statistics for PYLL).

[24] International Transport Forum, Org. for Econ. Coop. & Dev., *United States 1* (2019), https://www.itf-oecd.org/sites/default/files/united-states-road-safety.pdf (reporting figures for 2019).

[25] International Transport Forum, Org. for Econ. Coop. & Dev., *Road Safety Annual Report 2022*, at 35, https://www.itf-oecd.org/sites/default/files/docs/irtad-road-safety-annual-report-2022.pdf (reporting data for 2010–2019). This gap has widened since the onset of the pandemic. *See* Gregory H. Shill, *Regulating the Pedestrian Safety Crisis*, 97 N.Y.U. L. REV. ONLINE 194, 199–200 (2022).

One causal inference conundrum is that deaths per capita from a given activity are to an extent endogenous with the pervasiveness and intensity of the activity. Accordingly, researchers also sometimes consider deaths as a function of driving intensity, reported as vehicle miles traveled (VMT) per capita. Each year, by that measure, Americans travel in cars roughly two to four times the distance that residents of other high-income OECD countries do,[26] so – all else equal – one would expect more Americans to die in car crashes than their counterparts in peer countries. Historically this relationship explained a high percentage of elevated US roadway mortality (and, by extension, some of the life expectancy gap), but in this century the relationship has weakened somewhat as peers have cut deaths drastically while the US's VMT has grown only modestly and its traffic deaths remained elevated. In a recent three-year window, America's rate of per-capita deaths per VMT was 300 percent that of Norway, more than 200 percent that of the UK, Ireland, Switzerland, and Sweden, and about 165 percent that of Germany.[27] In other words, Americans do not simply die more on the roads because they drive more. The US road transportation system – a system that includes drivers, vehicles, and the roads themselves – claims more lives even on a VMT per-capita basis. The disproportionately young skew of roadway deaths converts this into a disproportionately high volume of PYLL.

20.1.2 *Maximizing the Value of Road Safety Interventions for Life Expectancy*

Organized national efforts to improve road safety in the US are at least a century old,[28] but success remains elusive for a variety of reasons, many of them legal and institutional.[29] A small package of high-value solutions would go a long way to reducing the drag that roadway mortality exerts on American life expectancy.

26 Cross-country comparisons are complicated by differences in data definitions and reporting, but these figures come from an estimate by the think tank Frontier Group that made an effort to account for these differences during the period 2011–2019. *See* Frontier Group, *Fact File: Americans Drive the Most* (Feb. 14, 2022), https://frontiergroup.org/resources/fact-file-americans-drive-most.

27 *Compare* International Transport Forum, *supra* note 24 (data for the US), *with* European Transport Safety Council, *Ranking EU Progress on Road Safety: 15th Road Safety Performance Index Report* 53 (2021), https://www.itf-oecd.org/sites/default/files/united-states-road-safety.pdf (data for European countries). Each of these reports measures deaths in vehicle kilometers traveled rather than VMT, but because they both use the metric denominator, the comparison's validity is unaffected.

28 *See Hoover Makes Plea for Traffic Safety*, N.Y. Times (Dec. 16, 1924) (discussing address by then Secretary of Commerce Herbert Hoover to the National Conference on Street and Highway Safety), https://www.nytimes.com/1924/12/16/archives/hoover-makes-plea-for-traffic-safety-forceful-corrective-action-is.html; Peter Norton, Fighting Traffic: The Dawn of the Motor Age in the American City (2008).

29 *See* Gregory H. Shill, *The Future of Law and Transportation*, 106 Iowa L. Rev. 2107 (2021); Shill, *supra* note 5; Jerry L. Mashaw & David L. Harfst, The Struggle for Auto Safety (1990).

Especially if the overall objective is to add years to US life expectancy, a major goal of safety measures must be to increase seatbelt use. In 2020, nearly half of all fatalities among US vehicle occupants were of people who were not wearing seat belts, and among the young these types of deaths are particularly prevalent.[30] After years of progress, restraint use has stalled, and a mix of enforcement (switching from secondary to primary enforcement, for example),[31] education, technology, and insurance incentives is probably needed to make further headway.

After decades of emphasizing personal responsibility as a route to improved safety, transportation agencies have in the past decade settled on a "safe system" approach that urges safer road designs – narrower or fewer vehicle lanes, protected bike lanes, traffic circles instead of conventional intersections – as a mechanism for improving outcomes. This approach, while important, is incomplete, and not only because physical design change is costly and requires navigating NIMBY ("not in my backyard") roadblocks:[32] It ignores the behavior of outliers – especially reckless drivers. It also overlooks the opportunity costs of forgoing incremental targeted changes in favor of wholesale physical transformation of the street. Given limited budgets and the imperative to save lives quickly, planners should reject design essentialism in favor of interventions that maximize the expected value of life-years saved per unit of time and money spent.

Speeding, for example, is associated with nearly one-third of traffic fatalities, about the same share as alcohol involvement.[33] While the latter generates considerable regulatory attention, speeding and other reckless behaviors do not attract the same opprobrium or official response. Most Americans don't drive double the speed limit or run red lights regularly, but there is reason to believe that the small minority who do are responsible for an outsize share of traffic fatalities. Their conduct should be a special focus of regulation.

Despite the obvious dangers connected to speed, populist opposition to enforcement of the speed laws is as old as speeding.[34] Creativity is needed to help defuse or sidestep this. Drivers could be required each year to buy a modestly priced bond (say $100) that is refundable conditional on an absence of grave speeding violations. (They could even be paid an above-market interest rate, subsidized by forfeited

[30] *See* Gregory H. Shill, *Transportation Safety in a Second-Best Environment*, Univ. of Minn. Ctr. for Transp. Stud., https://www.cts.umn.edu/research/featured/futureofmobility/shill (accessed Dec. 19, 2023) (collecting and analyzing National Highway Traffic Safety Administration data).

[31] *Id.*

[32] *See* Noah M. Kazis, *Transportation, Land Use, and the Sources of Hyper-Localism*, 106 Iowa L. Rev. 2339 (2021).

[33] Nat'l Safety Council, *Motor Vehicle Safety Issues: Speeding*, https://injuryfacts.nsc.org/motor-vehicle/motor-vehicle-safety-issues/speeding (accessed Dec. 21, 2023); Nat'l Safety Council, *Motor Vehicle Safety Issues: Alcohol Impaired Driving*, https://injuryfacts.nsc.org/motor-vehicle/motor-vehicle-safety-issues/alcohol-impaired-driving (accessed Dec. 21, 2023).

[34] *See* Sarah A. Seo, Policing the Open Road: How Cars Transformed American Freedom (2019).

bonds.) Or a portion of the revenue from speeding fines could be awarded to nonspeeding drivers – an experiment in Sweden doing just that yielded promising results by encouraging motorists to see safe driving as a possible economic windfall to them. Automated enforcement of speed limits and red lights, which have been shown to be effective at reducing serious crashes, should also be increased. Because they will help give back large numbers of life-years, prioritizing these and other reforms that reduce roadway mortality will have a disproportionately positive impact on life expectancy and open up the 100-year life to more Americans.

20.2 "GRAY TIEBOUT SORTING": A TRANSPORTATION-BASED RETIREE LOCATION MARKET

Although roadway fatalities and other causes of premature death restrict access to the 100-year life for many Americans, millions do enjoy extended longevity. Some projections suggest their ranks will swell in the coming years. Even among this fortunate group, however, many will not enjoy the full promise of their golden years because, nearly everywhere in the US, the built environment requires driving during a stage of life when driving is no longer safe. In fact, the season of life when those who live to 100 still have most of their faculties but can no longer drive safely is likely quite long – perhaps twenty years or more. To the extent that life expectancy climbs, the duration of this period will too.[35]

At present, the needs of Americans who outlive their ability to safely drive are underserved. A recent study concluded that "up to 60% of older adult drivers with mild cognitive impairment, and up to 30% with dementia, continue to drive,"[36] and fatal crash rates on a VMT basis "increase noticeably starting at age 70–74 and are highest among drivers 85 and older."[37] Because a fatal crash in old age does not take as many life-years as it does in youth, increasing older-driver safety, while imperative, will yield fewer dividends in terms of life expectancy. However, the prospect of extending and enhancing their independence will appeal to many seniors. Some would presumably be interested in ways of preserving their ability to access valued destinations later in life.

Recognition by local governments and developers of the benefits of increasing personal independence for seniors offers a way forward. This can mean many things. States like Florida, for example, famously offer master-planned retirement communities[38] that cater to the demands of retirees, including for

[35] As noted earlier, the period between the end of expected safe driving and expected lifespan was estimated early this century at seven to ten years on average; *see* Foley et al., *supra* note 4, and it is safe to assume that it grows as lifespan grows.

[36] Robert Toups et al., *Driving Performance in Older Adults: Current Measures, Findings, and Implications for Roadway Safety*, 6 Innovation in Aging 1, 1 (2022).

[37] *Id.* at 2. Elevated old-age mortality on the roads is likely attributable to a combination of causes, including increased physical vulnerability to trauma. *Id.*

[38] *See* Audra D. S. Burch, *The Villages, a Retirement Community in Florida, Was the Fastest-Growing Metro Area over the Last Decade*, N.Y. Times (Aug. 12, 2021), https://www.nytimes.com/2021/08/12/us/the-villages-census-florida-population.html.

independence.[39] Other localities and developers provide late-in-life independence through walkable dense areas, golf carts and shuttles (perhaps autonomous ones in the future[40]), and hyperlocal public or club amenities. So-called naturally occurring retirement communities in college towns, small cities, and some big-city neighborhoods provide access to a cluster of amenities without requiring a high degree of mobility. For municipalities, states, and developers, the financial benefits of attracting retirees are great, so in principle the incentives are already in place for what might be called transportation-based "gray Tiebout sorting."

The standard urban economics model of voting for local government services with one's feet is identified with an early exponent, Charles Tiebout.[41] Tiebout sorting posits the existence of a location market where individuals "move to the local government that best fits their preferences for public policies" through its particular mix of taxation and services.[42] Local governments offer different products – different bundles of services at different prices – that appeal to different location-consumers.[43] Locations that provide consistent access to desirable amenities in old age could (and to some extent already do) compete for a bigger slice of the retiree population pie. Although it targets movers, standard economic theory predicts that on the margin this process also benefits the great many retirees who prefer to stay put by exposing their localities to competition.

When it comes to transportation and land use, the challenge is not merely one of mobility – physical movement across space – but rather one known in the urban planning literature as accessibility,[44] which refers to connecting people with valued destinations. In the context of aging, this would allow them to continue to enjoy high quality of life and independence. These are high priorities for many retirees. As one indication, the AARP has taken up the cause of rating localities for their ability to "provide safe, walkable streets; age-friendly housing and transportation options; access to needed services; and opportunities for residents of all ages to

39 *See* Ira M. Sheskin, *Florida's Planned Retirement Communities: Marketing Age, Religion, Ethnicity and Lifestyle*, *in* ENGINEERING EARTH: THE IMPACTS OF MEGAENGINEERING PROJECTS (Stanley D. Brunn ed., 2010).

40 Planning for the 100-year life should not hinge on the development of automated vehicle technology, which, despite meaningful progress, remains experimental.

41 Tiebout, *supra* note 7.

42 *See* David Schleicher, *The City as a Law and Economic Subject*, U. ILL. L. REV. 1507, 1508 (2010) (summarizing Tiebout, *supra* note 7).

43 Robert M. Stein, *Tiebout's Sorting Hypothesis*, 23 URB. AFF. Q. 140, 157 n.2 (1987) ("A retired couple on a fixed income of $50,000 have different public-service demands than a family with the same income and two school-age children").

44 The concept of connecting people with valued destinations is known in urban planning parlance as accessibility. Jonathan Levine & Gregory H. Shill, *First Principles in Transportation Law and Policy*, *in* A RESEARCH AGENDA FOR US LAND USE AND PLANNING LAW (John Infranca & Sarah Schindler eds., 2023); JOE GRENGS, JONATHAN LEVINE & LOUIS A. MERLIN, FROM MOBILITY TO ACCESSIBILITY: TRANSFORMING URBAN TRANSPORTATION AND LAND-USE PLANNING (2019).

participate in community life" and introduced a Livability Index[45] to facilitate what might be called gray transportation-based Tiebout sorting.

The variety of ways to operationalize an independent lifestyle – mixed-use development, subsidized private shuttles, public transportation, greater access to delivery services, and so on – underscores the promise of the market metaphor. So does the potential of increased fiscal capacity for local governments and profits for private developers: For these players, retirees are in many ways an ideal group. They have assets and bring revenue in the form of property, consumption, and income taxes[46] but tend to underconsume widely subscribed local resources relative to their numbers. They do not attend or send their children to public schools. Meanwhile the cost of the services that they draw on disproportionately – physicians and hospitals, assisted living facilities – is borne primarily by the users themselves or by third-party payors like the federal government or private insurers. Others, like public libraries and parks, are provided at a relatively fixed cost such that increasing their use intensity is fiscally neutral.

Independence is only one component of the retiree location decision.[47] There is reason to believe, however, that seniors place an unusually high value on sustaining independent mobility in their final years (or, increasingly, decades) – and that doing so is necessary for maintaining access to essentials like medical appointments and food. Making changes to the transportation–land use bundle requires reform of both law and policy,[48] which runs into a thicket of Catch-22s. It is hard to make the case for public transit in an area that lacks the density to support it, but it is hard to grow the necessary density in an area that outlaws it through restrictive zoning or excessive parking requirements.[49] The market for retiree location offers a plausible mechanism to help resolve this.

[45] *See AARP Livable Communities: About*, AARP, https://www.aarp.org/livable-communities/about (accessed Dec. 21, 2023).

[46] Among states with an income tax, some tax Social Security income and distributions of tax-deferred retirement accounts like 401(k)s and traditional IRAs in whole or in part. *See* Katelyn Washington, *Taxes in Retirement: How All 50 States Tax Retirees*, Kiplinger (Oct. 30, 2023), https://www.kiplinger.com/retirement/602202/taxes-in-retirement-how-all-50-states-tax-retirees.

[47] *See* William Duncombe, Mark Robbins & Douglas A. Wolf, *Chasing the Elderly: Can State and Local Governments Attract Recent Retirees?* Ctr. for Pol'y Rsch. (Sep. 2000), https://surface.syr.edu/cgi/viewcontent.cgi?article = 1450&context = cpr.

[48] Examples of arguments in favor of law reform to facilitate mobility later in life include Michael Pollack & Lior Strahilevitz, *Property Law for the Ages*, 63 Wm. & Mary L. Rev. 561 (2021); Anne L. Alstott, *Lecture, A New Deal for Old Age*, 97 B.U. L. Rev. 1933 (2017); Katharine Silbaugh, *Distinguishing Households from Families*, 45 Fordham Urb. L.J. 1071, 1095–1097 (2016); and Israel Doron, *Municipal Elder Law: An Exercise in Legal Futurism*, 37 Wm. Mitchell. L. Rev. 80, 94 (2010).

[49] For more on the land use dimension of transportation reform, *see* Shill, *supra* note 5, at 535–555, and David Schleicher, *How Land Use Law Impedes Transportation Innovation*, *in* Evidence and Innovation in Housing Law and Policy (Lee Anne Fennell & Benjamin J. Keys eds., 2017).

Economists have observed that the quality of local amenities explains some of the housing price premium in high-amenity areas over and above differences in the opportunity to increase earnings.[50] A market for retiree location might be able to harness the same types of forces that render certain neighborhoods desirable to a particular demographic cohort. Just as some areas appeal to young professionals or families, others appeal to retirees. A deep market that offers a variety of ways of providing older residents ready access to amenities could stimulate intralocal or within-metropolitan competition for retiree market share. It might even be able to do this to a degree that generates spillover benefits to the general population. A catalyst of this sort might help areas that have struggled to overcome the inertia of the twentieth-century automobile planning paradigm to up their game.

A retiree location market already exists, and growing attention to longevity can provide a framework within which it can be cultivated further by profit-driven and public-minded forces alike. Not many places offer meaningful alternatives to automobility, and even doing so within a concentrated area requires combating decades of entrenched policy.[51] This is what makes the promise of the retiree location market intriguing: the potential for an efficient alignment of incentives. A well-defined cohort and geographic area lend themselves to narrower matching of services to needs. In the simplest case, a single owner, such as a private developer, stands to internalize the benefits of investment in accessibility-driven independence. In a more typical case, a small number of owners, some private and others public, may be able to coalesce around a common goal of improving accessibility within a given area. Many ingredients of success are present.

20.3 CONCLUSION

Broadly, extended longevity poses two policy challenges: making it feasible in the first place and enabling those who achieve it to thrive. Transportation policy is central to meeting both challenges.

In order to increase access to the 100-year life, it should be the policy of the US at all levels of government to grow life expectancy. There are many worthy ways to do that; this chapter emphasizes road safety interventions that target high-mortality crash factors – including failure to wear seat belts (associated with about half of crash deaths), speeding (about a third), and drunk driving (same). Each of these factors claims a disproportionate number of young lives, which means improving outcomes will reap outsize gains in life expectancy. They can also be rolled out in relatively quick and low-cost ways, using proven and experimental interventions that

[50] *See* Edward L. Glaeser, Jed Kolko & Albert Saiz, *Consumer City*, 1 J. ECON. GEOG. 27 (2001).

[51] *See* Shill, *supra* note 5, at 541 (contending that Tiebout sorting tends to be ineffective where a given locational attribute, such as automobility, is one that "a consumer-voter cannot move away from").

maximize gains in life expectancy by targeting those roadway behaviors that rob Americans of the most life-years. This focus may sound like common sense, but it rejects the fad of design essentialism that has swept roadway reformers in the past decade.

At the other end of the age distribution, a focus on helping seniors maintain access to valued destinations can enhance quality of life in the golden years. If local governments and property developers approach hyperlocal goods with the challenge of golden-years mobility in mind, they can stimulate transportation-based gray Tiebout sorting: residential self-selection by older Americans into locations that maximize mobility and independence. This, in turn, can create pressure on other places to increase their offerings. Thus, while skepticism is warranted about the potential for transportation-based Tiebout sorting in general, there are good reasons to expect one aspect of it – sustained independence past the age when one can drive safely – to hold more promise for some retirees.

21

Property and the 100-Year Life

Taisu Zhang

This chapter examines how property regimes are likely to respond to the significant increase in average life expectancy predicted by "100-year life" theories. It takes a relatively pessimistic position, arguing that the optimal institutional response to demographic aging will be very difficult to produce: Some countries, most notably the US, are likely to underrespond to the socioeconomic demands that demographic aging will probably impose on property law, whereas others, such as China and Japan, may well overrespond. This is because, within the realm of property rights and regulation, the economics and politics of demographic aging may well contradict each other: Aging potentially reinforces political opposition to public governance even as it creates economic demand for it.

21.1 SOCIAL MODELS OF THE "100-YEAR LIFE"

The first step of any intellectual exercise on the legal impact of a "100-year life" should, of course, be to unpack what such a significant gain in life expectancy would mean in broader socioeconomic terms. A society in which the top-income classes live on average to 100, but lower-income classes live only to seventy-five – which is increasingly where the US is headed[1] – obviously would have fundamentally different structural problems and institutional needs than one in which most people's life expectancy rises into the nineties – Japan, for example, seems headed more in this direction.[2] Furthermore, an aging society that is also shrinking in total population has a completely different set of problems than one that is demographically stable or expanding.

To make this exercise manageable, this chapter will focus on one specific set of circumstances: a society that is seeing life expectancy increase significantly across the board and that does not demographically contract. With some exceptions, most

[1] Aaron O'Neill, *Life Expectancy in the United States, 1860–2020*, Statista (June 21, 2022), https://www.statista.com/statistics/1040079/life-expectancy-united-states-all-time.

[2] Shoichiro Tsugane, *Why Has Japan Become the World's Most Long-Lived Country: Insights from a Food and Nutrition Perspective*, 75 Eur. J. Clinical Nutrition 921 (2021).

developed countries have yet to experience outright demographic contraction despite significant aging and may not experience it even in the future if they can sustain a reasonable amount of immigration.[3] Some of these societies also have a strong-enough welfare system that life expectancy gains are distributed somewhat equitably across economic classes – although many, including the US, do not.[4] The great majority of developing countries, in contrast, continue to expand demographically while seeing life expectancy increase across nearly all social classes. In other words, they age while not necessarily becoming smaller.

Under these general circumstances, the total amount of resources needed to sustain a society will increase if and only if aging dovetails with population growth, but the consumption and possession of those resources will inevitably shift toward the older end of the population. The ramifications of such a shift for general socioeconomic inequality are unclear:[5] On the one hand, longer life expectancy may increase economic inequality within age cohorts by amplifying the consequences of differences in physical endowment, intelligence, education, and inherited wealth. On the other, societal aging could also increase the economic returns to labor relative to capital and, therefore, reduce inequality.

Regardless of which of these scenarios materializes, an aging population will probably produce significant socioeconomic demand for urbanization and public infrastructure. Unless there is some fundamental breakthrough in medical technology, older populations will require more medical care than younger ones, even if they are not necessarily any less economically productive. Given that there are still enormous economies of scale in the provision of medical care, all else being equal, longer life expectancy will probably lead to more urbanization over the long run, which, all else being equal, will produce greater functional demand for public infrastructure.[6]

3 *See*, e.g., the European Union's ability to maintain low levels of population growth despite aging. Guillaume Marois et al., *Population Aging, Migration, and Productivity in Europe*, 117 PNAS 7690 (2020). The US also continues to expand demographically. *US Census: Five Key Takeaways on Population Trends*, BBC (April 26, 2021), https://www.bbc.com/news/world-us-canada-56896154.

4 Gary Burtless, *The Growing Life-Expectancy Gap between Rich and Poor*, BROOKINGS INST. (Feb. 22, 2016), https://www.brookings.edu/opinions/the-growing-life-expectancy-gap-between-rich-and-poor.

5 Xudong Chen et al., *Population Aging and Inequality: Evidence from the People's Republic of China* (Asian Dev. Bank Inst. Working Paper No. 794, 2017).

6 Donald O. Cowgill, *The Aging of Populations and Societies*, 415 ANNALS AM. ACAD. POL. & SOC. SCI. 1 (1974); Fabiane Ribeiro Ferreira et al., *Aging and Urbanization: The Neighborhood Perception and Functional Performance of Elderly Persons in Belo Horizonte Metropolitan Area: Brazil*, 87 J. URB. HEALTH 54 (2010); Theresa Grafeneder-Weissteiner et al., *Three Pillars of Urbanization: Migration, Aging, and Growth*, 168 DE ECON. 259 (2020); Louise Plouffe & Alexandre Kalache, *Towards Global Age-Friendly Cities: Determining Urban Features that Promote Active Aging*, 87 J. URB. HEALTH 733 (2010).

At the same time, longer life expectancy means that a smaller share of an individual's life will be spent living with his or her parents. In other words, older populations will likely consist of more households than younger ones – unless, of course, a significant share of elderly people move back in with their middle-aged children, which is rarely the case in developed countries and significantly less likely to be the case in developing countries now than it was several decades ago. This will produce greater demand for housing units in general, but perhaps less demand for large, single-family homes. There are obvious synergies between both of these trends and the aforementioned demand for urbanization.

All of these likely developments will place some institutional demands on property law, and particularly on its land-use subcomponents. Urbanization, demographic density, and housing unit availability are all intimately supported or constrained by various property rights systems, and any significant and durable shift in them will require corresponding adjustments in those systems. For the most part, a shift toward greater density and higher levels of urbanization will probably generate higher levels of socioeconomic demand for more "publicness" in property institutions, but not all legal systems will respond to this demand in a positive manner – and it is not even clear that it is always normatively desirable for them to do so.

21.2 PROPERTY REGIME TYPES

Property regimes deal with the demands of resource allocation and demographic management though varying levels of centralized regulation and private self-governance. Nearly all regimes make some use of both, but the specific combination differs sharply from country to country and region to region. On one end are highly centralized regimes, most often seen in smaller, more concentrated jurisdictions – Singapore may be closest of any country to this ideal type[7] – that rely primarily on state-driven planning and rule-making. In such regimes, the state enjoys high administrative and legal capacity within its geographical boundaries and, therefore, can regulate and control property relationships in relatively granular, socioeconomically contextualized ways through a combination of laws, rules, and executive actions. Scholars have sometimes labeled these "governance"-type regimes.[8]

Several East and Southeast Asian countries take a governance-oriented approach to property law. Land use in Japanese cities, for example, is controlled by a top-down yet nonetheless highly detailed legal structure in which the central government possesses ultimate authority over all local laws and regulations.[9] Much of this

7 *See*, e.g., ANNE HAILA, URBAN LAND RENT: SINGAPORE AS A PROPERTY STATE (2015).

8 Henry E. Smith, *Exclusion versus Governance: Two Strategies for Delineating Property Rights*, 31 J. LEGAL STUD. 453 (2002).

9 Byron Shibata, *Land-Use Law in the United States and Japan: A Fundamental Overview and Comparative Analysis*, 10 WASH. U. J.L. & POL'Y 161 (2002).

authority is delegated to lower-level governments, allowing for finessed adjustments based on local conditions, but there is a substantial amount of procedural uniformity throughout the system. Although the vast majority of property is indeed privately owned, the state, rather than private entities, supplies the lion's share of property and land-use institutions, enjoying very robust regulatory powers.

Despite being a theoretically "socialist" legal system in which the state nominally owns all nonrural land, the Chinese property system shares a large amount of functional common ground with the Japanese system: Land use rights are privately owned, used, and alienated, but laws and regulations govern these activities with very high levels of granularity, right down to exercising direct oversight over many homeowners' associations.[10] Private property owners are compensated for government expropriation but generally not for regulatory interference.[11] Given China's enormous size, there is significantly more regional institutional variation than one finds in Japan, but such variation stems primarily from provincial and local state activity rather than from self-governance by nonstate actors. More recently, the coronavirus pandemic has only seemed to strengthen the state's presence in and control over nearly all facets of urban life.

These institutional features carry substantial benefits but also major costs. On the one hand, they allow legal systems to effectively respond to market failures and impose public solutions for socioeconomic problems that belie private management. This is particularly valuable in urban settings where high population density and its socioeconomic consequences often require robust state action. It is no coincidence that East and Southeast Asia are now home to both a disproportionately high number of the world's largest – and often richest – megacities and some of the most aggressive and powerful property governance regimes. There is a strong functional correlation between the two. On the other hand, expansive governance powers can also be misused, leading to high levels of corruption and, occasionally, severe systemic misallocation of resources: China's often wasteful urban development over the past three decades is perhaps the most economically visible example of this.[12]

On the other end of the spectrum are weak state capacity regimes – relatively speaking, at least – in which the state lacks the ability to intervene effectively at the granular level and instead supplies a simple legal regime that provides a basic and highly standardized allocation of private rights and obligations upon which nongovernmental actors can layer supplementary social norms and self-governance institutions. Because the simplest and most effective basic allocation tends to be

[10] https://www.ft.com/content/efda9a15-13ae-4709-b741-e4f3599f431d; Shitong Qiao, The Authoritarian Commons: Divergent Paths of Neighborhood Democratization in Beijing, Shanghai and Shenzhen (in-progress book manuscript) (on file with author).

[11] Li Ping, Rural Dev. Inst., The Impact of Regulatory Takings by the Chinese State on Rural Land Tenure and Property Rights (2007).

[12] Yiping Xiao et al., *How Far Has China's Urbanization Gone?* 10 Sustainability 2953 (2018).

one that predominantly relies on private ownership, backed by strong rights of exclusion, these legal regimes are sometimes called "exclusion regimes."[13] One of the most prominent examples in the modern world is the US.

American property law and land-use law have historically been constructed around a fundamentally privatized paradigm, specifically, a fee-simple paradigm that is rooted in private land ownership by socioeconomically independent single-family households. American law therefore prioritizes private security, clarity of rights and obligations, and legal standardization over finessed governance.[14] Under this paradigm, property owners typically possess strong and clear rights of exclusion against trespassers of all kinds, sometimes backed by the right to claim exorbitant amounts of punitive damages against intentional trespassers. Governmental expropriation of land is, as a rule, both legally complicated and financially costly.

American property owners enjoy relatively expansive freedom to use their land as they please, only constrained by a relatively limited set of state-imposed usage regulations – for which the state must sometimes offer compensation, private covenants and easements, and a functionally unwieldy nuisance law.[15] The latter, in cases where neighboring property owners engage in mutually incompatible uses, typically grants legal priority to the highest value use through an amorphous balancing test. Finally, there are relatively few legal constraints on property alienation, allowing for a largely free and open real estate market. All three of these "sticks" – strong exclusion rights, relatively unconstrained use rights, and free alienation rights – are usually wrapped in a uniform fee-simple parcel that grants a single household perpetual and undivided ownership over a spatially condensed property parcel, usually a piece of land.

This kind of exclusion-oriented paradigm originated in a historical sociolegal context in which land was relatively plentiful and, therefore, cheap and sparsely populated: Due to a combination of relatively low population density and constant westward expansion, property law in the early American republic was often constructed without the kinds of scarcity rationales that drove – plagued, perhaps – contemporary European and Asian legal systems.[16] The abundance of arable land, often seized through armed conflict with indigenous peoples, meant that the law

[13] Smith, *supra* note 8.

[14] ERIC T. FREYFOGLE, ON PRIVATE PROPERTY: FINDING COMMON GROUND ON THE OWNERSHIP OF LAND (2007); David L. Callies and J. David Breemer, *The Right to Exclude Others from Private Property: A Fundamental Constitutional Right*, 3 WASH. U. J. L. & POL'Y 39 (2000); Larissa Katz, *Exclusion and Exclusivity in Property Law*, 58 U. TORONTO L.J. 275 (2008). *See also* the debate between Gregory Alexander and Henry Smith over how exclusion-oriented American property law is. Gregory S. Alexander, *The Social-Obligation Norm in American Property Law*, 94 CORNELL L. REV. 745 (2009); Henry E. Smith, *Mind the Gap: The Indirect Relation between Ends and Means in American Property Law*, 94 CORNELL L. REV. 959 (2009).

[15] Robert C. Ellickson, *Alternatives to Zoning: Covenants, Nuisance Rules, and Fines as Land Use Controls*, 40 U. CHI. L. REV. 681 (1973).

[16] *E.g.*, John G. Sprankling, *The Antiwilderness Bias in American Property Law*, 63 U. CHI. L. REV. 519 (1996).

could operate in general and relatively standardized terms without risking either significant loss of economic efficiency or grave sociopolitical tension over resource distribution and use. This allowed it to coalesce around a largely unified paradigm of private ownership and control, with weak constraints on usage rights and a comparatively limited role for the state.

Such a paradigm could no longer function well once the population became increasingly urbanized over the course of the late nineteenth and early twentieth centuries. The density of urban populations and the inherently greater need for public infrastructure in cities meant that the state had to take a more active role in property and land-use regulation, which eventually led to the rise of urban zoning in the 1920s. Even after these developments, however, American urban property regulation remained substantially more decentralized and privatized – more exclusion-oriented, in other words – compared to more governance-oriented legal systems. To this day, there is relatively little centralized rule-making or legislation, with cities, towns, and counties doing most of the regulatory work without top-down guidance.[17] Beyond that, an enormous swathe of socioeconomic rules come from private contracting and governance: homeowners' associations, condominium associations, cooperatives, corporations, and the like.[18]

This kind of institutional structure not only produces large amounts of regional variance but also gives abnormally large amounts of regulatory power to long-term local property owners, often at the expense of shorter-term residents, especially tenants. It therefore facilitates significant levels of NIMBYism ("not in my back yard"-ism), which aims to keep real estate scarce and local property values high, even if doing so produces serious housing shortages and escalating inequality.[19] This long-term owner-centric political economy functionally dovetails with the broader exclusion orientation of American property law, further privileging private control over public governance.

21.3 AGING, URBANIZATION, AND PROPERTY

One might imagine that demographic aging and the greater urban density it will likely create will exert a largely uniform force on property institutions – in favor of public governance and away from privatized exclusion – but that would be an oversimplification. It is almost certainly true that aging and urbanization will create greater functional demand for public governance, but it is unclear whether legal systems will actually respond to this demand. The political economy of aging may well prevent exclusion-oriented systems like the American one from breaking free of

[17] *See* SONIA A. HIRT, ZONED IN THE USA: THE ORIGINS AND IMPLICATIONS OF AMERICAN LAND-USE REGULATION (2015).

[18] Ellickson, *supra* note 15.

[19] David Schleicher, *City Unplanning*, 122 YALE L.J. 1670 (2012).

institutional path dependence. At the other end of the spectrum, although governance-oriented regimes will probably be able to ramp up governance and public legal infrastructure in response to demographic aging, there is also a distinct danger that they will do so too aggressively.

Consider first the range of possible political consequences of demographic aging in a democratic, relatively decentralized, exclusion-oriented system like the US: An aging population is not merely one that requires more health care and public goods but also one that will likely experience significant changes in political orientation and composition. Two specific changes are especially relevant for property governance: first, older populations are, all other things being equal, somewhat more conservative than younger ones, particularly with regard to property rights.[20] This may amplify resistance to public governance in societies that are politically conditioned to mistrust state authority. Second, older populations are also somewhat less geographically mobile ones,[21] which means that political capture by NIMBYism could worsen under some conditions.

The connection between aging and political conservatism is a fairly well-documented phenomenon. As people age and accumulate wealth, they often have more to lose from radical political and legal change and are, therefore, inclined to support stability over change, risk aversion over risk-taking – the very definition of Burkean conservatism. In particular, their relatively larger amounts of private wealth create stronger demand for secure and legally unburdened private property rights. The fact that most people will have exhausted their potential for upward socioeconomic mobility by middle age further intensifies this demand: If I feel there is no longer much room for me to rise on the socioeconomic ladder, but a significant amount of room to fall, then I will likely become more risk-averse and, therefore, more jealously protective of what I already have. Moreover, given that older generations naturally hold – relative to their demographic share – a disproportionately large share of societal wealth,[22] they are also less likely to be pro-redistribution than younger generations. These tendencies do not imply that older populations will necessarily become significantly more conservative across *all* ideological dimensions, but to the extent that property rights are a politically salient issue, they will likely lean toward classical conservative positions of strong private property rights and limited state intervention even if they lean liberal on other issues like race or gender.

[20] Norval D. Glenn, *Aging and Conservatism*, 415 ANNALS AM. ACAD. POL. & SOC. SCI. 176 (1974); Johnathan C. Peterson et al., *Do People Really Become More Conservative as They Age?* 82 J. POL. (2020).

[21] Anzelika Zaiceva, *The Impact of Aging on the Scale of Migration*, IZA WORLD LAB. (Nov. 2014).

[22] Guillaume Vandenbroucke & Heting Zhu, *Aging and Wealth Inequality*, ECON. SYNOPSES 2 (2017).

These inclinations are likely more powerful in societies like the US that have deep sociopolitical traditions of "state skepticism."[23] The relative lack, both historical and contemporary, of resource scarcity and high population density in the US meant that it could do without robust top-down governance for long periods of time – and that robust top-down governance was substantially more difficult to establish. Coupled with long-standing ideological inclinations toward decentralization and deregulation, these socioeconomic conditions render the American legal system inherently more hospitable to conservative-leaning positions on property rights and exclusion and, therefore, amplify the political influence of such trends whenever they emerge.

Furthermore, because demographic aging also tends to concentrate wealth in the hands of senior generations, it also grants them higher levels of sociopolitical status, often at a considerable cost to younger generations. In particular, unless significantly increased inheritance taxes get in the way, longer life expectancy naturally enhances the socioeconomic significance of inheritance, which increases intergenerational economic dependency, thereby further boosting the sociopolitical status of the elderly – a form of economically enhanced gerontocracy.[24] In other words, if demographic aging is the driving factor, then not only will the ideological composition of a society trend toward conservatism, but the political power of its more conservative components will also increase. Combined, these forces can easily produce an ideological swing that reinforces any preexisting institutional bias toward exclusion and privatization.

The impact of demographic aging on property is therefore inherently complex, perhaps even self-contradictory: At the economic level, it produces major demand-side pressures and incentives in favor of public governance, but at the political and ideological level, it will also produce significant trends that instead favor private exclusion. Now, one could argue that the former will, over the long run, produce changes in political perception that eventually neutralize the latter – that elderly property owners will eventually embrace the societal and personal need for more governance, given that they are some of the primary beneficiaries of it – but this assumes a fairly primitive version of economic determinism. In fact, it is not even clear that the economic calculus for senior property owners will be perfectly aligned in favor of governance: Seniors may have much to gain from stronger public governance, but by virtue of their stronger economic position, they also have less

[23] Andrew Fiala, *Political Skepticism and Anarchist Themes in the American Tradition*, Eur. J. Pragmatism & Am. Phil. 2 (2013); Matt Grossmann, *Americans Are Skeptical of the Government: Except When There's a Crisis*, FiveThirtyEight (Apr. 15, 2020).

[24] This is contested, but most studies seem to favor a positive correlation between aging and the importance of inheritance. *See* Harun Onder & Pierre Pestieau, *Inherited Wealth and Demographic Aging* (World Bank Pol'y Rsch. Working Paper No. 7739, 2016); Thomas Piketty & Gabriel Zucman, *Wealth and Inheritance in the Long Run*, *in* Handbook of Income Distribution 1303 (Anthony B. Atkinson and François Bourguignon eds., 2015).

to lose from sticking to an exclusion-oriented legal paradigm. As a result, the economic costs of indulging their ideological and political preferences are not necessarily that large.

Given this inherent political complexity, instead of seeing a universal shift toward governance as societies age, we may simply experience another couple of decades of institutional path dependency. There are at least two different ways to understand this: First, the relatively complicated bundle of institutional incentives that demographic aging produces, in which economics and politics have a tendency to cancel each other out, makes it somewhat less likely that the political benefits of a progovernance shift in property law will be large enough to clearly outweigh the costs of large-scale institutional change. Institutional inertia is, as scholars have long recognized, an inherently self-reinforcing force: It is always costly to overturn a long-standing institutional paradigm, both because of the administrative costs necessary for institutional change and because of the economic uncertainty it unavoidably generates.[25]

These costs are especially strong and salient in the context of property law: More so than other parts of the legal system, and perhaps even more so than other components of private law, property law places an enormous functional premium on institutional stability and economic predictability.[26] Given that property rights constitute the legal foundation of almost any economic exchange and any attempt to utilize an economic resource, any changes to property institutions are systemically magnified through the layers of contracting, tort rights, or organizational governance that are built upon that foundation. Reliance interests are therefore unusually strong in property law, both descriptively and normatively, even by the standards of private law. An exclusion-oriented property law may or may not be functionally superior to a governance-oriented one, depending on the socioeconomic context, but an institutionally stable property law is almost always functionally superior to a constantly changing one. As a result, property law tends to be unusually path-dependent, usually requiring an unusually large amount of political force to generate paradigmatic change. Demographic aging, with all its internal sociopolitical contradictions, is not especially likely to satisfy this requirement.

Second, how the institutional politics of aging play out in any specific society will depend heavily on what kind of political priors and leanings it carries into the process: In all likelihood, societies that are already institutionally and politically conditioned to favor exclusion over governance will likely assign greater amounts of perceived salience to the political costs discussed above, and less to the economic benefits; whereas those that are institutionally predisposed toward governance will

[25] Mariana Prado & Michael Trebilcock, *Path Dependence, Development, and the Dynamics of Institutional Reform*, 59 U. Toronto L.J. 341 (2009).

[26] Carol M. Rose, *Crystals and Mud in Property Law*, 40 Stan. L. Rev. 577 (1988); Henry E. Smith & Thomas W. Merrill, *Optimal Standardization in the Law of Property: The Numerus Clausus Principle*, 110 Yale L.J. 1 (2000).

likely do the opposite. When there are strong and complex forces both for and against an institutional change, which side wins out in the end will often depend on perception rather than objective significance – and therefore be subject to significant confirmation and framing biases that generally work in favor of path dependence.

To illustrate how these dynamics might play out in real life, consider what could happen if the US population reaches an average life expectancy of around ninety years in the near future – from around seventy-eight currently. Such a leap might seem overly optimistic given the stagnation and even decline of this statistic in recent years, but the country has experienced large gains in life expectancy after decades of stagnation before: From 1950 to 1970, American male life expectancy stagnated at around sixty-seven, and then leaped to seventy-three by 1990, and then to current levels by around 2008.[27] Imagine, then, a qualitatively similar but quantitatively more robust demographic trend emerging on the back of biomedical breakthroughs over the next two or three decades.

The last time this "sort of" happened, American politics underwent the Nixon era and the "Reagan Revolution," ending up, in most parts of the country, with a more conservative property regime that undid at least some of the progress toward fair housing and aggressive land-use regulation that had marked the 1960s.[28] Private exclusion never gave way to public governance as the population aged, and if anything, the trend was in the opposite direction. Demographic aging may well have had something to do with this: Even as younger, more mobile demographics flocked into large cities, older groups of long-term homeowners managed to successfully combat a considerable share of proposed public development projects and maintain privatized control over most parts of major American cities like New York and San Francisco.[29] Ironically, all of these cities are highly liberal in basic political orientation but nonetheless persistently conservative in how they have handled land-use regulation and property development.

History may well repeat itself if the American population undergoes yet another major round of aging: The elder generations in society, now more populous than they have ever been, flock to cities, towns, or the suburbs of major metropolitan centers in search of better health care, and as they do so, they are often wealthy enough to purchase title to property rather than rent. This drives up urban property prices, much to the delight of local property owners, new and old. When the city government attempts to construct affordable housing to accommodate the younger working population, which is increasingly being priced out of the real estate market, property owners rebel and manage to stall most of the projects. Infrastructure

27 Maureen Stanley, *1900–2000: Changes in Life Expectancy in the United States*, SENIOR LIVING (Dec. 21, 2023).

28 *See*, e.g., David A. Super, *The Rise and Fall of the Implied Warranty of Habitability*, 99 CALIF. L. REV. 389 (2011).

29 *E.g.*, Schleicher, *supra* note 19.

development meets with similar obstacles insofar as it requires some expropriation of private property, but homeowners are willing to pay the price of mediocre infrastructure if it means keeping the government away from their property assets, which are increasingly important to them as they age and become more reliant – both economically and psychologically – on those assets. In the end, the US becomes even more urbanized, but without any corresponding expansion in governmental regulatory authority or taking powers and without the expansion of affordable housing needed to ward off gentrification and escalating socioeconomic inequality, both of which intensify in the aftermath.

Contrast this with what might happen – indeed, has already happened – in an aging but governance-oriented society like China or Japan: Once demographic aging becomes a sociopolitically salient issue, multiple layers of government will likely claim that it presents societal challenges of caregiving and health services that can only be solved through public coordination and infrastructural renewal. This will give them political cover to pursue large-scale construction projects in metropolitan centers to accommodate the demographic influx into cities, and also to redraw land-use regulations to create the institutional space for those projects. The former will almost certainly require heavy use of eminent domain, which will in turn create political opportunities to expand that power and reduce the bargaining power of private property owners. In fact, the expansion of government regulatory and expropriation powers in urban centers is more or less what has already happened in Japan over the past two or three decades,[30] and is also what has been happening in China in the past five to ten years.[31] In the latter case, demographic aging only became a highly salient sociopolitical issue in the past decade, which has coincided with a partial reversal of the privatization and market-oriented property law reforms that characterized the 1990s and early 2000s. Instead, most Chinese cities now seem to be moving toward a property rights regime in which the government exercises tighter regulation over both land use and transfer and also continues to expropriate land with high regularity.

These measures have met with some resistance from urban homeowners, who have occasionally spoken out – or taken even more dramatic measures – against what they perceive as governmental encroachment on their rights and, perhaps more importantly, on the economic value of those rights.[32] Even so, their actions seem to have produced very limited concessions from the state, even before the COVID-19 pandemic made the expansion of state control all but irresistible in

30 Daisuke Akimoto, *Does Japan Need to Control Land Purchases by Foreigners?* DIPLOMAT (Mar. 23, 2021); Stephen Hesse, *New Land Law Still Ignores Public Voice*, JAPAN TIMES (Apr. 26, 2001); André Sorensen, *Land, Property Rights, and Planning in Japan: Institutional Design and Institutional Change in Land Management*, 25 PLAN. PERSPS. 279 (2010).

31 Wenjing Han et al., *Land Use Regulation and Urban Land Value: Evidence from China*, 92 LAND USE POL'Y 104432 (2020).

32 QIAO, *supra* note 10.

nearly every East and Southeast Asian country. There was, and is, no clear sociopolitical consensus in favor of shielding private ownership rights from state authority in many of these societies, some of which have clearly favored statist solutions to socioeconomic problems for decades. Once demographic aging becomes firmly embedded into political discourse and its economic effects are made clearer, it may even produce strong bottom-up social demand for more state intervention – which would likely baffle American property owners.

These sociopolitical conditions will almost certainly allow governance-oriented regimes to more robustly address the economic challenges of demographic aging than their exclusion-oriented peers, but that may very well prove to be a mixed blessing. In regimes where the accountability of government officials is relatively low and social distrust of them is relatively high, further expansion of public governance may lead to unsustainably high levels of corruption and eventually to strong public dissatisfaction. Moreover, too much state intervention is a distinct possibility in some of these regimes: State control and regulation is all too often an inherently self-reinforcing thing and could easily snowball in suboptimal ways if left to its own devices.

This can happen through at least two different mechanisms: First, government officials may simply enjoy the status and power that an expansion of governmental authority gives – including, perhaps, the rent-seeking opportunities it creates – and therefore seek more of it. As their power grows, it becomes more and more difficult to keep their self-interest in check, until eventually the system arrives at a breaking point. Second, and somewhat less nefariously, more state regulation may erode the self-governance and self-regulation capacity of some local communities: Neighborhoods or villages that previously produced robust social norms and covenants become reliant on the state for the regulation and coordination of socioeconomic behavior.[33] This produces even more demand for state intervention, which then erodes social institutions even further, generating a vicious cycle of constant governmental expansion. By creating strong demand for public goods and infrastructure that only the state can effectively provide, demographic aging could potentially set off either of these processes – or both – thereby producing too much state control over the long run.

China is arguably in the early stages of this: Over the past decade, the government has consistently expanded its regulatory and planning powers, often at significant cost to social or communal institutions like residents' associations.[34] Increasingly, it sees almost any type of social self-governance as a threat to its control and has attempted to formalize such self-governance into the state apparatus more fully.[35]

[33] For an illustration of these dynamics, *see*, e.g., JOEL S. MIGDAL, STRONG SOCIETIES AND WEAK STATES (1989).

[34] *See*, e.g., QIAO, *supra* note 10; Han et al., *supra* note 31.

[35] ELIZABETH ECONOMY, THE THIRD REVOLUTION: XI JINPING AND THE NEW CHINESE STATE (2015); Sangkuk Lee, *An Institutional Analysis of Xi Jinping's Centralization of Power*, 26 J. CONTEMP. CHINA 325 (2017).

While it is still too early to tell whether these trends will lead to measurable overregulation, things certainly seem to be headed in that direction. At the very least, it is extremely difficult to imagine how, under present circumstances, the expansion of state control can be halted, let alone reversed, which would seem to suggest that, if there is such a thing as too much governance, then China currently seems to be as good a candidate to eventually reach it as any in the modern world.

21.4 CONCLUSION

This chapter has discussed some possible property law and land-use regulation scenarios that could potentially emerge in response to certain forms of demographic aging. Regardless of the plausibility of its factual assumptions, it has attempted to tease out some of the likely interactions between demographics, economic demand, and political composition and to show that the economics and politics of demographic aging may well contradict each other when it comes to property law. The most likely institutional outcome therefore seems to be path-dependent: Countries that are currently exclusion-oriented will continue to be exclusion-oriented, and therefore underrespond to the economic demands of aging. In contrast, countries that are already governance-oriented will likely become even more so, to the point where overgovernance becomes a distinct possibility. The ideal balance between these two poles, like any optimal political economic equilibrium, may well prove highly elusive.

22

Scaling Down Senior Living

The Postpandemic Future of Housing for Elderly People

Joanna L. Martin and Lior Jacob Strahilevitz

There is a striking mismatch in contemporary society between the types of housing that elderly residents want and what the market delivers to them. Overwhelmingly, older Americans say they want to age in place. And if they must leave their current homes, most would like to stay in a home-like environment proximate enough to their present home to keep their existing social networks intact. In this chapter we examine legal rules that thwart the wishes of so many seniors to age in place and reside in homes that feel more residential than institutional. As recent history has shown, this desire to live in a scaled-down residential environment at the point in their lives when elderly people must lean on third parties to help with personal care is not merely a matter of personal preference. It can be a matter of life and death.

As the world approaches a half-decade since COVID-19 emerged, the horrific damage is plain to see. The elderly have been the hardest hit demographic group by far, with senior citizens representing more than three-quarters of lives lost to the disease in the US.[1] But the elderly are far from homogenous, and the variation in contagion risk has been especially pronounced based on where seniors lived. The majority of older adults will need caregiving support during their lifetimes.[2] Although 0.6 percent of the US population resides in assisted living or nursing home facilities, these residents account for up to 42 percent of COVID-19 deaths.[3]

[1] Calculation using data from *Weekly Updates by Select Demographic and Geographic Characteristics: Provisional Death Counts for COVID-19*, CDC (updated June 28, 2023), https://www.cdc.gov/nchs/nvss/vsrr/covid_weekly/index.htm (designating 859,497 of the 1,136,057 million American deaths from COVID as being among people aged sixty-five and older).

[2] Richard W. Johnson, *Later-Life Household Wealth before and after Disability Onset*, HHS Off. of The Assistant Sec'y for Planning and Evaluation, Off. of Disability, Aging and Long-Term Care Pol'y (Apr. 2019), aspe.hhs.gov/sites/default/files/migrated_legacy_files//188046/LifetimeRisk.pdf.

[3] G. Allen Power & Jennifer Carson, *The Promise of Transformed Long-Term Care Homes: Evidence from the Pandemic*, 35 Healthcare Mgmt. F. 25, 25 (2021); Sarah H. Yi et al., *Characterization of COVID-19 in Assisted Living Facilities: 39 States, October 2020*, 69 MMWR Morbidity & Mortal Wkly. Rep. 1730 (Nov. 2020), https://www.cdc.gov/mmwr/volumes/69/wr/mm6946a3.htm. *See* Yuchi Young, Ashley Shayya, Thomas O'Grady & Ya-Mei

Some research suggests that nursing home residents were nearly twenty-seven times as likely to die of COVID-related causes as senior citizens who did not live in nursing homes.[4] Elderly residents of single-family homes and apartments fared so much better in comparison as the disease spread rapidly through congregate living communities. The average nursing home resident is in poorer health than the average senior citizen, but even accounting for that difference the disparity in mortality remains striking.

Nursing homes differed greatly in terms of their success deploying COVID-19 countermeasures. As we will show, there were nursing homes that managed to protect their residents against the ravages of the pandemic much more effectively than their peers that followed more traditional models of elder care. There is some research suggesting that nursing homes that provide their patients with the highest levels of care did successfully protect their residents from COVID-related deaths in comparison to lower-quality facilities. But even the research suggesting that higher-quality facilities reduced COVID-related deaths indicates that this admirable performance was accompanied by a marked increase in non–COVID-related excess mortality. So it's possible that the higher-quality nursing homes saved residents from COVID-19 deaths while subjecting them to a higher risk of non-COVID deaths. This higher overall excess mortality may have resulted from the effects of isolation on the elderly.[5] Other research, including meta-analyses, finds no consistent relationship between nursing home quality metrics and COVID-19 mortality.[6]

So if it wasn't the highest-quality nursing homes that most successfully prevented deaths that resulted directly and indirectly from COVID-19, what kinds of nursing homes served their residents best? The answer is the Green House nursing homes, which do not necessarily have a higher quality of care than a typical nursing home but do offer a different benefit – they're small, with a typical resident population of ten to twelve per facility. These Green Houses, scattered across the country, appear to have largely avoided the worst harms of the pandemic. During the pandemic's first year, before vaccines became widely available, residents of Green House homes were about five times less likely than traditional nursing home residents to have

Chen, *COVID-19 Case and Mortality Rates Lower in Green Houses Compared to Traditional Nursing Homes in New York State*, 50 Geriatric Nursing 132 (2023).

4 Christopher J. Cronin & William N. Evans, *Nursing Home Quality, COVID-19 Deaths, and Excess Mortality* (NBER Working Paper 28012, 2020), at 1, https://www.nber.org/system/files/working_papers/w28012/w28012.pdf. Other research puts the ratio closer to 5:1. *See* Kevin A. Brown et al., *Association between Nursing Home Crowding and COVID-19 Infection and Mortality in Ontario, Canada*, 181 JAMA Internal Med. 229, 230 (2020).

5 Cronin & Evans, *supra* note 4, at 25; Elizabeth M. White, *Front-line Nursing Home Staff Experiences during the COVID-19 Pandemic*, 22 JAMDA 199, 201 (2021); Coronavirus Comm'n Safety & Quality in Nursing Homes, *Commission Final Report* (Sep. 2020), at 28, https://www.cms.gov/files/document/covid-final-nh-commission-report.pdf.

6 R. Tamara Konetzka, Elizabeth M. White, Alexander Pralea, David C. Grabowski & Vincent Mor, *A Systematic Review of Long-Term Care Facility Characteristics Associated with COVID-19 Outcomes*, 69 J. Am. Geriatr. Soc'y 2766, 2769 (2021).

contracted COVID-19, and about twenty times less likely to have died as a result of the disease.[7] This was true even though Green House residents were older and sicker than residents of other nursing homes, at least in some jurisdictions.[8] In Kansas, PEAK nursing homes that were not affiliated with the Green House movement but that practiced person-centered care and adopted some Green House policies, such as creating clusters of thirty or fewer residents who were consistently helped by the same nursing staff, saw COVID-19 infection rates 2.5 times lower than non-PEAK nursing homes.[9]

The reasons why Green Houses and similar scaled-down nursing homes performed relatively well when stress-tested by COVID-19 are straightforward. As we explain below, Green Houses adhere to several organizing principles, including ten to twelve residents per home and private bedrooms. These attributes provided significant resiliency against the disease. Fewer residents and fewer staff rotating through resulted in fewer potential sources of infection entry.[10] Not surprisingly, smaller nursing homes saw fewer infections and deaths than their larger counterparts.[11] Indeed, facility size and virus prevalence in the community were the two most powerful predictors of COVID-19 infection rates. In traditional nursing homes, private bedrooms and bathrooms are not the norm.[12] The importance of private bedrooms in limiting the spread of infections was well understood long before the pandemic. According to one estimate, converting all shared bedrooms into private bedrooms would have decreased COVID-19 mortality by 30 percent in nursing homes.[13] Moreover, Green House residents were able to do what residents of other nursing homes could not do – minimize the risk of contracting COVID-19 while still maintaining social ties with their fellow residents.[14] Green House homes are more than twice as likely to offer protected outdoor spaces for socialization, such as

[7] David C. Grabowski, *The Future of Long-Term Care Requires Investment in Both Facility- and Home-Based Services*, 1 Nature: Aging 10 (Jan. 2021); Rebecca Tan, *Nontraditional Nursing Homes Have Almost No Coronavirus Cases. Why Aren't They More Widespread?* Wash. Post (Nov. 3, 2020), https://www.washingtonpost.com/local/green-house-nursing-homes-covid/2020/11/02/4e723b82-d114-11ea-8c55-61e7fa5e82ab_story.html; *see also* Sheryl Zimmerman, Carol Dumond-Stryker, Meera Tandan, John S. Preisser, Christopher J. Wretman, Abigail Howell & Susan Ryan, *Nontraditional Small House Nursing Homes Have Fewer COVID-19 Cases and Deaths*, 22 JAMDA 489 (2021).

[8] Young et al., *supra* note 3, at 134.

[9] Meera Tandan, Migette L. Kaup, Laci J. Corneilison & Sheryl Zimmerman, *The Relationships between Person-Centered Care in Nursing Homes and COVID-19 Infection, Hospitalization, and Mortality Rates*, 51 Geriatric Nursing 253, 255–256 (2023). PEAK stands for Promoting Excellent Alternatives in Kansas nursing homes.

[10] Lauren W. Cohen et al., *The Green House Model of Nursing Home Care in Design and Implementation*, 52 Health Serv. Res. 352, 354 (2016).

[11] Konetzka et al., *supra* note 6, at 2769.

[12] Cohen et al., *supra* note 10, at 364.

[13] Power & Carson, *supra* note 3, at 27.

[14] Tan, *supra* note 7.

screened-in porches, compared to traditional nursing homes.[15] In short, residents could reduce the risk of the virus entering the facility, lower the risk of the virus spreading if one resident did become infected, and continue to socialize within their protective bubble rather than being isolated.

It's an open question whether the comparative data on COVID-19 mortality will spark a marked shift in the demand of well-resourced older Americans for Green House living arrangements. Rationally, elderly Americans should recognize that another pandemic is likely to hit the US in the decades to come. It is possible that memories of the pandemic will permanently alter consumer preferences and behaviors in ways that resemble the lifelong impact of the Great Depression on those who lived through it.[16] On the other hand, there is a possibility of survival bias. The present population weathered the last storm, and a focus on their own experiences may make them overconfident about their ability to survive the next deadly pandemic, even as changed health circumstances and age make them increasingly vulnerable over time. Assuming that salient experiences with COVID-19 do spark a shift in older Americans' preferences, the key questions are whether legal and financial obstacles to their creation will frustrate that demand.

Seniors living independently were more likely to survive COVID-19 than the institutionalized elderly. Retirees with the income and ability to remain at home in lockdown conditions, getting groceries and other life necessities delivered, generally were able to avoid infection until the vaccines arrived.[17] Given a preference, seniors consistently tell survey researchers that their paramount desire is to age in place until doing so is no longer feasible.

Accessory dwelling units (ADUs or, parochially, "Granny Flats") are a straightforward and easy way to satisfy that preference for aging in place as seniors' housing needs change during the course of their life cycles. While some jurisdictions have moved to make ADUs easier to build in recent years, there is still a great deal of resistance to land-use liberalization. As the pandemic has shown, zoning restrictions that constrain the development of these affordable units have likely contributed to the loss of life by forcing seniors into higher-risk living environments.

Our claim in this chapter is straightforward. Older Americans overwhelmingly prefer scaled-down living. That preference exists when they can live independently, and it remains when independent living is no longer realistic. This preference for living small may receive a further boost as seniors and their loved ones come to grips

[15] Cohen et al., *supra* note 10, at 365.

[16] *See generally* Glen H. Elder Jr., Children of the Great Depression: Social Change in Life Experience (1999); Lloyd H. Rogler, *Historical Generations and Psychology: The Case of the Great Depression and World War II*, 57 Am. Psych. 1013 (2003).

[17] Chinedum O. Ojinnaka et al., *Factors Associated with COVID-Related Mortality: The Case of Texas*, J. Racial & Ethnic Health Disparities 2 (Nov. 9, 2020); David J. Peters, *Community Susceptibility and Resiliency to COVID-19 across the Urban–Rural Continuum in the United States*, 36 J. Rural Health 446, 450 (2020).

with the data on infectious disease risk. Forms of housing that provided protection for their residents during the pandemic, especially Green House nursing homes and lower-cost, single-family residences such as ADUs, will become more desirable than they already were. Yet existing zoning laws in much of the US are a key impediment to developing the kinds of housing that seniors increasingly want at the scale that an aging society will need. We will discuss these impediments and identify promising reforms to satisfy this growing demand among the elderly for more intimate and protective housing arrangements.

22.1 THE GREEN HOUSE ALTERNATIVE

Geriatrician Bill Thomas pioneered the concept of the Green House long-term care facilities to address the shortcomings of traditional nursing homes. Green House homes are mostly nonprofit facilities.[18] Green House homes provide each of the ten to twelve residents with a private bedroom and en suite bathroom. The residents share an open kitchen, dining and living areas, and outdoor spaces.[19] Each house employs "Shahbazim," typically nurse's assistants who care for residents, do laundry, cook, clean, and order supplies. The available research suggests that Shahbazim are able to devote a higher percentage of their working hours to direct and indirect care of residents than is typical at traditional nursing homes, thanks in part to their ability to engage in tasks like cooking and cleaning while interacting with residents.[20] The Green House's founders deemed taboo traditional aspects of nursing homes – such as nursing stations, intercoms for paging healthcare professionals to rooms, and medication carts.[21] Residents of the Green Houses could set their own schedule for going to sleep and waking up, for receiving personal care, for eating, and for engaging in activities.[22] Where feasible, residents themselves would participate in cooking, laundry, gardening, and caring for household pets.[23] Housing concepts that share features similar to Green Houses have emerged in other parts of the developed world, including the Clustered Domestic model in Australia, the Butterfly model in Canada and the UK, and Dementia Villages in the Netherlands.[24]

[18] Christopher C. Afendulis et al., *Green House Adoption and Nursing Home Quality*, 52 Health Serv. Res. 454, 459 (2016).

[19] Cohen et al., *supra* note 10, at 354.

[20] Siobhan S. Sharkey et al., *Frontline Caregiver Daily Practices: A Comparison Study of Traditional Nursing Homes and the Green House Project Sites*, 59 J. Am. Geriatrics Soc'y 126, 130 (2011).

[21] Judith Rabig et al., *Radical Redesign of Nursing Homes: Applying the Green House Concept in Tupelo, Mississippi*, 46 Gerontologist 533, 534 (2006).

[22] *Id.*; Cohen et al., *supra* note 10, at 366.

[23] Rabig et al., *supra* note 21, at 534.

[24] Whitney Longstaff, Jody Filkowski & Melissa Severn, *The Small House Model to Support Older Adults in Long-Term Care*, 2 Can. J. Health Tech. 10–11 (2022).

In 2003, the first Green House homes opened in Tupelo, Mississippi, embracing the Green House movement's tripartite vision – providing a "real home," a "meaningful life," and an "empowered staff."[25] To facilitate evaluations of the model, efforts were made to ensure that the residents of the first Green Houses resembled those of comparable nursing homes insofar as possible, and all of the initial residents transferred from traditional nursing homes were managed by the same nonprofit.[26] There are now some 300 Green House homes in thirty-two different states, mostly organized as nonprofits.[27] At the same time, because of the small size of each home, the total population of all the Green Houses is approximately 3,200 people.[28] At least in the original Green House homes in Tupelo, African American seniors were more prevalent than in Tupelo's traditional nursing homes.[29] The reverse is true of New York's Green House homes, in which white residents are overrepresented.[30]

Though still relatively few in number, the Green Houses have been studied extensively by academics. The bottom line that emerges from this literature is that the quality of medical care delivered at the Green Houses is at least as good as what's available at traditional nursing homes, but the quality of life for residents is much better. For example, a differences-in-differences study using matching to try to minimize the effects of selection bias found that Green House homes had lower hospital readmission rates and saw statistically significant reductions in the percentage of patients who were bedridden, catheterized, or suffering from pressure ulcers.[31] Other indicators of medical quality were not significantly superior among the Green House residents.

It's with respect to measures of life satisfaction and patient autonomy that the Green House homes really shine.[32] Researchers have found marked differences in terms of satisfaction and overall emotional well-being, with residents' and their relatives' sense of their privacy, autonomy, and the physical environment at Green Houses rating significantly better than the traditional nursing home baseline.[33] The literature also suggests that turnover and absenteeism among staff are noticeably

[25] The Green House Project, *Who We Are*, https://www.thegreenhouseproject.org/about/vision mission (accessed Nov. 29, 2023).

[26] Rabig et al., *supra* note 21, at 535.

[27] Rob Waters, *The Big Idea behind a New Model of Small Nursing Homes*, HEALTH AFFS. 378, 379 (March 2021).

[28] Tan, *supra* note 7.

[29] Rosalie A. Kane et al., *Resident Outcomes in Small-House Nursing Homes: A Longitudinal Evaluation of the Initial Green House Program*, 55 J. AM. GERIATRICS SOC. 832, 836 (2007).

[30] Young et al., *supra* note 3, at 133 tbl. 1.

[31] Afendulis et al., *supra* note 18, at 459, 468–469.

[32] *Id.* at 470; Sheryl Zimmerman et al., *New Evidence on the Green House Model of Nursing Home Care: Synthesis of Findings and Implications for Policy, Practice, and Research*, 51 HEALTH SERV. RES. 475, 477 (2016).

[33] Kane et al., *supra* note 29, at 836; Terry Y. Lum et al., *Effects of Green House Nursing Homes on Residents' Families*, 30 HEALTH CARE FIN. REV. 35, 48 (2008–2009).

reduced compared to traditional nursing facilities.[34] Workers got to know residents better, and better continuity of care emerged, such that they had an easier time noticing changes in residents' health status quickly.[35] The private sleeping-quarters aspect of Green Houses is also a major selling point – surveys indicate that seniors prefer private bedrooms by a margin of twenty to one because these accommodations give seniors more privacy and control.[36]

The best evidence seems to indicate that Green Houses cost roughly the same to operate as traditional nursing homes, or perhaps a bit more. A 2016 study found that the average private-pay monthly cost of a Green House residence was 5 percent higher than the cost for a traditional nursing home.[37] Another study found that the operating expenses of Green House homes were approximately 7.6 percent higher than the national average, putting the homes in the sixtieth percentile for spending among nationwide nursing homes.[38] At the same time, there is evidence from an underpowered study indicating that Green Houses are associated with a decline in Medicare expenses of up to 30 percent, apparently because of decreased hospitalizations and transfers to skilled nursing facilities among Green House residents.[39]

Construction costs are likely to be significantly higher for Green House homes, though how much is difficult to estimate, with much of the differential driven by the fact that Green Houses allot more square footage to the average resident than traditional nursing homes with shared bedrooms.[40] The available evidence suggests that occupancy rates in Green House homes are much higher than in traditional nursing homes, which may offset the higher upfront capital costs.[41] Taken together, then, the data make it uncertain whether the total monetary costs to society associated with Green Houses will be higher than those associated with traditional nursing homes. It is more plausible that they entail somewhat higher costs, but also conceivable that there is no meaningful difference.[42]

34 Rabig et al., *supra* note 21, at 538.

35 Zimmerman et al., *supra* note 32, at 479; Cohen et al., *supra* note 10, at 370.

36 Brown et al., *supra* note 4, at E7.

37 Cohen et al., *supra* note 10, at 370–371.

38 Robert Jenkens et al., *Financial Implications of the Green House Model*, 19 Seniors Housing & Care J. 3, 12 (2011).

39 Zimmerman et al., *supra* note 32, at 484. Note that the 30 percent decrease study had a p value of .06, just narrowly missing the .05 standard for statistical significance notwithstanding the large size of the effect.

40 *Id.* at 14–19.

41 Waters, *supra* note 27, at 382; Robert Jenkens, Terri Sult, Newell Lessell, David Hammer & Anna Ortigara, *Financial Implications of the Green House Model*, 19 Seniors Housing & Care J. 3, 20 (2011); Alex Spanko, *How a Nursing Home Developer Made Green Houses Work: "It's Not Hard to Pencil Out,"* Skilled Nursing News (July 26, 2020), https://skillednursingnews.com/2020/07/how-a-nursing-home-developer-made-green-houses-work-its-not-hard-to-pencil-out/#:~:text=These%20%E2%80%9Csmall%2Dhouse%E2%80%9D%20style,work%20only%20within%20each%20cottage.

42 Jenkens et al., *supra* note 41, at 12 (placing the average cost per resident per day for Green House homes at the sixtieth percentile nationally among all nursing homes).

The Green House nursing home differs in one other respect from the traditional nursing home, and the difference looms large from a housing policy perspective. Green Houses are designed to have the profile of a large single-family home, and they can fit nicely into low-density residential neighborhoods. Their relatively small staff footprints also suggest that they could be situated in single-family neighborhoods without creating significant scarcity of street parking spots. As a result, there should be little principled opposition to efforts to zone them in any residential neighborhood where single-family homes predominate. To be sure, zoning opposition to projects in neighborhoods is often unprincipled, and some opposition to the siting of nursing homes and hospices in residential areas may reflect a perverse desire to keep aging and death out of sight, and therefore out of mind.[43]

Because the disabled are a protected class under the Fair Housing Act and many nursing home residents qualify as disabled, Green House developers should be in a strong position to challenge the denial of necessary zoning approvals under the Fair Housing Act.[44] Though judicial interpretations of existing law make it rather clear that a Green House can be built in most areas that are zoned single-family residential only,[45] Congress may wish to consider further amendments to strengthen the Fair Housing Act in a way that makes it crystal-clear that a municipality's refusal to treat small-scale nursing homes on equal terms with similarly sized single-family homes is unlawful.

22.2 ACCESSORY DWELLING UNITS

It turns out that the desire for continuity as people age is part of a broader phenomenon. At least in the US, older Americans strongly prefer to live in smaller versions of the single-family homes they lived in when they were younger. Thus, as the percentage of residents who are elderly in a community increases, demand for (and prices of) small, single-family homes tends to increase.[46] Older empty nesters and young families wind up competing for the same "starter" homes.

The preference for American seniors to "age in place" as much as possible is equally powerful.[47] Fully 83 percent of senior citizens agreed in a national survey

[43] A. Kimberly Hoffman & James A. Landon, *Zoning and the Aging Population: Are Residential Communities Zoning Elder Care Out?* 44 URB. L. 629, 643 (2012).

[44] *See*, e.g., Hovsons, Inc. v. Township of Brick, 89 F.3d 1096, 1103–1106 (3rd Cir. 1996). Developers seeking to site assisted living facilities in areas that are predominantly nonresidential may face an uphill battle, by contrast. *See* Forest City Daly Housing, Inc. v. Town of North Hempstead, 175 F.3d 144 (2nd Cir. 1999).

[45] Hovsons, Inc., 89 F.3d at 1096.

[46] Weijing Wang & Noah J. Durst, *Planning for Active Aging: Exploring Housing Preferences of Elderly Populations in the United States*, 38 J. OF HOUSING & THE BUILT ENVIRON. 795, 806 (2023).

[47] Jon Pynoos, *The Future of Housing for the Elderly: Four Strategies that Can Make a Difference*, 29 PUB. POL'Y & AGING REP. 35, 35 (2018).

that they wanted to remain in their current homes for as long as possible, and the overwhelming majority of these seniors agreed strongly with the sentiment.[48] Most seniors find the prospect of moving to nursing homes distasteful.[49] Senior citizens are especially likely to be tied to the community in which they live and the neighbors and relatives who surround them, making moves less desirable and less advantageous for the elderly than they are for younger citizens.[50] For seniors who are attached to their homes, that attachment represents a substantial component of their psychological well-being.[51]

While the community they've long resided in will have significant appeal, the house they've long called home might not be suited to the needs of elderly empty nesters. The home may have staircases that are difficult or dangerous to navigate for elderly residents whose mobility is impaired and who are at a greater risk of broken hips and other debilitating injuries. The home may be too large and expensive to maintain. New construction that is built for someone with impaired mobility and is right-sized for an elderly individual or couple will be ideal, but those sorts of dwellings are in rather short supply, especially in neighborhoods occupied largely by single-family homes.

Enter the ADU. ADUs are small houses built within the footprint of an existing parcel that already contains a single-family home. Some ADUs are apartments built over existing garages (i.e., coach houses). Others are new "tiny houses" built from scratch in backyards that resemble ground-floor studio apartments. Either kind of unit might provide great utility to a senior citizen who wishes to remain in place. An apartment built on top of a detached garage might be an ideal space for a caregiver to reside if an elderly resident wishes to remain in an existing single-family residence. And a ground floor unit might permit an elderly resident to stay in a beloved neighborhood while vacating the main house in favor of either a relative who can provide care and companionship, or a tenant who can supplement the senior's income.

Embracing ADUs is an important pillar of affordable and inclusive housing policy. Surveys of owners who have built ADUs in the Seattle area find that Black and Latino households are more likely than nonminority households to construct ADUs, and that these units are particularly likely to be built in middle-income communities.[52] The same study found that ADUs were especially common in those neighborhoods with a higher concentration of senior citizens. A separate study of

[48] Margaret F. Brinig, *Grandparents and Accessory Dwelling Units: Preserving Intimacy and Independence*, 22 ELDER L. J. 381, 385 (2015).

[49] *Id.* at 387–388.

[50] Michael C. Pollack & Lior Jacob Strahilevitz, *Property Law for the Ages*, 63 WM. & MARY L. REV. 561, 566 (2021).

[51] Gary W. Evans, Elyse Kantrowitz & Paul Eshelman, *Housing Quality and Psychological Well-Being among the Elderly Population*, 57 B J. GERONTOLOGY: PSYCH. SCI. P381, P382 (2002).

[52] Magda Maaoui, A *Granny Flat of One's Own? The Households that Build Accessory-Dwelling Units in Seattle's King County*, 30 BERKELEY PLANNING J. 102, 111 (2018).

ADUs in three high-cost cities on the west coast (Portland, Seattle, and Vancouver, BC) found that the average construction cost of ADUs was $156,000, putting them well within the reach of many seniors looking to downsize or supplement their income.[53] Fifty-seven percent of households living in ADUs consisted of one person, and another 36 percent comprised two people.[54] Approximately 28 percent of all American senior citizens currently live alone.[55]

There is circumstantial evidence consistent with the idea that those seniors who live near their children but not under the same roof benefit from that proximity. As Margaret Brinig has pointed out, senior citizens who live within eight minutes of the home of one of their children are among the seniors with the lowest mortality risks and the most satisfied mental states, but senior citizens who live in the same household as their adult children face high mortality risks and suffer from diminished mental states.[56] Obviously selection effects necessitate caveats – the elderly may need to cohabit with their children when their health declines or when a child's financial resources disappear, and both dynamics along with the inherent stress of adults merging households and losing privacy will correspond with declines in the quality of life for seniors.

Zoning laws are the main obstacle to the desirable arrangement whereby seniors live near, but not with, their children and grandchildren. The US generally zones for homogeneity, at least within neighborhoods. Not only are many residential neighborhoods uniformly so, but the quality and cost of housing is often uniform as well. For an elderly person with adult children and minor grandchildren living in a neighborhood of single-family homes, residential units that are right-sized for a single elderly person may be hard to find, or even nonexistent. And because of their lack of density, these neighborhoods are often not well served by transit options. So when elderly seniors who can no longer drive safely need to get around, they may be entirely dependent on relatives, or taxis and ride-sharing services if they are available. High-density neighborhoods also saw lower COVID-19 mortality rates during the pandemic, in part because they tend to have a higher-quality and more accessible medical infrastructure.[57]

If ADUs are desirable for seniors who wish to age in place but find a lack of other options in their beloved neighborhoods as their needs change, what is stopping them from being built? The answer is generally local land-use laws, though financing

[53] Karen Chapple, Jake Wegmann, Farzad Mashhood & Rebecca Coleman, *Jumpstarting the Market for Accessory Dwelling Units: Lessons Learned from Portland, Seattle, and Vancouver*, URB. LAND INST. (2017), at 16, https://ternercenter.berkeley.edu/wp-content/uploads/pdfs/Jumpstarting_the_Market_-_ULI.pdf.

[54] *Id.* at 18.

[55] John Infranca, *Housing Changing Households: Regulatory Challenges for Micro-units and Accessory Dwelling Units*, 25 STAN. L. & POL'Y REV. 53, 58 (2014).

[56] Brinig, *supra* note 48, at 390–391.

[57] Shima Hamidi, Sadegh Sabouri & Reid Ewing, *Does Density Aggravate the COVID-19 Pandemic?* 86 J. AM. PLANNING ASS'N 495, 496 (2020).

restrictions also play a role.[58] When researchers surveyed homeowners who had built ADUs, problems with the permitting process were the commonly identified causes of unanticipated delays and cost increases, and about one in every five survey respondents reported initially having their permit applications rejected.[59] The perceived hassle of obtaining the necessary permits emerged in interviews with landowners who had not constructed ADUs in other research as well.[60]

The legal scholarship bears out the difficulties for governments that wish to promote ADUs. In 2002, California enacted statewide legislation to require municipalities to permit the construction of ADUs in neighborhoods that were zoned single-family residential, but many local governments responded with regimes that de facto made ADUs extremely difficult to build.[61] The political economy behind these efforts and the resistance is interesting. The politically potent AARP strongly supported the statewide legislation and used its considerable clout in Sacramento to get the legislation enacted, forming a coalition with progressive advocates of affordable housing.[62] But at the local level, real estate developers, construction unions, and homeowners interested in maximizing their property values and maintaining the character of their communities became powerful obstacles blocking reform.

Even when statewide laws make it easier to construct ADUs, cities can thwart those policies by refusing to relax parking space requirements, insisting that ADU builders obtain conditional use permits, or requiring that ADUs be owner-occupied, though California's legislation thwarts several of these strategies.[63] Other communities, notably including Los Angeles, enacted ordinances that have facilitated the growth of ADUs and prompted their construction across wider swaths of the city, including in more affluent neighborhoods.[64] Nonetheless, ADUs remain more common in parts of Los Angeles that are close to light-rail stops, schools, and commercial districts, as well as neighborhoods with large

[58] For a survey of the widely varying local government approaches to ADU policy, *see* Katrin B. Anacker & Christopher Niedt, *Classifying Regulatory Approaches of Jurisdictions for Accessory Dwelling Units: The Case of Long Island*, 43 J. Planning Educ. & Res. 60 (2023).

[59] Chapple et al., *supra* note 53, at 22.

[60] Jamey M. B. Volker & Susan Handy, *Exploring Homeowners' Openness to Building Accessory Dwelling Units in the Sacramento Metropolitan Area*, 89 J. Am. Planning Ass'n 45, 54 (2023).

[61] Margaret F. Brinig & Nicole Stelle Garnett, *A Room of One's Own? Accessory Dwelling Unit Reforms and Local Parochialism*, 45 Urb. L. 519, 523–524, 547, 567 (2013); Infranca, *supra* note 55, at 70–84.

[62] Brinig & Garnett, *supra* note 61, at 539.

[63] Emily Hamilton & Abigail Houseal, *A Taxonomy of State Accessory Dwelling Unit Laws*, Mercatus Ctr. (Mar. 2023), at 2–4, https://www.mercatus.org/research/policy-briefs/state-accessory-dwelling-unit-laws.

[64] Dohyung Kim, S-Ra Baek, Brian Garcia, Tom Vo & Frank Wen, *The Influence of Accessory Dwelling Unit (ADU) Policy on the Contributing Factors to ADU Development: An Assessment of the City of Los Angeles*, 38 J. Hous. & Built Environ. 1585 (2023).

Latino populations. They are observed less frequently in parts of Los Angeles where large numbers of high-income residents live as well as in parts of the city where most of the residents are Black.[65] Policy decisions thus play a large role in determining whether ADUs become a viable tool for increasing housing supply and affordability, promoting dense development, and satisfying seniors' preferences to age in place.

To overcome local intransigence in cities and towns that have tried to keep ADUs out, more aggressive reforms will be necessary at the state level. Christopher Elmendorf has identified approaches to housing affordability in his other work that may be well adapted to the problem of ADUs.[66] Elmendorf envisions a series of steps whereby states create targets for localities to increase the housing supply; real estate developers and third-party interest groups gain new rights to sue localities that block applications for permits that would increase supply; and the state adds in financial penalties for localities that fail to increase the availability of housing over a predetermined number of years. These kinds of reforms could work well to promote the growth of ADUs. They have the advantage of altering the incentive structure for local governments from "how do we say no to these developments?" to "how do we get more approvals for these developments?" To comply with state mandates, local officials might even need to take steps to encourage single-family homeowners to consider construction of ADUs, which could help to overcome a major obstacle to their construction – which is residents' ignorance about the opportunity to build them.[67] Policymakers could also incentivize homeowners to build ADUs to help care for elders in their communities. For example, with proper supervision and regulation, single-family homeowners might become on-site caregivers for elderly residents of adjacent ADUs. In that way the homeowner could receive a stable source of income as both a landlord and a part-time caregiver, and the elderly resident would have assistance and companionship close at hand in the event of any emergencies.

To be sure, housing policy is only one important part of the necessary societal changes. Prior to the pandemic, advocates for the elderly pushed to increase the funding and availability for home-care services through Medicare, Medicaid, and perhaps nationalized long-term care insurance. Ways to improve further the prospects of seniors who want to age in place include increasing the availability of high-quality in-home caregivers and investing in highly skilled home-based primary care programs. Increasing the appropriate housing supply through ADUs is a necessary but not sufficient measure to facilitate that goal.

65 Sarah Thomaz & Jan Brueckner, *ADUs in Los Angeles: Where Are They Located and by How Much Do They Raise Property Value?* (unpublished manuscript), at 16.

66 Christopher S. Elmendorf, *Beyond the Double Veto: Housing Plans as Preemptive Intergovernmental Compacts*, 71 Hastings L.J. 79, 130–134 (2019).

67 Chapple et al., *supra* note 53, at 18.

22.3 CONCLUSION

People change as they age, but the stability of their housing preferences is rather remarkable. The elderly generally wish to remain in their long-time homes for as long as they possibly can, and when that option is no longer feasible, many of them desire a nursing care facility that will preserve the normality and privacy that characterized their earlier years. Despite the consumerist culture of the US, the market provides fewer options for late-in-life residential living than for any other life stage, and the options that the market does provide are mostly institutionalized and unappealing to large segments of the elderly population. Consider the heterogeneity of housing options available to a forty-five-year-old American. It is not obvious that the option set available to that person's parent, who is thirty years older, should be so much more restricted. Yet because the elderly are often paying indirectly for long-term care, through insurance or government entitlements, and because local laws substantially constrain the supply of housing, there is a mismatch between what seniors want (and arguably need) and what they get.

The COVID-19 pandemic may hasten a trend that was already underway, which is that many Americans wish to age in small housing units located within the neighborhoods they've grown attached to, or nursing homes that feel at least a little bit like home. To date, the nation has done a poor job of making these kinds of options broadly available to the elderly, and misguided land-use policies seem to be one major reason why. The pandemic underscores that some of the selling points of these housing arrangements are not merely matters of consumer preference but can be issues of life and death as well. COVID-19 may be the worst infectious disease of our lifetimes, but it will not be the last. As Americans begin living into their nineties and hundreds with increasing frequency, much of the existing resistance to the changes we anticipate here eventually will be overcome. Building the right housing now is an essential strategy to minimize the dislocation and anxiety that will occur when tens of millions of aging people discover that so many of their choices are unpalatable.

www.ingramcontent.com/pod-product-compliance
Ingram Content Group UK Ltd.
Pitfield, Milton Keynes, MK11 3LW, UK
UKHW040248200625
459886UK00007B/156
* 9 7 8 1 0 0 9 4 6 5 9 9 1 *